Balancing Strategy

What is the relationship between sea power, law, and strategy? Anna Brinkman uses in-depth analysis of cases brought before the Court of Prize Appeal during the Seven Years' War to explore how Britain worked to shape maritime international law to its strategic advantage. Within the court, government officials and naval and legal minds came together to shape legal decisions from the perspectives of both legal philosophy and maritime strategic aims. As a result, neutrality and the negotiation of rights became critical to maritime warfare. *Balancing Strategy* unpicks a complex web of competing priorities: deals struck with the Dutch Republic and Spain; imperial rivalry; mercantilism; colonial trade; and the relationships between metropoles and colonies, trade, and the navy. Ultimately, influencing and shaping international law of the sea allows a nation to create the norms and rules that constrain or enable the use of sea power during war.

Anna Brinkman is a lecturer in the Defence Studies Department at King's College London and co-director of the Corbett Centre for Maritime Policy Studies. She is a historian of eighteenth- and nineteenth-century maritime strategy and international law.

Cambridge Military Histories

Edited by

GREGORY A. DADDIS, USS Midway Chair in Modern US Military History and Director of the Center for War and Society, San Diego State University

HEW STRACHAN, Professor of International Relations, University of St Andrews and Emeritus Fellow of All Souls College, Oxford

GEOFFREY WAWRO, Professor of Military History and Director of the Military History Center, University of North Texas

The aim of this series is to publish outstanding works of research on warfare throughout the ages and throughout the world. Books in the series take a broad approach to military history, examining war in all its military, strategic, political, and economic aspects. The series complements *Studies in the Social and Cultural History of Modern Warfare* by focusing on the 'hard' military history of armies, tactics, strategy, and warfare. Books in the series consist mainly of single author works – academically rigorous and groundbreaking – which are accessible to both academics and the interested general reader.

A full list of titles in the series can be found at:

www.cambridge.org/militaryhistories

Balancing Strategy

Sea Power, Neutrality, and Prize Law in the Seven Years' War

Anna Brinkman

King's College London

Shaftesbury Road, Cambridge CB2 8EA, United Kingdom

One Liberty Plaza, 20th Floor, New York, NY 10006, USA

477 Williamstown Road, Port Melbourne, VIC 3207, Australia

314–321, 3rd Floor, Plot 3, Splendor Forum, Jasola District Centre, New Delhi – 110025, India

103 Penang Road, #05-06/07, Visioncrest Commercial, Singapore 238467

Cambridge University Press is part of Cambridge University Press & Assessment, a department of the University of Cambridge.

We share the University's mission to contribute to society through the pursuit of education, learning and research at the highest international levels of excellence.

www.cambridge.org
Information on this title: www.cambridge.org/9781009425568

DOI: 10.1017/9781009425599

First published 2024

A catalogue record for this publication is available from the British Library

Library of Congress Cataloging-in-Publication Data
Names: Brinkman, Anna, 1988- author.
Title: Balancing strategy : seapower, neutrality, and prize law in the Seven Years' War / Anna Brinkman, King's College London.
Description: Cambridge, United Kingdom ; New York, NY : Cambridge University Press, 2024. | Series: Cambridge military histories | Includes bibliographical references and index.
Identifiers: LCCN 2023045616 (print) | LCCN 2023045617 (ebook) | ISBN 9781009425568 (hardback) | ISBN 9781009425551 (paperback) | ISBN 9781009425599 (epub)
Subjects: LCSH: Prize courts–Great Britain–History. | Prize law–Great Britain–History. | Sea-power–Great Britain–History. | Neutrality–Great Britain–History. | Maritime law–Great Britain–History. | Great Britain. High Court of Admiralty. | Seven Years' War, 1756-1763. | War, Maritime (International law)
Classification: LCC KZ6660.G7 B75 2024 (print) | LCC KZ6660.G7 (ebook) | DDC 341.6/3–dc23/eng/20231002
LC record available at https://lccn.loc.gov/2023045616
LC ebook record available at https://lccn.loc.gov/2023045617

ISBN 978-1-009-42556-8 Hardback

This book is dedicated to the women who pulled me up and help me stand on their shoulders to this day, the women who shaped me as a scholar and a person:

Dr Kathryn Tolbert
Dr Regina Yando
Dr Ingrid Brinkman
Lori Fichter
Lise Pasterkamp
Kirsten Dolly

Thank you.

Contents

Acknowledgements

This book has been a labour of love for the past six years and there are two people without whom the entire project would never have come to fruition. They have been my intellectual and emotional rocks as this project has gone through conception, iteration, re-writing, and completion. My dear friend and colleague, Dr David Morgan-Owen, has read drafts of chapters and always gave me honest and considered feedback. He has had countless coffees, meals, and walks with me over which we discussed the book, its arguments, my ideas, and his suggestions. When I was at my lowest point and thought the book might never see the light of day, it was Dave who suggested a new approach and helped me through the herculean task of reconceiving the project. I cannot thank you enough, Dave. The other person to whom I owe enormous thanks is Dr Kathryn Tolbert, my mother and mentor. Kathryn has been a part of this project since its very first iteration as my PhD thesis. She has read and commented on every version of the manuscript and helped me talk through every idea, no matter how wild. Her input and questions always pushed me to be a better thinker and to engage more critically with the archival material. Whenever I struggled with how to convey what was in my mind, Kathryn could always help me find my voice. Thank you, Mom, I wish every historian had someone like you in their corner.

I also owe a very special thanks to Professor Michael Lobban at the LSE whose comments on early versions of the manuscript helped me hone the legal arguments. He pushed me to dig more deeply into the legal history and philosophy of this period and to expand my analyses beyond the four case studies. Working with Professor Lobban was like undertaking another degree and it has benefited my scholarship more than I could possibly convey.

The work of a historian is often portrayed as a solitary and lonely undertaking. But I think it takes a village to raise a history book, and I could not have asked for a better or more supportive village. My PhD supervisors, Professor Greg Kennedy and Professor Andrew Lambert, have always been just an email or a chat away and their unwavering faith in my scholarship has built my confidence from my very first year as a PhD student. In a field that is largely dominated by men and still full of misogynistic behaviour, they have never once made me feel that being a woman had any impact on how they thought of me or engaged with me. It is difficult to overstate how important this can be to building a strong sense of self in a young scholar. My students and colleagues at the Defence Studies Department have helped me develop my thinking around how historical work can be used to teach strategic thinking. I have often found that discussions with my students have provided moments of absolute clarity in my own intellectual development and much of that clarity helped craft the arguments in this book. I also want to thank Michael Watson and Professor Sir Hew Strachan, the editors at Cambridge University Press, who believed in this project and supported it. Finally, I want to thank my friend Eleanor McDonald who has been by my side since we undertook our MAs together. Her home and her couch have seen hours of writing, support, tears, and happiness around this project. Without your friendship Nellie, this book and my career would not have happened.

Introduction

Four Neutral Ships

The voyage from the Spanish port of La Coruña to San Sebastián was frequently undertaken by Biscayan traders and followed a route of 281 nautical miles almost due east along the coast of northern Spain. On 12 August 1756, as the Spanish ship *Jesús, Maria, y José* was sailing along this well-travelled route, she met with the British privateer, *Britannia*. Encountering no resistance, the *Britannia* took the Spanish ship and brought her into Bristol, with a view to having her declared lawful prize by the Admiralty courts. According to the crew of the *Britannia*, the *Jesús, Maria, y José* was carrying a cargo of French East India goods and French property. Four months later, the High Court of Admiralty determined that there was just cause for the seizure and condemned part of the cargo as contraband and, therefore, lawful prize of the crew of the *Britannia*. The ship itself and the rest of the goods were restored to the master of the Spanish ship. Neither party were satisfied with the outcome and both lodged an appeal.

Almost a year later, the Biscayan-owned ship *San Juan Baptista* was captured on 10 June 1757, by the Bristol privateer *Tartar*, near the end of her journey from Pasaia (a town slightly east of San Sebastián) to Nantes. Her cargo was similarly made up of French East India goods. On 23 September 1757, the High Court of Admiralty condemned the goods as lawful prize but restored the ship as Spanish property. The master (and part owner) of the *San Juan Baptista*, was not satisfied with the outcome and lodged an appeal.

The *Jesús, Maria, y José* and the *San Juan Baptista* were the first two Spanish ships to come before the Court of Prize Appeal during the Seven Years' War that had any bearing on Anglo-Spanish relations.[1] As the two

---

[1] They were, technically, the third and fourth Spanish ships to come before the court; the first was a ship egregiously captured on the Thames whilst lawfully trading with Britain. The second ship's case was never actually heard by the court. Thus, the *San Juan Baptista* and the *Jesús, Maria, y José* were the first two Spanish cases to come before the court that

cases moved through the prize court system, political relations between Spain and Britain deteriorated. Even with the best efforts of British ministers to use the court proceedings to help stabilise Anglo-Spanish relations through favourable judgments for Spanish ships, the two countries descended into war by 1762. Spanish neutrality, which British ministers considered strategically valuable in the war against France, was lost.

The *Maria Theresa* was a Dutch cargo ship captained by Tyerck Byaart. In August 1757, the ship undertook a voyage from Amsterdam to Cork, then from Cork to St Eustatius in the West Indies, and from St Eustatius back to Amsterdam. At St Eustatius, the *Maria Theresa* took on cargo before departing for Amsterdam. On the voyage across the Atlantic, the British privateer *Duke of Cornwall*, captained by David Jenkins, took the *Maria Theresa* as prize on 6 May 1758, and brought her into Falmouth. On 17 August, the prize case came before the High Court of Admiralty, where the goods were condemned as lawful prize. The ship was pronounced to belong to Dutch owners and was restored. The Dutch captain launched an appeal and, less than a year later, the case was heard by the Court of Prize Appeal on 22 March 1759. It was the first Dutch case to come before the appellate court in the Seven Years' War.

A few weeks after the *Maria Theresa* was taken by the *Duke of Cornwall*, HMS *Squirrel* was sailing in the North Sea slightly north-west of Amsterdam when she came across the Dutch ship *America*, captained by Louis Ferret. The captain of the *Squirrel*, Hyde Parker, ordered a shot to be fired so that the Dutch ship would heave to and Captain Parker could question her captain. Parker discovered that the ship had come from the French West Indies colony of St Domingue, and that there were no bills of lading or passes on board. Parker detained the ship on presumption of being French and took her as prize. Five months later, on 21 October 1758, the case went before the High Court of Admiralty, where the ship and cargo were condemned as French property. Ferret appealed the decision, and on 12 April 1759, the Court of Prize Appeal was convened to hear the case.

Because the two Dutch ships were the first Dutch cases to come before the Court of Prize Appeal, and in fairly close succession, the sentences that were passed carried implications of precedent for other Dutch cases that might come before the court during the war. As both cases moved through the British prize court system, political relations over neutral

had any bearing on neutral rights. See Part III, 'The Spanish Case Studies', for further detail.

rights between Britain and the Dutch Republic descended into crisis. The British ministry used the cases of the two Dutch ships in the Court of Prize Appeal to help end the crisis, and to both restore Dutch faith in Britain's commitment to Dutch neutral rights and the British prize court system's ability to be the safeguard of those rights.

The cases of the *Jesús, Maria, y José*, the *San Juan Baptista*, the *Maria Theresa*, and the *America* were four of the first cases to be brought before the Court of Prize Appeal during the Seven Years' War. They were intentionally used to establish how, and under what circumstances, the appellate court would protect and define Dutch and Spanish neutral rights. They were also used to establish the extent to which the appellate court would protect the rights of British warships and privateers. The journeys of these four ships through the prize court system unfolded within the contexts of British, Spanish, and Dutch maritime and political strategies of the mid-to-late eighteenth century. The sometimes neglected and downplayed actors in these imperial wars were the neutral nations, whose role was smaller than that of the belligerents, but vital in shaping strategic thinking.

In the maritime wars of the eighteenth century, neutral nations often served as the packhorses of belligerent commerce, both European and colonial. The role of a neutral nation was not passive, nor was it free from intervention. Neutrality meant only that a country was not an official belligerent; it did not mean that it was not heavily involved in the conflict, nor deeply engaged in continual negotiations with the belligerents to protect its own interests. During the Seven Years' War, these negotiations were especially critical for Britain in maintaining Dutch and Spanish neutrality. Equally important, and closely connected to diplomacy and strategy, were the sentences handed down by British prize courts, especially the Court of Prize Appeal in London. The court played a significant role within Britain's three-pronged maritime strategy for the war: maintaining foreign confidence in British maritime law and its court system, balancing the interests of British privateers and neutral carriers of commerce in the courts, and destroying French seaborne trade through commerce predation.

As a way to examine the singular role of the Court of Prize Appeal in maintaining Dutch and Spanish neutrality during the Seven Years' War, the particular fates of the first two Dutch and first two Spanish ships to come before the appellate court are chronicled in this book as they passed through the prize court system. Information gathered from the first-hand accounts of ministers and judges, court records, diplomatic and naval correspondence, pamphlets, and news articles is presented and analysed to show how the Court of Prize Appeal was crucial to both negotiations over neutrality and to British strategic thinking during the war. The wartime events surrounding the four ships and their journeys through the Court of Prize Appeal are also examined within their diplomatic, legal, and historical contexts.

The book seeks to argue that international law and domestic law – as expressed through the Court of Prize Appeal – were vital and complementary components of British maritime strategic thinking during the second half of the eighteenth century. British, French, Dutch, and Spanish strategic thinking during this period was influenced by ideas of a balance of power among Europe's maritime empires. This balance, however, was largely subjective and the strategic thinkers of each country sought to tip the balance in their favour without destabilising the entire system. It could be a delicate and fickle process where success was sometimes achieved through law and/or diplomacy, sometimes through war, sometimes all three. Balancing power in a time of war did not only mean striving for a new balance between belligerents; it also meant seeking an advantageous balance among belligerents and neutral nations without drawing the neutrals into the conflict as enemies. This could only be achieved if the actions taken by belligerents to alter the balance of power with neutrals during a war were accepted and seen by those same neutral nations as legitimate and grounded in the philosophies of international law. A legal consequence of pursuing legitimacy in the attempt to alter the balance of power was the creation of new rules, norms, and precedents within the British prize-law system. These new rules, norms, and precedents (introduced in Chapter 2) would serve to clarify and cement British interpretations of neutral rights without altering existing treaties or creating new legislation. Jurists in Britain's future maritime wars would turn to these rules, norms, and precedents to inform their own decisions in prize affairs and create a sense of consistency and legitimacy in prize court adjudications. This book also seeks to show that Dutch and Spanish neutrality was fragile, and its maintenance heavily dependent on the personalities, friendships, interests, and particular circumstances that worked to either hold it up or tear it apart.

British Strategic Thinking during the Seven Years' War

Britain sought to exploit the relationship between sea power and law during the Seven Years' War in an attempt to emerge from the conflict as the nation whose maritime courts, laws, and norms were accepted by other seaborne empires as internationally binding. A vital aspect of Britain's maritime strategy, and its connection with international law, was a focus on relations with neutral maritime nations who might become French allies and British enemies. The Seven Years' War was a period in which British maritime hegemony in the Atlantic world was ascending, but before strategic thinking and international law in war are usually considered to have emerged as formal disciplines. This does not mean, however, that strategic thinking and international law were absent from the conduct of war. The writings of international law philosophers such as Hugo Grotius, Cornelius van Bynkershoek, and Emmer de Vattel are widely acknowledged to have had a shaping influence on the European development of international maritime law. Their influence on the thinking and development of maritime strategic thinking during the Seven Years' War, however, is largely absent from histories of the conflict outside of some legal scholarship. Legal scholars such as Tara Helfman have used the Seven Years' War to explore the development of international legal scholarship, but the link to strategy and strategic thinking during the war are absent because it is not the purpose of the scholarship.[2] Similarly, scholarship on maritime strategic thinking has a tendency to ignore maritime strategic thought before the era of Clausewitz and the emergence of a 'modern', published, and European corpus on strategic thinking. Corbett, of course, is a notable exception to this, given his work on the Seven Years' War. However, even Corbett's writing does not necessarily make clear that the men who led Britain during the Seven Years' War – such as William Pitt and the Earl of Hardwicke – engaged in collective maritime strategic thinking. If, as Hew Strachan suggests, strategic theory in the pre-1945 era was knowingly retrospective, but strategy in practice is ultimately pragmatic,[3] then it makes sense to study the actions and thoughts of the men who prosecuted early-modern warfare as creators and inheritors of strategic thought. This remains the case even if those actions and thoughts were not collected into publications on war or strategy. More recent scholarship has begun to challenge this tendency such as Beatrice Heuser's book on strategy before the era of Clausewitz.[4] What is still missing, however, is a study of how maritime strategic thinking and international law were developed symbiotically during the Seven Years' War by the network of

---

[2] T. Helfman, 'Neutrality, the Law of Nations and the Natural Law Tradition', *Yale Journal of International Law*, 30:549 (2005), 549–84; and T. Helfman, 'Commerce on Trial, Neutral Rights and Private Warfare in the Seven Years War', in K. Stapelbroek (ed.), *Trade and War: The Neutrality of Commerce in the Inter-State System* (Helsinki Collegium for Advanced Studies, 2011), pp. 14–41.

[3] H. Strachan, *The Direction of War: Contemporary Strategy in Historical Perspective* (Cambridge University Press, 2013); p. 103.

[4] B. Heuser, *Strategy Before Clausewitz: Linking Warfare and Statecraft 1400–1830* (Routledge, 2017).

ministers and legal and naval minds who were charged with the conduct of the war. Without understanding these connections, and understanding how strategic thinking and law influenced one another, we cannot fully understand sea power in the eighteenth century.

In order to defeat France at sea during the Seven Years' War and therefore be in a position to achieve an advantageous shift in the European balance of power during peace negotiations, Britain needed to curtail the ability of neutral maritime nations like Spain and the Dutch Republic to carry French seaborne trade. Maritime commerce predation had been an element of British strategy for the entire period of colonial and imperial expansion. Because that strategy involved neutral nations and their maritime rights, negotiations over what constituted the rights of neutral nations were also central to British strategic thinking. Negotiations over neutral rights had clear strategic objectives for belligerents and neutrals during the Seven Years' War. From the British perspective, the strategic aim was to use negotiations over treaties of neutrality to manoeuvre the Dutch and Spanish governments into accepting an interpretation of neutral rights that limited the ability of neutral ships to carry French goods and gave British warships and privateers greater scope to police neutral ships. From the Dutch and Spanish perspectives, the strategic aim of negotiations over neutral rights was to prevent the British from interfering with their shipping generally and, specifically, their ability to carry French trade freely during times of war. It was also in the interest of Spain and the Dutch Republic that neither Britain nor France come out of the conflict with a strong enough position at the peace negotiations such that the balance of power could be dramatically shifted in either empire's favour.

As in many previous wars, it was paramount for Britain to keep France from obtaining a foothold in the Netherlands and setting up naval bases next to the Straights of Dover (the shortest crossing to England and a direct trade route into the Baltic).[5] As a maritime power without a particularly powerful army, Britain's best mode of securing the Netherlands against France was through diplomacy, and by making sure that the Dutch played the role of a neutral nation. At sea, Britain enjoyed superiority over France, which meant that when fighting in the colonies, where amphibious warfare and commerce predation were key factors, Britain had the upper hand. However, if Spain, with its large colonial presence in the Americas, became an ally of France, Britain's maritime superiority would come under threat.

---

[5] J. S. Corbett, *England in the Seven Years' War: A Study in Combined Strategy*, 2 vols. (Longmans, Green, and Co., 1907), vol. I, p. 18.

Spanish and Dutch neutrality was not necessarily a given when colonial hostilities began between Britain and France in 1754. Spain, like France, had an absolutist Bourbon king, and the two kingdoms were natural allies against a Protestant and parliamentary power like Britain. The Dutch, who were, in many respects, culturally closer to Britain than to France, did not wish for either country to emerge as the hegemonic victor.[6] If Britain had been perceived by other European powers as the aggressor and instigator of the conflict, it very well could have pushed Spain and the Dutch Republic into an alliance with France (a Franco-Spanish alliance was eventually formed in 1761). Such alliances would have changed the balance of power at sea and, in the case of the Dutch, given the French access to the Netherlands.[7] Once war was declared in 1756, however, both Spain and the Dutch Republic proclaimed their neutrality. The Dutch signed an agreement with France that kept the French out of the Low Countries and ensured that the Dutch would carry French trade in return.[8] Britain then focused on defeating the French at sea and, through her Prussian ally, defeating France on land in Europe. Britain's maritime predation strategy throughout the war would, however, be plagued by the constant task of maintaining Dutch and Spanish neutrality. This task was made increasingly difficult by what Julian Corbett called the 'law of maritime warfare' – the direct correlation between a country's increasing command of the sea and the likelihood of neutral powers becoming enemies.[9]

The first years of the war were not a resounding success for Britain in the maritime sphere but, by the end of 1759, France's colonial commerce had been all but eradicated. French Canada was under British control; France's navy was defeated, if not eliminated, in the battle of Quiberon Bay; and the islands of the French West Indies were falling prey to British invasion. Britain's increasing dominance over France at sea and in the colonial sphere directly affected the relationships between Britain, Spain, and the Dutch Republic. In order to ensure their neutrality, any rights or privileges enjoyed by the ships of neutral countries whilst at sea had to be upheld by the navies and privateers with whom they crossed paths on their voyages. Britain's increased maritime hegemony through the Seven Years' War meant that the warships and privateers with which neutral ships were most likely to interact, were British.

The behaviour of Britain's warships and privateers when interacting with neutral ships was, ostensibly, governed by bilateral treaties such as

---

[6] A. C. Carter, *The Dutch Republic in Europe in the Seven Years' War* (MacMillan and Co., 1971), p. xvi.
[7] Ibid. p. 83.   [8] Ibid. p. 34.   [9] Corbett, *England in the Seven Years' War*, vol. I, p. 5.

the Anglo-Dutch treaty of 1674, and the Anglo-Spanish treaty of 1667. However, it was ultimately impossible to control or police the actions of Britain's representatives at sea. Events between ships at sea were often completely isolated and the only witnesses were those involved in the encounter. News of an encounter could take weeks to reach authorities in Europe or London, by which time there was little that could be done to deter any diplomatic damage which the actions of British or neutral citizens might have sparked during a seaborne encounter. As a result, contentious incidents that occurred between British and Dutch ships, or British and Spanish ships, and which ended up in the prize courts, could not be treated as isolated incidents. They became an integral part of the reactive negotiations over neutrality and of Anglo-Dutch or Anglo-Spanish relations in general during the war.

Anglo-Dutch Relations in Context

At the end of the third Anglo-Dutch War, the marine treaty of 1674 was signed and, along with a previous treaty of 1667, re-established the Grotian principle of 'free ships make free goods' as a guiding principle for how neutral rights were understood between the two nations.[10] The treaty defined what goods were to be considered contraband and there-fore not covered by the 'free ships, free goods' principle. Subsequent Anglo-Dutch defensive treaties of 1678 and 1716 established a link between the armies of Britain and the Dutch Republic. In the event that Britain, or the king's possession of Hanover, was attacked, the Dutch were to provide a token fighting force of 600 men. If the Dutch were attacked, Britain would join the fighting as a Dutch ally.[11]

Disputes between the two countries arose during the Seven Years' War soon after the Dutch declared their neutrality and British privateers and warships began to take Dutch merchant ships as prizes. Because Britain deemed France the aggressor and attacker in the war, British ministers expected the Dutch to honour the treaty of 1678 and to deliver 600 troops. The Dutch, however, prevaricated over their obligation to Britain, and were more interested in keeping the French out of the Low Countries by not showing favour to Britain. For many British ministers and legal minds, the refusal of the Dutch to adhere to the treaty of 1678 was a good thing, because it made British adherence to the earlier treaty of 1674 moot. If the Dutch refused to honour one treaty, then Britain was under no obligation to honour the other previous treaty.

---

[10] Carter, *The Dutch Republic*, p. 4.   [11] Ibid.

The intellectual exercise of interpreting and disputing the two treaties preoccupied the minds of politicians and diplomats whilst at the same time the treaties were also being interpreted and acted upon in the prize courts across Britain and its colonies. The sentences passed on Dutch ships in these courts mainly focused on whether their cargo was being legally carried (i.e. whether the Dutch ships were violating the treaty and their neutrality by aiding the French, or whether the cargo being shipped was legal under the circumstances prescribed by the treaty). As the war progressed, the factions of the Dutch government that were anti-British, and the Dutch merchants mostly concentrated in Amsterdam and Rotterdam, became increasingly frustrated by the treatment of Dutch ships in the British prize courts. They began to doubt that the British prize system could, or would, protect their neutral rights.

By 1758, Anglo-Dutch relations had reached what Richard Pares called the 'Anglo-Dutch crisis'.[12] The crisis, from 1758 to early spring of 1759, encompassed the straining of Anglo-Dutch relations due to the condemnation of Dutch ships in the British prize courts and the inability of the two countries to agree how to define the neutral rights to be enjoyed by the Dutch. With no agreement outside of the prize courts on what constituted Dutch neutral rights, and with sentencing throughout the prize court system seen as inconsistent and arbitrary, the justice and due process of the prize courts were regarded with suspicion and contested by the Dutch government. The crisis, which almost led to open hostilities, was eventually resolved when Dutch grievances over neutral rights were allayed, largely, by the first two Dutch cases to come before the Court of Prize Appeal in March of 1759.

The Court of Prize Appeal worked to alleviate the Anglo-Dutch crisis by overturning or upholding sentences from lower prize courts involving Dutch ships, as necessary, to restore Dutch trust in the British government's commitment and ability to defend Dutch neutrality from the abuses of British warships and British privateers. It was in these early Dutch cases that one of the most important legal norms for defining neutral rights was brought into existence by the Court of Prize Appeal: the Rule of the War of 1756. This rule started to clarify how the British prize court system would understand the limits of neutral rights and begin to set legal precedents with the cases of the *Maria Theresa* and the *America*. The work of the Court of Prize Appeal was not limited to Dutch cases however, and the court, as well as the Rule, played an equally important role in Anglo-Spanish relations over neutral rights,

[12] R. Pares, *Colonial Blockade and Neutral Rights 1739–1763* (Porcupine Press, 1975), p. 75.

though unforeseen circumstances such as the death of kings and competition over resources in the Americas made the task of placating the Spanish immensely more complicated.

Anglo-Spanish Relations in Context

Anglo-Spanish relations followed a very different path from Anglo-Dutch relations during the Seven Years' War. The most glaring difference was that Britain pre-emptively declared war on Spain, in 1762, after Spain entered into an alliance with France. The Spanish empire, like many mercantilist states, did not open its colonial trade to extranational merchants except occasionally, during times of war, when enemy commerce predation made it a necessity. Britain's legal trade with the Spanish empire, therefore, could only go to, or through, the Iberian Peninsula. The Anglo-Spanish treaty of 1750 determined that Britain's trade could go through Cádiz and gave British merchants advantageous terms regarding tariffs. However, the 1750 treaty did not settle certain grievances that were left over from the War of Austrian Succession, such as the behaviour of British and Spanish privateers towards merchant ships, and whether British subjects had a right to make settlements and harvest logwood on the coast of Honduras. These issues were left in a murky state and continued to inflame diplomatic relations between the two empires.[13]

Like the Dutch Republic, Spain declared its neutrality after war broke out between Britain and France in 1756, but the interests linking Spain, France, and Britain were very different. France and Spain were closely related by their ruling families, both Bourbon, and both Catholic states. If France could convince Spain to join the war against Britain, their combined naval strength would surpass Britain's and the balance of power in the Americas would be dramatically shifted. Many of France's foreign policy efforts during the war were, therefore, spent trying to make an ally of Spain. For Britain, keeping Spain neutral was an important wartime strategic aim; a Spanish alliance with France could disrupt British aims to subdue France at sea and in the colonies, as well as cut off British trade through Cádiz, which was worth a lot of capital to the British government and to merchants, neither of whom wanted Spain as an enemy.

Spain, like most maritime countries, had grievances with Britain over its treatment of neutral shipping. Britain's war with France brought the opportunity for Spanish merchants to carry French trade in their neutral ships and provided British warships and privateers the opportunity to

---

[13] D. Baugh, *The Global Seven Years' War, 1754–1763* (Pearson, 2011), p. 98.

capture Spanish ships carrying French goods as potential prizes. British privateers showed an unfortunate zeal for taking Spanish prizes despite the efforts of British ministers to curb their excessive predatory actions.[14] The Spanish government and merchants retained little faith in the British prize court system as the war developed. By 1761, the skilful tactics of French ministers, the death of a trusted British foreign minister to Spain, and the accession of a new Spanish monarch who was staunchly anti-British, meant Spain was ready to renounce her neutrality and to enter into an alliance with France despite British efforts to maintain Spanish neutrality. The Franco-Spanish alliance in turn, led to the pre-emptive declaration of war by Britain against Spain.[15] It was, ultimately, the culmination of years of frustrated Anglo-Spanish negotiations. Whilst British ministers had tried to use diplomatic negotiations and the Court of Prize Appeal to restore Spanish confidence in the prize court system and Britain's commitment to neutral rights, it was not enough to bridge the gap between the two countries created by a host of long-running grievances and unfortunate circumstances. Spain, wary of Britain's rising maritime hegemony, sought redress for its complaints in the arms of a French alliance and an Anglo-Spanish war which it hoped could shift the balance of power in the Americas in Spain's favour. British strategic thinking with regard to Spain, realised through the Court of Prize Appeal, failed to secure neutrality for the duration of the Seven Years' War, but it did delay Spanish belligerence until after France had been crushed at sea, rendering the threat of a Franco-Spanish alliance in the maritime sphere surmountable. From a legal point of view, the Spanish cases that came before the Court of Prize Appeal helped to establish the Rule of the War of 1756 as applicable outside of an Anglo-Dutch context and thus a more universally relevant principle of British international legal thought. The early Spanish cases also proved important in establishing clear thinking and legal reasoning based on the doctrines of continuous voyage, transhipment, and adoption, that would shape British prize court decisions and strategic thinking in the American War of Independence, the French Revolutionary War, and the Napoleonic Wars.

British Maritime Hegemony, Neutrality, and Prize Law in Historical Context

The growth of British maritime hegemony in the eighteenth century meant that British prize law increasingly became the international norm

---

[14] Pares, *Colonial Blockade*, p. 28.   [15] Baugh, *Global Seven Years' War*, p. 514.

by which neutral maritime rights were governed. As Sophus Reinert remarked in the essay *Rivalry: Greatness in Early Modern Political Economy*, 'a growing fear in eighteenth century Europe was that it would be Great Britain to give the world its laws, either through the power of its navies or of its manufactures'.[16] If the British prize court system was to be an arbiter in disagreements over maritime neutral rights in any conflict that involved British sea power, then the neutral nations had to trust that the system was fair, legitimate, and would protect the rights of their seaborne citizens. If this trust and legitimacy were lost, if the prize courts failed to uphold neutral rights, then Corbett's law of maritime warfare would come to its natural conclusion, and neutral nations in Britain's wars would become belligerents.

The concept of trust and legitimacy is crucial when looking at British attempts to define and uphold neutral rights in order to suit strategic aims during the war. Xabier Lamikiz, in his book *Trade and Trust in the Eighteenth-Century Atlantic World*, argued that in early-modern commerce, trust was largely dependent first on the 'efficiency of the legal system in enforcing contracts and second, on the availability of information, which was closely linked, but not exclusively linked, to the frequency and quality of communications'.[17] Lamikiz's argument can be easily translated to apply to prize courts and neutrality. Efficiency in upholding and enforcing neutral rights through the prize court system was paramount to fostering trust in Britain's ability to be considered a legitimate international arbiter of neutrality. During the Seven Years' War, maintaining Dutch and Spanish trust in the prize court system to assure their neutrality was, therefore, a critical part of the larger British maritime strategy of commerce predation, which was dependent on the neutrality of other nations that were significant players in the maritime sphere.

In the mid-eighteenth century, neutral rights were negotiated and interpreted mainly through bilateral treaties which were supposed to be upheld by both signatories in times of war. The concept of maritime neutrality, as expressed in the treaties which governed Anglo-Dutch and Anglo-Spanish relations during the Seven Years' War, began to emerge around 1650, with treaties containing the Grotian principle that 'free ships make free goods';[18] that is, goods carried in neutral ships, except those goods designated as contraband of war, were free from

---

[16] S. Reinert, 'Rivalry: Greatness in Early Modern Political Economy', in P. Stern and C. Wennerlind (eds.), *Mercantilism Reimagined: Political Economy in Early Modern Britain and Its Empire* (Oxford University Press, 2014), p. 352.

[17] X. Lamikiz, *Trade and Trust in the Eighteenth-Century Atlantic World* (Boydell Press, 2013), p. 13.

[18] C. Kulsrud, *Maritime Neutrality to 1780* (Little Brown and Co., 1936), p. 155.

confiscation, even if those goods belonged to an 'enemy'. These treaties usually contained stipulations that a belligerent had the right to board neutral merchant ships and search for contraband goods.[19]

The principle of 'free ships make free goods' was derived from the concept of the law of nations, of which there were two kinds. The first is contractual in nature; it arose from an 'agreement between states and is therefore binding *only* upon states that are actually parties to the agreement in question'.[20] The other was also contractual in nature, but was of 'universal application, arising out of a "general agreement" between states'.[21] The law of nations was a man-made law that applied only between man-made states, as distinct from a natural law which was derived from the divine will and the idea that God had granted the 'boons of creation' to all of humanity collectively. Natural law could be divided into categories based on how humans derived ownership of the boons of creation without harming others or taking possession of that which was already owned.[22] These definitions were derived from the work of seventeenth-century writers on law and war, the Spaniard Francisco Suárez and the Dutchman Hugo Grotius.[23] It was through Grotius's publication *On the Law of War and Peace* of 1625, that the concept of the law of nations came into popular use.[24] It would be almost exclusively Grotian principles that were used and interpreted by jurists in the Court of Prize Appeal to justify and legitimise their decisions.

Another Dutch legal thinker, Cornelius Van Bynkershoek, is important to note because of his place in some of the legal historiography of the Seven Years' War. Writing in the first half of the eighteenth century, he produced his *Dissertation on the Dominion of the Sea* in 1703 and *Questions of Public Law* in 1737. Both works were relevant to discussions over maritime neutrality. In contrast to Grotius, Bynkershoek argued in *Questions of Public Law* that the seizure of enemy property in times of war for the purpose of destroying an enemy was just, but not linked to natural law. For Bynkershoek, war meant that normal social obligations no longer applied and any means used to destroy an enemy was just: 'the reason that justifies war justifies every method of destroying the enemy'.[25] As far as the activities of neutrals were concerned, he argued that a neutral nation had every right to protect their commercial interests

---

[19] Ibid. p. 159.
[20] S. Neff, *Justice Among Nations: A History of International Law* (Harvard University Press, 2014), p. 156.
[21] Ibid. p. 171.
[22] Hugo Grotius, *The Free Sea*, ed. D. Armitage (Liberty Fund, 2004), p. xiii.
[23] Neff, *Justice Among Nations*, p. 142.   [24] Ibid. p. 158.
[25] Helfman, 'Neutrality, the Law of Nations and the Natural Law Tradition', pp. 559–60.

and that belligerents and neutrals must come to an agreement on how each other's rights were to be acknowledged and legitimised.[26] In their work, Tara Helfman and Koen Stapelbroek argue for the influence of Bynkershoek's ideas on the development of ideas and doctrines within the British prize court system during the Seven Years' War.[27] Helfman in particular argues that a shift occurred during the course of the war from the ideas of Grotius and the natural law tradition to the ideas of Bynkershoek and the beginnings of modern legal positivism.[28] Her argument is largely founded on examining British pamphlets produced during the war and the examination of some Anglo-Dutch diplomatic correspondence. Whilst her argument is convincing in terms of the pamphlets reflecting much of Bynkershoek's thinking on neutrality, she does not delve into the archival material of the prize court cases themselves. The arguments made in this book rely more heavily on the ideas of Grotius because it is his ideas that are discussed in the notes of the judges and lawyers examined in the following chapters. There is almost no mention, and no direct engagement, with Bynkershoek in the court cases here examined.

In England, the standard in matters of maritime law was Charles Molloy's 1676 book *De Jure Maritimo et Navali* which went through ten editions, the last of which appeared in 1778. Molloy presented the idea that, in accordance with the law of nations, neutral property found on board an enemy ship did not belong to the enemy and could not, therefore, be considered the legitimate prize (property) of the captor.[29] In 1758, Emerich de Vattel, a Swiss scholar, published his *Droit des gens* in which he argued that the property of neutrals found in an enemy ship should be returned to the original owners if the enemy ship were captured as prize. The captors had no right to confiscate the neutral goods.[30] Vattel sought to make natural law philosophy more accessible to practitioners, such as diplomats, who might find it useful in their negotiations. Vattel believed that the law of nations had its foundation in natural law

---

[26] Ibid. p. 561.

[27] Helfman, 'Neutrality, the Law of Nations and the Natural Law Tradition'; Helfman, 'Commerce on Trial'; K. Stapelbroek, 'The Rights of Neutral Trade and its Forgotten History', in K. Stapelbroek (ed.), *Trade and War: The Neutrality of Commerce in the Inter-State System* (Helsinki Collegium for Advanced Studies, 2011), pp. 14–41; K. Stapelbroek 'The Foundations of Vattel's "System" of Politics and the Context of the Seven Years' War: Moral Philosophy, Luxury and the Constitutional Commercial State', in K. Stapelbroek and A. Trampus (eds.), *The Legacy of Vattel's Droit des gens* (Palgrave Macmillan, 2019).

[28] Helfman, 'Commerce on Trial', p. 16.   [29] Kulsrud, *Maritime Neutrality*, pp. 122–3.

[30] Ibid. p. 153.

but that it was also a positive law.[31] The ability of states to exert their 'neutral' rights during a time of war was therefore governed by a combination of natural law tradition and legal positivism.

The diplomats and politicians of the second half of the eighteenth century who were negotiating and interpreting the bilateral treaties that dealt with maritime neutrality were likely to be well versed in the law of nations and the concept of 'free ships, free goods' as discussed and interpreted by men like Grotius, Bynkershoek, and Vattel, and they used these principles to define how neutral goods and ships were to be treated when captured during times of war. When it came to enforcing the law of nations and protecting neutrality, it was the prize courts of various nations that largely took on the task. Britain's prize courts were very active in this regard, as the nation was almost continually involved in maritime wars with other European nations from the 1650s through 1815.

The ability of British prize courts to enforce the law of nations and treaties on neutrality as fledgling international law was rooted in the independence of the courts. In 1692, the first British Prize Act was passed and it guaranteed that a captor had the legal right to present his case in a prize court in which adjudication was free from political interference.[32] In terms of neutral rights, this meant that the British government was, technically, unable to interfere in cases of captured neutral ships or cargo at the request of the neutral nation's government. The prize courts in Britain were, at least on paper, independent from politics, and served only to carry out the letter of the law as prescribed by treaties dealing with neutrality. In practice, however, the independence was not complete, nor was following the letter of the law always a clear-cut matter. Before the War of the Austrian Succession (1740–8), treaty provisions about 'free ships, free goods' were not widely enforced and, even after 1740, there was political interference in the enforcement.[33]

After the War of the Austrian Succession, the Seven Years' War, and the American War of Independence, all of which were global wars involving European maritime empires, many treaties involving neutrality were simply renewed by Britain. Consequently, by the time of the French Revolutionary and Napoleonic Wars, the main treaties regarding neutrality still in place were from the seventeenth century. However, each conflict did produce cases and arguments that could serve as precedents in future conflicts. Even cases that were 'dropped' by the court or where

---

[31] K. Stapelbroek and A. Trampus, 'The Legacy of Vattel's *Droit de gens*: Contexts, Concepts, Reception, Translation and Diffusion', in K. Stapelbroek and A. Trampus (eds.), *The Legacy of Vattel's 'Droit des gens'* (Palgrave Macmillan, 2019), pp. 2–3.
[32] Neff, *Justice Among Nations*, p. 35.   [33] Kulsrud, *Maritime Neutrality*, p. 155.

the appeal was ultimately withdrawn, could produce a large amount of written opinion and discussion from the judges and advocates that contributed to the formation of a collective thinking, or *communis opinio*, that could be called upon in future cases. Thus, the corpus of legal thought that helped judges interpret and enforce prize law grew with each war even as the treaties remained stagnant. During the Seven Years' War it was the Anglo-Dutch treaty of 1674 and the Anglo-Spanish treaty of 1667 that had the most bearing on Spanish and Dutch neutrality, whilst the most important developments in legal precedents and legal thinking about neutral rights would emerge in the form of the Rule of the War of 1756 and the doctrines of continuous voyage, transhipment, and adoption.

A Case-Study Approach

To analyse the inner workings, successes, and failures of the Court of Prize Appeal as a facilitator of both wartime strategy and negotiations over neutrality, the first two Dutch, and the first two Spanish, prize cases to come before the appellate court were selected as case studies. This case-based research allowed for an in-depth study of the Court of Prize Appeal, the men involved in it, the men running it, and how they all related to one another. Each case is a microcosm of British wartime strategy in action. Each court case spanned several years, and was shaped by factors specific to the case, but also general in nature. The judges, particularly Lord Hardwicke, took great care to use these first cases in order to aid negotiations over neutral rights and to establish guiding precedents and principles that the court would use throughout the Seven Years' War – and the Napoleonic Wars. The four ships are unique in their exact circumstances and trajectories, whilst also being illustrative of how the court carried out its legal and political work. The case studies also illustrate how the interpersonal and professional relations of men on the court or in government were of paramount importance to the success or failure of a strategy that tried to maintain a balance between maritime neutral rights and maritime predation.

A case-study methodology complements previous statistical studies with large samples that have been previously carried out. David Starkey, in his research on privateering and prize law during the eighteenth century, used a very large selection of evidence from the records of the High Court of Admiralty. Richard Pares selected sources from the High Court of Admiralty, the Court of Prize Appeal, and the colonial Vice Admiralty courts in his work on the colonial blockade and maritime warfare in the West Indies. E. S. Roscoe, in his extensive works on the history of prize law and prize courts, used Admiralty and High Court of

Admiralty records.[34] These historians have made valuable and extensive contributions to the history of the prize courts. Their work on trends, developments, and consistencies in eighteenth-century prize courts and prize-taking has laid a foundation from which a much more nuanced and detailed research approach can be launched without the fear of coming to general erroneous conclusions based on too small a sample. The detailed examination of the first prize appeal cases to come before the court offers information regarding the inner workings and politics of the Court of Prize Appeal and presents compelling evidence for the court's role in the strategic aims of keeping Spain and the Dutch Republic neutral throughout the Seven Years' War. It also offers the ability to trace how, and why, the foundations for precedents and principles that shaped British conceptions of neutral rights and international maritime law for more than fifty years, were laid in these first four cases.

In order to put together the micro-histories of the four court cases, several avenues of investigation had to be explored. The first task was to explore the connections between ministers, judges, civil law lawyers, merchants, and foreign diplomats; a veritable who's who of prize law and foreign policy for the war. The search began in the official and private correspondences of government ministers and judges who were invested in the Court of Prize Appeal. As the first four cases to come before the court stirred debate in political and legal circles, these connections emerged in letters between ministers and confidants, in official memorandums for certain departments, or private memorandums written for future reference. The book relies heavily on the notes of Lord Hardwicke as the leading judicial voice on the Court of Prize Appeal. His notes on the court cases are also the most complete and thorough. The limitation of relying on Hardwicke's notes for parts of the analysis is that they represent the thinking of the Court of Prize Appeal as understood by one man. In order to mitigate this, the correspondence of other influential members of the court have been used wherever possible in order to illustrate their own thoughts and ideas. Ministerial writing was plagued by veiled references and an aversion to proper nouns. In almost all instances, the names of the neutral ships involved in Court of Prize Appeal cases did not appear in personal correspondence or memorandums. Despite rarely mentioning names, however, ministers were usually scrupulous in dating their letters and memorandums. Putting together

---

[34] See also D. Starkey, *British Privateering Enterprise in the Eighteenth Century* (Exeter University Press, 1990); Pares, *Colonial Blockade*; R. Pares, *War and Trade in the West Indies 1739–1763* (Frank Cass and Co., 1963); and E. S. Roscoe, *Studies in the History of the Admiralty and Prize Courts* (Stevens and Sons, 1932).

the dates, the facts of the case under discussion, and the people involved, it was possible to assemble a clear trail of the four court cases through the correspondence of the men involved.

A second line of investigation was a close review of contemporary public sources. Through the use of the seventeenth– and eighteenth–century-focused Burney Collection Digital Newspaper Archive, and the Eighteenth-Century Digital Database (two research tools recently compiled by the British Library and not available to most prior prize-law historians) it was possible to find a wide variety of public references and debates about the court cases and the issue of neutral rights. The names of specific ships sometimes appeared in articles applauding and condemning the actions of the courts and ministers. Pamphlets published by judges and lawyers (not coincidently, at the same time the cases were being tried) either defended or condemned Britain's strategy regarding neutral maritime countries.

A methodological problem that arises when using newspapers as sources is how to sort through the material that was printed in newspapers during the Seven Years' War. It is sometimes thought that the answer to this question is provided to historians when institutions like the British Library began to digitise their newspaper collections and make them searchable through OCR (optical character recognition) technology. The problem is the unreliability and frequent inaccuracy of OCR.[35] The accuracy of OCR is dependent on the quality of the image available, and many of the images that make up the digital collections used in this book are of a poor quality. Research based on search hit-rates to make an argument is, therefore, largely suspect, if using the digital collections.[36] For this book, however, the newspapers that needed to be searched were bounded by time, and whether they discussed maritime affairs and neutrality. This greatly limited the number of newspapers that had to be read and searched. It was possible, therefore, to read the publications in their entirety and search for articles without relying heavily on OCR searches.[37]

---

[35] S. G. Brandtzæg and P. Goring and C. Watson (eds.), *Travelling Chronicles: News and Newspapers from the Early Modern Period to the Eighteenth Century* (Brill, 2018).

[36] A. Prescott, 'Searching for Dr. Johnson: The Digitisation of the Burney Newspaper Collection', in S. G. Brandtzæg and P. Goring and C. Watson (eds.), *Travelling Chronicles: News and Newspapers from the Early Modern Period to the Eighteenth Century* (Leiden: Brill, 2018), p. 62.

[37] For further research into newspapers and eighteenth century politics in Britain see A. Brinkman-Schwartz, 'The *Antigallican* Affair: Public and Ministerial Responses to Anglo-Spanish Maritime Conflict in the Seven Years War, 1756–1758', *The English Historical Review*, Nov. (2020), 1132–64; A. Brinkman-Schwartz, 'The Heart of the Maritime World: London's Wartime Coffee Houses 1756–1783', *Historical Research*, 94 (2021), 508–31; and H. Barker, *Newspapers, Politics, and Public Opinion in Late Eighteenth Century England* (Oxford University Press, 1998).

In terms of court material, there is a considerable amount still extant on each ship in both the High Court of Admiralty and Court of Prize Appeal records. These records are held at the UK National Archives. Additional archives which supported the case studies include the Hardwicke Papers at the British Library and the New York Public Library; the Shelburne Papers at the Clements Library at the University of Michigan, which includes a wealth of letters and documents on Anglo-Spanish relations during the Seven Years' War from colonial, official, and mercantile perspectives; the Archivo General de Indias in Seville, which contains correspondence between Spanish ministers and colonial ministers; and the Archivo Histórico Nacional in Madrid, which contains correspondence between Spanish ministers. Consequently, it has been possible to reconstruct the court cases amid the political, legal, personal, maritime, wartime, and commercial factors that contributed to their specific outcomes with a level of detail and understanding not previously found in the historiographies of prize affairs that are based on much broader, quantitative, data samples.

The micro-histories of the four court cases demonstrate how British strategy and law regarding neutrals was developed and implemented through the mechanism of the Court of Prize Appeal. These histories also demonstrate the necessary links between diplomacy, strategic thinking, domestic legal systems, and international law philosophy, in order to negotiate the terms of neutrality and how neutral rights were actually interpreted. These four cases are important to study not because they dramatically changed legal history or drastically revolutionised strategic or legal thinking, but because they were considered vitally important to the success of British strategic aims at the time. That success was seen to depend on whether Spain and the Dutch Republic could be convinced that their neutral rights were being protected by the Court of Prize Appeal. The first few cases offer the possibility of understanding the concerns and thinking of the ministers, diplomats, judges, and advocates and how their work laid the foundation for how neutral rights would be conceived of and treated for the rest of the Seven Years' War and subsequent conflicts.

Structure

The body of this book is divided into three parts. Part I, 'Sea Power and Its Relationship to Strategy and Law', contains Chapters 1 and 2. These are dedicated to analysing the relationship between sea power, strategy, and law and how this relationship has been considered by sea power theorists. Part II, 'The Dutch Case Studies', is dedicated to the case studies of the Dutch ships, the *Maria Theresa* and the *America*, and their progression through the prize court system. In this part, Chapter 3 presents the wider context of Anglo-Dutch relations during the Seven Years' War and introduces the two Dutch prize court cases and their participants. Chapters 4 and 5 analyse the Dutch court cases as they passed first through the High Court of Admiralty and then the Court of Prize Appeal, culminating in the end of the Anglo-Dutch crisis and continued Dutch neutrality. Part III, 'The Spanish Case Studies', is dedicated to the case studies of the Spanish ships, the *San Juan Baptista* and the *Jesús, Maria, y José*. Chapter 6 introduces the context of Anglo-Spanish relations during the Seven Years' War and how it differed from the Anglo-Dutch context. Chapters 7–9 follow the two Spanish ships through the High Court of Admiralty and the Court of Prize Appeal and demonstrate how the policy of upholding neutral rights in the prize courts, which worked to ease Anglo-Dutch tensions, was not sufficient to resolve Anglo-Spanish conflicts.

The conclusion notes the contrast between the outcomes of Britain's negotiations with these two neutral nations and serves to show that a strategy of upholding neutral rights through the Court of Prize Appeal, which was so successful with the Dutch, could not be successfully applied in all circumstances. The nuances of the negotiations, legal arguments, court proceedings, unforeseen national events, and the interpersonal relations of the men involved were critical elements of success or failure. The case studies presented in the following chapters are microcosms of those relationships and the negotiations upon which the attempt to build a successful British strategy concerning neutral nations depended.

Part I

Sea Power and Its Relationship to Strategy and Law

Framework

What is the relationship between sea power, law, and strategy? How can a state harness both the law and sea power in order to further its strategic aims? These questions have occupied maritime strategic thinkers for centuries. Much modern writing on the subject has been influenced by the work begun by Julian Corbett in *Some Principles of Maritime Strategy* and in his treatment of the Seven Years' War, *England in the Seven Years' War* – works which elevated Britain's eighteenth-century wars as often idealised cases in which law and maritime power were used to achieve strategic effect. Other prominent maritime strategists, namely Alfred Thayer Mahan and Sir Herbert Richmond, have also approached the subject, but their work is rarely as explicit on how law and sea power relate to and influence one another, leaving Corbett's work as one of the most enduring statements on the question.[1]

Law and sea power cannot be divorced for two principal reasons. First, sea power is the vehicle through which a state is able to transform domestic law into international maritime law by using its power and influence to establish the status quo. Secondly, the strategic aims and considerations of sea powers drive negotiations over maritime international law in attempts to either constrain, or expand, the impact of sea power. The extent to which maritime nations are able to influence those negotiations depends on the relative qualities/strengths of their sea power. This dual dynamic was central to the exercise of maritime strategy during the Seven Years' War, although not always in the ways in which Corbett and others interpreted those conflicts. This first part of the book is divided into two chapters. Chapter 1 will address the relationship between sea power and strategy, with a focus on how that relationship

---

[1] J. S. Corbett, *England in the Seven Years' War: A Study in Combined Strategy*, 2 vols. (Longmans, Green, and Co., 1907); J. S. Corbett, *Some Principles of Maritime Strategy* (Longmans, 1911); A. T. Mahan, *The Influence of Sea Power upon History* (Little Brown and Co., 1890); H. Richmond, *Statesmen and Sea Power* (Little Clarendon Press, 1946).

has been understood by scholars of strategy with particular reference to the Seven Years' War. Chapter 2 will address the relationship between law and sea power with a focus on how legal scholars and legal philosophers have understood the development of international maritime law during the Seven Years' War. Overall, the two chapters will suggest that the place of the law–sea power nexus in the Seven Years' War, and thus the cannon of British maritime strategic thought, has not been sufficiently considered.

1   Sea Power and Strategy

The intended meanings behind the terms, strategy, maritime strategy, and naval strategy, have not always been consistent and are often used interchangeably. It is worth taking a moment to consider how these terms and concepts have been used over time and how their meanings have changed. What, if any, are the distinctions between strategy, maritime strategy, and naval strategy? During the eighteenth century, strategy, as both a word and concept, was something reserved for generals and land campaigns and was primarily applied to the use of armies and the conduct of battle. Clausewitz, who did not write about the sea specifically but was writing about the final European war of the long eighteenth century, has had his definition of strategy neatly summarised by Hew Strachan; 'Clausewitz defined strategy as the use of the battle for the purposes of the war: in other words, he aimed to link tactics to a wider objective and ultimately, of course, to link strategy to policy.'[1]

If Clausewitz and other thinkers, like Jomini, used the wars of the long eighteenth century in an attempt to create a theoretical framework for the conduct of warfare on land, why was not the same thing done for war at sea? Strachan points out the following, 'Nobody who fought at sea in the Napoleonic Wars subsequently used those wars ... to develop thinking about strategy.'[2] This observation is correct, but it raises three avenues of discussion that have a direct bearing on our understanding of the development of maritime strategic thinking during the Seven Years' War and the wider eighteenth century. First, does Clausewitz's definition of strategy – 'the use of the battle for the purpose of the war' or 'what generals did' – translate to the maritime environment and to admirals? Or is there another way to conceive of strategy in the maritime sphere in the eighteenth century? Secondly, is the intellectual development of maritime strategic thought limited to the work of admirals and commanders who

---

[1] H. Strachan, *The Direction of War: Contemporary Strategy in Historical Perspective* (Cambridge University Press, 2013), p. 152.
[2] Ibid.

have participated in war? Thirdly, and closely related to the second, is the development of strategic thought defined only as the public or formal discourse created by published works on the subject which use the language of 'strategy'?

Strachan addresses the first avenue in *The Direction of War*. He argues that in the eighteenth century (and the early-modern period more broadly) the thinking that shaped attitudes about the use of the sea in times of war, and about the expansion of empires, was rooted in economic and legal considerations.[3] Imperial expansion and colonialism went hand in hand with the rise of mercantilism, the transition to early capitalism, and European-centric international law.[4] The sea provided the connection between Europe and colonies and was the highway upon which trade, people, and information flowed. Access to the sea (and the control of that access), therefore, had to be protected, but that protection was not a purely military endeavour – it was legal, political, economic, military, and naval:

> Those concerned with the exercise of maritime power in the seventeenth and eighteenth centuries had to contend much more directly with the legal framework for its exercise than did commanders in land warfare. Practices at sea, therefore, combined naval (in the narrowly military sense) with maritime developments, peace with war, and economic and legal practices with national power.[5]

Can the exercise of maritime power (or sea power), then, be called strategy? Not, as Strachan makes clear, in the eighteenth-century sense of the word. However, a more contemporary definition of strategy reflects an eighteenth-century and nineteenth-century conception of the relationship between trade, politics, law, and the sea in both times of peace and war:

> Strategy today is applied in peace as well as in war; it encompasses the preparation of plans and equipment for conflict, aspects which Clausewitz saw simply as ancillary; and it includes the economic capacity of a state and its people's political and social commitment to wage war. The intellectual roots of that definition derive from maritime power, not land power, and are a manifestation of the influence of sea power on strategic thought.[6]

If the current understanding of the Euro-centric discourse on strategy is based on an eighteenth- and early nineteenth-century understanding of how sea power could be exercised in the pursuit of national policies, then

---

[3] Ibid.
[4] L. Campling and A. Colás, *Capitalism and the Sea* (Verso, 2021); and R. S. Du Plessis, *Transitions to Capitalism in Early Modern Europe: Economies in the Era of Early Globalization, c.1450–c.1820* (Cambridge University Press, 2019), pp. 4–8.
[5] Strachan, *Direction of War*, p. 153.   [6] Ibid. p. 155.

it is logical to study the maritime wars of that period, like the Seven Years' War, in order to fully understand how and why strategic thinking was developed, influenced, shaped, and implemented by the actors and factors involved. It is a historical study of practical strategy rather than strategic theory.[7] The men collectively developing maritime strategy during the war did not seek to leave behind a treatise that would help subsequent generations think about and prosecute wars. However, the material they did leave behind allows students of strategy to delve into their thinking and thus enlighten their own understanding of how strategies are made and implemented.

In addressing the first avenue of inquiry, the second has been partially covered. Taking Strachan's definition of strategy mentioned above means that the intellectual development of maritime strategic thought could not be limited to the work of admirals and commanders who have participated in war. Ministers, ambassadors, judges, government officials, as well as the First Lord of the Admiralty and his allies, all participated in the development of maritime strategic thinking during the Seven Years' War. N. A. M. Rodger points out that, in this period, there were no formal forums or dedicated spaces in which strategy was formed and discussed.[8] However, the absence of a formalised space dedicated to strategic thinking does not preclude the collective act of strategic thinking. The spaces in which strategic development and thinking took place during the Seven Year's War were what today we might consider informal. In other words, outside a dedicated space such as a national security council or a staff college. Maritime strategic thinking during the war was done through the writing of letters and memorandums, through conversation and the recording of such conversations in personal notes or journals, in the marginalia of official documents, and in orders sent to officials overseas. The source material for maritime strategic thinking in the eighteenth century is vast and varied. It is also spread across global archives and, for the most part, never neatly collated under the banner of 'strategy'. In order to understand how and why maritime strategic thinking developed in the way that it did, the informal spaces in which strategic thinking took place must be considered and investigated. Many historians of the Seven Years' War, such as Richard Pares and

---

[7] This idea is explored by Hew Strachan in his 2019 article H. Strachan, 'Strategy in Theory; Strategy in Practice', *Journal of Strategic Studies*, 42:2 (2019), 171–90.
[8] N. A. M. Rodger, 'The Idea of Naval Strategy in Britain in the Eighteenth and Nineteenth Centuries', in G. Till (ed.), *The Development of British Naval Thinking: Essays in Memory of Bryan McLaren Ranft* (Routledge, 2006), p. 20.

Daniel Baugh, have already contributed greatly to this area.[9] This book adds to the historiography of the war and maritime strategy by investigating the spaces where legal thinking and action intersected with the maritime world to influence and shape maritime strategy.

When the Seven Years' War drew to a close, there was no great public intellectual reckoning of the like provided by Jomini and Clausewitz in the post-Napoleonic period. However, does this lack of formal and public discourse mean that strategic thinking during the Seven Years' War had no impact on future strategic thinking? Only if the development of strategic thinking is measured in published works. This third avenue of discussion has been explored recently by Beatrice Heuser in her book *Strategy Before Clausewitz*, in which there is a chapter dedicated to command of the sea and its origins as a strategic concept.[10] Only a few paragraphs are dedicated to the eighteenth and nineteenth centuries, and they link the origin of 'command of the sea' to the writings of legal philosophers such as John Seldon and Cornelis van Bynkershoek. Heuser does not, however, link these philosophers to the maritime strategic thinkers of the eighteenth century. Nor does she link the legal thinking to the wider concept of sea power.[11] How was strategic thinking passed on in the eighteenth century if not through published works? If the development of collective strategic thinking took place in letters, conversations, journals, etc. how was it passed on to those prosecuting the next conflicts? The answer lies in how the sources for maritime strategic thinking were collected, and by whom.

The archival collections used in this book are those of the men who were in charge of prosecuting the Seven Years' War, and those of their networks and allies. Much of this material is correspondence in which the practical problems of strategy are addressed. However, a considerable part of the material in the collections consists of the memos, correspondence, court cases, and data from previous wars and previous ministers, judges, officers, etc. For example, William Petty, Second Earl of Shelburne, who served as the Secretary of State for the Southern Department from 1766 to 1768, was in charge of Britain's relations with Spain, which involved a good amount of negotiation over maritime affairs both in Europe and in the Americas. His collection of papers at the Clements Library includes copies of the correspondence between the

---

[9] R. Pares, *War and Trade in the West Indies 1739–1763* (Frank Cass and Co., 1963); R. Pares, *Colonial Blockade and Neutral Rights 1739–1763* (Porcupine Press, 1975); and D. Baugh, *The Global Seven Years' War, 1754–1763* (Pearson, 2011).

[10] B. Heuser, *Strategy Before Clausewitz: Linking Warfare and Statecraft 1400–1830* (Routledge, 2017), pp. 117–35.

[11] Ibid. pp. 129–30.

Secretaries of State for the Southern Department and the ambassador to Spain during the Seven Years' War. They also include material on intelligence gathered from foreign courts, material on the economic and political affairs of various Caribbean islands and settlements in Spanish territory, and naval intelligence.[12] Maritime strategic thinking in this period was not passed on through formal publications, but through the informal collation of materials relevant to one's position or office. The development and progression of strategic thinking in this period was not driven by overarching theory, but by practical considerations and problem solving.[13] The men in charge of Europe's wars in the eighteenth and early nineteenth centuries were engaged in practising strategy as described by Strachan 'The most important single task for strategy is to understand the nature of the war it is addressing. Its next task may be to manage and direct that war, but it cannot do that if it starts from a false premise.'[14] The arguments presented in this book form a history of the practice of maritime strategy during the Seven Years' War and why that history needs to consider the influence of the law in order to fully understand sea power during the second half of the eighteenth century.

How has the concept of sea power been understood by strategic thinkers and how does it apply to the eighteenth century? For Julian Corbett, sea power boiled down to the ability of a nation to have control of communications at sea.[15] This phrase, 'control of communications' is likely well known to those familiar with sea power theory, but it is still worth interrogating what it actually meant for Corbett and what it implies for the relationship between law and sea power during the Seven Years' War. Corbett approached the concept of sea power by asking the basic question – what does the sea offer to an empire? The answer varies somewhat, nation to nation, based on its geography, national resources, and relations with other states. For Corbett, the general answer was as follows:

The only positive value which the high seas have for national life is as a means of communication. For the active life of a nation such means may stand for much or it may stand for little, but to every maritime State it has some value.

---

[12] CL, Shelburne Papers.

[13] Andrew Lambert makes a similar argument for the British navy in his chapter 'The Development of Education in the Royal Navy: 1815–1914', in G. Till (ed.), *The Development of British Naval Thinking: Essays in Memory of Bryan McLaren Ranft* (Routledge, 2006), pp. 35–7.

[14] H. Strachan, *The Direction of War: Contemporary Strategy in Historical Perspective* (Cambridge University Press, 2013), p. 103.

[15] Corbett, *Some Principles of Maritime Strategy*, pp. 91–106.

Consequently, by denying an enemy this means of passage we check the movement of his national life at sea.[16]

From this concept, Corbett deduced that controlling this 'means of passage' was vital when engaged in a war, and that 'Command of the sea means nothing but the control of maritime communications, whether for commercial or military purposes. The object of naval warfare is the control of communications.'[17] How then, does a nation achieve control of communications and what role does the law play in achieving this control? Control of communications, and therefore sea power, is much more than simply having a powerful and dynamic navy (though this is an important component). Trade, finance, intelligence, port infrastructure, labour forces, shipbuilding industries, market access, freedom of navigation, and geography are all important aspects of gaining control of communications and creating advantageous conditions for the safe passage of a nation's ships and goods. Not all of these elements are directly related to international law in the period under examination in this book. However, each of these elements has been, is, and can be, subject to international law – underlining the value of law as a means of interpreting both historical and contemporary maritime strategy.[18]

In the mid-to-late eighteenth century, trade, market access, and freedom of navigation were the most relevant elements to maritime international law in times of both peace and war. European empires functioned within a largely mercantilist system in which access to colonial markets was heavily protected, and foreign access to such markets was heavily restricted and regulated by bilateral treaties or agreements. Examples of such treaties include the Treaty of Utrecht which contained the *Asiento de Negros* – the contract that granted a private individual, company, or government, the right to trade enslaved Africans into Spanish colonies in the Americas. Spain had no African colonies and could choose to open the trade to foreigners. At the end of the War of the Spanish Succession (1701–13), Britain refused to enter into peace negotiations until a contract was granted for the *Asiento de Negros*. Having acquired this bilateral agreement during negotiations in Madrid in 1713, British ministers were subsequently sent to Utrecht to negotiate the

---

[16] Ibid. p. 93.   [17] Ibid. p. 94.
[18] See, among others, L. Campling and A. Colás, *Capitalism and the Sea* (Verso, 2021); I. Urbina, *The Outlaw Ocean* (Knopf, 2019); I. Hull, *A Scrap of Paper: Breaking and Making International Law during the Great War* (Cornell University Press, 2014); G. Frei, *Great Britain, International Law, and the Evolution of Maritime Strategic Thought, 1856–1914* (Oxford University Press, 2020).

broader peace. The new *asiento* contract granted Britain a monopoly on slave trading to Spanish America for thirty years through the South Sea Company which was created for this purpose.[19] Along with the slave trade, Britain was granted the right, under the Treaty of Utrecht, to bring one 500-ton ship a year to the annual trade fair in Portobello (present-day Panama) without having to pay any charges normally applied to foreign imports. However, due to the ineffectual nature of the Spanish navy in the Americas at that time, the single ship was often resupplied by smaller vessels overnight during the week-long fair and British imports to Portobello greatly exceeded the limits imposed by the treaty. Tensions over the management and execution of the *asiento* would eventually lead to the War of Jenkins' Ear.[20]

The relative qualities of Britain's and Spain's sea power were at play in the granting and implementation of the *Asiento de Negros*. The *asiento* was favourably negotiated by Britain, in part, because, in this instance, Britain had greater control of maritime communications than did Spain, and Spain could not access enslaved people through its own use of the sea. Spain lacked the required seaborne access to African colonies where men and women were enslaved and then shipped across the Atlantic. In the Americas, Spain lacked the naval forces to prevent British ships and merchants from exploiting their access to the Portobello fair. Britain had the available financial capacity within the maritime sphere for the South Sea Company to be created, and the merchant shipping capacity to conduct the slave trade in large volume.

The example of the *asiento* is an illustration of how sea power and law can interact during a period of transition between war and peace, but Corbett's definition of sea power as the control of communications can also be applied in peace and wartime and it allows for the concept to be adapted to the specific circumstances and contexts of maritime nations. The end of a conflict does not necessarily bring with it new clarity on international maritime law or an end to negotiations between nations. This is often because negotiations over whether international law should constrain or expand the rights of sea powers are often conducted between belligerents and neutral nations. The dynamic between belligerent and neutral sea powers is succinctly summarised again by Corbett and his law of maritime warfare: the direct correlation between a country's increasing command of the sea and the likelihood of neutral powers becoming

---

[19] A. Weindl, 'The Asiento de Negros and International Law', *Journal of the History of International Law*, 10 (2008), 229–58, p. 244.
[20] Ibid. p. 246.

enemies.[21] A state whose command of the sea increases throughout a conflict (like that of Britain during the Seven Years' War) can attempt to shape maritime law to expand its own rights at sea in order to better defeat its maritime opponents via economic warfare strategies such as commerce predation or blockades. These strategies will almost certainly require interacting with neutral maritime nations, who choose to trade with either belligerent nation, because neutral ships will be affected by both commerce predation and blockades. The role of the law, then, becomes twofold for the nation whose command of the sea is increasing. It must expand the ability to destroy the enemy's maritime commerce, but it also must convince the neutral nations that its increasing command of the sea does not pose a threat to the rights of the neutral to engage in maritime trade. From the perspective of the neutral nation, maritime law can be used to expand access to the maritime trade of belligerent nations (this is particularly relevant in any type of mercantilist or protectionist system) and to protect this wartime access from belligerents engaging in economic warfare. This is what the Dutch and the Spanish each sought to do whilst Britain and France fought the Seven Years' War.

Sea Power Theorists: Engaging with Law and the Eighteenth Century

The importance of law to maritime strategy began to be codified in what became the canonical works in the field from the late nineteenth century and into the twentieth century. The Seven Years' War featured prominently in these writings, and thus in the process of how law began to be understood within the framework of maritime strategy. However, the war mostly serves as an idealised example of when Britain ascended into the role of maritime global hegemon. The works do not offer a critical examination of how law shaped maritime strategy both during the Seven Years' War and in subsequent conflicts.

In *Some Principles of Maritime Strategy*, Corbett (who was trained in the law) discusses commerce predation but does not overtly tie it to questions of law. For Corbett, part of controlling communications during times of war is having the right to forbid seaborne commerce from transiting through areas where one has command of the sea. 'Now the only means we have of enforcing such control of communications at sea is in the last resort the capture or destruction of sea-borne property.'[22]

---

[21] J. S. Corbett, *England in the Seven Years' War: A Study in Combined Strategy*, 2 vols. (Longmans, Green, and Co., 1907), vol. I, p. 5.

[22] Corbett, *Some Principles of Maritime Strategy*, p. 9.

Corbett goes on to state his dislike of the term 'commerce destruction' and what he considers the more accurate description of the strategic idea, 'commerce prevention'. This small discussion of Corbett's (it takes up merely a few paragraphs of *Some Principles*) is interesting and worth further examination. Corbett refers to the capture and destruction of seaborne commerce as the 'last resort' of commerce prevention and to the capture of seaborne commerce specifically as the form of warfare that causes the least human suffering: 'It is more akin to process of law, such as distress for rent, or execution of judgement, or arrest of a ship, than to a military operation.'[23] He makes the important distinction, however, that when privateering was involved, the practice of commerce prevention was riddled with 'cruelty and lawlessness'. For Corbett then, commerce prevention should be something that is governed by law, lacks cruelty, and is highly organised. Writing in 1911, for the contemporary British navy, Corbett made the point that abolishing privateering allowed for better and more effective commerce prevention: 'A riper and sounder view of war revealed that what may be called tactical commercial blockade – that is, the blockade of ports – could be extended to and supplemented by a strategical blockade of the great routes.'[24] The capture and destruction of seaborne commerce outside of blockade structures is a 'last resort' because it is the least efficient and effective form of commerce prevention. Because Corbett's discussion of commerce prevention is geared towards the strategic merits of commercial blockades and written after privateering was abolished by the Declaration of Paris (1856), he does not indulge in a discussion of how the capture and destruction of commerce by privateers and warships was shaped by, and shaped, maritime law. Nor, however, does he discuss how strategic thinkers and political leaders should approach, or consider, the law when employing a strategy of commerce prevention.

Corbett's use of eighteenth- and early nineteenth-century maritime wars in his writing had a very practical educational purpose. He was writing for the officers of the Royal Navy under the influence of his friend John Knox Laughton, a man who had both served in the navy and had then become a highly influential naval educator in the 1860s. Laughton believed that the study of history was critical for the Royal Navy:

The educational system Laughton demanded would be based on history, because only history could contribute hard evidence to the process ... In the absence of personal experience the only way to learn the business of modern war was to profit from the experience of others, in earlier ages and other navies. Only by such

---

[23] Ibid. p. 98.   [24] Ibid. p. 102.

preparation would commanders acquire the understanding and judgement required to meet the unknown, respond to changing conditions in wartime, and develop the capacity to think at a higher level.[25]

Historical study would form the foundation of strategic thinking. Corbett lectured to the Naval War Course that was set up in 1901. By 1907, Corbett was also teaching strategy and publishing historical analyses aimed at influencing contemporary policy. In 1905, Corbett delivered a course at the Army Staff College that addressed 'the function of the Army in relation to gaining command of the sea, and in bringing war with a Continental Power to a successful conclusion'.[26] Corbett did this through an analysis of this same principal during the Seven Years' War. The lectures that Corbett gave to the army and navy that year were subsequently published as his book *England in the Seven Years' War*. Lambert describes the book as a 'Clausewitzian analysis of a major conflict as a template for the development of contemporary strategy.'[27] Corbett's use of the Seven Years' War, and the age of sail in general, always had a contemporary focus aimed at helping current officers develop their understanding of operations, strategy, and the role of the navy in both. The Seven Years' War was a tool; an example of how the moving parts of sea power came together to shape strategy. Questions of why those moving parts were related, and how they were thought of by strategic thinkers in the eighteenth century, as well as questions of how and why law influenced sea power in the eighteenth century, were not part of Corbett's educational aims.

Subsequent sea power scholars have analysed Corbett's writing on sea power with a similarly instrumental approach to the eighteenth century and a skirting of the influence of law. One dominant vein in Corbettian scholarship is the idea of a British school of naval thinking. This is closely tied to ideas around the 'British way of warfare'. The aim here is not to debate the concept of a British way of war and whether it exists or remains relevant. This has been done in many other spaces and is not relevant to the arguments presented in this book.[28] Geoffrey Till described Corbett's conclusions about British sea power as focusing on the combination of naval and military power in order to achieve strategic effect and influence the balance of power in Europe. 'This they had done

[25] Lambert, 'The Development of Education in the Royal Navy', p. 47.   [26] Ibid. p. 52.
[27] Ibid.
[28] See e.g. B. Liddell Hart, *The British Way in Warfare* (Faber and Faber Limited, 1932); M. Howard, *The British Way in Warfare: A Reappraisal* (Cape, 1975); A. Lambert, *The British Way of War: Julian Corbett and the Battle for a National Strategy* (Yale University Press, 2021).

by the controlled and careful application of maritime power in peace and in war. Because the secret of British success lay in the combination of land- and seapower ...'[29] Barry Hunt made a similar point when he wrote that for Corbett, 'This "British Way in Warfare" required that her [Britain's] statesmen, entrepreneurs and military leaders understood what it could and could not achieve.'[30] Hunt goes on to describe the instrumentalisation of the Seven Years' War when he writes about Pitt's system. This is a reference to the leadership and strategic thinking of William Pitt as the de facto British prime minister during the Seven Years' War. 'Corbett evidently settled on the theme of the Elder Pitt's "system" of war making on a global scale because it so aptly illustrated his lectures on limited war and combined operations. Indeed it was the premier case study ...'[31] Hunt then goes on to quote Corbett about the Seven Years' War 'there is none beside Pitt's war which is so radiant with the genius of a maritime state, and none which was so uniformly successful'.[32] Hunt, with Corbett's help, makes the Seven Years' War into the ideal example of how Britain should fight maritime wars and of how its leaders should conceive of maritime strategy without actually delving into the conflict itself. Hunt, like Till and other maritime thinkers, are not historians of the Seven Years' War, nor were they attempting to be. However, the instrumentalisation of the Seven Years' War in their analysis of Corbett's strategic thinking has meant that the war itself is rarely engaged with in the field of strategic thinking within its own historical context.

Corbett's American contemporary, Alfred T. Mahan, was a sea power theorist who wrote about the history and theory of sea power in order to help US policy makers and strategists find a successful American approach to sea power. Much of Mahan's writing focuses on economics and economic warfare, but he never fully delves into the role played by law and lawmakers. In his book *The Influence of Sea Power upon History*, Mahan discussed the Seven Years' War largely by recounting what happened in chronological order. Near the end of the section on the war he engages with neutrality, but it is brief and not a critical examination: 'Without a rival upon the ocean, it suited England to maintain that enemy's property was liable to capture on board neutral ships, thus

---

[29] G. Till, 'Corbett and the Emergence of a British School', in G. Till (ed.), *The Development of British Naval Thinking: Essays in Memory of Bryan McLaren Ranft* (Routledge, 2006), p. 71.

[30] B. Hunt, 'The Strategic Thought of Sir Julian S. Corbett', in J. Hattendorf and R. Jordan (eds.), *Maritime Strategy and the Balance of Power: Britain and America in the Twentieth Century* (Palgrave Macmillan, 1989), p. 111.

[31] Ibid. pp. 118–19.   [32] Ibid. p. 119.

subjecting these nations not only to vexatious detentions, but to loss of valuable trade ...'[33] More broadly in his work, he discussed Anglo-Spanish maritime relations during the eighteenth century and specifically the diplomatic problems caused by British ships smuggling in Spanish colonies, Spanish coastguards capturing English/British ships, and British ships searching or seizing Spanish ships.[34] Spain viewed British sea power, and the economic encroachment it enabled, as a threat to its American colonies and empire. Britain actively used its sea power to expand its commercial interests in Spanish America through its greater ability to control communications in the Atlantic and Caribbean. Whilst describing commercial and trade disputes between the two empires, Mahan makes the observation that 'It chiefly concerns our subject to notice that the dispute was radically a maritime question, that it grew out of the uncontrollable impulse of the English people to extend their trade and colonial interests.'[35] But Mahan does not then engage in a discussion of how maritime law, both in wartime and peacetime, was used in partnership with sea power in order to further Britain's colonial interests and, from the Spanish perspective, to try to constrain British sea power and commercial influence.

Mahan's lack of engagement with the relationship between sea power and the making of international maritime law leads him to some unexamined conclusions about that relationship and how international maritime law and sea power influenced one another during the eighteenth century. When discussing British maritime hegemony in the Americas at the end of the eighteenth century, Mahan wrote: 'The very lawlessness of the period favoured the extension of their [Britain's] power and influence; for it removed from the free play of a nation's innate faculties the fetters which are imposed by our present elaborate framework of precedents, constitutions, and international law.'[36] Whilst Mahan was, overall, making a point about how American sea power would have to emerge in a different context from that of Britain in the early-modern period, he missed a critical point about the development of British sea power. It did not develop and emerge out of a 'lawless period' where British enterprise and 'innate faculties' could run rampant. Rather, British sea power at the end of the early-modern period was the product of a long-lasting process in which national ambitions, maritime strategy, and the making of international law, were understood by policy makers to be critical elements of

---

[33] Mahan, *The Influence of Sea Power upon History*, p. 312.
[34] A. T. Mahan, *The Complete Works of Alfred Thayer Mahan* (Shrine of Knowledge, 2020), p. 284.
[35] Ibid.   [36] Ibid. p. 642.

balancing power between empires and, if possible, tipping that balance in one's favour.

Scholars of Mahan have written about the eighteenth century in much the same way as scholars of Corbett. In summarising Mahan's strategic thought, John Hattendorf emphasised the idea of continuity between the age of sail and the practise of naval warfare during Mahan's period. For Mahan, the eighteenth century was still relevant in the new age of steam because 'the principal impetus behind the need for a navy was the need to protect merchant shipping'.[37] The study of history could therefore be 'a guide to the present and future employment of naval forces'.[38] In the same volume, Donald Shurman gives an appraisal of how Mahan used British history in order to serve his contemporary purpose of turning US strategic attention towards sea power:

The British suited Mahan's purpose because they continued to grow in a naval and maritime way until their general sea supremacy and wide range of action were everywhere acknowledged. It looked like a planned development carried out, from 1588 to 1815, by a people who had taken their instruction from Jomini. The history contained in the selected British time span exactly suited the Mahanite purpose of 'scientific' cause and effect.[39]

Despite Schurman's veiled criticism of Mahan's selection of history, he falls into making a teleological argument about British sea power in the age of sail. Shurman describes the factors that contributed to making Britain a sea power as naturally culminating in British maritime supremacy in 1815.[40] There is no critical examination of this grand British arc of sea power and minimal engagement with the conflicts in question in order to analyse the strategic thinking occurring at the time. The purpose of Shurman's engagement with history in the chapter is, rather, to demonstrate how Mahan's thinking holds up with the realities of the period after 1815. Once again, the eighteenth century and, in this particular case, the Napoleonic Wars, are held up as an unexamined ideal of British maritime hegemony.

Following in the footsteps of both Mahan and Corbett, the interwar strategic thinker, Sir Herbert Richmond, wrote that sea power was dependent upon three things, 'shipping, colonies or overseas possessions,

---

[37] J. Hattendorf, 'Alfred Thayer Mahan and his Strategic Thought', in J. Hattendorf and R. Jordan (eds.), *Maritime Strategy and the Balance of Power: Britain and America in the Twentieth Century* (Palgrave Macmillan, 1989), p. 87.

[38] Ibid. p. 86.

[39] D. Schurman, 'Mahan Revisited', in J. Hattendorf and R. Jordan (eds.), *Maritime Strategy and the Balance of Power: Britain and America in the Twentieth Century* (Palgrave Macmillan, 1989), p. 97.

[40] Ibid. p. 99.

and a fighting force capable of overcoming the opposition of an enemy armed force and of exercising control over the movements of sea traffic'.[41] This can be read as a combination of Corbettian and Mahanian thought expressed neatly in one sentence. Richmond continued his statement with a neat summation up Corbett's law of maritime warfare:

It [a sea power] must do this in accordance with the recognised laws which have evolved to govern conduct at sea, and in a manner which will be acceptable to nations not engaged in the dispute, that is to say, in accordance with what is called the Law of Nations: for unless it does so it will bring recruits to the forces of its enemy.[42]

Like his predecessors, Richmond understood that the law was a critical part of sea power and that it played a unique role when it came to relations between belligerent and neutral sea powers. The abolition of privateering and the changes in technology from sailing ships, to steam engines, to oil engines, or submarines does not negate the relationship between law and sea power, but it can influence the character of that relationship. For Richmond, economic warfare was at its most efficacious when not relying on captures of trade at sea, but rather when enemy commerce was prevented from even being upon the sea.[43] This view led Richmond to consider the relationship between belligerents and neutrals in terms of international law:

The interest of the neutral must be to contrive to ... take advantage of the abnormal situation which war brings into existence to extend his own commerce of all kinds. Hence a state possessing sea power almost of necessity finds itself in conflict with the private interests of neutral states, and the Governments of those states tend to place such interpretations upon the Law of Nations as will further the interests of their citizens.[44]

It is important to note here that Richmond is using the phrase 'Law of Nations' as a synonym for international law, which he explains further on in his text. Richmond's description of the relationship between neutrals, belligerents, and international law in the abstract is sound. He even goes on to quote A. Pearce Higgins in his *Cambridge History of the British Empire* to make clear that British policy and British prize courts had a great influence on the formation of international maritime law.[45] However, Richmond's subsequent discussion of the legal maritime norms that emerged in the eighteenth century betrays a lack of discernment. While Mahan described the early-modern period as one of 'lawlessness', Richmond describes the end of that period too neatly in terms of maritime law. For Richmond, the Rule of the War of 1756 and

[41] H. Richmond, *Sea Power in the Modern World* (G. Bell and Sons, 1934), p. 38.
[42] Ibid.   [43] Ibid. p. 49.   [44] Ibid. p. 63.   [45] Ibid. p. 64.

the doctrine of continuous voyage (discussed more widely in Chapter 2) emerge and are based upon 'objective principles' such that they 'become the basis of sea policy of the two greatest maritime struggles of the nineteenth and twentieth centuries – the American War of Secession of 1861 and the War of 1914'.[46] Richmond is correct that both the rule and the doctrine of continuous voyage are important in subsequent maritime conflicts; however, his assertion that they are founded on objective principles leads the reader to assume that their emergence and international acceptance was achieved without years of negotiation, strife, and herculean efforts by strategic thinkers, lawyers, and judges to forge legal norms that furthered British strategic maritime aims. In looking for the origin of the international law that he sees as governing the most recent maritime conflict (World War I), he ascribes an objectivity and clarity to the creation of international law that goes against his own theoretical understanding of how sea power and strategy shaped its creation.

Richmond's biographer and strategic thinker in his own right, Barry Hunt, describes Richmond's *Statesmen and Sea Power* and *The Navy as an Instrument of Policy* as efforts to 'paint a broad-brush picture of the unchanging fundamentals of maritime strategy. Setting aside the operational detail of his earlier histories, he placed overall British policy within the wider context of naval, military, economic, political, and international considerations ...'[47] Here again is the sweeping use of history to educate current practitioners of strategy. Hunt, however, does not engage with Richmond's analyses of the early-modern period, nor does he engage with Richmond's ideas on the interplay between law and sea power. All three strategists – Corbett, Mahan, and Richmond – relied heavily on historical analysis of the eighteenth century, and all three made arguments about the relationship between law and sea power. Subsequent work that analyses the thinking of these three theorists largely fails to engage with the eighteenth century in any truly critical way and fails to draw out the importance of international maritime law in its relation to commerce predation and questions of neutrality.

An important legacy of the sea power theory discussed above is the Anglo-centric nature of much sea power writing. Corbett, Mahan, and Richmond – but Corbett in particular – engaged with the historical sources of other nations involved in the eighteenth-century wars upon which they founded much of their thinking. They tried to understand the influence that non-British thinking had on the development of sea power

---

[46] Ibid.
[47] B. Hunt, *Sailor-Scholar: Admiral Sir Herbert Richmond, 1871–1946* (Wilfrid Laurier University Press, 1982), p. 233.

and the balance of power during the eighteenth and early nineteenth centuries. The keepers of their legacies in strategic thinking have, for the most part, left that element of historical analysis behind, and focused largely on how the three thinkers shaped British and American maritime traditions of strategic thinking – and whether those traditions exist or not. As Strachan states in his chapter, 'The Limitations of Strategic Culture', 'The challenge for strategy is how best to link past, present and future: how to apply the context of the past in order to understand the present and to inform an awareness of the future.'[48] This can only be done if the context of the past is fully examined without a teleological lens. For students and practitioners of maritime strategy, the Seven Years' War is currently an idealised moment in British maritime history used by sea power theorists as an example of what British sea power can achieve if applied 'correctly'. The irony is that the strategic thinking – and the factors involved in shaping that thinking – that took place during the war, remain largely unexamined in the field of strategic thinking. The following chapters aim to provide a history of how maritime strategic thinking during the Seven Years' War was heavily shaped by considerations of neutrality and international law. By doing so, this book offers a new account of the relationship between sea power, law, and strategy in the second half of the long eighteenth century and shows the need for a more critical engagement with the Seven Years' War in the field of strategic thinking.

This discussion of Corbett, Mahan, Richmond, and their subsequent interpreters is included here not to discredit them as sea power thinkers or to suggest that their work no longer has a use in the study of strategy and sea power. It serves, rather, as a starting point and as a suggestion that there are still areas in which their work can be expanded and built upon. This book could not have been written without their contributions to maritime strategic thinking, and it is through their theoretical and foundational work on sea power that the relationship between strategy, law, and sea power can be further explored in its eighteenth-century and early-modern context. The next chapter turns to international law and the rules, precedents, and norms that will be analysed in the subsequent chapters through the case studies of four ships in the Court of Prize Appeal during the Seven Years' War.[49]

[48] Strachan, *The Direction of War*, p. 139.
[49] For further examinations of sea power and its intersection with international law see, among others, H. Bourguignon, *Sir William Scott, Lord Stowell: Judge of the High Court of Admiralty 1798–1828* (Cambridge University Press, 1987); Hull, *A Scrap of Paper*; Frei, *Great Britain*; C. Kulsrud, *Maritime Neutrality to 1780* (Little Brown and Co., 1936); S. Kinkel, *Disciplining the Empire: Politics, Governance and the Rise of the British Navy* (Harvard University Press, 2018).

2   Law and Sea Power

Rules, Precedents, and *Communis Opinio*

Sea power can be leveraged to create, shape, and influence maritime international law. As with the example of the *asiento* used in the previous chapter, sea power can be leveraged in the negotiation of treaties that govern maritime affairs. Treaties, however, are not always as binding or final as their preambles may declare, because they are subject to interpretation by subsequent lawyers, judges, and policy makers. These interpretations can create their own legal entities in the form or rules, precedents, doctrines, and *communis opinio* (communal opinion/understanding). Treaties such as the Anglo-Dutch treaty of 1674 and the Anglo-Spanish treaty of 1678, were interpreted differently, and to varying advantages, as Anglo-Dutch and Anglo-Spanish strategic relationships, and relative sea power, changed throughout the eighteenth century.

Rather than re-negotiate existing treaties, sea powers can use the maritime court systems already empowered by the treaties in order to expand or constrict the rights contained in the treaty. In this case, treaties function as a starting point for new legal entities that reflect new or changing dynamics between sea powers. The creation of new legal entities is the result of adjudications over confrontations at sea, where one side claims their actions are sanctioned by the treaty, and the other claims that their rights under that same treaty have been violated. Law and legal entities, then, are made, and purposefully constructed, using myriad materials such as previous judgments, treaties, philosophical writings, and diplomatic correspondence. Anne Orford in her book *International Law and the Politics of History*, describes this process as follows:

For lawyers, the relation of the world of evidence and the work of interpretation is … complicated. Debates over the relationship between fact and narrative in the work of legal argument can be traced back to at least eighteenth-century controversies amongst lawyers and beyond … Evidence, fact-finding, and inference play a central role in the interpretation and practice of law more broadly, and determining which facts are relevant to a legal analysis is not simply an empirical process. The presentation of facts has a normative effect. As trial lawyers have pointed out, 'the statement of the facts is not merely a part of the argument, it is more often than not the argument itself'. Once the facts of a legal case are assembled, much of the normative work has been done. The distinction between questions of fact and questions of law is both central to legal thinking and at the same time slippery and often unsustainable. The 'glue' that holds together reasoning about facts or evidence and the legal conclusions drawn from those facts is made up of background generalisations, processes of story-telling and narrative, and other forms of inferential reasoning and interpretation ... Which version of the facts we believe is not just a matter of probability and logic but also a matter of which narrative we find persuasive.[1]

Analysing the cases of the *Maria Theresa*, the *America*, the *San Juan Baptista*, and the *Jesús, Maria, y José*, reveals in practice the process described by Orford. It is the examination of why, and how, lawyers present their arguments. Examining the making of maritime law also entails analysing how, and why, judgments were made and how facts and narratives were chosen by the judges of the British Court of Prize Appeal:

In situations of a dispute over facts, a key question for law is always 'who determines the facts?' and 'who determines which facts are relevant?' Facts cannot simply be found and disagreements over the facts are often central to legal disputes. The removal of ambiguity through the writing of facts and the determination of whether evidence is relevant is central to the practice of judgement. In international law, where states are reluctant to submit disputes to international adjudication, there is often an ongoing struggle to establish facts and a repeated refusal by powerful states to give up the sovereign authority to determine which facts are relevant ... Without an authoritative decisionmaker, the facts become as if they were alive as a series of uncoordinated concentrations of state powers.[2]

Who the judges of the British prize court system were, then, is a critical aspect of understanding the creation of international maritime law. Trying to understand why they made the decisions they made, and their relationship to policy makers, is critical to understanding the relationship between law and sea power. Law, precedent, rules, and *communis opinio* were *made* in the Court of Prize Appeal in order to best serve the maritime strategic interests of Britain. From the Seven Years' War, the most important legal entities that emerged, and that would carry into

---

[1] A. Orford, *International Law and the Politics of History* (Cambridge University Press, 2021), pp. 219–20.
[2] Ibid. pp. 222–3.

future conflicts, were the Rule of the War of 1756, the doctrine of continuous voyage and transhipment, and the *communis opinio* that emerged around how these entities might be applied in future cases with neutral nations.

The Rule of the War of 1756 has enjoyed some discussion in the scholarship surrounding neutrality in the eighteenth and nineteenth centuries.[3] As the name suggests, the rule was developed during the Seven Years' War, but it did not become part of British prize court decisions until 1758, when Anglo-Dutch tensions over neutral rights were high, and the first Dutch cases came before the Court of Prize Appeal. The rule itself was simple and intended to curtail the neutral carriage of French colonial goods by stating that any trade which had been prohibited to a neutral during times of peace (in this case French colonial trade) would be prohibited during times of war. It was a logic rooted in mercantilist thinking and tradition, wherein European colonial powers usually did not allow other nations to trade directly with their colonies.[4] The rule itself was of Lord Hardwicke's invention but developed from a widely accepted principle of neutrality. Hardwicke was one of the leading judges on the Court of Prize Appeal during the Seven Years' War. The principle on which he based the Rule of the War of 1756 was as follows: if a neutral ship sailed under an enemy pass (in other words a belligerent sanctioned a neutral vessel to partake in commercial activity to which the neutral did not normally have access), it was considered to have forfeited its neutral status because it had, for all intents and purposes, become a ship of the enemy.[5] Hardwicke's Rule can be seen as a semi-extension of this principle. Rather than address individual ships with enemy passes, Hardwicke's Rule would apply a blanket ban on neutrals carrying French colonial trade. However, the rule did not go so far as to claim that these neutral vessels would be treated blanketly as enemy vessels, only that carrying the French cargo would not be permissible. This was a critical omission from the principle and would be an important point of discussion in Prize Appeal cases

[3] This includes R. Pares, *Colonial Blockade and Neutral Rights 1739–1763* (Porcupine Press, 1975); C. Kulsrud, *Maritime Neutrality to 1780* (Little Brown and Co., 1936); H. Bourguignon, *Sir William Scott, Lord Stowell: Judge of the High Court of Admiralty 1798–1828* (Cambridge University Press, 1987); S. Neff, *Justice Among Nations: A History of International Law* (Harvard University Press, 2014); S. Neff, 'James Stephen's *War in Disguise*: The Story of a Book', *Irish Jurist*, 38 (2003), 331–51; and M. Abbenhuis, *An Age of Neutrals: Great Power Politics 1815–1914* (Cambridge University Press, 2014), among others.

[4] Neff, 'James Stephen's *War in Disguise*', p. 332.   [5] Ibid. p. 333.

when it came time to set precedents on whether neutral ships should be condemned as enemy vessels.

From Hardwicke's correspondence, it is clear that he began to think about the rule at the start of the war, but it was in the Dutch cases of the *Maria Theresa* and the *America* where the rule emerged and began to set precedents.[6] The decision in the *Maria Theresa* established that Dutch ships carrying French trade from a Dutch colony to a Dutch port in Europe would not have the cargo condemned as lawful prize. The decision in the *America* established that Dutch ships carrying French trade from a French colony to a port in France *would* have the cargo condemned as lawful prize. Together, the two cases laid the groundwork for the application and boundaries of the Rule of the War of 1756 during the Seven Years' War, and its subsequent application in Britain's maritime wars through the end of the Napoleonic Wars.

The rule did not only affect Dutch cases. The first two Spanish ships to come before the Court of Prize Appeal, the *San Juan Baptista* and the *Jesús, Maria, y José*, created an opportunity to set precedents that would help establish the more universal application of the Rule of the War of 1756. Unexpected twists and turns in the case of the *Jesús, Maria, y José*, meant that the painstakingly thought out and considered sentence crafted by Hardwicke and his allies was never actually passed. However, the tens of pages of notes left by Hardwicke, and the verbal discussions that took place during the course of the case, both in and out of the court room, contributed to a more nuanced understanding of how the rule could be applied in cases similar to that of the *Jesús, Maria, y José*. This nuance and application to Spanish ships would be accessible to future judges who had been present when the case was argued, or who might have access to Hardwicke's notes through legal and social networks. It was not the creation of precedent, but it was the creation of a *communis opinio* that might eventually lead to firmer precedents. The fact that the rule was applied, or could be applied, to multiple neutral nations, helped establish it as a British doctrine that would become an integral element of Britain's approach to, and negotiations over, neutral rights for the rest of the long eighteenth century.

---

[6] Helfman argues that the Rule of the War of 1756 marks a shift from Grotian influence to Bynkershoekian influence in the British prize court system. It is true that Hardwicke's thinking about the Rule has Bynkershoekian overtones in terms of his idea that neutral nations should not help or hinder either belligerent by gaining access to new markets during wartime. However, in the correspondence and notes examined for this project, neither Hardwicke nor his correspondents call upon the ideas of Bynkershoek when discussing the Rule. See T. Helfman, 'Neutrality, the Law of Nations and the Natural Law Tradition', *Yale Journal of International Law*, 30:549 (2005), 549–84.

Closely related to the Rule of the War of 1756 were the doctrine of continuous voyage and the concept of transhipment. Transhipment referred to the act of taking goods from one vessel and placing them into another vessel, usually for the purpose of continuing to transport the goods. There were various types of transhipment of French colonial goods that came to the attention of the prize courts during the war. A French ship might carry French goods from French colonies to Dutch colonies in order to place the goods into Dutch ships for the voyage across the Atlantic to France or the Dutch Republic. Alternatively, a Dutch ship might carry French colonial goods from French colonies to Dutch colonies in order to tranship the goods into a different Dutch ship for the voyage across the Atlantic. The Court of Prize Appeal's interest in these two types of transhipment was based on the intention behind the transhipment. If the purpose of stopping in the neutral port to transfer French goods into a Dutch ship was to evade capture by the British, then the voyage could be considered a continuation of the original voyage and the Rule of the War of 1756 could be applied.[7] However, ascertaining the intent behind the transhipment was not always clear cut. Cases before the Court of Prize Appeal might drag on for years while the commissioners sought evidence that proved whether goods had been imported into a Dutch colony and therefore had become Dutch goods, or whether they remained enemy goods disguised as neutral goods. The first few cases to come before the appellate court set some precedents that established the doctrine of continuous voyage and how it should be applied by the lower prize courts.[8] French colonial goods that had been taken to a Dutch port and purchased, such that they became Dutch property, could not be condemned as enemy goods on the voyage across the Atlantic, even if the eventual receiver of the goods was French. Practically, this meant that after the Rule of the War of 1756 and the doctrine of continuous voyage were established, almost no goods travelling between Dutch colonies and the Dutch Republic were condemned in the High Court of Admiralty.[9] This had a positive, and tension-relieving, effect on Anglo-Dutch relations.

Another type of transhipment that concerned the Court of Prize Appeal was the transfer of French colonial goods into Spanish ships off the coast of Spain for the purpose of transiting the goods into France. As in the Dutch cases, the crux of the problem was the ownership of the goods, and therefore the applicability of the Rule of the War of 1756 and

---

[7] Neff, 'James Stephen's *War in Disguise*', 336.   [8] Pares, *Colonial Blockade*, 216–17.
[9] Ibid.

the doctrine of continuous voyage. In the Spanish cases, there was also more debate as to whether the ships themselves should be condemned as enemy ships because they were being used deliberately to avoid British capture on the last leg of a French journey. After the first Spanish case came before the Court of Prize Appeal, a loose precedent was set, wherein the doctrine of continuous voyage was clearly applicable to all neutral nations who violated the Rule of the War of 1756. It constituted a 'loose precedent' because the case notes left behind are very minimal, and the reasoning behind the decision is not fully discussed. This would have made it harder for future judges to draw on these cases when making subsequent arguments rooted in the concept of continuous voyage. The second Spanish case did leave behind a large volume of opinion, but the sentence was not declared, so it could not serve as precedent. Both Spanish cases, however, laid the groundwork for the doctrine of continuous voyage to be applied in subsequent non-Dutch cases, both in the Seven Years' War and in future conflicts. The doctrine of continuous voyage surfaced again in Britain's ensuing wars against France. During the French Revolutionary and Napoleonic Wars, the doctrine would become critical in British prize court treatment of American ships acting as neutrals. The precedents set in the Seven Years' War by the first Dutch cases, and the *communis opinio* created by the first Spanish cases in the Court of Prize Appeal, would shape the thinking and actions of prize court judges and political commentators in order to establish the limits of neutrality and preserve Britain's ability to engage in commerce predation against France.

The Evolution and Operation of the Prize Courts

To fully explore the role of the British Court of Prize Appeal in the maintenance of neutrality during the Seven Years' War, it is helpful to explain how the prize court system actually worked. It is an elusive topic in terms of the secondary literature, and one that often remains little understood. The purpose of the prize courts was to adjudicate cases of ships captured at sea and taken as prize by British warships and British privateers. The legality of the seizure was the crux of each case and depended upon the interpretations of existing treaties and British prize law. The men interpreting the law and treaties were the judges, proctors, and advocates of the prize courts.[10] Prize law fell under the umbrella of

---

[10] Proctors and advocates were the practitioners of the civil law system, which was separate from the common law system. Advocates were the civil law counterparts to common law serjeants, and proctors were the counterparts of attorneys. A clear and concise

Admiralty law, which was a branch of civil law. Over time, however, the Admiralty court would be influenced by both the civil law and common law traditions of England.

The common law system was, and is, in essence, the tradition that was developed in England and applied within England. The civil law was developed from the Roman civil law tradition, widely used in Europe, and from canon law. Under the Tudors, the Admiralty court's work focused on three areas related to maritime affairs: prize cases, criminal jurisdiction, and instance jurisdiction (suits brought by a private party). The latter covered mercantile and shipping affairs and, under the aegis of Henry VIII, the Admiralty court handled all aspects of maritime business such as contracts made outside of England, charter parties, insurance, cargo damage, freighting issues, etc.[11] Over the course of the late sixteenth century, common law courts began to encroach upon Admiralty courts by challenging their jurisdiction over matters that did not occur at sea (such as contracts and matters of ownership).[12] By the start of the seventeenth century, Admiralty courts only had jurisdiction over matters and disputes that occurred at sea, such as prize-taking and privateering. Though the civil law tradition and the jurisdiction of the Admiralty courts had been much reduced in Britain by the time of the Seven Years' War, matters of prize still fell under their purview.[13] It was argued by Chief Justice Lee in 1742, that the jurisdiction in prize-law cases was given to the Admiralty courts because prizes were a matter concerning the 'law of war' and the 'law of nations' and not concerning the municipal (common) law of a country.[14] Advocates who practiced in civil courts were doctors of civil law and most joined the civilian equivalent of the Inns of Court, which was Doctor's Commons, based in London, near St Paul's. It was here that the High Court of Admiralty was convened, and the Court of Prize Appeal was often convened (the Court of Prize Appeal was also sometimes convened at Whitehall).

Before anything could be adjudicated in the prize courts, some form of sanctioned maritime predation had to take place, and prizes had to be brought into port by privateers or warships for adjudication.[15] Fitting out

---

description of them can be found in J. Baker, *An Introduction to English Legal History* (Oxford University Press, 2019), p. 180.

[11] Bourguignon, *Sir William Scott, Lord Stowell*, pp. 5–6.   [12] Ibid. p. 7.

[13] Baker, *An Introduction to English Legal History*, pp. 131–3.

[14] J. Oldham, *English Common Law in the Age of Mansfield* (University of North Carolina Press, 2004), pp. 177 and 180.

[15] By the mid-eighteenth century, a privateer was defined as a private ship of war (often converted merchant ships but sometimes built for purpose) that held a commission from the Lords of the Admiralty to capture enemy ships and commerce. A privateer could also

a ship for commerce raiding required no small amount of preparation and capital for would-be privateers. When war was declared in 1756, King George II issued a Royal Proclamation and Declaration which, when enacted by Parliament, allowed general reprisals against the vessels and goods of France.[16] The king's proclamation opened up privateering for the duration of hostilities. For all of the men (and occasionally women) involved, privateering was first and foremost a high-risk financial investment in a time of war. Its purpose was to make money for the owners, investors, and crew, with a convenient dose of patriotism and contribution to the war effort on the side. Risk and initial investment were high, and usually spread amongst multiple owners or investors. In the mid-eighteenth century, every private ship fitted out for commerce raiding, regardless of size, had to fulfil certain legal requirements before going to sea. Ships were granted letters of marque (a commission from the Admiralty) to legalise prize-taking activity. In order to obtain these, the commander of a ship had first to request a warrant from the Lords Commissioners of the Admiralty, and then present himself at Doctors' Commons and declare before the judge of the High Court of Admiralty the details of the ship, the owners, the intended voyage, and the crew. If all were in order, the commander of the privateer would receive the letter of marque or commission. The last and, arguably, most important thing the commander needed to produce before going to sea was bail or bond with two guarantors. The Anglo-Dutch treaty of 1674 declared that the bail should be £3,000 for a ship of 150 men or more, and £1,500 for a smaller ship.[17] The bond was intended as a guarantee of good (or at least legal) behaviour on the part of the privateers. If a case were brought against them in an Admiralty court and they were fined or ordered to pay damages to an injured party, the money would come out of the bond. Once all of these requirements had been met, a private ship of war was ready to sail. In 1756, requests for letters of marque could not legally be denied as long as the stipulated conditions were met, though this would change in 1759, with the passing of a new Privateers Act.

The rules governing prize-taking in His Majesty's Navy were not quite as complex as those for privateers, in part because the Navy was already a well-regulated and well-administered body. All royal warships were allowed to take prizes, though it was not the primary task of most.

refer to armed merchant vessels that had been granted letters of marque that allowed them to capture enemy vessels should the occasion arise during their normal commercial ventures. The meaning of 'privateer' and 'letter of marque' changed over the course of the centuries and the history is well covered by David Starkey in *British Privateering Enterprise in the Eighteenth Century* (Exeter University Press, 1990), pp. 20–2.

[16] Ibid. p. 22.   [17] Ibid. p. 23.

Frigates were the best suited to prize-taking because of their speed to armament ratio, and they were often sent out on cruises where their primary task was to harass enemy commerce and shipping. Once a prize was taken, it would be given a skeleton British crew to take it, and the original crew, back to the closest, or preferred, prize court.[18] Throughout the colonies, Vice Admiralty courts served as prize courts during times of war. For prize cases tried in Vice Admiralty courts, appeals could be lodged at the High Court of Admiralty and, subsequently, the Court of Prize Appeal, both in London.

The High Court of Admiralty was presided over by a judge, trained in the civil law tradition, who was appointed for life by the Lords Commissioners of the Admiralty. The judges of the Vice Admiralty courts did not necessarily have legal training or a legal career and could be removed and replaced at will by the Admiralty.[19] Many of the Vice Admiralty judges, for example, were governors of the colonies in which the court was located, and when war was declared, they were required to receive permission from the Admiralty in order to begin adjudicating prize cases. This protocol was not always followed however, and many governors adjudicated prizes without permission from the Admiralty.[20]

When a prize case was being argued at the High Court of Admiralty, the advocates and proctors worked with the law, and with the facts of the case that had been gathered when the prize was brought into port. A single case could easily contain a mountain of paperwork that ranged from the depositions of both crews to the papers and passports found on board the seized vessel. Cases often took weeks to adjudicate. If the judge found in favour of the captor, then the prize, and/or the goods, would be sold at public auction for profit. Each crew member received the portion that had been agreed in his contract, minus fees, and navy sailors would get a percentage set by the Admiralty. These transactions were handled by prize agents. If the judge found in favour of the captured plaintiff, then the captured ship, or the goods, or both, would be restored to the owners. Damages sustained by the wronged party would be assessed by the court and paid out by the captor from his bond. In the event of the captive losing the case, they could choose to undertake the cost of an appeal. From the High Court of Admiralty there was only one court in which to appeal: the Court of Prize Appeal, presided over by the honourable Lords Commissioners of Prize Appeal.

---

[18] N. A. M. Rodger, *The Wooden World: An Anatomy of the Georgian Navy* (Norton, 1996), p. 136.
[19] Pares, *Colonial Blockade*, p. 84.   [20] Ibid.

By law, all privateer crews retained the services of advocates and prize agents. It was the job of the prize agent to handle the administration of bringing a prize to trial, and the job of the advocate to win the case. Both agent and advocate worked on commission, which was often a percentage of the prize value.[21] If the owners of a ship taken as prize wished to contest the seizure, they would also retain the services of an advocate or proctor to try to establish that the ship had been taken illegally. If an appeal was lodged, the ship and goods which had been taken as prize would be sold, and the proceeds kept by the court until the appeal was completed and they were awarded to one of the parties. This was done in large part to deal with perishable goods, or goods whose value fluctuated on the market.[22]

Whilst prize courts were part of England's civil tradition, the Court of Prize Appeal occupied a legal space that straddled both the civil law and common law traditions. This was not done by design but, rather, it was an accident made possible by having two law traditions whose jurisdictions, as they developed and jostled for primacy over time, occasionally overlapped. The concept of appeals, and the right to an appeal, was not part of the early development of the common law tradition in England. The idea gained traction early on in the seventeenth century and was conceived of as an important element of the constitution by the second decade of the eighteenth century.[23] In the fifteenth and sixteenth centuries, appeals from the Admiralty courts were heard by commissioners appointed on each occasion by the monarch and their council. The commissioners were drawn from practitioners of civil law and, usually, the Privy Council.[24] By the start of the eighteenth century, the Lords Commissioners of Appeals were drawn from the members of the Privy Council and some judges such as the Lord Chancellor and the Lord Chief Justice. There is little indication within the prize court historiography of exactly when the commissioners appointed to adjudicate prize appeals began to be known as the Lords Commissioners of Prize Appeal or the Court of Prize Appeal. However, the critical point is that this was not a 'court' in the usual sense; it was a tribunal which occupied a distinct place in the legal world and was made up of lawyers from both the civil and common law traditions. The terms 'Lords Commissioners of Prize Appeal' and 'Court of Prize Appeal' were in common use during the War

[21] Starkey, *British Privateering*, p. 77.
[22] E. S. Roscoe, *A History of the English Prize Court* (Lloyd's, 1924), p. 37.
[23] Baker, *Introduction to Legal History*, p. 145.
[24] W. Senior, *Doctors' Commons and the Old Court of Admiralty: A Short History of the Civilians in England* (Longmans, Green and Co., 1922), pp. 52–53.

of the Austrian Succession and the Seven Years' War. During the latter conflict, it was Lord Chief Justice Mansfield and the recent ex-Lord Chancellor Hardwicke who guided the appellate court's decisions.[25]

Given that the Court of Prize Appeal commissioners were appointed by the Crown, government and monarchical interference in appellate cases was not uncommon, especially when the case was of diplomatic importance. However, the passing of a Prize Act in 1708 (which was subsequently renewed at the start of conflicts throughout the century including the Seven Years' War) made it impossible for the government to overtly interfere in prize affairs. The Prize Act of 1708 declared that captured ships and goods which were declared legal prize were, in their entirety, the property of the captors.[26] Until this Act, some portion of prize property had belonged either to the Crown or to various other Crown appointed officials. The Act had implications for ministerial interference because of the tradition defending property rights in English law. Statutes in the medieval period began to protect an Englishman's right to property and to curtail the Crown's ability to interfere with that property.[27] Since the Prize Act of 1708 took away the Crown's share of prize property, it meant that the Crown, and by extension the ministry, could no longer have a say in how that property was disposed of and had to allow the prize adjudication process to be completed. Political interference in the prize courts was, ostensibly, at an end. However, ministries, including the one in place for most of the Seven Years' War, understood that prize affairs were an important part of negotiations over neutral rights, and were not willing to forego all of their influence. Because of the appointment process for the Lords Commissioners of Prize Appeal, it was not difficult for the ministry to have influence in the Court of Prize Appeal as long as the appointees were chosen from among a long list of ministerial allies on the Privy Council, and amongst those holding higher judicial offices, such as Lord Chancellor and Lord Chief Justice.

Ministerial influence in the Court of Prize Appeal was not obvious, nor was it present in every case that came before the Court. However, the men in government responsible for the conduct of the war, such as William Pitt and the Duke of Newcastle, did take an interest in prize cases that came before the Court of Prize Appeal. In particular, they took an interest in the first Dutch and Spanish cases to come before the court, because they were instrumental in demonstrating to the Dutch and Spanish that their concerns over British abuses of their neutral rights

[25] Pares, *Colonial Blockade*, pp. 101–2.   [26] Ibid. p. 6
[27] Baker, *Introduction to Legal History*, p. 105.

were being concretely, and fairly, addressed by the appellate court. The first few cases served as a blueprint for how subsequent cases would be handled, and it was, therefore, critical that they proceeded in a manner that was favourable to British strategic aims and the maintenance of Dutch and Spanish neutrality. Early sentences would either set precedents to deter the neutral country from carrying French goods under certain circumstances or would restore ships and goods to the neutral nation in order to demonstrate that the court would respond favourably under circumstances where the court acknowledged that neutrality had been violated by British ships. This element of British strategy required close co-ordination between the ministry and the judges interpreting British prize law, treaties, and international legal philosophy in the appellate court. It only functioned if the relevant members of the government, Admiralty, and the Court of Prize Appeal could work together in pursuit of a strategy that convinced both the Dutch and the Spanish that their neutral rights were being protected, while at the same time allowing Britain to destroy French seaborne commerce.

Throughout the war, the small group of men in power concerned with neutrality and strategy were often closely linked by family, profession, education, and society. These close ties were not always harmonious, and sometimes led to internal conflicts and ambitions that adversely affected wartime relations with neutral nations. Nonetheless, the close relationships provided an informal means for sharing information and points of view that helped to affect the desired political outcomes through the Court of Prize Appeal. While the actions of privateers and the actions of the judge of the High Court of Admiralty were difficult for British ministers to influence or control, the Court of Prize Appeal afforded members of the government a way to directly affect the implementation of prize law in pursuit of maintaining Dutch and Spanish neutrality. In order to influence the outcome of prize appeal cases, ministers acted through their allies and cronies who regularly attended the Court of Prize Appeal. It is true that some ministers attempted to distance themselves from certain cases, but a closer look into the matter indicates that ministers did indeed directly influence the decisions of the court and used that influence to great effect in pursuing strategic objectives. In the first few cases that were heard by the Court of Prize Appeal during the Seven Years' War, it was Lord Hardwicke's reasoning that guided the court's decisions. Hardwicke was at the heart of a social, political, and legal network that included the men who directed Britain's war effort and British strategic thinking. Hardwicke was, therefore, perfectly placed to ensure that the Court of Prize Appeal was, during this conflict, established as an institution that worked towards British strategic aims whilst presenting itself as an impartial guardian of neutral rights.

The relationships between British ministers and their Dutch and Spanish counterparts were equally important. In order for negotiations over neutral rights to be successful, the rapport between British and foreign ministers had to be strong, lest promises and assurances be dismissed as unsubstantiated gestures and attempts at prevarication. These relationships also allowed critical knowledge of neutral countries' internal pressures to become part of the decision-making process in deciding the outcomes of cases before the Court of Prize Appeal.

When a case came before the Lords Commissioners, the protocol seems to have been very similar to that followed in the lower courts. In an appellate case, the person (or persons) who first filed an appeal would be named as the Appellant. The other party was named the Respondent. Each side was assigned two or more advocates who would represent them, formulate arguments, and deliver those arguments before the judges. The Appellant's case would generally be delivered first. The arguments would be made before the judges, and the judges could ask questions and had the ability to request that further information or evidence be gathered. Advocates could also ask for certain allowances from the judges, such as time to gather depositions or evidence from overseas. After the Appellant's case was heard, the advocates for the Respondents would have their turn to make their arguments before the judges. Once both sides had delivered their arguments, the judges would gather to discuss the case and come to a sentencing agreement. Sentences passed in the Court of Prize Appeal were reached by consensus at a meeting of the commissioners at the end of the hearings. The number of commissioners varied from case to case and even meeting to meeting. Usually, there were between four and twelve commissioners present.[28] In order to weigh in on the judgment, however, a commissioner had to attend all of the hearings and the final meeting. A case could take anywhere from one day to a few months to be presented and decided upon.

From Micro to Macro and Back Again

Understanding the relationship between sea power, law, and strategy in any given period requires the ability to delve into both micro and macro

[28] Lists of commissioners in attendance are not always included with the case material, but there are lists of many cases in the case papers found in the National Archives (TNA), HCA 42/52–109; TNA HCA 48/7; TNA HCA 45/1–5; and BL Add MS 36208–15.

history. Understanding the relationship from a theoretical perspective requires the ability to pick out what are enduring characteristics of that relationship and what are period-specific characteristics. There is no set formula for doing this, and though the arguments in this chapter have offered some ideas regarding how to think about the enduring character-istics of the relationship between sea power, law, and strategy, the overall purpose of the following chapters is to demonstrate how that relationship and the individuals involved in that relationship thought about and created both law and strategy during the Seven Years' War. From this examination, it is hoped that similar analyses and examinations might be made of the relationship between sea power, law, and strategy in other conflicts, building on methods and ideas presented in the following chapters.

Part II

The Dutch Case Studies

3   Personalities and Policies
The Anglo-Dutch Context

Britain's Dilemmas

Like many of the subsequent cases concerning Dutch ships during the Seven Years' War, both the case of the *Maria Theresa* and the case of the *America* hinged on interpretations of the Anglo-Dutch treaty of 1674 and on the Grotian concept of 'free ships, free goods'. The two cases shared many similarities when they came before the prize courts because both ships were on homeward bound voyages from the West Indies. The deliberations of the court were most concerned with whether the treaty, and Grotius's concept, applied in the Americas the same way that they applied in Europe. This possible distinction in the treaty's application was put forward by Lord Hardwicke at the start of the war as a way to curtail Dutch carriage of French colonial goods, and it would become ever more important as a point of negotiation and contention as Anglo-Dutch relations deteriorated in the first years of the war.

Destroying or capturing goods from the French West Indies was a vital component of British maritime strategy that could be easily undermined if those goods were allowed to be carried in neutral Dutch ships. However, Dutch anger over the real or perceived violation of their neutrality had to be addressed, lest it spill over into outright hostility and war. The stability of Anglo-Dutch relations was ultimately ensured by the legal credibility of decisions handed down by the Court of Prize Appeal, and that credibility was initially established by the cases of the *Maria Theresa* and the *America*. The decisions clarified the British position on neutral trading in French West Indian goods through the enshrinement of what would come to be known as Hardwicke's Rule of the War of 1756, which stated that any trade closed to neutral countries in times of peace should remain closed in times of war. Taken together, the outcomes of both cases and their contribution to ameliorating the Anglo-Dutch crisis were ultimately a legal and strategic victory for British ministers. Dutch carriage of French West Indian trade was curtailed for the rest of the war without pushing the Dutch Republic into the conflict and an alliance with France. The favourable resolution of the crisis and the restoration of Dutch faith in the British prize court system was made possible largely due to the specific individuals involved on both sides and their ability to work coherently together. This chapter builds on the existing British and Dutch historiographies of the mid-eighteenth century and makes the overarching argument that, in order to understand how maritime empires negotiated during wartime, it is imperative that legal and political spheres be analysed together, with a specific focus on the networks and connections of the men responsible for negotiating.[1]

A Winning Government

To best understand how the cases of the *Maria Theresa* and the *America* contributed to a successful British strategy regarding Dutch neutrality and neutral rights, it is important to examine the relationships between the members of the British Court, the Court's relationships with the representatives of the Dutch Republic, and the Court's relationships to the privateers who helped carry out commerce predation. It is also important to understand what drove the foreign policy aims of the Dutch ministers.

By the time the Anglo-Dutch crisis was at its height in late 1758 to early 1759, a functional wartime British government had been firmly established and had successfully been conducting the war against France since June 1757. As its de facto leader and prime minister, the government had the formidable Mr William Pitt, who held the post of Secretary of State for the Southern Department.[2] He was joined by the previous prime minister and long-time veteran of British governments, Thomas Pelham-Holles, Duke of Newcastle, as First Lord of the Treasury. Both men were instrumental in shaping British wartime strategy, although they were sometimes at odds with each other over how best to carry it out. Their allies, both in and out of government, served to back their policies and to offer advice in the pursuit of upholding Dutch and Spanish neutrality whilst crippling France at sea.

---

[1] See L. Benton and L. Ford, *Rage for Order: The British Empire and the Origins of International Law 1800–1850* (Harvard University Press, 2016); L. Benton and R. J. Ross, *Legal Pluralism and Empires, 1500–1850* (New York University Press, 2013); R. Pares, *Colonial Blockade and Neutral Rights 1739–1763* (Porcupine Press, 1975); R. Pares, *War and Trade in the West Indies 1739–1763* (Frank Cass and Co., 1963); P. J. Stern and C. Wennerlind (eds.), *Mercantilism Reimagined: Political Economy in Early Modern Britain and Its Empire* (Oxford University Press, 2014).

[2] The office of prime minister in this period was not an official position but was, rather, an appellation given to the strongest or most influential minister. Usually, this unofficial title fell on the shoulders of the First Lord of the Treasury, but it was not always so.

Newcastle had been a powerful figure in politics since at least 1724 and was part of the 'Establishment Whig' political tradition that is closely associated with Robert Walpole and with policies of naval deterrence, fiscal restraint, and maintaining the balance of power amongst European states. Establishment Whigs were, as a general rule, not in favour of expanding Britain's maritime empire through the acquisition of more colonies, nor were they in favour of large, drawn-out, and expensive wars.[3] Due to Newcastle's long career as a politician, and the influence of his family in local and national politics, he had built up considerable control over certain types of patronage, which he used astutely to advance the careers of his friends and allies.[4] Two of the members of the Privy Council who were appointed Lords Commissioners of Prize Appeal and who regularly attended court proceedings were Newcastle's relatives. Charles Cornwallis, Earl Cornwallis, was Constable of the Tower and Newcastle's nephew-in-law by virtue of marrying Elizabeth Townshend, Newcastle's niece. Constable of the Tower was not a powerful political position, but it did give him the ability to be appointed a commissioner to the Court of Prize Appeal. Charles Townshend, Treasurer of the Chamber and also a member of the Privy Council, was the son of Newcastle's sister, Elizabeth Pelham. Newcastle also had several allies in the government who were involved in the Court of Prize Appeal. His closest friend and lifelong ally was Philip Yorke, Earl Hardwicke, who had been involved in politics and law since the reign of George I, and who, as previously mentioned, carried immense weight in legal spheres. Hardwicke held the post of Lord Chancellor from 1737 to 1756, when he resigned voluntarily. However, the position of Lord Chancellor remained vacant until 1761, and Hardwicke remained on the Privy Council as High Steward of the University of Cambridge. Hardwicke's son-in-law, also a member of the Privy Council, was Lord Anson, First Lord of the Admiralty. Father and son-in-law were very close, and though Anson did not always hold Newcastle in the highest

---

[3] S. Kinkel, *Disciplining the Empire: Politics, Governance and the Rise of the British Navy* (Harvard University Press, 2018), pp. 56–66 and 124.

[4] R. Browning, *The Duke of Newcastle* (Yale University Press, 1975), p. 188. There is an interesting and important linguistic point that should be highlighted here and is expertly made by Naomi Tadmor. Her research expands our understanding of how the term 'friend' had a very expansive meaning in eighteenth-century politics and included people who were considered to owe, or considered themselves as owing, political allegiance or favours to a patron-like figure such as the Duke of Newcastle. Tadmor in fact used the Duke of Newcastle as an example of this in her chapter on political friendship. In my own writing I use the phrase 'friends and allies' in order to capture this broader understanding of friendship. N. Tadmor, *Family and Friends in Eighteenth Century England: Household, Kindship, and Patronage* (Cambridge University Press, 2001), pp. 216–36.

regard, he would listen to Newcastle at Hardwicke's behest.[5] Another close friend of Newcastle's, William Murray, Earl of Mansfield, also came from the legal sector, and was Lord Chief Justice of the King's Bench from 1756 to 1788, the highest judicial position after Lord Chancellor. Both Hardwicke and Mansfield took a keen interest in the affairs of the prize courts and were the dominant voices amongst the commissioners.

In contrast to Newcastle, William Pitt was part of the 'Patriot Whig' faction within whiggish politics. The Patriot Whigs were largely defined by their opposition to the corruption of British society that came from the political and social upper echelons. In order to combat corruption, the Patriot Whigs supported wider access to political power; breaking up commercial monopolies in order to broaden access to Britain's commercial world; and the expansion of Britain's empire, based on a libertarian model rather than a centrally controlled and managed one.[6] Pitt's Patriot Whig supporters in the government who also attended the Court of Prize Appeal were not numerous. He had only two: Richard, Earl Temple, the Lord Privy Seal, and Lord Lyttelton, who had been Chancellor of the Exchequer in 1756, and was a new member of the Privy Council. Temple was Pitt's brother-in-law and Lyttelton was the nephew of one of Pitt's mentors who owed his career to Pitt. Though Pitt did not share as close a friendship with Hardwicke and Mansfield as did Newcastle, he and the two judges did enjoy a mutually respectful professional relationship, which grew closer as the war continued. Outside of the Pitt and Newcastle camps was Robert Darcy, Earl of Holdernesse, and Secretary of State for the Northern Department. Though he could not be said to be an ally of either Pitt or Newcastle, they did share the goal of maintaining Dutch neutrality and, as it was Holdernesse's office that officially dealt with Anglo-Dutch relations, his willing co-operation was instrumental to the success of any Anglo-Dutch related strategy.

Pitt and Newcastle's Strategies

There are very decided opinions within the historiography of the Seven Years' War regarding the actions taken by William Pitt and the Duke of Newcastle during their tenure as leaders of the wartime government. Pitt is often described as an energetic, industrious, and egomaniacal leader who had an extremely good grip on the strategies and policies that led

[5] J. S. Corbett, *England in the Seven Years' War: A Study in Combined Strategy*, 2 vols. (Longmans, Green, and Co., 1907), vol. I, p. 51.
[6] Kinkel, *Disciplining the Empire*, p. 93.

Britain to ultimate victory. Daniel Baugh, in describing Pitt's leadership, wrote '[H]e insisted on taking the lead in directing the war ... In respect to grand strategy he took his cues from unfolding events and circumstances, but the wish to contain or diminish French power, especially at sea or overseas, always dominated his thinking.'[7] Part of diminishing French power involved denying it the benefits of colonial trade, which could only be done if Britain prevented neutral countries from carrying it. Julian Corbett's take on Pitt was similar to Baugh's, though he concentrated on Pitt as a wartime strategist. Corbett's high praise for Pitt was based on his strategy of combining land and sea forces to attack France and to deny it, as much as possible, the use of the sea.[8] Corbett was well aware of the delicate balance between an aggressive maritime strategy and a wartime foreign policy with neutral nations rooted in contentious treaties. He described Pitt in 1759, when relations with the Dutch were frayed, as being made uneasy only by the question of neutral powers:

There was, however, one factor in the situation which caused Pitt real anxiety, and that was the uncertain and even menacing attitude of the neutral sea power ... what oppressed his mind from the first was a vision of the three northern powers [Dutch Republic, Denmark, and Sweden] uniting to protect their trade ... join[ing] hands with the French fleet, and declare[ing] war.[9]

Corbett painted Pitt as being painfully aware of the thin line that separated a neutral country from a belligerent one when maritime predation was part of wartime strategy. Nonetheless, Pitt pursued an aggressive policy of maritime predation and British naval supremacy, counting largely on the British prize system and the Court of Prize Appeal to manage disputes that might arise between Britain and neutral maritime nations.

In contrast to Pitt, the Duke of Newcastle is often disparaged for his conduct in the early years of the war, when he was, in effect, prime minister, and the war was going badly. Corbett's analysis of Newcastle is that his methods were not the best, but his strategy was sound. However, he believed Pitt to be the superior minister.[10] Newcastle's view on strategy during the war was, in many ways, more concerned with events on the Continent than Pitt's because he was much closer to King George II. The king's concerns, as the ruler of Hanover, had been Newcastle's concerns for many years and thus lent his policies and goals a more Continental approach. Baugh described Newcastle as an

---

[7] D. Baugh, *The Global Seven Years' War, 1754–1763* (Pearson, 2011), pp. 25–7.
[8] Corbett, *England in the Seven Years' War*, vol. I, p. 100.   [9] Ibid. pp. 5–7.
[10] Ibid. p. 15.

extremely active, hardworking man, who knew everyone and was concerned with everything, but he also acknowledged that Newcastle, having been the Secretary of State for thirty years, had a firm grasp on British politics. '[He] was the leading minister during almost the entire war ... At the centre of power, and fond of activity, the duke played a vital coordinating role: in effect, he functioned as the cabinet secretariat.'[11] Pitt and Newcastle had radically different personalities with mostly different views on strategy and the specifics of wartime policy. Pitt, as Secretary of State for the Southern Department, was more concerned with Spain and the Americas than with the Dutch Republic. Newcastle, who was closely tied to the Hanoverians, was always concerned with events in Northern Europe. Their focus on different geographic areas had a bearing upon their dealings with the Court of Prize Appeal, but the impending possibility of a Dutch declaration of war in 1759 aligned their concerns more closely in an effort to make sure that the court was able to maintain Dutch neutrality.[12]

Government Connections to the Court of Prize Appeal

Pitt and Newcastle also had friends and allies amongst the prestigious legal brotherhood of Doctors' Commons who argued before the Court of Prize Appeal as doctors of civil law (also called civilians). The membership of Doctors' Commons were not very numerous: in the English Registry of 1759 there were listed four judges, and seventeen advocates.[13] Of these men, three were involved in, and instrumental to, the cases of the *Maria Theresa* and the *America*: Dr George Hay, His Majesty's Advocate General; Dr R. Smalbroke, Advocate; and Dr John Bettesworth, His Majesty's Advocate in his office of the Admiralty. Two more men, not members of Doctors' Commons, but holding high legal office and more political sway, were Charles Yorke, Solicitor General; and Charles Pratt, Earl Camden and Attorney General. Both of these important legal positions were often stepping-stones to becoming Lord Chancellor. Little seems to be known about Dr Smalbroke, but Dr Hay was the King's Advocate and the chief advocate of the British privateers in both the *Maria Theresa* and *America* cases.[14] He would eventually become judge of the High Court of Admiralty in 1773, and was

---

[11] Baugh, *Global Seven Years' War*, pp. 18–19.
[12] For further discussion on William Pitt as a politician see J. Black, *Pitt the Elder* (Cambridge University Press, 1992).
[13] No Author, *The English Registry, for the year of our Lord, 1759; or A Collection of English Lists* (Printed for John Exshaw, 1759), pp. 68–9.
[14] Pares, *Colonial Blockade*, p. 199.

appointed a Lord of the Admiralty in November of 1756, a post which he held until April of 1757. In his capacity as a Member of Parliament during the war he was an ally of both Pitt and Newcastle and a vocal supporter of the Pitt–Newcastle administration in the House.[15] Much more is known about Charles Pratt and Charles Yorke. Pratt had befriended Pitt at Eton, and they remained friends in their professional lives. Pitt often consulted Pratt in legal matters, and when he became Secretary of State, in 1757, he offered the position of Attorney General to Pratt, passing over Charles Yorke, who was then Solicitor General. Pratt sat firmly in the Pittite camp and was an advocate for the British privateers in both the case of the *Maria Theresa* and the *America*.[16] Charles Yorke was a son of Philip Yorke, Earl of Hardwicke. Hardwicke, as Lord Chancellor, had helped boost his talented son's career, sometimes to the detriment of others such as Pratt. Charles Yorke's close connection to his father made him a Newcastle ally, and he was the chief advocate for the Dutch appellants in the cases of the *Maria Theresa* and *America*.

The Privateering Lobby

Interest in the proceedings of the Court of Prize Appeal was not confined to ministers and lawyers. Ordinary British citizens also followed the court cases and those most interested would likely have been the captains, sailors, and investors, who relied on the prize courts to award them prize money when a captured ship was brought into port. Though these citizens would have had very little individual contact with men like Pitt and Newcastle, as a group they were able to exert some political influence because a successful privateering arm was an important component of Britain's commerce predation strategy. The ubiquity of newspapers and their accessibility through distribution in coffee houses gave privateers and their investors a wide-reaching platform.[17] Britain's maritime community could be stirred by the privateering lobby, either to laud or to condemn the government's actions when it came to neutral rights and the rights of privateers. It is extremely unlikely, however, that the privateering lobby could have posed a political threat to the government's stability and support in Parliament through public shows of discontent

---

[15] J. Brooke and L. Namier (eds.), *The History of Parliament: The House of Commons 1754–1790*, 3 vols. (Boydell and Brewer, 1964), vol. II, pp. 512.
[16] BL Add MS 36208, Hardwicke Papers, Notes on the *Maria Theresa*.
[17] A. Brinkman-Schwartz, 'The Heart of the Maritime World: London's "Mercantile" Coffee Houses in the Seven Years' War and the American War of Independence, 1756–1783', *Historical Research*, 94 (2021), 508–31.

intended to stir up the maritime community.[18] Nonetheless, if privateers did not trust in the government and in prize courts to protect their interests, they could choose to engage less actively in commerce predation, which would be detrimental to Britain's maritime strategy against France. It was in the government's interest to make sure that privateers had full confidence in the impartiality and fairness of prize law and the prize courts.

The privateer that took the *Maria Theresa* as a prize, *The Duke of Cornwall*, was what David Starkey has described as a 'Deep Water' private ship-of-war.[19] These were large ships that could vary from roughly 100 to 500 tons, and preyed upon enemy or neutral merchant ships returning from the colonies, laden with goods for Europe. Because their cargos were of great value, many merchant ships were well armed and/or travelled in a convoy. They were a dangerous target that required weaponry and suitable manpower of 100 men or more to subdue. Deepwater privateering was a hazardous and expensive venture that offered the possibility of a large pay-off or a large loss. With such significant capital and manpower requirements, deep-water privateers needed cities with a large maritime labour force and available investors for their base.[20] London and Bristol were both cities that fit the requirements and, indeed, The *Duke of Cornwall* was a Bristol ship. The men who were likely to invest in a deep-water privateering venture were those already well versed in maritime commerce and, indeed, shareholders tended to come from within the maritime community. When Britain entered into a state of war, merchants were able to shift their money and focus to privateering from whatever peacetime trade they normally plied.[21] The privateering interest during wartime, therefore, was largely the same as the maritime commercial interest during peace, if slightly smaller. When these merchants from Bristol or London chose to stand together as a political body, they could resist ministerial pressure and, sometimes, exert influence of their own. The political aims of the privateering lobby are not particularly difficult to discern; as members of a venture capital scheme, they disliked legislation that attempted to impose rules or

---

[18] J. Black, *Parliament and Foreign Policy in the Eighteenth Century* (Cambridge University Press, 2004), pp. 7–9. It is also important to note that the privateering lobby was only one of many lobbies, or groups, with the ability to sway or worry the government. See e.g. D. Hancock, *Citizens of the World: London Merchants and the Integration of the British Atlantic Community, 1735–1785* (Cambridge University Press, 1995) and S. Haggerty, *Merely for Money? Business Culture in the British Atlantic, 1750–1815* (Liverpool University Press, 2012).

[19] David Starkey, *British Privateering Enterprise in the Eighteenth Century* (Exeter University Press, 1990), p. 40.

[20] Ibid. p. 42.   [21] Ibid. p. 67.

restrictions that hindered their chances of a high return on their investment. This generally meant that they opposed legislation that protected
the rights of neutral ships.

Pitt and Newcastle were not strangers to the privateer and merchant
lobbies. Pitt was often considered a favourite of the privateers because he
looked out for their interests. Many of the people who supported the
Patriotic Whigs were drawn from the urban and commercial population;
the same sort of demographic that would support privateering during
times of war.[22] From Pitt's political and ideological perspective, it made
sense to champion the privateers' cause. Though Pitt tried to keep the
privateers happy and working for the interest of British strategy, he found
it very difficult to influence or control them. There was, of course, no
way to control their behaviour at sea, since there was no way to police the
actions of privateers once they had left port. All checks on abuses were
necessarily reactive and after the fact. Even when the political situation
with the Dutch Republic was dire, Pitt was only able to threaten privateers with the due process of the law.[23]

Part of the reason Pitt could only issue threats was there were no legal
sanctions that could be applied to privateers before a prize case went
through the court system. The Prize Act of 1708 gave the captors a
statutory right to their prizes and to all of the proceeds gained from
condemnation – in other words, prizes became a matter of private property. The Act deprived the Crown of any control over the administrative
or judicial procedures in prize affairs. Attempts to return powers of
administration over prize affairs to the Crown in subsequent prize acts
were shunned by governments for fear that such a move would provide
fodder for parliamentary opposition and accusations that the Crown was
trying to erode Parliament's authority.[24] The king's ministers were left
with few choices outside of the prize courts, but it is well to note one
apparent extrajudicial solution, which was used sparingly, and only in
extreme situations. If ministers believed that captured neutral ships
needed to be released quickly in order to patch up relations with a neutral
country, the government could pay the value of the prizes to the captors
and thereby have the prizes released into their care. This allowed the
government to circumvent the courts, pay the privateers, and release
captured neutral property quickly. The government applied this method
in 1758 in the case of several captured Dutch ships from Suriname.[25]
It was, however, not a long-term or financially prudent solution to the
problem of privateers violating neutral rights.

[22] Kinkel, *Disciplining the Empire*, pp. 125 and 138.
[23] Pares, *Colonial Blockade*, pp. 69–70.   [24] Ibid. pp. 66–9.   [25] Ibid. p. 71.

Many of the problems over neutral rights and the rights of privateers were caused by the arbitrary nature of decisions in the High Court of Admiralty and the over-zealous enthusiasm with which some privateers indiscriminately pursued prizes. The judge of the High Court of Admiralty, Sir Thomas Salusbury, did not enjoy a good reputation, and was known for indiscriminately condemning neutral property as lawful prize.[26] In terms of the privateers, '[T]he excessive zeal with which many privateersmen conducted their examinations, the pillage of innocent vessels, and the inconsistencies displayed by the Prize Court in the adjudication of seized property, increasingly served to jeopardise Britain's relations with the neutral states.'[27] Julian Corbett, ever Pitt's champion, described the relationship between Pitt and the privateers almost as one would the relationship between a parent and a troublesome child: 'He was honestly doing his best to check the abuses, but the privateers were incorrigible.'[28] Richard Pares, a historian particularly concerned with the effects of commerce predation on colonies, saw privateers as being less useful than they should have been:

The privateers were less serviceable to the nation than they were supposed to be. There were some ways in which they were an actual nuisance ... There was a much worse and more present danger that the privateers would involve the nation in diplomatic difficulties with neutrals.[29]

It was this ever-present danger that ministers like Pitt and Newcastle attempted to mitigate through the adjudications of the Court of Prize Appeal. With respect to the Dutch Republic during the Seven Years' War, ministerial attempts to maintain Dutch neutrality were successful, in large part due to the efforts of this appellate court.

Dutch Strategy and Neutrality

Britain was closely connected to the Dutch Republic by virtue of being a Protestant country, and through the House of Orange. William IV, Prince of Orange, and husband of Anne, the eldest daughter of King George II, was elected stadtholder of the Republic in 1747. The stadtholderate had been vacant since the death of William III in 1702 when the States of Holland had decided to leave the position unfilled.[30] William IV was proclaimed stadtholder on 3 May 1747, only after a small French

[26] Ibid. pp. 85, 121, and 132.   [27] Starkey, *British Privateering*, p. 39.
[28] Corbett, *England in the Seven Years' War*, vol. II, p. 7.
[29] Pares, *Colonial Blockade*, p. 43.
[30] J. Israel, *The Dutch Republic: Its Rise, Greatness, and Fall 1477–1806* (Oxford University Press, 1995), p. 959.

army had invaded the Republic and touched off a revolution rooted in anger and resentment over the economic decline of the past half-century. By the middle of May, William IV was the first stadtholder of every province in the Union.[31] The stadtholder was chosen by the States General, and though he was not the ruler of the Republic, he could be powerful so long as he had enough political and public support. He presided over the provincial states (assemblies) and had command of the provincial armies. William IV died in 1751 and left behind a 3-year-old son, William V. The position of stadtholder had been made hereditary, but because William V was too young to assume responsibility, his Hanoverian/British mother became regent.

Aside from the stadtholder, there were three officers who held the most powerful positions in the Dutch Republic when it came to foreign affairs. These officers were the Grand Pensionary, the Greffier, and the Treasurer General of the Union. Together with the stadtholder, they helped shape Dutch foreign policy during the Seven Years' War. At the time of the Anglo-Dutch crisis, the Grand Pensionary was a man named Pieter Styn. He was tasked with maintaining an unofficial correspondence with Dutch ministers in foreign countries. Though unofficial, the correspondence was extremely important for maintaining Dutch policy, as a hint or instruction given by the Grand Pensionary was not lightly ignored. The office of Greffier was held by Hendrick Fagel, who conducted the Republic's official correspondence with foreign representatives.[32] The last member of the Dutch government power quartet was Johannes Hop, the Treasurer General of the Union. He handled the budgeting needs of any policy and advised the States General how, and from where, to raise funds when they were needed.[33] Hop came from an influential anti-Orangeist family in Amsterdam. He had two cousins, Cornelis and Hendrik Hop. Cornelis was a well-known Amsterdam merchant, and his brother Hendrik was the Dutch representative to the British Court.[34] The British representative in the Dutch Republic was a son of Lord Hardwicke, Major General Joseph Yorke, who had been Minister Plenipotentiary to the United Provinces since 1751, and kept himself well informed of Dutch affairs.[35] Joseph carried on a constant correspondence with both his father and the Duke of Newcastle, often dealing with questions of Dutch neutrality and ship seizures.

[31] Ibid. pp. 1067–9.
[32] A. C. Carter, *The Dutch Republic in Europe in the Seven Years' War* (MacMillan and Co., 1971), p. 24.
[33] Ibid. p. 26.   [34] Ibid.   [35] Ibid. p. 76.

Much like the British ministers, the Dutch officials were concerned with neutrality. At the start of official hostilities in 1756, Dutch policy was to remain neutral by keeping France out of the Low Countries, and by staying out of British military actions in Hanover and Germany. The maritime commercial interests of the Dutch Republic did not want to see Britain emerge as the dominant world sea power. That being said, if France were to obtain total victory and overthrow the Hanoverians in the name of the Catholic Stuarts, the Protestant Republic would be flanked by potentially hostile Catholic powers.[36] Neither outcome was desirable. Neutrality was the best course: it was a position in which wartime resources were not expended, the French carrying trade was picked up, and the possibility of assisting in peace settlements before either belligerent became too powerful, was possible. The Republic's policy of neutrality was not, however, only governed by strategic prudence. The Dutch Republic was unable to finance a major European war after 1713, due to the tax burden it would impose on its small population, and to the large amount of debt that it had incurred whilst fighting in the War of the Spanish Succession.[37] Neutrality, which bolstered the Dutch carrying trade and therefore increased the wealth of Dutch citizens, was a much better fiscal option.[38] However, it became increasingly difficult to maintain this course as Dutch officials perceived that Britain's privateers and ships of war were continually violating Dutch neutrality.

The Anglo-Dutch Treaty of 1674

The Anglo-Dutch treaty of 1674 was negotiated at the end of the third Anglo-Dutch war and was designed, in part, to address issues raised by the effect of the British Navigation Acts on Dutch trade. Britain's ability to wage a war at sea was partially dependent on naval supplies from the Baltic region, and, as England developed triangular trading patterns between the North Sea, Baltic, and American colonies in the seventeenth century, the protectionist Navigation Acts increasingly excluded Dutch merchants and ships from the Anglo-Baltic trade.[39] However, the increasing frequency of naval warfare in the eighteenth century also played a role in excluding the Dutch from Anglo-Baltic trade because, in times of war, the trade was much more of a risk to neutral carriers given the importance of naval supplies to any belligerent country.

---

[36] Ibid. p. xvi.   [37] Israel, *The Dutch Republic*, p. 86.
[38] D. Ormrod, *The Rise of Commercial Empires: England and the Netherlands in the Age of Mercantilism, 1650–1770* (Cambridge University Press, 2003), p. 23.
[39] Ibid. p. 278.

The Navigation Acts encompassed the concept that 'unfree ships make unfree goods', in other words, any neutral goods found inside of an enemy ship would be considered enemy goods and could be declared lawful prize.[40] It is possible to read the treaty of 1674 as a concession to the Dutch which, under some of the articles, inverted the concept of 'unfree ships make unfree goods' espoused in the Navigation Acts to one of 'free ships make free goods', giving the Dutch the ability to carry enemy cargoes safe from seizure except for the explicitly named contraband goods.[41] The inversion of 'unfree ships make unfree goods' in portions of the treaty was partially in line with what Grotius had written in his 1625 work *De jure belli ac pacis* ('On the Laws of War and Peace') but actually went further than Grotius did in granting protection to enemy goods so long as they were carried by neutral ships. Grotius did not specifically address the question of whether enemy goods found on a neutral ship were protected from seizure. Grotius claimed only that non-enemy goods found within an enemy's territory (here it is possible to extrapolate that an enemy's territory could apply to an enemy's ship) did not make a lawful prize.[42] He also stated:

The observation usually made, that all things on board an enemy's ships are to be deemed an enemy's goods, ought not to be received as a standing and acknowledged rule of the law of nations, but only as a maxim, indicating the strong presumption that both goods and vessel belong to the same owner, unless clear proof to the contrary can be brought.[43]

For Grotius, the blanket concept of 'unfree ships make unfree goods' was not universally applicable as part of the law of nations. It was more of a starting baseline that allowed a nation to rightfully presume that the goods found on board an enemy's ship would be lawful prize unless clearly proven to belong to non-enemies. As 'unfree ships make unfree goods' was not an acknowledged rule of the law of nations – but rather a deviation – the rule could only exist as part of an agreement, contract, or treaty, entered into by two or more nations.[44] A possible extension of Grotius's thinking on 'unfree ships make unfree goods' would have been that a similar maxim existed for neutral ships wherein all things found on board neutral ships were presumed to be neutral unless proven otherwise; in other words, a softer version of 'free ships make free goods'. In order to achieve an absolute version of 'free ships make free goods', nations would have to enter into a specific treaty – such as

---

[40] Ibid. pp. 298–9.   [41] Ibid.
[42] H. Grotius, *On the Law of War and Peace*, Bk 3, Ch. 6, s. 6. (Anodos Books, 2019), p. 196.
[43] Ibid.   [44] Ibid.

the Anglo-Dutch treaty of 1674. Philosophically, there was no problem with entering into a treaty where goods carried in Dutch ships were protected from British seizure. The issues arose when it came to enforcement and the specific protections that the treaty offered to the private property of both neutral and enemy actors. When examining the treaty itself, it becomes clear that what it offered was indeed a soft version of 'free ships make free goods' which left a lot of room for interpretation on the subject of how property was to be defined.

The first article of the treaty broadly proclaimed that English and Dutch subjects would have the reciprocal freedom to conduct any manner of commerce with any kingdoms, countries, or estates, without interference.[45] The rest of the treaty was, essentially, a series of caveats that narrowed down the parameters of this freedom and how it was to be ensured. Article 2 made it clear that the freedom to trade could not be interfered with even when one of the two signatories was involved in a war; in other words, when one of the parties was a neutral and the other a belligerent. The only exception to the freedom from interference was if the goods being traded were on the list of contraband goods which was enumerated in Article 3 and was exclusively related to weapons of war.[46] Article 5 was related specifically to seaborne commerce and ports of entry. Any English ship entering and subsequently leaving a Dutch port, or any Dutch ship entering and subsequently leaving an English port, was required only to show a passport (otherwise known as a sea-brief) to authorities in order to legitimise the voyage. The form for the passport was attached to the treaty.[47] If vessels belonging to one signatory were encountered on the open sea (the term was not defined specifically by the treaty) by warships or privateers of the other, then the ships were to keep 'a convenient distance' and the warship or privateer was only allowed to send a boat with up to three men to check the passport. If the passport was shown and correct, the ship could not be searched and had to be allowed to continue its voyage.[48] The next two articles were related to neutral ships travelling to ports under the control of a signatory's enemy. If it were found that a neutral ship was travelling into an enemy port, then that ship needed to provide the aforementioned passport as well as a bill of lading in order to ensure that the ship was not bringing contraband goods into an enemy port. If the paperwork was not in order or indicated

---

[45] Anglo-Dutch treaty of 1674, Oxford Historical Treaties, https://opil.ouplaw.com/view/10.1093/law:oht/law-oht-13-CTS-255.regGroup.1/law-oht-13-CTS-255?rskey=M7VBVj&result=25&prd=OHT, p. 2.

[46] Ibid. For those not intimately familiar with the treaty of 1674, the rest of Article 2 will be discussed further later in this section.

[47] Ibid.   [48] Ibid.

that contraband goods might be on board, it was still not possible to search the ship.[49] If it was indeed suspected that a ship was carrying contraband goods, the whole ship and all of the property held within were to be taken to a port where Admiralty or prize courts could determine if any of the goods were indeed contraband and/or lawful prize. Article 7 gave further clarification on how enemy goods and enemy ships were to be treated. Any enemy goods carried in neutral ships were to be considered free goods unless they were contraband. However, any goods, even neutral goods, found on board an enemy ship were liable to confiscation and condemnation as lawful prize.[50] Article 7 was a declaration of Grotius's maxim and the portion of the Navigation Acts that declared 'unfree ships make unfree goods'. However, at the same time, it also declared that in most cases 'free ships make free goods'.

The articles of the 1674 treaty were highly favourable to the nation transporting goods in a state of neutrality rather than to the nation trying to ensure that no illegal goods were being carried to aid its enemies. The limitations on searching vessels meant that successfully carrying contraband was dependent on carrying the correct paperwork, even when heading to an enemy port, which was not particularly onerous or stringent. The limitations also meant that neutral ships could carry the goods of any nation without having to justify or explain who owned them. In a situation where Britain was at war and the Dutch remained neutral, any nation or merchant could ship their goods in Dutch ships with the reasonable expectation that they would remain free of British interference. It was indeed a soft version of 'free ships make free goods' that came fairly close to an absolute version of the concept. But what of enforcement? How was the broad freedom accorded to neutral vessels to be protected from abuse by privateers or warship captains bent upon taking prizes? As mentioned earlier, abuses could only be addressed after the fact through court proceedings because it was almost impossible to police abuse of the treaty at sea. The framers of the treaty clearly understood the issues of enforcement, because they took some precautions to deter abusive behaviour. Article 9 of the treaty claimed that all subjects who set out in warships or privateers and committed abuses 'shall be punished, and moreover be liable to satisfy all costs and damages, by restitution and reparation, upon pain and obligation of person and goods'.[51] This meant that, should it be proven and declared in the British prize courts that British warships or privateers abused the treaty, they would be held fiscally responsible for all damages. Further to this,

---

[49] Ibid.   [50] Ibid.   [51] Ibid. p. 7.

Article 10 decreed that privateers whose crew was less than 150 men had to give a security of £1,500 before being granted a commission. Those with crews of over 1,500 men had to give a security of £3,000.[52]

Whilst it may seem that the treaty was clear and specific about what did, or did not, constitute Dutch trading rights as neutrals in Britain's wars, the treaty did not address what would become a critical issue for Anglo-Dutch negotiators during the Seven Years' War: how were enemy ships and enemy property to be defined? The question is not as pedantic as it may first appear, because the answer did not exist in a legal philosophical vacuum. The answer was dictated by British and Dutch strategic aims which, for the sake of legitimacy, needed to be rooted in mutually agreed definitions of enemy property. For the English, the concession of 'free ships make free goods' would have meant that English merchants could be saved high wartime freight rates by shipping their goods in neutral Dutch ships. However, most ministers agreed that such a boon was not worth the risk that Dutch neutrality might prolong Anglo-French conflicts by allowing French trade to be safely carried by Dutch ships, thereby making an English strategy of commerce predation more difficult.[53] As Britain's maritime hegemony grew, ministers became increasingly concerned about neutral nations carrying the trade of Britain's enemies and less concerned about how neutrals might aid Britain's trade in a time of war. The type of French trade being protected by Dutch ships that most alarmed British ministers during the Seven Years' War was that between French colonies and France. Whilst the treaty of 1674 had come into being largely as a result of the Anglo-Baltic trade, the frictions which its interpretation caused in Anglo-Dutch affairs during the Seven Years' War were a result of West and East Indian colonial trade. The treaty had not been specifically designed to address Dutch carriage of French colonial goods, but a slight ambiguity in Article 2 left an opening for British interpreters of the treaty to attempt to put a stop to this type of trade. The article is short but worth quoting in full:

Nor shall this freedom of navigation and commerce be infringed by occasion or cause of any war, in any kind of merchandizes[sic], but shall extend to all commodities which shall be carried in time of peace; those only excepted which follow in the next article, and are comprehended under the name of Contraband.[54]

The ambiguity which the British would successfully argue for and exploit during the Seven Years' War was that the article could be interpreted as meaning that the type of neutral commerce protected by the treaty was

---

[52] Ibid. p. 8.   [53] Ormrod, *Rise of Commercial Empires*, p. 306.   [54] Ibid.

the commerce that the neutral nation was legally allowed to engage in with belligerents when there was no war. This reading or interpretation of the treaty was not unknown. At the time of negotiating the treaty the Grand Pensionary had expressed to the English envoy that the English had enforced such a principle at the beginning of the century.[55] In the specific circumstances of the Seven Years' War, this would mean that the Dutch would be allowed to carry French commerce in Dutch ships if they had been allowed to do so before the war. A possible, and logical, extension of Article 2 was that Dutch ships and their cargo were not protected by the treaty if they engaged in French commerce that had only been opened to them after, and because, an Anglo-French war had begun. The refinement and use of this very restrictive interpretation of Article 2 to curtail Dutch carriage of French goods was spearheaded and developed by Lord Hardwicke with the help of Lord Mansfield. Eventually, it became known as the Rule of the War of 1756 and successfully constrained the concept of 'free ships, free goods' by declaring that any trade which was prohibited to a country in peacetime was prohibited during wartime. Since France operated in a largely mercantilist system, its laws allowed French colonial trade to be conducted only by Frenchmen and in French ships. According to the Rule of the War of 1756, the Dutch could not legally carry French colonial trade when France was at war because they were not allowed to do so when France was at peace. This represented a clever way of curtailing the neutral rights granted by the treaty of 1674 without actually altering the treaty in any way, and it was the court cases of the *Maria Theresa* and the *America* in the Court of Prize Appeal that would establish the boundaries of, and set precedents for, the Rule of the War of 1756. Before these two court cases and the acceptance of the Rule of the War of 1756 by Dutch ministers as a constraint on neutral rights, Dutch mistrust of Britain's ability to protect Dutch neutrality was only increasing, and tensions between the two maritime nations were reaching breaking point. By the end of August 1758, when the *Maria Theresa* was brought before the Court of Prize Appeal, the Dutch Republic and Britain were headed towards a fourth Anglo-Dutch war.

Many scholars of the Seven Years' War and international law have written about the Rule of the War of 1756, and about the case of the *Maria Theresa*. Some approaches to the subject have focused on the Rule of the War of 1756 as the beginning of modern conceptions of neutral rights and as a rejection or deviation from Grotian principles in

---

[55] C. Kulsrud, *Maritime Neutrality to 1780* (Little Brown and Co., 1936), p. 99.

international law.[56] Perhaps the best and most expansive treatments of the Rule of the War of 1756 are found in Kulsrud's *Maritime Neutrality to 1780* and in Richard Pares's *Colonial Blockade and Neutral Rights 1739–1763*. Kulsrud dedicates a chapter to the subject. He makes the important point that the Rule of the War of 1756 was not new in its conception and that it was based on early seventeenth-century precedents where trade closed during peacetime was denied to a neutral nation during times of war.[57] Pares's treatment of the Rule of the War of 1756 is based on his wide engagement with the prize court papers and with the diplomatic correspondence of both the War of the Austrian Succession and the Seven Years' War. Pares focused somewhat on the distinction between trading *with* the enemy and trading *for* the enemy. Such a distinction mattered to neutral rights because it was the difference between profiting as a neutral from trade enjoyed with countries during times of peace and profiting from enemy trade that was only opened up so that an enemy could avoid enemy capture.[58] The latter situation gave extra profit to the neutral nation and benefited one belligerent over another. What is often lacking in scholarship on the Rule of the War of 1756 is the explicit connection to Lord Hardwicke and the strategic aims he was supporting as the leader of the Court of Prize Appeal. It is perhaps too easy to look back on a legal development such as the Rule of the War of 1756 and ascribe to it importance because of subsequent developments in international legal philosophy. However, it is equally important to examine it as a product of its time and as a practical answer to a problem that held strategic, legal, and diplomatic dimensions. The importance of the rule and Hardwicke's use of it during the war to manage Dutch anger over neutral rights deserves a closer exploration.

The treaty of 1674 had not been specifically designed to address Dutch carriage of French colonial goods, but it had been written with enough deliberate ambiguity that it could be favourably interpreted by the British such that Dutch neutral rights were curtailed when it came to French commerce. Nonetheless, Dutch interpretations of the treaty could just as easily expand Dutch neutrality to encompass French colonial trade. British negotiations with Dutch officials over the rights granted by the treaty would require a boost of legal legitimacy which appeased both sides and more concretely defined Dutch neutral rights without altering the treaty. This boost was provided and refined by Lord Hardwicke in the first two Dutch cases to come before the Court of Prize Appeal.

---

[56] T. Helfman, 'Trade and War: The Neutrality of Commerce in the Inter-State System', in K. Stapelbroek (ed.), *Trade and War: The Neutrality of Commerce in the Inter-State System* (Helsinki Collegium for Advanced Studies, 2011), p. 15.
[57] Kulsrud, *Maritime Neutrality*, p. 99.   [58] Pares, *Colonial Blockade*, pp. 182–3.

4   Whose Goods Are These?

The *Maria Theresa* and the *America* in the High Court of Admiralty

It is evident from the correspondence amongst British ministers involved in Anglo-Dutch relations that they were concerned about the behaviour of British privateers and the effect that the capture of Dutch prizes would have on Dutch neutrality. In a meeting that included Newcastle, Holdernesse, Lord Anson, Charles Pratt, and Lord Hardwicke, on 1 July 1756 (two months after war had been declared on France), the first steps were taken to ensure that the actions of privateers at sea would not jeopardise Dutch neutrality. The meeting was called in order to make a decision about Dutch ships that had been seized since the declaration of war. Three suggestions were put forward, all of them extrajudicial, as there was very little that the ministers could do to interfere with the workings of the lower prize courts. The first suggestion was that the captured Dutch ships that did not include naval stores (considered contraband under the 1674 treaty) as part of their cargoes should be immediately released.[1] How this would be achieved was not included in the notes on the meeting, but it would have required the privateers to drop their claim. The second suggestion was that any ships that did contain naval stores should be bought for the use of the British navy.[2] Such a move would be an effective way of keeping naval stores out of the hands of the French, whilst at the same time appeasing the Dutch merchants and avoiding lengthy trials in the prize court system. It was a tactic that had been used in the previous war. However, it was not a solution that prevented the Dutch from carrying naval stores to Britain's enemy, nor was it a check on the behaviour of British privateers. The third suggestion was directly related to the treaty of 1674, and a subsequent treaty from 1678 that was directly tied to the former. The treaty of 1678 was a defensive treaty, which required the Dutch Republic to send 600 soldiers to Britain if Britain were ever attacked. Should the Dutch

---

[1] BL Add MS 32997, Newcastle Papers, Note Written at the Cockpit by Newcastle, 1 July 1756, f. 22.
[2] Ibid.

fail to fulfil the requirements of the 1678 treaty, the articles of the 1674 treaty would become void.[3] The ministers agreed that orders should be sent to Charles Yorke, British representative at the Hague, to inform the Dutch ministers that the treaty of 1674 would be considered void unless the Dutch Republic was willing to adhere to the Anglo-Dutch treaty of 1678.[4] Since British ministers had painted France as the aggressor in the current war, they invoked the treaty of 1678, but the Dutch had yet to signal any intention of sending soldiers to Britain. Britain did not need the soldiers, and it is clear that the ministers were calling on the 1678 treaty in order to avoid discussions and disputes over the limits of Dutch neutrality. Newcastle's notes from the meeting included the following about the instructions for Yorke:

His Majesty, from His great friendship towards the States General, will not be averse to enter into a new treaty of trade and navigation, or into some reasonable modification of the treaty of 1674. And, that the Lords of the Admiralty should give Orders to the Captains of His Majesty's ships, not to seize and detain any more Dutch Ships, unless loaded with contraband goods, or Naval stores, till further orders.[5]

The aim of these early overtures to the Dutch Republic was not about acquiring troops, but about making sure that the Dutch remained neutral. The orders sent out to the ships of the Royal Navy were an extra precaution, one that the ministers wanted the Dutch to be aware of as a token of British commitment to the protection of Dutch neutral rights.

An official memorandum with formalised versions of the suggestions put forward at the July meeting was presented to the ministers of the Dutch Republic on 2 August 1756, by Joseph Yorke. It contained, as an additional concession, a two-month grace period during which time Britain acknowledged and granted to the Dutch all of the rights given by the treaty of 1674. After the two-month period, if the Dutch had not adhered to their duties as prescribed by the treaty of 1678, the Crown reserved the right to declare the treaty of 1674 to be void.[6] The memorandum remained unanswered by the Dutch ministers and, instead, after the two-month grace period, Lord Holdernesse received numerous complaints from Hendrick Hop, the Dutch representative in London, demanding that Britain adhere to the terms of the 1674 treaty and correct

---

[3] A. C. Carter, *The Dutch Republic in Europe in the Seven Years' War* (MacMillan and Co., 1971), p. 55.

[4] BL Add MS 32997, Newcastle Papers, Note Written at the Cockpit by Newcastle, 1 July 1756, f. 22.

[5] Ibid.

[6] BL Add MS 32886, Newcastle Papers, Letter from Holdernesse to Yorke, 28 November 1758, ff. 54–65.

the behaviour of British privateers.[7] It is unnecessary to delve into the details of the exchanges between Holdernesse and the Dutch ministers during 1756 and 1757, because no diplomatic progress was made. Holdernesse refused to engage with Dutch complaints until the question of the 1678 treaty was addressed. The Dutch ministers refused to engage with questions on the treaty of 1678 and demanded that Dutch commerce be left free of interference as prescribed by the treaty of 1674. Tensions were consistently ratcheted up until the first Dutch ship, the *Maria Theresa*, came before the Court of Prize Appeal. However, early on in the war, whilst Anglo-Dutch tensions were building, Lord Hardwicke had already begun to think of Dutch neutrality in terms that would lead to the creation of the Rule of the War of 1756.

By September 1756, Hardwicke had split Franco-Dutch trade into five categories which needed to be addressed by British ministers and the prize courts: contraband trade, the trade in naval stores, the coastal trade, trade to and from French colonies, and the general carrying trade for France. The first three, Hardwicke considered, were covered by the treaty, though he advocated a wider definition of contraband. The fourth and fifth categories troubled Hardwicke the most and were the genesis of his Rule of the War of 1756. Of the colonial trade, he wrote:

[I]t can by no means be tolerated. All the European nations exclude foreigners from their American colonies, and so things stood at the time of making the treaty of 1674. It is the general rule still, and cannot possibly be varied, except as a new invention fraudulently to screen French efforts from capture and the question is whether England shall suffer them to trade thither, in time of war, without seizure, when the French themselves will not suffer them to trade thither, in time of peace, without seizing them on most any account.[8]

Hardwicke's appreciation for the connection between the 1674 treaty and the Navigation Acts is clear, as is his understanding that in past conflicts trade prohibited in peacetime had been prohibited in wartime. His objection to the French colonial trade articulated the foundation for the Rule of the War of 1756, but it relied on what he believed was a generally accepted rule. If European nations did not allow foreigners to trade with their American colonies in times of peace, then the British should not allow the trade to exist in times of war. Hardwicke's thoughts on the fifth category of trade, the general carrying trade for France, were rooted in the concept of 'free ships, free goods'. Once again, his main worry was about the carriage of French colonial goods in Dutch ships

[7] Ibid.
[8] BL Add MS 32997, Newcastle Papers, Hardwicke's Notes Relating to the Dutch Trade with France, September 1756, ff. 48–51.

but, in this case, he was concerned with French goods which had been landed in other neutral ports, such as Spain or Portugal, and then put on Dutch ships for the final leg of the voyage expressly to avoid capture from British ships. Such fraudulent practices were considered by Hardwicke to be a 'continuation and completion of the original [French] voyage, and ought to be liable to the like capture although the vessel is collusively changed and the goods transhipped. These ought to be subject to condemnation on proof that the goods are French property ...'[9] Hardwicke's reasoning about the transhipment of French goods also contributed to the Rule of the War of 1756 and to what would come to be known as the doctrine of continuous voyage. The doctrine of continuous voyage, and transhipment, Hardwicke would argue in the appellate court, made neutral rights contingent upon the intent of the voyage and the original ownership of the goods found on board the ship.[10] The doctrine of continuous voyage was not the same as transhipment, because, in continuous voyage, the goods do not change ship but the ship calls at various neutral ports in order to cover its origin in enemy ports. Transhipment is changing the goods from an enemy ship to a neutral ship in order to elude capture and seizure. One of the ways to justify British seizure of Dutch ships carrying French colonial goods out of neutral ports was to claim that the shipment of French colonial goods into any country other than France was illegal under French law during times of peace and should therefore be illegal in times of war. By the same token, any French colonial goods that were illegally imported into a neutral country could not legally be shipped out to France in a Dutch ship because the intent of the voyage was to deceive the British and aid France rather than to simply, and neutrally, benefit Dutch trade. Hardwicke's argument of transhipment as a non-neutral, and therefore not protected, practice would be tested in the Spanish appellate cases examined in the second half of this book and go a long way towards concretely establishing the Rule of the War of 1756 as precedent. The arguments put forward in the Dutch and Spanish appeals were forged from those made before the judge at the High Court, and Anglo-Dutch discussions about neutrality changed dramatically after the *America* and the *Maria Theresa* were sentenced. They were the first Dutch cases in which the claimants sought an appeal, and the appeal presented British and Dutch ministers with an

---

[9] Ibid.

[10] T. Helfman, 'Trade and War: The Neutrality of Commerce in the Inter-State System', in K. Stapelbroek (ed.), *Trade and War: The Neutrality of Commerce in the Inter-State System* (Helsinki Collegium for Advanced Studies, 2011), p. 15. The doctrine of continuous voyage is thoroughly discussed by Tara Helfman, and in R. Pares, *Colonial Blockade and Neutral Rights 1739–1763* (Porcupine Press, 1975).

avenue for resolving disputes that was not centred around the deadlock
of the treaty of 1678.

The America in the High Court of Admiralty

On 21 October 1757, about two months after HMS *Squirrel* brought the
America into Yarmouth, the case was heard in London at the High Court
of Admiralty. The Honourable Sir Thomas Salusbury, judge of the
court, was presiding. Captain Louis Ferret of the *America* claimed that
the voyage of his ship had begun before war was declared between Britain
and France, with the purpose of taking goods from Amsterdam to Port-
au-Prince, in St Domingue. After unloading the cargo at Port-au-Prince,
they purchased a cargo of goods grown on the island consisting of indigo
and sugar and were on the voyage back to Amsterdam when it was taken
as prize.[11] Once in Yarmouth, Captain Ferret, his mate, and the boat-
swain were given preparatory examinations (a standard set of questions
given to officers and sailors of prize vessels when they were first brought
into port). There were some incriminating statements made by Ferret
during these initial examinations. He declared that once he had reached
Port-au-Prince and was ready to leave for Amsterdam, the governor of
St Domingue delayed the *America*'s departure because British ships were
known to be near the island, and he did not want the *America* to be taken.
Ferret went on to declare that when he was 3 leagues from Shetland, off
the coast of Scotland, some of his sailors wanted to put into port in order
to take on more sailors because more than twenty had died on the voyage
across the Atlantic. The captain, however, refused to stop because he
feared that 'if he carried his Ship into Shetland, or any British port, he
believed that the cargo of the said ship, being French goods, would be
taken by the English, as prize'.[12] Ferret also swore, however, that he, the
sailors, the cargo, and the ship were all Dutch. He also gave an explanation as to why no papers were found on board other than a passport for
the voyage, when the *America* was stopped by the *Squirrel*. According to
Ferret, a few days after leaving Port-au-Prince, he was chased by a ship
which he thought to be English and, per the instructions of the owners of
the cargo should this happen, he threw the bills of lading overboard to be
destroyed.[13] On this evidence Judge Salusbury condemned both the ship
and the goods as French and as lawful prize. Captain Ferret lodged an
appeal, hoping that the ship and cargo would be restored. He also hoped

---

[11] BL Add MS 36208, Hardwicke Papers, Notes on the *America*, ff. 180–98.   [12] Ibid.
[13] Ibid.

that Captain Parker of the *Squirrel* would be condemned to pay damages and the court costs for an unlawful seizure.

Ferret's advocates, the Solicitor General, Charles Yorke (brother of Joseph Yorke and son of Lord Hardwicke) and J. Bettesworth, cited three reasons for why the appeal was lodged. The first reason given by the Appellant's advocates invoked the treaty of 1674 and declared that 'though the voyage was made to and from a French settlement, yet it was justified by the Treaty, which allows Freedom of Navigation and Commerce to the subjects of the States General [Dutch Republic], not restrained to Europe, but extended to all countries of the World, with which they are at Peace'.[14] This was likely the first time, in a formal legal capacity, the treaty of 1674 was declared to apply specifically outside of Europe and to the Americas. It would prove to be a big part of the deliberations of the Lords Commissioners of Appeal in many Dutch cases, and to have a large impact on how neutral rights were interpreted through the treaty. It is perhaps noteworthy that it was Hardwicke's son, Charles Yorke, who, in his role as a Dutch advocate, specifically brought up the point of the treaty applying outside of Europe. There is no direct evidence to suggest that father and son discussed the affair and deliberately set out to put the question of jurisdiction before the appellate court. However, Hardwicke had corresponded with another son, Joseph Yorke, about how the treaty should not be allowed to apply to French trade coming out of the American colonies.[15] It is very possible that if he discussed the issue with one son, he would have discussed it with Charles in his capacity as Solicitor General and advocate in the Court of Prize Appeal. The advocates did not make a point of stating that the voyage had begun before the declaration of war, and it is possible that this fact was purposefully omitted, with the knowledge that French colonial trade was prohibited to Dutch ships during times of peace, and that the entire voyage, from its inception, was illegal.

The second reason for the appeal in the case of the *America* was that the goods could not be proved to be French because they did not have a French passport, nor were they bound to a French port. The third and last reason cited addressed Ferret's action of throwing the bills of lading overboard. It was claimed by the advocates that such a practice was usual and done through an excess of caution. It was not an admission of

[14] Ibid.
[15] Letter from Hardwicke to Col. Yorke, Draft, 17 September 1756, in P. C. Yorke (ed.), *The Life and Correspondence of Philip Yorke Earl of Hardwicke*, 2 vols. (Cambridge University Press, 1913), vol. II, p. 312.

unlawful practice, and though it gave probable cause for a seizure, it did not lay sufficient grounds for a condemnation in the court.[16]

The Respondent in the appellate case, Captain Parker, had the advocates George Hay (King's Advocate) and Charles Pratt (Attorney General) to argue his case. They responded to the Dutch appeal with a cross-appeal requesting that the appellate court uphold the decision passed by the High Court of Admiralty, and that they might condemn the Dutch Appellant to pay the costs of the court cases. In support of their appeal, they cited the laws of France, which prohibited foreign ships to trade in French ports in America, and they cited Ferret's initial examinations, in which he claimed that the cargo was French.[17] By rooting their arguments in the laws of France and on whether the treaty applied in America, the advocates on both sides were opening up the possibility for the court to make a ruling that would incorporate the ideas behind Hardwicke's Rule of the War of 1756, and whether the treaty of 1674 applied in the Americas. The case of the *America* would, along with that of the *Maria Theresa*, pressure the Court of Prize Appeal to make concrete interpretations of the 1674 treaty, and to take a position on the neutral rights of the Dutch as far as British prize law was concerned.

The *Maria Theresa* in the High Court of Admiralty

The case of the *Maria Theresa* came before the High Court of Admiralty on 17 August 1758. According to the records of the Court of Prize Appeal, when the *Maria Theresa* was taken, all of her paperwork was in proper order. It had on board bills of lading from Cork and from St Eustatius, but, more importantly, it had the passport required by the treaty of 1674, declaring that the ship was Dutch property and that its voyage was lawful. The treaty also required that the passport be signed by the rulers or officials of the city in the Republic from which the ship had sailed.[18] The passport of the *Maria Theresa* was signed by the Greffier of the Dutch Republic, Hendrick Fagel. The ship carried an additional document from the Dutch West India Company that granted the ship the right to trade in St Eustatius and to bring all its cargo back to the Netherlands.[19] Given that all of the papers were in order and in

---

[16] BL Add MS 36208, Hardwicke Papers, Notes on the *America*, ff. 180–98.   [17] Ibid.

[18] C. Jenkinson, *A Collection of Treaties of Peace, Commerce, and Alliance, between Great-Britain and other Powers, from the Year 1619 to 1784* (Printed for J. Almon and J. Debrett, 1781), p. 57.

[19] BL Add MS 36208, Hardwicke Papers, Notes on the *Maria Theresa*, ff. 128–50.

accordance with the treaty, it is impossible to say why Captain Jenkins of the privateer *Duke of Cornwall* thought that the Dutch ship would make a lawful prize. It was, perhaps, an example of the zealous nature of many privateers during the war. Seizures in the vicinity of the English Channel of Dutch ships coming from St Eustatius did not really begin until early 1758, and they became increasingly common after the cargo of the *Maria Theresa* was condemned in the High Court of Admiralty.[20] It is possible that the news emboldened privateers to expand their activities and more actively pursue Dutch ships as they returned to Europe from the West Indies.

Once the *Duke of Cornwall* and the *Maria Theresa* reached Falmouth, examinations (interviews and statements) were taken based on the preparatory interrogatories (the standard set of questions given to officers and sailors of prize vessels). Only Captain Tyerck Byaart and two sailors were examined. No reason was given as to why. Two interesting revelations about the *Maria Theresa*'s cargo came out of the examination of Byaart, and they are both underlined in Lord Hardwicke's notes on the case. The first revelation was that upon reaching St Eustatius, the ship unloaded most of its cargo on shore, but the rest was unloaded onto two ships in the same port. Byaart stated that he did not know the nationality of either ship, and that he never found out.[21] St Eustatius was an island without good natural harbours, so the lading and unlading of ships was done by smaller craft that would come out to the ships, take on small portions of cargo and convey them to shore.[22] With such a cumbersome system of unloading cargo that required multiple small crafts, it would have been easy to parcel out the *Maria Theresa*'s cargo into boats or canoes that were going to shore and into those that were going to waiting ships anchored nearby. In the hustle and bustle of a port whose inhabitants and visitors were well versed in a contraband trade with French and British islands, such activity would likely have gone purposefully unnoticed.[23]

The second revelation involved a third mysterious ship. Of the cargo that the *Maria Theresa* took on in St Eustatius, part of each commodity was loaded from shore and the rest was taken from a Dutch frigate then in port and another ship, which Byaart claimed not to have identified.[24] The examination of one of the sailors of the *Maria Theresa* (which was

---

[20] Pares, *Colonial Blockade*, p. 211.
[21] BL Add MS 36208, Hardwicke Papers, Notes on the *Maria Theresa*, ff. 128–50.
[22] L. M. Rupert, *Creolization and Contraband: Curaçao in the Early Modern Atlantic World* (University of Georgia Press, 2012), p. 122.
[23] Ibid.
[24] BL Add MS 36208, Hardwicke Papers, Notes on the *Maria Theresa*, ff. 128–50.

completely underlined by Hardwicke) is slightly more revealing. The sailor, Peter Retti, claimed that both ships from which the *Maria Theresa* took on cargo were French, and that the cargo itself was French. His knowledge came from the fact that he had been sent onto one of the ships to help with the transfer of goods. All of the people on that ship, he declared, were French, and he had heard the captain say that they had just come from a French settlement.[25] This was perfectly plausible since St Eustatius was close to both Guadeloupe and Martinique and the contraband trade between the Dutch and the two French islands enjoyed great success.[26] The revelations about the nature of the *Maria Theresa*'s cargo would prove her undoing in the High Court of Admiralty. It was a stroke of luck for Captain Jenkins, as there was no way that he could have known this information before the examinations, because the bills of lading found on the *Maria Theresa* only had the names of Dutch merchants based in St Eustatius. Salusbury condemned the goods as lawful prize because they were presumed to belong to enemies, but declared that the ship was indeed Dutch and should be restored.[27] From this decision, Captain Byaart appealed and wished that the condemned goods be restored and that the privateers be condemned to pay damages and all of the court costs. The appeal was not lodged for several months. The reasons given for lodging the appeal were drawn up by Charles Yorke, and R. Smalbroke, the two advocates who would represent the case before the Court of Prize Appeal.

The first reason cited for lodging an appeal was that all of the ship's papers had been in order and in accordance with the treaty of 1674, including a passport that showed that no contraband goods were on board, and bills of lading that showed the cargo to be the property of Dutch subjects in Amsterdam. The paper proofs were contradicted only by the hearsay of one sailor whose claims about French goods being put onto the *Maria Theresa* were impossible to confirm. The advocates of the Appellant claimed that hearsay was not enough to override the legal paper evidence presented by Byaart.[28] The second reason allowed that there was, of course, a slim possibility that some of the goods on board the ship came from French colonies. However, the advocates argued that this did not mean, nor was there proof, that they were shipped on French account or owned by Frenchmen, which meant that they had still to be

[25] Ibid.
[26] W. Klooster and G. Oostindie, *Realm Between Empires: The Second Dutch Atlantic 1680–1815* (Cornell University Press, 2018), pp. 42–3.
[27] BL Add MS 36208 Hardwicke Papers, Notes on the *Maria Theresa*, ff. 128–50.
[28] Ibid.

considered neutral property.[29] The last reason given for appeal was that the capture of the *Maria Theresa* was illegal even if the goods on board had been shipped on French account and owned by Frenchmen, because it contravened the treaty of 1674, wherein it was granted that that subjects of the Dutch Republic could freely trade with the enemies of Great Britain.[30] By tying the appellate case directly to the treaty of 1674 and the right to trade with the enemies of Britain, the Appellant's advocates opened the discussion as to whether the treaty granted access to trade that was denied to the Dutch during times of peace. It opened, in other words, a discussion on whether Hardwicke's Rule of the War of 1756 would be brought to bear. No cross-appeal was filed by the Respondent, Captain Jenkins of the *Duke of Cornwall*, which might explain why there were no corresponding reasons given by the Respondent's advocates, George Hay and Charles Pratt, as to why the appellate court should uphold the sentence passed by the High Court of Admiralty.[31] It is likely not a coincidence that the advocates in this case and that concerning the *America* included the King's Advocate (George Hay), the Solicitor General (Charles Yorke), and the Attorney General (Charles Pratt). These three men held high and important legal offices, and often came together to work on cases or matters that were relevant to the Crown or government's interests and involved international law and foreign relations.[32] Their involvement in these two first cases before the Court of Prize Appeal is an indication of their importance to Britain's strategy and the impact that the legal arguments could have on present and future Anglo-Dutch relations. That being said, all four men were involved in Court of Prize Appeal cases throughout the war, another indication of the importance of the court to Britain's strategic and legal pursuits during the war. Of the approximately 139 cases that were adjudicated by the Court of Prize Appeal during the war, George Hay, Charles Yorke, and Charles Pratt, acted as advocates together in 77 of them. At least one of them acted as an advocate in 137 of the cases. Charles Yorke acted as advocate in 121 of the cases.[33]

Given the evidence that French ships had interacted with the *Maria Theresa*, and the clear evidence that it was a Dutch ship, Salusbury's

---

[29] Ibid.   [30] Ibid.

[31] It is not clear from the court documents, or the proceedings, whether a cross-appeal always had to be filed in order for a Respondent's advocates to make specific arguments rather than just respond to those made by the Appellants.

[32] A. D. McNair et al., 'The Debt of International Law in Britain to the Civil Law and the Civilians', *Transactions of the Grotius Society*, 39 (1953), 183–210, p. 203.

[33] BL Add MS 36208–14, Hardwicke Manuscripts, Notes on Cases of the Court of Prize Appeal.

sentence did not cause a public uproar amongst Britain's maritime circles. The High Court of Admiralty's decision in the case of the *America* did not create a stir either, because the case had gone in favour of the British naval captain. However, in the time that elapsed between their hearings in the High Court of Admiralty and their hearings in the Court of Prize Appeal, Anglo-Dutch negotiations moved away from the deadlock of the early war years and began to rapidly descend into an Anglo-Dutch crisis in the summer of 1758. There was no particular catalyst for the somewhat sudden resumption and rapid deterioration of Anglo-Dutch negotiations. However, it came at a time when Pitt's military focus shifted, in part, to operations in the West Indies, and it is useful to set the shift in Anglo-Dutch negotiations within the context of Pitt's wartime strategy.

A Strategic Shift to the West Indies

Pitt's ultimate focus in the Seven Years' War was victory in North America, because he believed that victory over France in Europe relied on victory over France in North America first. Victory in North America against the French had also been on the agenda of the 'patriotic' branch of the Whig party, to which Pitt belonged, since the previous war.[34] By 1758, Britain's combined naval and land forces were well on their way to securing that victory, and Pitt began to cast his eye towards eccentric attacks in the West Indies that would add weight to the main attack in North America. He developed a plan against Martinique with the intention of gaining a bargaining chip for Minorca (which had been lost to the French at the beginning of the war) and crippling the French colonial trade.[35] In the summer of 1758, the commander of the Leeward Islands Station set up a blockade of Martinique in preparation for the attack. However, it soon became clear that the island was mostly being supplied from St Eustatius, and so a blockade was set up there as well.[36] Commerce raiding in the West Indies was increased and, as a result, neutral Dutch ships were targeted. This inevitably increased tensions between the two countries: 238 Dutch St Eustatius ships were captured by 1761 through the efforts of British privateers and warships.

[34] S. Kinkel, *Disciplining the Empire: Politics, Governance and the Rise of the British Navy* (Harvard University Press, 2018), pp. 125–7.
[35] J. S. Corbett, *England in the Seven Years' War: A Study in Combined Strategy*, 2 vols. (Longmans, Green, and Co., 1907), vol. I, pp. 371–4.
[36] Ibid.

The estimated financial damages caused by those captures was 3 million guilders.[37]

Up until the point when Pitt's strategic eye was cast upon the West Indies, the Duke of Newcastle, Secretary of the Treasury; Lord Holdernesse, Secretary of State for the Northern Department; and Joseph Yorke, British representative at The Hague, had been working at cross-purposes with Dutch officials. The Dutch position maintained that the capture of Dutch ships violated the treaty of 1674, which granted Dutch merchant ships immunity from British interference during peace or war.[38] The British position was that the treaty did not apply since the Dutch had not complied with the defensive treaty of 1678, which promised Dutch soldiers be sent to Britain if it were 'attacked'. By 1758, partly in support of Pitt's strategy, British ministers were interested in stopping the Dutch trade with the French colonies in the Americas and, with the support and aid of Lord Hardwicke, took up the position that the treaty of 1674 did not apply to trade in America. Hardwicke based his position on Article 2 of the treaty, which stated: 'Nor shall this freedom of navigation and commerce be violated or interrupted ... but such freedom shall extend to all commodities, which might be carried in time of peace.'[39] As far as Hardwicke was concerned, the treaty was always meant to exclude trade prohibited during times of peace. In a letter to Joseph Yorke from September 1756 (that closely resembles the wording from his notes on the Dutch trade with France discussed earlier) he wrote in respect of Article 2 that freedom from interference only applied to trade open to the Dutch during times of peace and that this had always been the case and the intention behind the treaty.[40] The French colonial trade, being based on a mercantilist system, was not open to the Dutch, or any non-Frenchmen, during peacetime, and thus was not covered by the treaty. On 27 August 1758, ten days after the High Court of Admiralty handed down the sentence in the case of the *Maria Theresa*, the Dutch ministers sent a proposal to the British Court asking for full rights under the treaty of 1674 and the release of all Dutch ships that had been taken as prize for trading to French colonies in the Americas. In return, Dutch officials would 'hint' to their merchants that trade with the French colonies should not be continued.[41] It is likely that Britain's strategic shift to more actively attacking the French in the West Indies,

[37] Klooster and Oostindie, *Realm Between Empires*, pp. 47–8.
[38] Jenkinson, *Collection of Treaties*, p. 51.   [39] Ibid.
[40] Letter from Hardwicke to Col. Yorke, Draft, 17 September 1756, in Yorke (ed.), *The Life and Correspondence of Philip Yorke Earl of Hardwicke*, vol. II, p. 312.
[41] BL Add MS 32886, Newcastle Papers, Letter from Holdernesse to Yorke, 28 November 1758, ff. 54–65.

and thus more actively interfering with Franco-Dutch trade, prompted the sending of the Republic's proposal. The proposal, however, was rejected by Newcastle and Holdernesse in no uncertain terms, with Holdernesse writing that

His Majesty must give up the question by delivering up the ships already taken for carrying on that unwarrantable practice [trading to French colonies], and depend for the future upon what? Not upon an Act of State, not even upon an avowed transaction, but upon an insinuation privately given and which it would have been in the breast of every trader to have complied with, or not, as suited his inclination or his interest.[42]

Holdernesse clearly had no intention of granting more concessions to the Dutch by freeing more ships extrajudicially as he had done at the beginning of the war. Such a concession would, at this advanced stage in the war, defeat the purpose of Britain's policy, because the Dutch would not guarantee a cutback on future Franco-Dutch colonial trade in return for restoring Dutch ships. Though British ministers might appease Dutch anger through such a move, it would ultimately do nothing to safeguard Dutch neutrality, because it did not address the disputes over whether the ships were legally taken within the constraints of the treaty of 1674. The same situation would likely arise again after more Dutch ships were captured by British warships and privateers.

A few weeks after the Dutch proposal was received by the British ministers, Lord Hardwicke penned a letter to Holdernesse on 7 September 1758, in which he described his distress over the Dutch disputes. Unlike Holdernesse, Hardwicke believed it was time for a solution, and that Britain should make overtures to the Dutch Republic.[43] Ever since 1756, Hardwicke wrote, he had been pushing for an amendment to prize law that would grant the Crown, and thereby the interested members of the Privy Council, the power to release captured neutral ships without going through the usual legal motions of a trial. He suggested to Holdernesse that the Dutch ships that had recently been taken be released, and that this gesture of goodwill would cause the Dutch to give up carrying French trade to and from the West Indies. He claimed that had his proposal been enacted, 'Much of this mischief might then have been prevented',[44] and he proposed that his amendment be considered once more.

---

[42] Ibid.
[43] BL Add MS 3431, Leeds Papers, Letter from Hardwicke to Holdernesse, 7 September 1758.
[44] Ibid.

Hardwicke's solution to the Dutch disputes, as espoused in the letter, was threefold: first, the Crown should be given more power to release neutral ships; secondly, the Dutch would have to give up carrying French trade to and from the Americas, but as a token of friendship Britain would be lenient and forgiving of their trade with France in Europe; and thirdly, restrictions would have to be placed on British privateers for 'otherwise they will put their kind at war with all the world'.[45] Hardwicke's approach would give the Crown more power, and would allow Newcastle, Pitt, and Holdernesse to alleviate tensions immediately by releasing Dutch ships when their seizure by British privateers caused an uproar in the Dutch Republic. However, giving the Crown the additional power to bypass laws put in place by Parliament would likely also cause an uproar in Parliament and amongst the privateers, as it would encroach on parliamentary authority and the rights of privateers granted by the 1708 Prize Act. Nonetheless, Hardwicke's suggestion convinced Holdernesse and Newcastle to make overtures to the Dutch Republic in the winter of 1758–9.

On 28 November 1758, Holdernesse wrote a letter, seen and approved by Newcastle and Hardwicke, to Joseph Yorke, along with a proposal for ending the animosity between the two countries. It is clear from Holdernesse's wording however, that he viewed the proposal as an overture made to bring unreasonable men to the negotiating table. It is worth quoting him in full because his obvious frustration with the Dutch comes out strongly:

When the minds of men are actuated by passion and interest; when their prejudices are increased and their passions irritated, by faction, and when the most delusive arts are used to inflame their temper, and misguide their judgment, there is but little room to hope that Reason and Argument will take place; and this is but too true a description of the situation of the Dutch.[46]

The proposal sent to the Dutch, and the concessions made therein, were not to Holdernesse's liking; but he recognised that it was one of the only possible ways to resolve the disputes over the treaty of 1674 and the capture of Dutch ships. Per Hardwicke's suggestion, the memorandum required that the Dutch give up the French trade to and from the Americas. If the Republic agreed, then Britain would grant the Dutch the benefits of the treaty of 1674. In terms of redressing potential wrongs done to Dutch merchants by British privateers, Holdernesse suggested

---

[45] Ibid.
[46] BL Add MS 32886, Newcastle Papers, Letter from Holdernesse to Yorke, 28 November 1758, ff. 54–65.

and encouraged the Dutch merchants to appeal cases to the Lords Commissioners of Prize Appeal in order that the mistakes of the lower courts could be rectified. If the appeal proved too expensive for some merchants, the Republic should assume the costs:

And the Dutch merchants could do no greater pleasure to the King, than by enabling His Majesty to trace such offenders [misbehaved privateers] and bring them to justice ... In like manner, the complaints that are raised against the dilatory and expensive proceedings of the inferior courts of Admiralty, are only to be rectified by the court of appeals, who can, and would control the inferior courts, if any irregularity or injustice in their proceedings could be made to appear.[47]

This, he suggested, would alleviate the 'rage' felt by Dutch merchants and go a long way towards a reconciliation of the two nations.[48] However, Holdernesse's claim that the appellate court could control the lower courts within the British prize system was optimistic. Whilst decisions and precedents in the appellate court should have served as a guide to the lower courts, there was no way for ministers to guarantee that they would be followed. The High Court was, at least, in the same city as the appellate court, but regarding all the Vice Admiralty courts in the empire, which, in many cases, were not even presided over by legally appointed judges, it would be an impossible task to ensure that they followed precedents set by the Court of Prize Appeal.

The proposal was, nonetheless, perfectly in line with Britain's wartime strategic aims of maintaining Dutch neutrality without compromising the predation strategy that was defeating the French at sea. Destruction of French West Indian commerce was a necessary part of Pitt's strategy to reduce French power and gain bargaining chips for future peace negotiations. Allowing the Dutch to carry French commerce within European waters, as defined by the treaty of 1674, would not have been detrimental, as Hardwicke had identified at the beginning of the war. Holdernesse's letter was also the first time that a British official suggested that the Dutch use the appellate process to address their mercantile grievances. Though it is unclear whether the suggestion to use the appellate court came out of Hardwicke's wish to grant the Crown more power, it is certainly a possibility. Having the Dutch seek recourse in the appellate court would grant ministers the ability to rectify both the abuses carried out by privateers at sea and the decisions made in the High Court of Admiralty that threatened Dutch neutrality. Commerce predation could continue, but the ministers would also be able to claim that

[47] Ibid.   [48] Ibid.

Dutch grievances were being addressed by the prize system. A reliable Court of Prize Appeal that was seen as a defender of Dutch neutral rights could bolster Dutch faith in the British legal system and its ability to be an arbiter of international maritime disputes.

Dutch faith in Britain's commitment to the Republic's neutrality was not the only problem for the British ministers in the winter of 1758; there was also the question of whether British ministers, and the British public, trusted that the Dutch would not abuse their neutral rights as granted by the treaty of 1674. Holdernesse did not believe that the Dutch could be trusted, and in the last paragraph in his letter to Joseph Yorke about the British proposal to the Dutch, he wrote that thorough examinations of Dutch ships were necessary in order to prevent Dutch fraud. Such examinations were normally conducted at sea but, if there was doubt, then the Dutch ship should be brought into a British port for further assessment. Holdernesse acknowledged that the topic of Dutch fraud and his suggested response would cause great annoyance within the Republic:

> [T]he moment you come to touch upon this topic, it will be treated by our adversaries in Holland as a proof of our intention to annoy every Branch of the Dutch Commerce, though, at the same time, no regulation whatsoever that can be made, is to be depended upon, unless a verification of the voyage and cargo of a ship is, some how or other attained ...[49]

The treaty of 1674 heavily restricted the right of search as long as the required papers for any given ship were presented when detained. This was in keeping with the concept of 'free ships make free goods' but it would have been extremely frustrating for ministers who believed that the Dutch were fraudulently carrying French trade to the detriment of British strategic interests. Since the letter was seen and approved by Newcastle and Hardwicke, it is reasonable to assume that the two men agreed, at least to some extent, with Holdernesse's assessment of Dutch fraud. Neither country's ministers were willing to believe that the behaviour of the other's agents could be controlled at sea. British ministers did not believe that Dutch ships would not commit fraud, despite regulations emanating from the officials of the Republic. Dutch officials did not believe that British ministers could control the abuses of privateers or warships when stopping Dutch ships to enquire about fraud, despite assurances about adherence to the terms of the treaty of 1674. As a result of such mistrust, and the fact that it was indeed impossible to police the actions of captains and sailors at sea, the only assurances Britain gave

[49] Ibid.

relied on correcting abuses after the fact, through the Court of Prize Appeal. The question of controlling behaviour at sea was acknowledged by British ministers to be one that was best avoided until further notice. 'His Majesty thinks it most advisable that you should not speak it out at once … [until] it shall be discussed in what manner the King may be assured that the terms agreed upon with the State can be faithfully executed.'[50] However, as much as the British ministers wished to avoid the issue of Dutch fraud, the British commercial community were aware of it and it was, according to Holdernesse, having a detrimental effect on the London Stock Exchange.

Dutch Money for a British War

The commercial and financial worlds of Britain and the Dutch Republic were strongly connected in the mid-eighteenth century. The British community in Dutch cities like Rotterdam was well integrated, with a large portion of it intermarried and strongly identifying as Dutch.[51] In financial terms, the Dutch had a large stake in Britain's national debt, worth approximately £20 million by 1762.[52] This figure was equivalent to about 20 per cent of the total national debt. The Dutch owned 30 per cent of the national debt that was held in bank stock.[53] With a heavily integrated commercial sector, it is not surprising that adverse Anglo-Dutch relations and accusations of Dutch fraud at sea could be reflected in the London Stock Exchange. The connection was not lost on the British ministers negotiating Anglo-Dutch affairs, and on the same day that Yorke received Holdernesse's letter from 28 November 1758, he also received a different communication that was labelled 'Separate and Secret'; in it was a small note from Holdernesse about the London Stock Exchange and the Dutch. Resentment against the Dutch for their conduct during the disputes was indeed having an adverse effect on the Stock Exchange and was getting worse. Holdernesse wrote, 'it is highly to be wished, that this troublesome affair were happily and speedily ended and it is with this view, His Majesty has gone as far as possible towards an accommodation …'[54] but that no more concessions could be made. Money was on the mind of the ministers and for good reason; the

---

[50] Ibid.
[51] D. Ormrod, *The Rise of Commercial Empires: England and the Netherlands in the Age of Mercantilism, 1650–1770* (Cambridge University Press, 2003), p. 95.
[52] Ibid. p. 80.   [53] Ibid. p. 323.
[54] BL Add MS 32886, Newcastle Papers, Letter from Yorke to Holdernesse, Separate and Secret, 28 November 1758, f. 67.

new year was coming and, with it, the need for the government to raise money for the year's expenses.

Newcastle, as Secretary of the Treasury, was in charge of raising funds and making sure there was enough money to support Britain's war effort. Dutch banks and merchants were key lenders to Britain in addition to owning a considerable portion of the national debt. It is not surprising, then, that Newcastle wrote to Joseph Yorke on 1 December asking for information on the Dutch banking houses. He revealed to Yorke that the expenses for the coming year would exceed £12 million and asked 'Can you send me any account of the French supplies, for the next year? Will any of the great Houses in Holland subscribe to our Loan?'[55] Without waiting long enough for Yorke to return an answer, Newcastle repeated his question in a letter on 8 December. It is clear that, in the minds of both Newcastle and Holdernesse, funding the British national debt was part of the motivation for repairing relations with the Dutch and maintaining their neutrality. Richard Pares also attributed Newcastle's concerns over the Dutch, in part, to having to raise enough money for the coming year. 'He [Newcastle] was always particularly tremulous at the season of raising the supplies, and he was more anxious than ever for the success of this year's loan and for the prestige of the Government stocks ...'[56] In order for Pitt's strategy against the French to succeed, the treasury had to be able to foot the bill, an endeavour that was more easily accomplished with Dutch goodwill and financial aid.

Unfortunately, by mid-December 1758, the situation between Britain and the Dutch Republic had not improved. Joseph Yorke wrote to Newcastle on 12 December that, in order for the French carrying trade to the Americas to be given up by the Dutch, more concessions would need to be granted by the British ministers in terms of the Franco-Dutch trade that was not concerned with the Americas, and regarding British visitation of Dutch ships:

The article of visiting and bringing up their [Dutch] ships upon suspicion is the most delicate but provided the others can go down and that to save the Princess and her family, England could show a little mercy upon the ships already taken, I do not despair of showing them that in the manner we propose, they will not in reality be such great sufferers.[57]

[55] BL Add MS 32886, Newcastle Papers, Letter from Yorke to Newcastle, 1 December 1758, ff. 98–9.
[56] Pares, *Colonial Blockade*, p. 70.
[57] BL Add MS 32886, Newcastle Papers, Letter from Yorke to Newcastle, 12 December 1758.

It was perhaps slightly dramatic for Yorke to imply that the princess needed saving; nonetheless, it does indicate that Dutch relations with Britain were putting a strain on the Stadtholder Party and hurting the Regent's power. Yorke, as usual, was vague in his wording, but it is possible that 'the manner we propose' referred to dealing with Dutch ships in the Court of Prize Appeal or to having them released extrajudicially. Yorke also reported that some of the Dutch trading houses in London were making matters worse in Holland by writing to their Dutch counterparts that the ships already taken by the British would not be released.[58] Such a claim, if true, would do nothing but hurt Dutch confidence in the British prize system and Britain's commitment to Dutch neutrality.

Some of the British public were also feeling uneasy over the rise of Anglo-Dutch tensions in 1758. Henry Holding, a man from Bristol, wrote a memorandum on 28 July 1758, to Earl Granville, Lord President of the Privy Council. In it, Mr Holding mentioned that the merchants of Bristol had fitted out fifty-one privateers with more than 6,000 sailors, and that twenty-seven Dutch ships with a total value of £300,000 brought in by these privateers would likely not be restored by the prize courts.[59] Whether these numbers are accurate, and what time-span they apply to, is impossible to say. Along with the memorandum there is a list of twenty-seven Dutch ships taken by Bristol privateers, and the *Maria Theresa* is amongst the names. It is unclear whether the list was sent along with the memorandum or drawn up independently. However, whether accurate or no, Mr Holding found these numbers cause enough for alarm. The memorandum was a condemnation of the actions of British privateers and the harm they were doing to relations between Britain and the neutral Dutch Republic. Holding was particularly worried about how the Dutch would react to such zealous privateering:

[I]f the practice of bringing up Dutch ships without distinction of cause be continued, the Dutch must of necessity take measures to defend their trade or cease to be a nation ... there hath been several [British] privateers fitted out with no other intention and with orders from their owners to bring up all Dutch ships they meet I can positively assure your lordship.[60]

Again, whether this statement was true is largely irrelevant. Mr Holding, believing it to be true, demonstrating that some of the British population were concerned and aware of Anglo-Dutch tensions. Some of the population, like Mr Holding, were also willing to appeal directly to ministers

---

[58] Ibid.   [59] TNA PRO 30/8/78, Bristol Memorandum, 1758.   [60] Ibid.

in order to condemn the privateers in an effort to save Britain from a fourth Anglo-Dutch war.

On the same day as Yorke's letter, almost as if in answer, Newcastle wrote to the British representative that Britain's position was very clear in terms of Dutch neutral trade:

The points are shortly these; If the Dutch will renounce their trade to, and from, the French Colonies, which they pretend they would do, and the transhipping, which is a consequence of it; and also include two, or three species more in the contraband; then they shall have their treaty of 1674, without our insisting upon the subsequent one of 1678; which is equally binding upon all parties, and subsequent to the other; and upon the execution of which treaty we have insisted, and from which we have never departed.[61]

This was a very strong statement from Newcastle, which lent an air of consistency to Britain's demands as well as implying that Britain was being conciliatory by not insisting on the treaty of 1678. The most important point of contention remained Dutch carriage of French colonial trade and transhipment. Newcastle also raised the point of releasing Dutch ships without having them go through the British prize courts. 'It is not in the King's Power to do it [release the ships]; but we may, and I hope we shall, set about to endeavour to get the captors consent, and to bring on the trials of those, who will not consent, as soon as possible.'[62] The Dutch ships could not be released at the king's demand as the Dutch officials wished, but Newcastle was trying to point out that there were ways to work with the prize system that would be to the benefit of Dutch merchants, and that British ministers were working to make that system as efficient and speedy as possible. However, the problem of trust still remained because, until Dutch ships underwent trials in the Court of Prize Appeal, British promises of justice for abuses committed at sea were impossible to substantiate. Luckily for Newcastle, the first Dutch trial in the Court of Prize Appeal was only three months away.

On 15 December, Newcastle responded to Yorke's letter of the 12th and wrote a letter to William Bentinck, a close advisor of the Regent and a principal architect of the Orangeist Revolution. In his communication with Bentinck, Newcastle made it abundantly clear that, if the Dutch agreed to renounce the French trade to the Americas, the detained ships that did not participate in that trade could be released extrajudicially by

---

[61] BL Add MS 32886, Newcastle Papers, Letter from Newcastle to Yorke, 12 December 1758.
[62] Ibid.

getting the consent of the privateers.[63] In his letter to Yorke, he enclosed a copy of his letter to Bentinck and added that, should the Dutch agree to British terms, in the future the release of captured ships not trading to the Americas could be arranged, and that an alteration to the Prize Act could be made. He concluded by writing that Pitt had introduced the idea of altering the Prize Act in the House of Commons that day and that it went well.[64] This was the genesis of the Privateers Bill of 1759, which would be passed by Parliament after the cases of the *Maria Theresa* and the *America* had come to the Court of Prize Appeal. Pitt had agreed to displease the privateering lobby and the Patriotic Whigs because he feared that the Dutch would join the French and launch an attack on Britain, an event that posed a much greater threat than that of any political discontent amongst British merchants.[65]

The British ministry spent the early months of 1759 discussing, drafting, and passing what would come to be known as the Privateers Act of 1759. The Act was a collaborative effort between William Pitt, the Duke of Newcastle, Lord Holdernesse, and Lord Hardwicke, aimed at curtailing the abuses that privateers committed against neutral shipping. It created restrictions on issuing letters of marque. Whereas the 1708 Prize Act had declared that any person who applied for a letter of mark would be granted it, the new Act made the issuing of letters of marque a discretionary power of the Lords of the Admiralty for certain types of vessels. Any vessel under 100 tons with fewer than forty men and twelve 4-pounder guns, was no longer entitled to a letter of marque. Any vessel that met this description, and had previously obtained a commission, would have to reapply for one after 1 June 1759. In addition, the Act declared that owners of privateers were no longer able to act as guarantors for the conduct of their vessel and crews, which meant that they would have to find other members of the community willing to take on the financial burden of guaranteeing their conduct.[66] Despite the curbing nature of privateering, it was mostly a political response to Dutch anger over British privateering abuses and the Anglo-Dutch crisis. The Act was passed in May 1759, about a month after the appellate cases of the *Maria Theresa* and the *America*, and it is worth pointing out that in British public channels, there was largely silence on the Privateers Act.

[63] BL Add MS 32886, Newcastle Papers, Letters from Newcastle to Yorke, 15 December 1758, ff. 319–20.
[64] Ibid.
[65] BL Add MS 32886, Newcastle Papers, Memorandums for the King, 22 December 1758, f. 431.
[66] David Starkey, *British Privateering Enterprise in the Eighteenth Century* (Exeter University Press, 1990), p. 163.

According to Corbett's brief treatment of the Privateers Act, 'The resistance of the privateer owners was violent and formidable.'[67] However, the English newspapers of May and June 1759 contained almost no discussion of the Privateers Act and no reports of anger aimed at its passage. The only references to the Act were found in two London newspapers. In the *Lloyd's Evening Post* edition of 28 May, there was a small notice on page six stating that several bills were expected to receive Royal Assent the coming Saturday. Six bills were then briefly described, one of which was the Privateers Bill. It was described in such a way, however, as to almost mask its content, '[A bill] to amend the Act for more effectually manning his Majesty's navy, with respect to commissions to be granted to privateers.'[68] On 5 June, in the *London Chronicle* there appeared a very similar notice on the front page that listed acts that had been granted Royal Assent. Amongst the list of thirty-nine acts was, once again, the opaque description of the Privateers Act which had appeared in the *Lloyd's* newspaper, with the added clarification that the Act was also for 'the better prevention of piracies and robberies by the crews of private ships of war'.[69] Neither of these notices stand out in the newspapers, nor do they go into detail about the particulars of the Act or the repercussions it would have on privateering ventures. If there was, as Corbett claimed, a large amount of opposition to the Act, it did not play out very publicly in newsprint.

In contrast to Corbett, David Starkey makes an argument that may go some way to explaining why there was apparently such little public outcry over the new Act. According to Starkey, French seaborne commerce had been largely eradicated by early 1759 and, as a result, there was little incentive for new privateers to seek a commission.[70] It is possible that Pitt, Newcastle, Holdernesse, and Hardwicke wished to keep news of the Act to a minimum in order to avoid any possible expressions of wrath from the privateering lobby. It is also possible that British ministers understood that the Act amounted to no more than continued promises to improve the conduct of the privateers.

In late December 1758, as the Privateers Act was in its nascent stages, Newcastle revealed to Yorke that Pitt had secured the support of Dr Hay, King's Advocate, member of Doctors' Commons, and an MP, to help the new privateer bill along. He also made clear to Yorke that once the Dutch openly declared that they would give up the French trade to the Americas, then all of Britain's promises would come to pass. As to

[67] Corbett, *England in the Seven Years' War*, vol. II, p. 8.
[68] *Lloyd's Evening Post and British Chronicle*, 28–30 May 1759.
[69] *London Chronicle*, 2–5 June 1759, no. 380.   [70] Starkey, *British Privateering*, p. 167.

the matter of future captured Dutch ships and the Court of Prize Appeal, Newcastle, with a natural tendency towards obfuscation in his writing, implied that Pitt had a scheme for the success of the new privateers bill and for cases in the appellate court which relied on the co-operation of Dr Hay, who was one of the advocates in both the case of the *Maria Theresa* and the *America*. Newcastle wrote to Yorke that he believed in Pitt's scheme but that

> You [Yorke] must do your part, on your side. Bring them to say openly, what they have already said in private. Yield to our three points, and then we shall, and will, do our part. – we are all now sensible, that it is our interest so to do. – I have enquired as to the facts relating to appeals lodged, and the pretence alleged, that they never have been brought to a hearing. The fact I hear, is this, (but I don't give it absolutely as fact,) some appeals are lodged, but the Appellants have never proceeded upon them, and, if so, the council could not bring them to trial.[71]

Everything was ready on the British side for Dutch cases to be treated in the Court of Prize Appeal to the satisfaction of the Dutch; however, it was up to Yorke to make sure that the appeals lodged by the Dutch were actually brought to trial. Without this crucial last step, the appellate court could not fulfil its promise. It is possible that the late appeals launched in the cases of the *Maria Theresa* and the *America* were a result of Yorke's push to get Dutch merchants to use the appellate court. Newcastle ended his letter with the following parting advice about captured ships: 'prove those ships detained, and which you want to be released, not to be in that case [French trade to the Americas], or under that Description; and then we shall see whether we cannot, some way or other, get them released'.[72] This statement perhaps tempered his previous one by making it clear that ships which traded to French colonies would not be released, but as long as they could be proved innocent of the French colonial trade, then the court, or ministers, would see to their release. More negotiations between the two countries at this point would not help Anglo-Dutch relations over neutrality progress any further. Action was needed, and that action would come from the British Court of Prize Appeal. The stage was set for the Anglo-Dutch crisis to wind down. The Privateers Act of 1759, along with the extrajudicial release of a few ships, and the promise of future swift justice in the Court of Prize Appeal, would be the trifecta that Newcastle's and Holdernesse's policy needed to succeed smoothly. As Alice Clare Carter wrote about adjudication of cases in the appellate court:

---

[71] BL Add MS 32886, Newcastle Papers, Letter from Newcastle to Yorke, 22 December 1758, f. 429.
[72] Ibid.

Thereafter, domestic tensions in the Republic relaxed and there was no further need to make political capital out of the trade disputes, which returned to their earlier guise of vexatious problems needing a settlement, so that trade could continue under conditions of safety.[73]

However, in order for tensions to remain low, Newcastle and other interested ministers had to make sure that sentences passed in prize cases coming before the Court of Prize Appeal maintained a good balance between the Dutch merchants and the British captors. The *Maria Theresa*, and the *America*, came before the Lords Commissioners in March and April of 1759, respectively, and their paths through the appellate court demonstrated how this balance was to be kept.

---

[73] Carter, *Dutch Republic*, p. 105.

5   Quelling the Crisis
The Court of Prize Appeal and the Fate of the
Maria Theresa and the *America*

Lloyd's Evening Post and British Chronicle, a newspaper known for its reliable shipping and maritime news, came out every Monday, Wednesday, and Friday in 1759, and could regularly be found in Lloyd's Coffee House on Lombard Street, a stone's throw away from the Bank of England, and a short walk from Doctors' Commons where the Court of Prize Appeal often convened. In the edition of Wednesday, 21 March 1759, the paper ran two articles and one notice dealing with British captures of Dutch ships. One of the articles included a reprint of a petition sent to the States General of the Dutch Republic by the merchants of Amsterdam and Rotterdam, after hearing news of the condemnation of several Dutch ships in the High Court of Admiralty on 24 February 1759. The merchants feared that the decisions in the court would lead to more ships being condemned and have a 'fatal effect on the trade'[1] of the provinces. They implored the members of the States General to 'employ every method'[2] to hinder the sentence and to prevent future sentencing. Two members of the States General were sent to London to negotiate the matter and, not long after they were sent, Joseph Yorke received a resolution from the Dutch 'requesting the British Ministry to suspend the execution of the sentence passed on the cargoes of the Dutch ships'.[3] Printed immediately below the article in *Lloyd's Evening Post* was a notice simply informing the reader that a Dutch ship named *Maria Theresa* had come before the Court of Prize Appeal the day before, and that after six hours of full hearings, the Lords Commissioners delayed the sentencing until the following Thursday. It concluded with the statement 'By the determination of the above Appeal, a number of Dutch cargoes will be condemned or acquitted.'[4] The notice hinted that the case of the *Maria Theresa* would set a precedent for future Dutch cases but there was no suggestion that the information in the notice, and the article that preceded it, were intimately

---

[1] *Lloyd's Evening Post and British Chronicle*, 21–23 March 1759, no. 262.   [2] Ibid.
[3] Ibid.   [4] Ibid.

connected to the extremely tense state of Anglo-Dutch relations. With seemingly no awareness of the connection, *Lloyd's Evening Post* was reporting on the Anglo-Dutch crisis and, separately, on a court case that had the potential to lead the ministers of both countries to a resolution of that crisis.

The Dutch Appellate Case

At eleven o'clock, on the morning of 22 March 1759, some of the Lords Commissioners of Prize Appeal, Lord Hardwicke amongst them, filed into the main hall at Doctors' Commons for the first hearing on the *Maria Theresa*. The arguments presented by both sides were much the same as those given before the High Court of Admiralty, but more heavily detailed. The Dutch Appellant's advocates, Charles Yorke and R. Smalbroke, maintained that, at the time of her capture, the *Maria Theresa* was a Dutch ship making a voyage from the Dutch island of St Eustatius to Amsterdam carrying goods which she took on board at St Eustatius. They argued that the cargo should never have been con-demned by the High Court of Admiralty and rooted their arguments in five of the articles of the treaty of 1674: Articles 1, 2, 5, 6, and 8. Article 1 of the treaty stipulated that it was legal for the subjects of the States General of the United Provinces (the Dutch Republic) to freely

exercise all manner of traffic, in all other Kingdoms, Countries and Estates, ... so that they shall not be any way hindered or molested ... by the military forces, ships of war, or any other vessel whatever, belonging either to the said King [British] or to his subjects, upon account or under pretence of any hostility or quarrel now subsisting, or which may hereafter happen, between his said Majesty and any other Princes or Peoples whatever, which are or shall be in peace, amity, or neutrality, with the said Lords of the States [Dutch Republic].[5]

Whilst Yorke and Smalbroke were arguing that the *Maria Theresa* was trading between a Dutch colony and a Dutch city, they made the point that Article 1 of the treaty covered the possibility that the ship had French West Indian goods as part of her cargo because it allowed Dutch subjects to trade with the enemies of Great Britain. This point would later be addressed by Hardwicke and the Lords Commissioners in their deliber-ations, because it had direct implications as to whether the treaty of 1674 applied in the Americas, a point which Hardwicke still believed was crucial to successful Anglo-Dutch relations and a successful strategy of commerce predation against the French.

---

[5] BL Add MS 36208, Hardwicke Papers, Notes on the *Maria Theresa*, ff. 128–50.

The next argument invoked by the Appellant's advocates was based on Article 2 of the treaty, which ostensibly concerned contraband goods. It stipulated that the freedom granted in Article 1 to all kinds of merchandise could not be interrupted by any war and that 'such freedom shall extend to all commodities which might be carried in time of peace, those only excepted which are described under the name of contraband goods'.[6] The *Maria Theresa* was not carrying contraband goods, nor did either side claim she was; however, the importance to the case of Article 2 was not the contraband section but, rather, the section about the freedom to carry goods which were carried in times of peace. By inserting Article 2 into their arguments, the advocates for the Appellant were possibly giving the court an opportunity to make a ruling that could incorporate Hardwicke's Rule of the War of 1756, which declared that neutral ships in times of war could only carry goods that were allowed them in times of peace. By specifying goods carried in times of peace, the article could be interpreted to mean that only goods that were allowed to be carried in times of peace were protected by the freedom of commerce granted in Article 1. Although there was no real need for this article to be invoked in the case of the *Maria Theresa*, because it did not add more weight to their case than that provided by Article 1, it did, however, open up the possibility of making the Rule of the War of 1756 a precedent, able to be invoked in future cases and future diplomatic discussions.

Article 5 of the treaty was more relevant to the case of the *Maria Theresa*, because it declared that a ship trading between one Dutch port and another was only obliged to show a passport if stopped by a British ship. Yorke and Smalbroke maintained that the privateers who captured the *Maria Theresa* had also demanded to see its bills of lading, even though it was going between two Dutch ports, and that such an action made the entire seizure illegal.[7] In order to bolster the point, the advocates also called on Article 6, which stipulated that if a Dutch ship were going to or from an enemy port then a passport and bill of lading had to be provided if stopped by a British ship. The *Maria Theresa* had on board both a passport and a bill of lading and, therefore, had more documentation than was required for a voyage from St Eustatius to Amsterdam.[8]

The last article called upon in the Appellant's case was Article 8, which covered the concept of 'free ships makes free goods'. In other words, goods of Britain's enemies (contraband excepted) found inside a Dutch

[6] Ibid.   [7] Ibid.   [8] Ibid.

ship were protected and considered free by virtue of the ownership of the ship.[9] This final article was the crux of the case from the Appellant's point of view, because it countered any accusation that the goods found inside of the *Maria Theresa* were French West Indian goods and that they had been taken on directly from a French ship. This was an argument that would open up the question of transhipment, and whether there was a difference between trading *with* the enemy and trading *for* the enemy to the detriment of British attempts to destroy French commerce. Would the treaty protect Dutch ships if they set out with the intention of carrying French trade in order to deceive British ships and thereby explicitly aid the French war effort? Could this be considered a breach of neutrality? It was also, however, an argument that would be rendered useless if the court ruled that the treaty of 1674 did not apply in the Americas. The advocates made it clear that they did not believe that the goods found inside of the Dutch ship could be considered by the court to be French property on the hearsay of one single sailor and in contravention of the documentation required by the treaty. Once the Appellant's case had been made, it was left to the advocates of the British Respondent, Captain David Jenkins, to make theirs. The Respondent's advocates were George Hay and Charles Pratt, both close allies of William Pitt.

The British Respondent's Case

The Respondent's advocates began their arguments with a fairly lengthy story about French colonial commerce throughout the war and how it had been systematically destroyed by British efforts. The advocates claimed that the French had tried to get around British commerce predation by using the ships of neutral nations 'under pretence of trading with their own colonies indirectly, to carry on the enemy's trade'.[10] In other words, trading *for* the enemy. The neutral ships were to be laden in Europe and voyage to St Eustatius where, without landing the cargo, it was transferred into French ships bound for French colonies. The French ships then returned to St Eustatius with cargo from the French islands and, without landing it, loaded the cargo into the empty neutral vessel, which would carry it back to France.[11] It was a good story, and one which painted Dutch ships and traders who handled French West Indian goods as complicit in purposefully deceiving the British, and in acting in such a way that was beneficial to France's war effort and

---

[9] Ibid.   [10] Ibid.   [11] Ibid.

detrimental to Britain's. It was also perfectly true.[12] Such behaviour was open to the interpretation of not being very neutral. The advocates then proceeded to paint the *Maria Theresa* as one of the ships that was complicit in helping France fight its war against Britain. They accused the Appellant of taking on a cargo of French West Indian goods from French ships at St Eustatius, all of which were French property. They failed to mention that only one witness, the sailor Rotti, claimed that the ship and goods from which they took on part of the cargo were French, and they failed to mention that none of the witnesses knew who the owners of the cargo were, French or otherwise.[13]

At the end of their argument, the Respondent's advocates referred to the treaty of 1674 and tried to create a scenario in which the concept of 'free ships make free goods' did not apply to the *Maria Theresa*. They claimed that 'The subterfuge to which the Appellant has had recourse in support of his claim to carry on this hurtful and pernicious trade, is the treaty of 1674, which declares, that free ships shall make free goods.'[14] The wording used by the advocates shone an unfavourable light upon the treaty as a tool of subterfuge to help the French protect their West Indian trade. The advocates followed with a declaration that every state that owned colonies had the right to exclude other countries from trading with said colonies and that admitting foreigners into a country's closed colonial trade was akin to naturalisation. Anyone who traded directly or indirectly with the French colonies should therefore be considered French and was not protected by any treaty of neutrality.[15] Under this logic, the transhipment of French colonial goods in a Dutch ship turned the ship into a French vessel for all intents and purposes. Equally, by this logic, the treaty of 1674 could not be applied because Dutch ships became French ships as soon as they partook in the transhipment of French colonial goods. On the surface, this was a highly mercantilist argument, but it was also an argument that invited closer scrutiny about the limits of 'free ships make free goods' and the limits of neutral rights.

From a practical legal and strategic point of view, the limits of neutral rights had to be more clearly defined during the Seven Years' War in order to prevent Anglo-Dutch relations from deteriorating into an actual conflict. Once defined for practical purposes, they could then be incorporated into international legal philosophy and serve as precedents in

---

[12] W. Klooster and G. Oostindie, *Realm Between Empires: The Second Dutch Atlantic 1680–1815* (Cornell University Press, 2018), p. 75.
[13] BL Add MS 36208, Hardwicke Papers, Notes on the *Maria Theresa*, ff. 128–50.
[14] Ibid.   [15] Ibid.

future conflicts.[16] It is important here to note that thinking around the limits of neutrality and how neutral rights should, or could, be universally defined was not confined to the workings of the British prize court system. At the same time that the first Dutch ships were going through the Court of Prize Appeal, Emer de Vattel was writing and publishing *The Law of Nations* in which he aimed to clearly define the limits of a state's ability to impose upon the freedom of trade of other nations.[17] Nonetheless, the practical legal thinking that took place in the Court of Prize Appeal had the direct purpose of supporting British strategic aims and setting legal precedents as required by the circumstances of the conflict.

The idea behind the advocates' argument was very much in line with Hardwicke's thinking, because it boiled down to the same effect as the Rule of the War of 1756 (any trade prohibited to neutrals during peace-time should be prohibited to them during wartime) without actually falling under the circumstances of the Rule. In other words, if Dutch ships acted like French ships, they would be treated as French ships and could be condemned. This was, in fact, more severe that the Rule of the War of 1756 or a case of 'continuous voyage' because, if the ships themselves were treated as French, then the ships, not just the cargo, could be condemned as lawful prize. It was on this last note that the advocates closed their arguments and hoped that the sentence issued by the High Court of Admiralty would be affirmed by the Lords Commissioners of Prize Appeal.

---

[16] T. Helfman, 'Commerce on Trial, Neutral Rights and Private Warfare in the Seven Years War', in K. Stapelbroek (ed.), *Trade and War: The Neutrality of Commerce in the Inter-State System* (Helsinki Collegium for Advanced Studies, 2011), pp. 14–15.

[17] Emer de Vattel, *The Law of Nations*, ed. B. Kapossy and R. Whatmore (Indiana, 2008), p. xv. For Vattel, this was ultimately about a balance of power between European states. From Christian Wolff, Vattel had borrowed the idea that mutual aid among states was a basic principle of natural law. However, Vattel thought that the existing commercial competition between states was unnatural and had arisen because national economies had not been integrated enough. This lack of integration led belligerents to interfere in the trade of other states in order to derive an advantage, rather than to promote mutual aid. Vattel proposed that Wolff's idea about mutual aid among states be considered from a political point of view, so that the integration of national economies had the aim of a balance of power between European states rather than commercial dominance. Commerce, and, by extension, competition between states, should be subservient to the political goal of balance and integration. Commercial treaties would be forged by states in order to preserve the balance of power and protect the principal of mutual aid between states. K. Stapelbroek and A. Trampus, 'The Legacy of Vattel's *Droit de gens*: Contexts, Concepts, Reception, Translation and Diffusion', in K. Stapelbroek and A. Trampus (eds.), *The Legacy of Vattel's 'Droit des gens'* (Palgrave Macmillan, 2019), p. 13.

The approaches used by the advocates in the Appellant's and Respondent's arguments were strikingly different. The Appellant's case was completely grounded in the treaty of 1674 and bent on showing how the taking of the *Maria Theresa* violated the treaty. The Respondent's case, however, was weaker, and relied mostly on a story that turned the captain of the Dutch ship into an accomplice in France's war effort, on the evidence of one sailor, and on a claim that trading to French colonies was the same as being French. It is possible that the stark difference between the arguments was intentional. As mentioned above, George Hay and Charles Pratt were close allies of Pitt, and Newcastle had alluded, in his letter from 22 December, to a plan that would bring satisfaction to the Dutch if only Joseph Yorke could get Dutch merchants to bring cases before the Court of Prize Appeal. The implication of a conspiracy to make the Respondent's case weaker, but still in line with Hardwicke's thinking, in order to make it easy for the Court of Prize Appeal to find in favour of the Dutch Appellant, is speculation. However, the result of the two sets of arguments presented before the Court of Prize Appeal was that Hardwicke and his fellow commissioners gathered to address the specific arguments put forward by both sides which had direct bearings on the negotiations over the treaty of 1674 and the Rule of the War of 1756. The decision taken by the court would, therefore, have its own bearing on the resolution of the Anglo-Dutch crisis.

The Court's and Hardwicke's Deliberations

Once each side had presented its case, the Lords Commissioners retired to offices in Whitehall to deliberate. They spent six hours in deliberation but postponed passing sentence until 29 March. During those six hours, Hardwicke took detailed notes on the discussion.[18] From the section on Dr Hay's arguments for the Respondent, it is clear that Hardwicke believed the case to hinge on two questions. If, as Dr Hay asserted, the ship should have been treated as a naturalised French ship coming from a French island (because it allegedly took on board French cargo from St Domingue) was it lawful for a British privateer to seize it? It would depend, Hardwicke wrote, on the treaty of 1674. The second question

---

[18] R. Pares, *Colonial Blockade and Neutral Rights 1739–1763* (Porcupine Press, 1975), used Hardwicke's notes on the *Maria Theresa*, amongst many other accounts of ships, in order to help make his argument that the Rule of the War of 1756, and the Doctrine of Continuous Voyage, were developed because the wars from 1739 to 1763 were colonial conflicts. His analysis is entirely correct, but it is very broad, and he does not delve into how the case of the *Maria Theresa* was used by British ministers and Lord Hardwicke as an instrument of wartime strategy regarding neutrality.

was, did the treaty remain in effect under the circumstances put forward by Dr Hay; and, if it did, was it applicable to the voyage in question?[19]

Hardwicke highlighted two points from Charles Yorke's argument on behalf of the Appellant. The treaty of 1674, according to Yorke, subsisted, and therefore made the question of who owned the property immaterial because the Dutch were free to carry enemy goods. This argument would presuppose that the treaty applied to colonies in America, but Hardwicke did not presume this to be established or necessarily true. The second point that Hardwicke highlighted was Yorke's contention that 'the privilege of the ship was the privilege of the cargo',[20] another way of stating that free ships make free goods. Hardwicke made one more important note; he believed that the presumption of property was to be taken from the origin of the voyage. It is unclear if at this stage in his notes he meant the origin of the ship's voyage or the origin of the voyage of the goods. A crucial distinction.[21] No more notes were taken until 29 March, when the case was to be decided. Outside of Doctors' Commons, most ministers, and the interested public of London, waited out the week with little to write or read about the *Maria Theresa*. However, Newcastle, ever the prolific writer, had much to say in a memorandum on neutrality and prize affairs by the end of the week.

The day before a decision was given by the Court of Prize Appeal, Newcastle wrote a memorandum to himself, whilst at home, that took the form of a diary entry. In it, he related that Earl Granville (President of the Privy Council, a long-time politician, generally an ally of Pitt, and one of the most frequent attendees at the Court of Prize Appeal) was not happy with Charles Yorke's performance in the case of the *Maria Theresa*, and that there would soon be published a paper that would justify the sentence passed by the High Court of Admiralty.[22] It is not a far leap to assume that Granville was not happy with the way things were turning out in the appeal because he did not see eye to eye with Newcastle and Holdernesse on the matter of Dutch foreign policy. Granville lamented that he was not able to attend the first hearing of the *Maria Theresa* in the appellate court due to illness. His absence at the first hearing barred him from attending the subsequent discussions. He would, however, attend the hearings in the case of the *America*.[23]

---

[19] BL Add MS 36208, Hardwicke Papers, Notes on the *Maria Theresa*, ff. 128–50.
[20] Ibid.   [21] Ibid.
[22] BL Add MS 32889, Newcastle Papers, Newcastle Memorandum, 28 March 1759, ff. 272–3.
[23] BL Add MS 36208, Hardwicke Papers, Notes on the *Maria Theresa*, ff. 128–50.

Granville's presence would hardly have made a difference, since a large proportion of the commissioners were allies of Newcastle and not Granville. It is nonetheless interesting to note that Newcastle's memorandum implies that a decision in the case had been taken on the first day of the hearing, before the court reconvened on the 29th. It also revealed that the case was discussed outside of the hearing amongst members of the Privy Council. Lord Bute, future Secretary of State for the Northern Department and favourite of the Prince of Wales, had not attended the hearing, but was very much in favour of finding against the Dutch and awarding the cargo as lawful prize to the privateers. Newcastle related in his memorandum that

My friend said that ... he reasoned with him, (Lord Bute) – showed him the consequences of breaking with Holland both at present, and hereafter. – And talked so much, and so strongly to him, upon that head, that Lord Bute acquiesced; and promised not to meddle at all in this matter.[24]

It is likely that Newcastle's 'friend' was Lord Hardwicke, or a close ally of Hardwicke's on the court, as he would have had intimate knowledge of the arguments and had worked with Newcastle and Holdernesse on Dutch appeasement throughout the war. The conversation, as retold by Newcastle, also suggests that the court intended to find in favour of the Dutch Appellant in order to preserve Dutch neutrality. The memorandum, which only discussed the Dutch appeal, ended with the following line, which also suggests that a decision had already been taken in the case of the *Maria Theresa*: 'My friend told me that every thing went well – that the resolution was taken, or that it was determined; and that he would tell me the particulars in the course of this week.'[25] Again, it is likely that Newcastle was referring to Lord Hardwicke or another Commissioner who had attended the appellate court, and that 'the resolution taken' overturned the earlier decision made in the High Court of Admiralty.

Newcastle's own involvement in the decisions at the Court of Prize Appeal, in spite of his attempts at secrecy in his memorandums, is made abundantly clear by his memorandum for the king on 29 March, the day the decision on the *Maria Theresa* was announced. Hardly any of the documents found in the collections of ministers have a time stamp, so it is impossible to know if Newcastle's memorandum was written before or after the decision at the court was taken. Nonetheless, it shows, in very

---

[24] BL Add MS 32889, Newcastle Papers, Newcastle Memorandum, 28 March 1759, ff. 272–3.
[25] Ibid.

few words, that Newcastle and his allies had a plan about how the Court of Prize Appeal would be used to secure the success of their foreign policy concerning Dutch neutrality. Newcastle wrote: 'The appeal. Dutch Ship ... This Ship for the Dutch. The next probably against them. Then the time for proposals of accommodation.'[26] The means to ensuring the success of Newcastle and Holdernesse's policy had been set in motion; it only remained to be seen if its implementation, through the appellate court and the cases of the *Maria Theresa*, followed by the *America*, would be successful in instituting Dutch faith in the British prize court system and in putting an end to the discussions about the treaty of 1674.

When the Lords Commissioners reconvened to finish the business of the *Maria Theresa*, Hardwicke once again took detailed notes. He began by questioning the assumption that some of the goods were French property, and by coming to the conclusion that suspicions about property could not be equal to proof. 'It may amount to a suspicion; but suspicion don't make proof, much less presumption in law.'[27] Hardwicke did not believe that the hearsay of one sailor presented in the examinations was enough to consider some of the goods to be French. Taking the matter further, he determined that 'the *Place or Dominion* from wherever the goods are brought, does by no means determine the property ... But I take it to be rightly laid down on the other side, that the right presumption of the *property of the Cargo* is to be taken from the *property of the ship*.'[28] This was clear support of the contention in Article 8 of the 1674 treaty that goods found on board Dutch ships were to be considered as Dutch goods. To back up his conclusions, Hardwicke turned once again to Grotian thinking on a maxim which contended, in part, that goods aboard a ship are to be presumed to belong to the same country as that of the ship unless otherwise stipulated by a treaty. It was another way of stating that free ships are presumed to make free goods. Hardwicke described it as follows:

goods found on board the ship of the friend is property of friends, goods found on board the ship of an enemy is presumed the property of enemies. Here the property of the ship admitted to be Dutch. Then Grotius adds ... Lamen validis in contrarium probationibus possit elidi – it turns the onus of the proof on the one side or the other reciprocally.[29]

---

[26] BL Add MS 32889, Newcastle Papers, Memorandum for the King, 29 March 1759, f. 291.

[27] BL Add MS 36208, Hardwicke Papers, Notes on the *Maria Theresa*, ff. 128–50.

[28] Ibid.

[29] Ibid. Author's translation of the Latin: Those who wish to prove contrary must provide the proof.

If the Respondent wished to claim that the goods were not Dutch, contrary to the maxim, then he must furnish the proof. The hearsay of one Dutch sailor did not qualify as proof in the face of the ship's passport and the bills of lading as prescribed by the treaty. Having determined that the maxim applied in this case because the 1674 treaty did not stipulate anything different, he reasoned that the goods found on board were therefore to be presumed and treated as Dutch property. Hardwicke then turned to the problem of setting a precedent based on the treaty of 1674.

Assuming that Hardwicke and Newcastle had decided that the case of the *Maria Theresa* must come out in favour of the Dutch, but that no agreement had been reached amongst the British ministers as to whether the treaty of 1674 should apply in the Americas, the least controversial ruling that the Court of Prize Appeal could make was one that did not hinge on the treaty at all. Hardwicke, possessed of an acute legal mind, managed to produce that very outcome with little effort. After establishing that the case was covered by Grotius's maxim if the goods could be proven to be French, he only had to show that the goods were not French and that therefore the treaty did not apply. If the goods were Dutch, then there would be no right to take them under the law of nations because they would not be enemy goods. The treaty regulated permitted trade with enemies, so if the goods were Dutch, then no trade with enemies was taking place and the treaty would not apply. Grotius's maxim, and the treaty, only applied to enemy goods found in neutral ships or neutral goods found in enemy ships. It did not apply to neutral goods found in neutral ships. Hardwicke reasoned that in order for the treaty to apply, the law of nations had to apply because the treaty was an alteration (Hardwicke used the word 'inversion') to the conditions of the law of nations. Hardwicke, in the case of prizes, took the law of nations to mean that enemy goods found inside a neutral ship were lawful prize and neutral goods found inside an enemy ship were not lawful prize.[30] This reasoning was again rooted in Grotian principles because Grotius had written that the law of nations applied universally between states unless stipulated differently by a treaty.[31] Hardwicke had only to reason that the case of the *Maria Theresa* did not present a situation covered by the 1674 treaty. He wrote:

But this leads to the last point ... to consider this case upon the treaty of 1674. In this case, no occasion to enter into that treaty; for, if no ground of capture by the laws of nations, there can be none by virtue of that treaty, in this particular

---

[30] Ibid.
[31] S. Neff, *Justice Among Nations: A History of International Law* (Harvard University Press, 2014), pp. 156 and 171.

instance. The treaty inverts the Law of Nations into instances – *In Prejudice* of the neutral power, where the goods of their subjects are found on board an enemy's ship – prize … In favour of the neutral power … where the goods of enemies are found on board a neutral ship – *not prize*.[32]

According to Hardwicke's interpretation, the treaty of 1674 only applied to cases where enemy goods were found on Dutch ships or when Dutch goods were found in enemy ships. Under any other circumstance, the treaty did not come into play. This interpretation left the circumstance of the *Maria Theresa* outside of those covered by the treaty because Hardwicke had already determined that it was a Dutch ship carrying Dutch goods. Therefore, under the law of nations, there was no reason for the *Maria Theresa* to have been taken as prize, and no reason for the case to be examined through the lens of the treaty. Hardwicke's argument completely bypassed the question of whether the treaty applied in the Americas and did not set a precedent based on any interpretation of the treaty. However, he did make the point, in his notes, that had the goods been satisfactorily proved to be French West Indian goods, then a discussion would have had to take place about the treaty of 1674, and that he was not convinced that its privileges would apply.[33] Fundamentally, Hardwicke's judgment was based on the simple contention that the word of one Dutch sailor could not be taken as fact. His interpretation of the law of nations, and of the treaty of 1674, allowed him to implement Newcastle's strategy of keeping the Dutch neutral by giving them hope that they could seek justice and reparations through the Court of Prize Appeal. The sentence for the appeal of the *Maria Theresa* was passed that same day. The cargo and ship were restored to their Dutch owners, and the privateer was ordered to pay the cost of the trial in the High Court of Admiralty but not the cost of the appeal, as it had technically been filed outside the allotted timeframe within which appeals were supposed to be filed.[34]

The *Maria Theresa* Decision Made Public

There was bound to be some political and public fall-out from the decision in the case of the *Maria Theresa*, because it was the first sentence passed on a Dutch ship by the Court of Prize Appeal in the Seven Years' War, and some newspapers in London thought that it would set a precedent for all future Dutch ships taken as British prizes. Many of the London newspapers printed articles about the acquittal of the *Maria*

---

[32] BL Add MS 36208, Hardwicke Papers, Notes on the *Maria Theresa*, ff. 128–50.
[33] Ibid.   [34] Ibid.

Theresa the day after, or a few days after the sentence was pronounced. All of the articles printed were critical of the decision taken by the Court of Prize Appeal. The *Gazetteer and London Daily Advertiser* ran two articles. The first, a very short article, correctly informed readers that the ship had been restored because the cargo was not proved to belong to the enemy. The author speculated that if all enemy cargo that had been taken in Dutch ships by British privateers was restored, it would affect 100,000 Britons and that the value of all that enemy cargo was nearly £2 million.[35] Where the statistics came from is not cited, but despite the fact that their veracity is questionable, they would have been alarming to privateers and citizens concerned with prize-taking. Just beneath this little article was a much longer article titled 'The Present State of the Question between Great Britain and Holland' that described the affairs between Britain and the Republic to date with a very favourable view of Britain's conduct, and the assertion that Britain had made several concessions to the Dutch whilst it had received none in return:

Thus the affair [Anglo-Dutch relations] is reduced to a very great simplicity. England offers the Republic the enjoyment of her treaty of 1674, and the rule, That a free ship shall make free goods in all parts of the world, excepting those ships only which come from St. Eustatius and Curacao, to prevent Dutch merchants from becoming carriers to her enemy; ... What doth England ask in return for these proofs of friendship? Nothing.[36]

The assessment in the article was misleading. Britain had not offered the full privileges of the treaty of 1674, and the judgment on the *Maria Theresa* specifically avoided confirming or denying the rights allowed by the treaty in America. As to the concept of 'free ships, free goods', Hardwicke had upheld a maxim of the law of nations, but only in so far as Dutch goods found on Dutch ships remained free. He had also made very clear that the maxim was altered when under the umbrella of the treaty. Such nuances about legal arguments were lost in the newspapers, and the impression given by the article to any reader was that all of the privileges of the treaty had been given to the Dutch and that, except for trade coming out of two Dutch islands, goods found in Dutch ships were protected and considered free.

Another paper, the *Universal Chronicle or Weekly Gazette*, put forward such an egregious misrepresentation of the case that it came to the attention of Lord Hardwicke himself. The article read, 'We hear that the Lords of Appeal have determined the case of the Dutch ships taken this war, that they shall be all restored, and that the Owners of those ships

[35] *Gazetteer and London Daily Advertiser*, 30 March 1759, no. 5456. [36] Ibid.

that took them shall pay all costs.'[37] Given that Hardwicke apparently worked quite hard to develop a sentence that did not set widely applicable rules as to the specific circumstances under which Dutch ships would be released, and that Newcastle had determined the next sentence would go against the Dutch, this article was especially misleading, and ran counter to the ministers' strategy. When Hardwicke read it, he wrote the same day to Holdernesse, expressing concern that the article had been printed 'maliciously in order to raise a clamour'.[38] He asked Holdernesse if he could print a paragraph in a few of the London papers to contradict it. Hardwicke feared that if the story were not contradicted, the public would be very much inflamed. No rebuttal seems to have been printed though, which suggests that Holdernesse did not share Hardwicke's concerns about the public or, at least, did not mind that the Commissioners of Prize Appeal would bear the brunt of any fall-out.

One more article, printed on 31 March, is worth noting, because the author did not contest the restoration of the *Maria Theresa* but was, rather, concerned with how the High Court of Admiralty would be regarded by other countries in the wake of the restoration. The author, pen-named Britannicus, was a frequent contributor to the patriotic leaning *London Evening Post* and wrote libertarian and patriotic articles throughout the war.[39] He commended the Lords Commissioners for their decision and declared that it did not set a precedent for future cases in the Court of Prize Appeal. He feared, however, that decisions taken by the High Court of Admiralty would no longer carry the same weight and that the prestige of the court would suffer in Europe:

[W]hen they [the countries of Europe] shall perceive that the Judgment, given on such captures, by our Court of Admiralty, (a Court, that have ever hitherto been held in the highest esteem for their justice and impartiality) hath been reversed by the Lords of Appeal, they will be apt to have a less opinion of the weight and importance, at least, if not of the justice and impartiality of the determination, of that Court ...[40]

It is difficult to say where Britannicus got the idea that the High Court of Admiralty was held in high esteem and known for its impartiality, as its judge was known for incompetence and for having been appointed to the post only by virtue of being the son-in-law of the previous judge.[41] As to a

---

[37] *Universal Chronicle or Weekly Gazette*, 30 March 1759, no. 52.

[38] BL Add MS 3431, Leeds Papers, Letter from Hardwicke to Holdernesse, 30 March 1759.

[39] B. Harris, 'The London Evening Post and Mid-Eighteenth-Century British Politics', *The English Historical Review*, 110 (1995), 1135–99.

[40] *London Evening Post*, 31 March 1759, no. 4900.   [41] Pares, *Colonial Blockade*, p. 132.

reputation for impartiality, the High Court enjoyed the opposite reputation amongst the other maritime nations of Europe.[42] Newcastle,
Holdernesse, and Hardwicke's efforts in the Court of Prize Appeal were
aimed at achieving what Britannicus alleged already existed, a reputation
for justice and impartiality for the British prize court system. The author
of the article seemed unable, or unwilling, to understand that such a
reputation required righting the abuses of the lower courts and finding in
favour of foreign plaintiffs as well as domestic ones in order to maintain
Dutch neutrality alongside a strategy of commerce predation.

Britannicus went on to declare that the case of the *Maria Theresa* had
indeed not set a precedent, because the decision was based on unusual
circumstances, but his comment was inflammatory nonetheless:

[W]as it [the decision] to be looked upon in another light, was it to be esteemed
as a precedent for all the other vessels, condemned by our Court of Admiralty,
would it not be showing the most amazing favour to the Dutch, who now act as
avowed enemies to his Majesty ... would it not be a most severe blow ... and
would it not put a final period to all our privateering?[43]

The Dutch were condemned in his comment as enemies, and the
implied threat was clear. If another decision were made in the court
similar to that in the case of the *Maria Theresa*, then all privateering
would come to an end and the enemies of Britain would flourish. His
final say in the matter concluded that at least the case did not set a
precedent, and that 'from its judgment being reversed in this long-
disputed, well-known, and weighty Matter, [the powers of Europe
would] conclude, it should not be depended upon as final in any other'.[44]
Without seeming to realise it, Britannicus had gleaned the crux of
Newcastle's foreign policy: taking power away from the High Court of
Admiralty and granting to the ministers and judges on the Court of Prize
Appeal the ability to regulate how prizes were adjudicated. In the view of
Britannicus, and perhaps much of the 'patriot' leaning population,
weakening the High Court of Admiralty weakened Britain's position as
a European power and the power of the maritime population. In the view
of Newcastle and his allies, however, it strengthened Britain against the
possibility of accumulating another enemy.

From the various articles in the London press that immediately
followed the case of the *Maria Theresa*, it is clear that London's populace
was interested, but not always accurately informed, about either the
proceedings of the Court of Prize Appeal or the precarious relations
between Britain and the Dutch Republic. Whilst some of the articles

---

[42] Ibid.   [43] *London Evening Post*, 31 March 1759, no. 4900.   [44] Ibid.

and sentiments were inflammatory, they never went beyond discontented grumblings, and never incited more than the occasional petition from the privateering lobby. Nonetheless, some ministers, mostly Pitt's allies who were associated with the Court of Prize Appeal, shied away from the decision. Earl Temple, Richard Grenville (a cousin, brother-in-law, and political ally of Pitt) and even Pitt both distanced themselves from Hardwicke's sentence after it was made public. Newcastle claimed that it was their intention to 'blame' the affair on Hardwicke, Newcastle, and Lord Mansfield and 'expose them to the resentment of the nation and to rise upon the advantage thus given to them'.[45] No doubt Newcastle was still feeling the sting over the court martial and execution of Admiral Byng and was in no hurry to once again shoulder the blame for a ministerial mishap. Even Hardwicke threatened to have nothing more to do with the Court of Prize Appeal if he were to take all the fall-out for decisions that were carefully and correctly made.[46] Pitt, as the Secretary of State for the Southern Department, would necessarily have been less involved in the Dutch cases than his counterpart Holdernesse. However, it is clear from his involvement in the Privateers Bill and his association with Dr Hay that he was involved in the Anglo-Dutch crisis to an extent, and that he was aware of its importance.[47] Pitt's, Hardwicke's, and Newcastle's fears, however, were unfounded, and did not last long. When the case of the *America* was decided a few weeks later, it became clear that the Court of Prize Appeal had indeed not set a precedent of restoring all Dutch cargo, and that British maritime predation could still flourish under the judgments of the Court of Prize Appeal.

Unlike the gloom heralded in the London newspapers on 30 March, Newcastle's letters from that day were full of elation. He wrote to Joseph Yorke that the court's actions were honourable and that the favourable outcome was completely the doing of Lord Hardwicke and Lord Mansfield. He proceeded to advise Yorke on how the news should be used:

I doubt not but you will make good use of this great advantage, which is put into your hands, not only to undeceive the weak, credulous, but well intentioned part of the Republic, but to frighten those, who are ill-disposed, and to stop the ill effects of the lies, which they have spread in all the foreign courts, who have any concern in maritime affairs.[48]

---

[45] BL Add MS 32890, Newcastle Papers, Newcastle Memorandum, 12 April 1759, ff. 41–3.
[46] Pares, *Colonial Blockade*, p. 106.   [47] Ibid.
[48] BL Add MS 32889, Newcastle Papers, Letter from Newcastle to Yorke, 30 March 1759, ff. 299–300.

Newcastle's point was clear. The decision in the case of the *Maria Theresa*, orchestrated by Newcastle and his allies, was intended to restore Britain's international credibility when it came to prize affairs and arbitration in maritime affairs. It was also meant to dent the influence of the anti-British factions in the Dutch Republic. Newcastle mentioned he was pleased that the court did not award the Dutch Appellant the costs of the appeal, because it would spur other Dutch owners to file appeals sooner, in order to avoid that outcome due to late filing.[49] If more prize cases were appealed, Newcastle's strategy of using the appellate court to ensure Dutch neutrality would have a greater chance of success. His letter also contained an assurance that Hop, the Dutch representative at the British Court, had promised to put the case in the most favourable light to his counterparts in the Republic.[50] From a memorandum written later that day by Newcastle, it is also clear that because of the decision in the case of the *Maria Theresa*, the Dutch banking houses could be approached for money to fund Britain's war.[51]

Yorke's reply to Newcastle was not written until 6 April, but it was equally jubilant and full of confirmation that Newcastle and Hardwicke's policy was working. 'You can have no doubt of the reception this news met with here where it has entirely changed the language of the whole country and as much commendation is bestowed upon us now, as there was abuse before, the two countries seemed to have changed sides.'[52] Yorke's letter conveys a certain amount of relief as all of the Anglo-Dutch tensions seemed finally to be relieved. Even the fact that the Appellant had not been awarded costs for the appellate case was well received:

[T]he condemning the appellant in his own costs upon the appeal is disapproved by nobody, on the contrary people find it as it is consistent with justice, and disapprove the delays which they themselves have occasioned ... it shall improve this favourable appearance and I don't doubt but as the wrath against us subsides, the jealousy against France will increase ... I cannot say enough for the applause that is given here to the candour and equity of the court of appeals ...[53]

The Anglo-Dutch crisis was well on its way to resolution and towards a system that seemed to ensure a continued solution. Friendly Anglo-Dutch relations could be maintained through consistent appeals filed by the Dutch and guided by the hand of Hardwicke and his allies on the Court of Prize Appeal.

[49] Ibid.   [50] Ibid.
[51] BL Add MS 32889, Newcastle Papers, Memorandum for the King, 5 April 1759, f. 363.
[52] BL Add MS 32889, Newcastle Papers, Letter from Yorke to Newcastle, 6 April 1759, ff. 372–3.
[53] Ibid.

The *America* Comes before the Court

Dutch faith in the British prize court system was being restored, but there
was much left to do for the Court of Prize Appeal. The voices of doubt
coming from within Britain's maritime population also still needed to be
addressed. The clamour in the press was that the days of preying on
Dutch ships were over, and the question of the treaty of 1674 had not yet
been addressed by the Court of Prize Appeal.[54] However, two weeks after
the decision on the *Maria Theresa* was handed down, the case of the
America came before the Commissioners of Prize Appeal, and the concerns of the privateers were fully addressed. In terms of the treaty of
1674, some clarification was provided over the concept of 'free ships
make free goods', but no firm precedent would be established as to
whether the treaty applied in America. The case did, however, support
Hardwicke's Rule of the War of 1756. As Richard Pares noted, decisions
from the Court of Prize Appeal, which dictated strict interpretations of
the treaty or set strict precedents were 'too dangerous politically, nor
would [they] have had such far-reaching results as the Rule of the War of
1756'.[55] Encouraging the Dutch to abandon the French carrying trade
was important, but leaving the Court of Prize Appeal free to decide cases
based on the political needs of the moment was crucial to the maintenance of Dutch neutrality.

On 12 April 1759, Lord Hardwicke, along with nine other members of
the Privy Council, sat down to hear the Appellant's and Respondent's
arguments in the case of the *America*. The Dutch Appellant's arguments
were presented first and were delivered by the advocates Charles Yorke
and J. Bettesworth. Their contention was that the voyage of the Dutch
ship was legal under the treaty of 1674, and that the goods laden at Port-
au-Prince were protected by virtue of the ship being Dutch. They
invoked the concept of 'free ships make free goods'. The arguments were
based on Articles 1 to 5 and 8 of the 1674 treaty and were very similar to
those made in the case of the *Maria Theresa*. Article 1 was invoked in
order to argue that the treaty allowed Dutch ships to trade with any
countries which were at peace or war with Britain and that they were to
be unmolested in their trade.[56] This article was of particular relevance to
the *America* because her voyage was acknowledged to be from
Amsterdam to the French colony of St Domingue. The advocates went
on to argue that, according to Article 5 of the treaty, any Dutch ship met

---

[54] *London Evening Post*, 31 March–3 April 1759, no. 4900.
[55] Pares, *Colonial Blockade*, p. 190.
[56] BL Add MS 36208, Hardwicke Papers, Notes on the *America*, ff. 180–98.

by a British privateer or ship of war must have on board a passport which showed that the ship was Dutch property. When the *America* was taken, it had such a passport on board, so it should never have been taken as prize by Captain Parker.[57] It is worth noting that, unlike in the case of the *Maria Theresa*, the advocates did not invoke Article 6 of the treaty, which stipulated a Dutch ship trading to a port of Britain's enemy must have a bill of lading, as well as a passport on board. In the case of the *America*, Captain Ferret had thrown the bill of lading overboard when he was chased by a ship a few days out of Port-au-Prince and so did not have one on board when stopped by Captain Parker. By not having a bill of lading on board, the ship was legally liable to capture, but not necessarily condemnation in the courts. This point was conceded by the advocates at the end of their arguments, but without specific reference to Article 6.

The most interesting argument put forward by the Dutch Appellant's advocates was based on Article 8 and its stipulation that 'free ships make free goods'. The argument itself was extremely close to that put forward by Hardwicke in his notes on the *Maria Theresa*. This is not surprising as Charles Yorke was involved in both cases as was Hardwicke's son, so it is possible that Charles and his father discussed the cases, and it is even possible that Charles had looked through his father's notes. Yorke declared that

The Law of Nations confiscates the goods of an enemy in the ship of a friend, and exempts the goods of a friend in the ship of an enemy; but the Marine Treaty between England and Holland inverts this Rule, and confiscates Dutch effects on board the ship of an enemy, and protects the goods of an enemy on board a Dutch Ship.[58]

It had been fairly easy to declare that the treaty of 1674 did not apply in the case of the *Maria Theresa* because it was a Dutch ship carrying Dutch goods. However, the *America* came under one of Hardwicke's instances where the law of nations was inverted, because it was a Dutch ship carrying French goods from a French colony. If the treaty applied in the Americas, as the Appellant's advocates decreed it did from Article 1, then the *America*'s voyage was protected by the inversion of the law of nations and was not liable to condemnation by the British prize courts. In order to boost their arguments, the advocates also pointed out to the court that in the previous war, many Dutch ships trading to the French colonies had been released by the Court of Prize Appeal.[59]

The last avenues of arguments put forward in the Appellant's case were based on Articles 2, 3, and 4 of the treaty, and were related to

[57] Ibid.   [58] Ibid.   [59] Ibid.

contraband and the freedom to carry all commodities during times of peace. Since the *America* had left Amsterdam before war was declared between Britain and France, the advocates argued that, although the ship did not have a licence from the French king, it was on a voyage that was sometimes allowed by the French in times of peace from a French colony to Holland. The advocates, however, provided no proof that this type of voyage was allowed by French laws in peacetime.[60] As to contraband, the argument was put forward that the treaty only considered implements of war as contraband and that Article 4 specifically excluded sugar and all other goods not named in Article 3 as free goods. Since the *America* carried a cargo of only sugar and indigo, there was no cause for the ship to have been stopped and seized per the wording of Article 2: 'Nor shall this freedom of navigation and commerce be violated or interrupted, by reason of any war, as to any kind of Merchandize ... except contraband goods.'[61] With no contraband goods found on board and the voyage itself covered by the right granted by the treaty to carry enemy trade, the advocates ended their arguments by asking that the court restore the ship and goods to the Dutch Appellant and condemn Captain Parker to pay the costs of all proceedings.

The arguments made on behalf of the Respondent, Captain Parker, were based on proving that both the ship and the cargo were, or should be treated, as French property. Whilst the treaty of 1674 was mentioned, it was not as thoroughly relied upon as it had been in the Appellant's case. The first argument made by the Respondent's advocates, George Hay and Charles Pratt, was that the laws of France did not permit the Dutch, or any foreigners, to trade with its colonies in the East or West Indies. To support their contention and to demonstrate the strictness of the French laws, they quoted the letters of marque, which the French Crown granted to merchant ships and privateers. French privateers were allowed to prey on 'the ships, barks, and vessels, as well French as foreign, carrying on a foreign and a prohibited trade to the French islands in America'.[62] If the Dutch were not legally allowed to trade with the French colonies, and the *America* had done so openly and at French invitation, then it must be considered a French ship. The advocates admitted that, originally, the ship had indeed been Dutch property, but ceased to be so when it was chartered to go to the French island of St Domingue with a cargo consigned to residents of the French island. Once in Port-au-Prince, the *America* had taken on cargo owned, according to Captain Ferret's examinations, by Frenchmen. The ship

---

[60] Ibid.   [61] Ibid.   [62] Ibid.

and its cargo were well known to the French governor, as it was he who delayed their departure from the island until it was thought that there were no British ships in the area.[63] If the governor knew about the ship and its voyage enough to personally delay its departure, then it was clear that the Dutch ship was being used, knowingly, by French officials in order to evade British capture.[64] The ship was being treated as a French ship by the French officials of the island, and so should be treated as French by the court. The last argument made on behalf of the Respondent was that the destruction of the bills of lading by Captain Ferret was a strong indication of guilt and a desire to avoid the scrutiny of British ships. The advocates finished their arguments by asking the Court or Prize Appeal to uphold the decision of the High Court of Admiralty and to condemn both the ship and the cargo as French and lawful prize.

Deliberations

Once all of the arguments had been presented, the Commissioners of Prize Appeal withdrew to deliberate and, once again, it is Lord Hardwicke's notes which have survived. The deliberations hinged primarily on the questions of whether the ship was to be considered a French or a Dutch ship. If it were considered a Dutch ship, as Charles Yorke argued forcefully that it should be, then the treaty of 1674 would have to be discussed, and a decision made as to whether it applied in America.[65] On the other hand, if the ship were considered a French ship, then the treaty of 1674 did not have to be applied. Hardwicke's notes give the impression that he was much more interested in proof that the ship could be considered a French ship, because a large portion of the notes are dedicated to that end. Hardwicke first called on the fact that the French governor at Port-au-Prince had not wanted the ship to depart, for fear that it would become the prey of British ships: 'this is looking upon her as a French ship, and adopting her'.[66] He further reasoned that if the ship had headed to a port that was open exclusively to French trade, then the ship ceased to be considered a neutral and became an adopted French ship. Here Hardwicke cited four previous cases from the last war in which that principle had been upheld and the 'neutral' ships had been considered adopted French ships.[67] In answer to the point made in the Appellant's case that the *America* had left Amsterdam before the war between Britain and France broke out, Hardwicke wrote that it did not matter, because she left Port-au-Prince several months into the war with

[63] Ibid.   [64] Ibid.   [65] Ibid.   [66] Ibid.   [67] Ibid.

full knowledge that a state of war existed between France and Britain. Under these conditions, Hardwicke considered that the ship could be treated as a French ship.

The next section of Hardwicke's notes addressed a request from Charles Pratt that the court consider the case using the treaty of 1674. In order to do this, Hardwicke first made a distinction between the cargo and the ship. In terms of the cargo, which was admitted to be French and owned by Frenchmen, it could only be condemned if the 1674 treaty did not extend to America. He contended that the wording of Article 8 (free ships make free goods) was too general, and the answer as to whether it applied in America lay in the intent of the treaty's authors, which he could not speak to. It is interesting that Hardwicke wrote this given that in previous correspondence with Joseph Yorke he had very firm opinions on the intention of the treaty and the fact that it did not permit trade that was prohibited during times of peace. Nonetheless, he went on to write that even if trade to America had been under contemplation by the authors of the treaty of 1674, a Dutch voyage to St Domingue sanctioned by French officials was a clear breach of Dutch neutrality and would condemn the cargo.[68] This was because it became a matter of transhipment and a case of trading *for* the enemy rather than *with* the enemy. The cargo, which was French and French owned, had been placed in a Dutch ship in order to avoid capture.

Moving next to the question of the ship under the treaty of 1674, Hardwicke declared, as the Appellant's advocates had argued, that there were isolated instances in which the French had allowed Dutch ships to trade to their colonies, but this did not amount, in his opinion, to a constant permission to trade with French colonies during times of peace. Therefore, he returned to the contention that the ship should be considered an adoptive French ship and be treated as a French ship. The transhipment of the French cargo, and the intent behind the transhipment, had been enough to convince Hardwicke that the ship itself should be treated as an enemy.

The final decision handed down by the Court of Prize Appeal was that the *America*, whilst originally being a Dutch ship, should be considered by law a French ship, because it was freighted on French account to a French port in the West Indies with the sanction of the French government.[69] At Port-au-Prince, the ship had taken on board French cargo, and had destroyed the bills of lading when chased by a presumed British ship. As a French ship carrying French goods, the sentence from the

[68] Ibid.   [69] Ibid.

High Court of Admiralty was upheld, and it, along with the goods, was condemned.[70] Once again, no firm precedent had been set by the Court of Prize Appeal when it came to the treaty of 1674 and whether it applied in America, but the court had made it clear that Dutch ships which traded directly with French colonies were likely to be condemned as French. This created diplomatic space for Anglo-Dutch negotiations to continue over whether the treaty applied in America, but the ruling had also created a precedent that lower prize courts could call on whereby Dutch ships trading directly with French colonies would be condemned. The sentence also likely served to boost the confidence of the British privateers because, unlike the allegations by the press after the *Maria Theresa* decision, Dutch ships could still be condemned in the highest court of the British prize system.

After this case, a precedent would be set whereby Dutch ships carrying French cargo from a French colony would be condemned as lawful prize in British prize courts. Hardwicke's reasoning was very much in line with the practical intent behind what would come to be known as the Rule of the War of 1756, which was to prevent neutrals from carrying French colonial trade that they were not permitted to carry in times of peace. It is important here to stress two things. First, the Rule of the War of 1756 was not tied to the Anglo-Dutch treaty of 1674 or the political negotiations surrounding it. It was created by the precedents established in the cases of the *Maria Theresa* and the *America*. Secondly, the Rule of the War of 1756 was created by Hardwicke, and approved by ministerial allies, in order to achieve the effect of preventing neutral nations from carrying French colonial trade and establishing the circumstances under which Dutch ships and their cargo would, or would not, be condemned in British prize courts.[71] In other words, it would help establish trust and understanding with the Dutch and the British privateers whilst negotiations over the treaty were ongoing.

Public and Ministerial Reaction to the Two Cases

It is difficult to precisely quantify the level of resentment and worry amongst merchants and privateers caused by the sentencing of the *Maria Theresa*, because the few sources available from which to gauge public opinion on such an issue are the surviving newspaper articles and pamphlets which were circulated around the taverns and coffee, houses

---

[70] Ibid.   [71] Pares, *Colonial Blockade*, pp. 186–90.

of the maritime community.[72] It is fairly clear from the newspapers, however, that there was indeed some amount of anxiety. One of the few pieces of evidence which points to action being taken by the privateering lobby was printed on the day that the *America* went before the Lords Commissioners. In the *Gazetteer and London Daily Advertiser* of 12 April 1759, there was a notice printed prominently on the front page that stated in big letters 'Prize-Causes. The Owners and Managers of Privateers'. It then went on, in smaller letters:

and others interested in the capture of Dutch, or other neutral ships, carrying on a Trade directly or indirectly to or from the French Colonies, are desired to meet at the King's Arms Tavern in Cornhill on Wednesday the 25th of this instant April ... to consider of a proper application for redress.[73]

Given the timing of the article and the fact that only one Dutch ship had so far come before the Court of Prize Appeal, the meeting was likely called to address the sentencing of the *Maria Theresa* and how it might hurt the prospects of British privateers. Since the notice called for a consideration of redress, the men who called the meeting were clearly not confident that the Court of Prize Appeal would do justice to the ships, which they believed had been justly brought in as prize. The sentence pronounced in the case of the *America* the same day that this notice appeared in the press would have gone a long way to alleviating any concerns scheduled to be brought up in the meeting a week-and-a-half later. A testament to the easing of anxieties within the privateering lobby is the small amount of attention that the *America*'s sentence received in the press. In contrast to the articles printed about the *Maria Theresa*, the *America* was rarely mentioned. One article, on 13 April, in *Lloyd's Evening Post*, merely recounted, accurately, what had passed in the appellate court and why the ship and cargo had been condemned. There were no predictions about what the sentence meant for the future of privateering, and no accusations that Britain had conceded too many favours to the Dutch.[74] There was quiet in the press about Anglo-Dutch

---

[72] Some of the pamphlets published during the war which dealt with the issue of Dutch neutrality were James Marriott's *The Case of the Dutch Ships Considered*, 1759; Malachy Postlethwayt's *Britain's Commercial Interest Explained and Improved*, 1757; and Charles Jenkinson, *A Discourse on the Conduct of the Government of Great-Britain, in Respect to Neutral Nations, During the Present War* (R. Griffiths, Pater-Noster Row, 1758). Marriott was a member of Doctors' Commons and future judge of the High Court of Admiralty; Postlethwayt was one of the most influential economic writers of the late eighteenth century; and Jenkinson had been paid by Newcastle and Holdernesse to produce his pamphlet.

[73] *Gazetteer and London Daily Advertiser*, 12 April 1759, no. 5460.

[74] *Lloyd's Evening Post and British Chronicle*, 11–13 April 1759, no. 271.

affairs and the Court of Prize Appeal. It would remain quiet until the next Dutch ship, the *Novum Aratrum*, came before the appellate court in May, but the anxiety produced by the case of the *Maria Theresa* did not emerge again in the press through the remainder of the war.

Much like the quiet reaction of the press, ministerial reaction to the sentencing of the *America* was subdued. It is possible that this was, in part, due to negotiations within the ministry regarding the Privateers Bill, which was debated in April and May of 1759. Whatever the reason, the effect of the Court of Prize Appeal on Anglo-Dutch affairs was not discussed in ministerial correspondence until mid-May, when Newcastle received a letter from Joseph Yorke in which the satisfaction of the Dutch officials was conveyed:

> The Dutch Deputies continue to write favourably and to express the deepest sense of the civility and regard which is shown them ... I have always said and think, that if the Prize Bill passes, and the Court of Appeals decides in favour of what is really Dutch Property, that their merchants will have as much real security as fair traders can desire in time of war.[75]

According to the British representative in the Dutch Republic, Newcastle and Hardwicke's strategy continued to work, and the Anglo-Dutch crisis continued to wind down. As long as the Court of Prize Appeal continued to make decisions similar to those made in the cases of the *Maria Theresa* and *America*, then Dutch neutrality would be maintained. The Privateers Bill, which would pass in June, would also contribute to raising Dutch faith in the British legal system and Britain's commitment to Dutch neutral rights. The bill, which became an Act once it was passed, constrained the actions of privateers by prohibiting owners of privateering vessels to act as guarantors for their voyages and decreed that the commission of any vessel under 100 tons was null and void as of 1 June. Any further commission of a vessel under 100 tons was at the discretion of the Lords of the Admiralty.[76] The Act was largely a symbolic gesture because, as David Starkey's analysis of privateering ventures during the war shows, by 1759 Britain's strategy of commerce predation had been very successful, and there was virtually no French commerce left on the seas for privateers to prey upon. 'The 1759 Act, therefore, was a corrective measure designed to placate the neutral powers, by restricting the

[75] BL Add MS 32891, Newcastle Papers, Letter from Yorke to Newcastle, 18 May 1759, f. 165.
[76] David Starkey, *British Privateering Enterprise in the Eighteenth Century* (Exeter University Press, 1990), p. 163.

unbridled assault on their shipping. Its timing, however, suggests that it was little more than a gesture.[77] The gesture was effective though, and in combination with the decisions made in the Court of Prize Appeal, which continued to keep a good balance between finding in favour of the Dutch ships and the British privateers, a fourth Anglo-Dutch war was avoided.

Hardwicke and Strategy

The ultimate purpose of the first cases that came before the appellate court was to demonstrate to the Dutch ministers and merchants, as well as their British counterparts, that Dutch neutral rights would be respected by the Court of Prize Appeal but that those rights did not extend to carrying and protecting French colonial trade that had been prohibited during peacetime. From a maritime strategy perspective, this would satisfy both the aim of making sure the Dutch Republic remained a neutral power during the war and that France's profitable colonial trade could be destroyed through maritime predation. From a legal perspective, the decisions in the first two cases enabled Hardwicke to create precedents that could guide lower prize courts in their future decisions on Dutch prize cases – precedents that would continue to be set by the Court of Prize Appeal and eventually become known as the Rule of the War of 1756. They also allowed Hardwicke to side-step any concrete rulings based on the treaty of 1674 and thus avoid constraining negotiations over whether the treaty applied in the Americas. Hardwicke believed that the original intention of the treaty was that neutral nations should not be able to carry French colonial trade that had been forbidden during times of peace, but he was cognisant that the Dutch were not inclined to see eye to eye on this point.[78]

Unable to foresee or choose which cases would be the first to come before the appellate court, Hardwicke had to have a flexible approach to cases in order to make sure that the judgments handed down by the appellate court supported the government's strategic aims and laid the groundwork for more consistent sentencing by the lower courts. Hardwicke's long tenure in the Chancery Court likely helped him

---

[77] Ibid. p. 163.
[78] Letter from Hardwicke to Joseph Yorke, Draft, 17 September 1756, in P. C. Yorke (ed.), *The Life and Correspondence of Philip Yorke Earl of Hardwicke*, 2 vols. (Cambridge University Press, 1913), vol. II.

navigate the complex, and often intrigue-filled, cases. As in the Chancery Court, prize appeal cases were examined on an individual basis, without a jury, and the judges had the ability to make a decision after a thorough investigation of the presented evidence and arguments.[79] The sentences and reasoning in the Court of Prize Appeal cases carried legal weight that future judges and policy makers could call upon to justify their actions both within the prize court system and in diplomatic negotiations. Precedents and authority were a vital part of the English law tradition and in the early-modern period there was a shift towards precedents being set via judicial decisions rather than formal sources of law. Within these judicial decisions, it was the legal reasoning that led to a judge's decision that was given primacy and authority.[80] With the cases of the *Maria Theresa* and the *America*, Hardwicke was starting the set of precedents that would eventually become known as the Rule of the War of 1756, and was using his judicial reasoning based on international law philosophy to give the rule its authority. Setting the precedents in the first cases to come before the appellate court without involving the Anglo-Dutch treaty was vital to Britain's strategic success, to the establishment of Britain as a perceived legitimate protector of neutral rights, and to Britain's ability to continue negotiations over the limits of the 1674 treaty.

It mattered that Hardwicke's judicial reasoning in the early appellate cases was rooted in international law philosophy because he was, ultimately, using English legal traditions to forge precedents whose legitimacy needed to be accepted by non-English and non-British actors. The authority of these precedents had to be recognised by neutral nations in order to successfully further British strategic aims. Prize law, rooted in civil law, was supposed to be distinct from other law traditions. However, the influence of the English law traditions in the Court of Prize Appeal is clear when the role of men like Hardwicke and the Solicitor General are taken into account. Hardwicke's success in marrying his experience as Lord Chancellor to his role as judge on the Court of Prize Appeal shows that legal traditions could be brought together in the pursuit of solving strategic maritime and political issues. The maritime aspect here is worth

[79] J. H. Langbein, 'Bifurcation and the Bench: The Influence of the Jury on English Conceptions of the Judiciary', in P. Brand and J. Getzler (eds.), *Judges and Judging in the History of the Common Law and Civil War* (Cambridge University Press, 2015), p. 73.

[80] D. Ibbetson, 'Authority and Precedent', in M. Godfrey (ed.), *Law and Authority in British Legal History, 1200–1900* (Cambridge University Press, 2016), pp. 74–5.

commenting upon further, because international law in the maritime sphere was a bit nebulous in the early-modern period due to the understanding that the sea was largely and naturally free to navigation and not subject to enforceable possession.[81] International maritime law was 'not a settled body of legal principles or precedents but a global patchwork of imperial legal and political contestation'.[82] Maritime law was a legal philosophy that lent itself to being influenced by a variety of legal traditions because, as Matthew Crow has argued, 'maritime affairs are a matter of praetorian jurisdiction, which is to say judgement followed from a general consideration of balancing principles of equity in natural law with regional custom and the facts of a specific case'.[83] This was Hardwicke's approach to the Court of Prize Appeal. His success in using the Court of Prize Appeal to pursue British strategic aims regarding neutral rights was possible because prize law, international law philosophy, diplomacy, and strategic thinking were all interconnected. The Court of Prize Appeal was the crucible for the successful negotiation of Anglo-Dutch affairs and neutral rights.

Conclusion to Part II

There were still, as in all negotiations, wrinkles in Anglo-Dutch affairs throughout the rest of the war, such as a disagreement about under what circumstances British ships had a right to stop and search Dutch ships. Confusion, wilful or no, amongst Dutch officials, also continued to exist about whether the king had the power to release ships extrajudicially.[84] Nonetheless, tensions never again rose to the levels of the winter of 1758–9, even though no firm decisions were ever made in the appellate court or through diplomatic channels regarding the treaty of 1674. The clarity and precedents laid down by the cases of the *Maria Theresa* and the *America*, which declared that Dutch ships caught participating in French trade under certain circumstances forbidden during peacetime would be condemned, was enough to ease the tension. Dutch merchants, Dutch officials, and British captains now had a better understanding of what to expect when cases came before the Court of Prize Appeal.

---

[81] M. Crow, 'Littoral Leviathan: Histories of Oceans, Laws, and Empires', in E. Cavanagh (ed.), *Empire and Legal Thought* (Brill, 2020), p. 365. These ideas are articulated in the work of philosophers such as Alberico Gentili and Hugo Grotius.
[82] Ibid. p. 367.   [83] Ibid. p. 369.
[84] BL Add MS 32891, Newcastle Papers, Letter from Newcastle to Yorke, 22 May 1759, f. 222.

Hardwicke had demonstrated that each case would be judged on its merits, and that there was method to the court's deliberations that did not rely on the 1674 treaty.

The next Dutch case to come before the Court of Prize Appeal was that of the *Novum Aratrum*, which had been carrying goods from St Eustatius to Amsterdam. The court declared that the goods were in fact Dutch and restored them, using similar arguments as those presented in the case of the *Maria Theresa*. Throughout the war, almost no goods travelling from St Eustatius to the Dutch Republic were condemned as prize and even the lower courts stopped condemning this type of trade as lawful prize.[85]

Of the approximately 139 cases which came before the Court of Prize Appeal during the war, 76 were Dutch ships.[86] The groundwork laid in the first few cases allowed the rest of the Dutch cases to be adjudicated in a manner pursuant to British strategy, and helped keep a second Anglo-Dutch crisis from forming. Alice Clare Carter attributed the success of averting the Anglo-Dutch crisis without renegotiating the treaty of 1674 to the changing realities of neutrality in the second half of the eighteenth century. The treaty, Carter argued, 'had been made at a time when neutral traders had not yet the power to favour so greatly one nation against another as to enable one to retain indefinitely colonial advantage of the other'.[87] France no longer had the ability to compete with Britain in a maritime war whose success greatly relied on commerce predation. In such a situation, the neutral carrying capacity of the Dutch served as an advantage to France but served very little purpose in Britain's commerce. Setting precedents that clarified the legal rules of commerce predation without recourse to the treaty was effective enough for those precedents collectively to become known as the Rule of the War of 1756 and remain relevant to international maritime law through the mid-nineteenth century. The sentences handed down by the Court of Prize Appeal allowed the British ministers to contain any damage done to Dutch neutrality by actions taken at sea, whilst making sure that French colonial commerce did not contribute to France's war effort. The flexibility of the appellate court in its approaches to individual cases was vital for the success of Newcastle and Hardwicke's strategy and Pitt's desire to completely subdue France outside of Europe. The decisions passed in

---

[85] Pares, *Colonial Blockade*, pp. 215–17.
[86] Compiled from TNA HCA 45 and BL Add MS 36208–8214.
[87] Carter, *Dutch Republic*, p. 107.

the cases of the *Maria Theresa* and the *America* demonstrate that the court, under Hardwicke's guidance, allowed for ministerial influence in the British prize court system, in order to pursue British maritime strategic aims. The court's decisions also allowed Dutch officials and Dutch merchants to begin to trust that their rights as neutral carriers would be clear, and consistently protected by Europe's emerging hegemonic sea power.

Part III

The Spanish Case Studies

6 Kings and Merchants
The Legal, Political, and Domestic Contexts of Spanish Foreign Policy

The *San Juan Baptista* and the *Jesus, Maria, y Jose*

As the Anglo-Dutch crisis was winding down in the summer of 1759, the case of the Spanish ship, *San Juan Baptista*, was being prepared for argument before the Court of Prize Appeal. It was, technically, the third appellate case dealing with a Spanish ship to come before the appellate court during the war but, for all intents and purposes, it was the first to have any bearing on Anglo-Spanish relations. The first Spanish appellate case concerned the ship *Nuestra Señora del Rosario* (also known as *La Felicite*) and had been heard on 29 June 1758. This had been a very unusual case which was of little use for setting broader precedents, because the ship had been captured at anchor in a British harbour after completing a voyage from a Spanish port to London. British customs officials had been on board at the time of seizure, and the privateer captain, William Death, was dead by the time of the appeal. Both the ship and cargo were restored respectively to their Spanish and British owners.[1] A second case, that of the ship *San José*, had also been scheduled to be heard in the summer of 1758, but the case notes do not indicate that the appeal actually took place, nor is there any indication that a sentence was actually passed. There is some limited material on the *San José* in Hardwicke's notes, but the case does not exist in the official case books of the Court of Prize Appeal.[2] It is possible that this case was settled extrajudicially or that the appeal was withdrawn for unknown reasons. In the year between the scheduled hearing for the *San José* and those for the *San Juan Baptista*, no other Spanish cases came before the Court of Prize Appeal.

---

[1] BL Add MS 36208, Hardwicke Papers, Notes on the *Nuestra Señora del Rosario*.
[2] BL Add MS 36208, Hardwicke Papers, Notes on the *San José*. The official case notes should be found in TNA HCA 45/1 but are not there. The first case is *Nuestra Señora del Rosario* in HCA 45/1/1 followed by the *Maria Theresa* in HCA 45/1/2.

The *San Juan Baptista* was a Biscayan-owned ship that had been captured on 10 June 1757, near the end of her journey from Pasaia[3] (a town slightly east of San Sebastián) to the French port of Nantes. Her cargo was made up of French East India goods such as tea, coffee, and logwood. On 23 September 1757, the High Court of Admiralty had condemned the goods as lawful prize but restored the ship as Spanish property. The master of the ship, José Arteaga, was not pleased with the outcome of the High Court case, because he had lost the entire cargo and been condemned to pay the court and docking costs. Arteaga lodged an appeal. John Shaw, the captain of the British privateer *Tartar* that had taken the *San Juan Baptista* as prize, did not lodge an appeal.

Not long after the case of the *San Juan Baptista* was heard in the Court of Prize Appeal, a fourth Spanish case came before the appellate court. This fourth case dealt with the ship *Jesús, Maria, y José* which had been captured by the British privateer *Britannia*, during a voyage between La Coruña and San Sebastián. The *Jesús, Maria, y José* had been carrying saltpetre (a contraband good) as part of its cargo and, based upon this, the High Court of Admiralty had condemned the saltpetre as lawful prize and declared the seizure lawful. Because it had been deemed a lawful seizure, the Spanish master, José Ezenarro, was also condemned to pay the expenses of the court and of having his ship docked. Neither the British captain, Charles Davids, nor José Ezenarro were satisfied with the decision in the High Court and, when Ezenarro lodged an appeal, the commander of the *Britannia* joined him and lodged a cross-appeal.[4]

Following the progress of the *San Juan Baptista* and the *Jesus, Maria, y José* through the British prize court system offers a detailed account of how British ministers and their extrapolitical allies tried to use the Court of Prize Appeal as a vehicle to foster Spanish trust in Britain's commitment to neutral rights, whilst making sure that the interpretations of international treaties used in prize cases remained favourable to Britain's overall maritime strategy. An analysis of these two cases also illustrates the numerous factors – such as pressure from the British privateering lobby, French pressure in the Spanish Court, and the internal intrigues of both the Spanish and British Courts – with which Britain's ministers had to contend in their attempt to maintain Spanish neutrality, win the war against France, and further their own political ambitions.

Before delving into the legal cases of the *San Juan Baptista* and the *Jesús, Maria, y José*, and the machinations of the Britons and Spaniards

---

[3] 'Pasaia' is the Basque name. The town is also called 'Pasajes' in Spanish and 'Passages' in English.

[4] BL Add MS 36211, Hardwicke Papers, Notes on the *Jesús, Maria, y José*.

involved with the Court of Prize Appeal, it is of particular importance to understand the Spanish and British political and domestic contexts within which the proceedings took place. This first chapter of Part III is dedicated to an examination of the factors that shaped Spanish foreign policy during the Seven Years' War and the period of the Bourbon reforms. Chapter 7 analyses the two court cases through the decisions handed down by the High Court of Admiralty, and lays out how Britain's political, mercantile, and legal worlds determined British wartime strategic thinking concerning Spain in the early stages of the war. Chapters 8 and 9 are an analysis of the progress of each of the two cases as they went through the appellate court, and the ultimate failure of Britain's attempt to maintain Spanish neutrality through the Court of Prize Appeal.

The Anglo-Spanish Treaty of 1667 and Prize Affairs

In both appellate cases, the arguments laid before Lord Hardwicke and his colleagues were based on the Anglo-Spanish treaty of 1667 and the Rule of the War of 1756. The treaty was largely a commercial treaty that granted British merchants limited rights to trade with the Spanish empire and access to some markets without having to pay customs fees, a lucrative concession given the mercantilist tendencies of the era. Unlike the Anglo-Dutch treaty, the 1667 Anglo-Spanish treaty did not have that much to say about neutral rights or prize affairs, and it did not explicitly grant any version of 'free ships make free goods'. Nonetheless, there are several treaty articles that would support the crux of the arguments put forward in the cases of the *San Juan Baptista* and the *Jesús, Maria, y José*. Article 14 laid out the rules of conduct for merchant ships of one country when they encountered either warships or privateers of the other. Ships were not to come within cannon-shot of one another, and only a small boat with two or three men could visit the merchant ships. The merchant ship need only to have passports and sea-letters that listed the ship's lading, the nationality of the ship, and the owner and master's names. The article also specified that the paperwork would be given credibility, but that countersignatures (from port authorities or other officials) should be included if found necessary.[5] The article does nothing to establish clarity in terms of what circumstances would necessitate countersignatures on the ship's paperwork. The ambiguity of the wording left

---

[5] Article 14, Anglo-Spanish treaty of 1667, Oxford Historical Treaties, http://opil.ouplaw .com/view/10.1093/law:oht/law-oht-10-CTS-63.regGroup.1/law-oht-10-CTS-63?rskey= ALzNqM&result=4&prd=OHT.

an opening for warships and privateers to take merchant ships as prizes if the paperwork was not countersigned.

Articles 21 to 25 were perhaps the most relevant to neutral rights because they established freedom of navigation and declared that 'unfree ships did not make unfree goods'. Articles 21 and 22 declared that Spanish and English ships had the freedom to sail to, and trade with, any countries in a state of peace or neutrality with Spain or England. By that same token, this freedom was not to be curtailed if either Britain or Spain entered into a state of hostility with another country.[6] In other words, neutral ships could not be stopped from trading with Spanish or English enemies or carrying their goods. It was a roundabout way of stating that 'free ships make free goods'. Article 23 qualified the preceding articles by stating that should any contraband goods be found on board, then those specific goods – and only those specific goods – were to be confiscated and taken out of the ship. The rest of the goods and the ship were to be left at liberty and not seized as prize.[7] This would become an important point in prize appeal cases, because often the British captains would argue that the ship should be condemned, as well as the cargo, for violating the treaty.

Article 26 was a very clear statement of Grotius's maxim about the law of nations wherein unfree ships make unfree goods. All neutral goods (in the case of this treaty either British or Spanish goods) found on board enemy ships were to be liable to confiscation and condemnation.[8] This would also become an important point in Anglo-Spanish prize disputes because, in combination with Article 23, it created a circumstance where the association of the ship – enemy or neutral – could determine whether the ship and all of the cargo, or just part of the cargo, could be condemned. It particularly arose in cases of transhipment (transferring goods from an enemy ship into a neutral ship for the purposes of shielding the goods from lawful capture) where prize courts could declare a neutral ship to be acting, effectively, as an enemy ship, due to the nature and intent of its voyage. These arguments would come up in the cases of both the *San Juan Baptista* and the *Jesus, Maria, y José*.

The final article of the treaty relevant to Anglo-Spanish negotiations over neutral rights was Article 38, which stated that Spanish and British subjects were to enjoy the same rights and privileges as those granted to the subjects of the Dutch Republic via any treaty.[9] In effect, this would mean that in prize disputes, Spanish appellants would be able to call on the privileges of the Anglo-Dutch treaty of 1674. However, it also meant

---

[6] Ibid. Articles 21 and 22.   [7] Ibid. Article 23.   [8] Ibid. Article 26.
[9] Ibid. Article 38.

that British appellants would be able to call on arguments based on that treaty such as the unresolved question of whether it applied outside of Europe.

The crux of both the *San Juan Baptista* case and the *Jesus, Maria, y José* case was the true ownership of the cargo, because both ships had been carrying French East India goods when they were captured. The advocates for the Spanish Appellants argued that the goods had first been landed in Spain, purchased by Spanish owners, and shipped out again as Spanish owned cargo. The advocates for the British privateers argued that the cargo had been placed into the captured Spanish ships directly from a French East India Ship and remained French owned goods. Without an abundance of deliberation, the Court of Prize Appeal reversed the sentence pronounced by the High Court of Admiralty in the case of the *San Juan Baptista*, and returned the goods plus damage costs to José Arteaga. Despite the similar circumstances of the two cases however, contradictory evidence and the cross-appeal lodged by the *Britannia*'s captain mired the hearings and complicated the judgment on the *Jesus, Maria, y José* such that the proceedings dragged on until February 1761, when the original High Court of Admiralty sentence was upheld.

A Crumbling Neutrality

Unlike the Anglo-Dutch crisis of 1759, which was resolved, largely, through the Court of Prize Appeal, British ministers and their policies failed to secure Spanish neutrality for the duration of the Seven Years' War. Though British ministers and their allies tried to use the appellate court to ease growing tensions and to appease the Spanish Court, the differences and grievances between the two countries were ultimately too numerous and deep seated to be smoothed over by the politic treatment of Spanish ships in the highest prize court. Three main factors played into the loss of Spanish neutrality: Spanish and British grievances left unresolved from previous conflicts, a growing fear on the part of the Spanish Court that British success against the French would alter the balance of power in the Americas, and the ascendance of the anti-British king, Charles III, to the throne of Spain in August of 1759. These factors, and all of the complications they spawned, created an environment of deep mistrust in the Spanish Court regarding British intentions in the Americas should Britain obtain a resounding victory against the French.

The Court of Prize Appeal was called upon initially by ministers of both countries to help gain the Spanish Court's confidence in Britain's prize court system as a fair arbiter of maritime neutrality. The British ministers and their allies ultimately failed to allay Spain's fears. While the court found ways to reverse many High Court of Admiralty decisions in favour of the Spanish, it was not enough, or soon enough. It was their inability to allay Spanish fears and inspire faith in Britain's commitment to Spanish neutrality that ultimately led to the outbreak of war between Spain and Britain. However, it is worth noting that though the British were unable to preserve Spanish neutrality for the duration of the conflict, the strategy of keeping Spain as a neutral actor did delay Spain's entrance into the war. By the time a Franco-Spanish alliance was forged, Britain had done enough damage to France in the maritime sphere that a Franco-Spanish alliance was not an insurmountable threat. Britain was still able to fight against Spain and bring both France and Spain to the negotiating table in favourable circumstances.

The Spanish Court and Relations with Britain

In the first half of the Seven Years' War, Spanish foreign policy concerning Britain was governed by various existing trade treaties and, on the Spanish side, was conducted by the Spanish king, the Secretary of State, and the minister in London. The Spanish Secretary of State and first minister was actually an Irish-born man known as Don Ricardo Wall, who was raised to the position in 1754 and maintained it throughout the war. The son of two Jacobite refugees, Wall was born in Nantes in 1694 and, through the good favour of French nobility, was sent, in 1716, to Spain, as a page to the household of Cardinal Alberoni, the leading Spanish minister at that time. It was under Alberoni's patronage that Wall joined the Spanish navy and, later, the army. Through a successful military career and various other avenues of patronage, Wall was sent as Minister Plenipotentiary to London to help settle the peace between Britain and Spain in 1749.[10] Wall's dedication to the international interests of the Spanish Crown and his friendship with the British ambassador, along with accusations of Anglophilia, would both shape and plague his political career. As with many politicians, his actual beliefs and character are, perhaps, less important and less interesting than what other men presumed about them. Since part of British wartime strategy was keeping Spain as a neutral power, the British government's perception of the atmosphere in the Spanish Court was a valuable gauge for how British actions might influence Spanish neutrality.

---

[10] D. Alarcia Téllez, *El Ministerio Wall: La 'España discreta' del 'ministro olvidado'* (Ediciones de Historia, 2012).

The British ministers with whom Wall had the most contact were the ambassadors in Madrid who safeguarded British interests. For the first half of the war, the British ambassador was Sir Benjamin Keene, who maintained a very friendly and respectful relationship with Wall. He described Wall as a man interested in maintaining peace, but brought low by the weight of his responsibilities: 'Wall hates his office, and suffers at these matters as much as myself; he sees, as well as I do, the Danger Two Great Crowns are in, from matters of so insignificant a nature compared with their peace.'[11] The insignificant matters to which Keene referred were the captures of British ships by the Spanish, and vice versa. Keene believed, until his death in 1758, that Wall worked with him in earnest to maintain Spanish neutrality, but that the internal squabbles of the Spanish Court, and French influence, were against them.[12] The man who replaced Keene as ambassador in 1758 was Lord Bristol who, in a letter to William Pitt from August 1761, described Wall as a friend of England, but made it clear that this was a problem for the minister:

I am persuaded he is too good a Spaniard not to be a friend to England, but if he acted in the manner we have reason to expect he should. – He thinks his conduct would be attributed to that predilection, he has ever been accused of towards Great Britain, and that no one would believe he was influenced by Spanish principles.[13]

Even though Wall may have believed that peace remained Spain's best course of action, British ministers were concerned that Spanish Court politics and a growing anti-British atmosphere in Spain were forcing him to take decisions against the British in order to safeguard his position. This loss of faith in Wall's pro-British actions, merited or not, contributed to the more bellicose attitude that British ministers exhibited towards Spain in the latter stages of the war.

In contrast to Wall, the Spanish minister in London, Juan Felix D'Abreu, elicited no descriptions or strong feelings from the ministers in London. He was sent to London by King Ferdinand VI in early 1756, whilst a counterpart was sent to Versailles. They were tasked with serving as arbiters between the French and British Courts in order to avoid a war.[14] Unsuccessful in his task, D'Abreu stayed at the British Court after the Anglo-French declaration of war and played the role of ambassador

---

[11] CL M-66, Shelburne Papers, vol. 22, Letter from Keene to Pitt, 6 March 1757, ff. 471–7.
[12] Ibid.
[13] New York Public Library, Hardwicke Paper 129, Letter from Bristol to Pitt, 31 August 1761.
[14] AHN ESTADO 2891, Jaime Massones to Wall, 12 March 1756.

in all but name. It is clear from the British correspondence that the ministers had confidence in D'Abreu's desire to keep both countries at peace. In a letter to Keene, Pitt described D'Abreu's desire to clear up a misunderstanding about prizes between the two Courts:

> as far as may be judged of mons. D'Abreu's real sentiments on this extraordinary proceeding, and the unhappy impression which he sees it has made here, it is hardly to be doubted but that this minister will represent things in the properest light to determine his Court to accelerate and expedite a reparation so essential to the good will and harmony between the two Nations.[15]

As the war progressed, D'Abreu's correspondence showed very little variation in his stance and position on Anglo-Spanish affairs. Other ministers commented that he never expressed any opinion other than that which he was told to express by his masters in Spain. His letters to Wall are straightforward and devoid of anything other than fact and a regurgitation of his conversations.[16] He was, perhaps, the perfect intermediary, in that his own ideas appear, for the most part, not to have coloured his behaviour. The most remarkable thing about D'Abreu is that he was an unremarkable minister. D'Abreu's king, Ferdinand VI, was, however, a monarch worthy of note, who sought peace with Britain in the early years of the war but was plagued by a fractious Court.

Ferdinand VI is variously described as 'gentle', 'weak', and 'inward looking' by historians of eighteenth-century Spain.[17] He had assumed the throne in 1746, after being sidelined from politics for most of his youth. Perhaps as a conscious contrast to the policies of his father and his powerful Italian stepmother, Ferdinand generally favoured peace as the aim of Spanish foreign policy. Staying out of European conflicts allowed him to focus on internal politics and reforms.[18] Like most monarchs, however, he was influenced by his ministers, and the British ambassador, Keene, feared that he could be persuaded to question the benefit of Britain's friendship. In April 1757, in the midst of a small crisis over a British privateer, the *Antigallican*, whose crew was imprisoned by Spanish officials in Cádiz, Keene described Ferdinand in a letter to Pitt:

> [T]he King of Spain's wrath you will have perceived quickly subsided, as it always will, where insinuations and assurances are made to him by certain persons that

---

[15] CL M-66, Shelburne Papers, vol. 22, Letter from Keene to Pitt, 5 April 1757, ff. 479–87.

[16] AHN ESTADO 2891.

[17] A. J. Kuethe and K. Andrien, *The Spanish Atlantic World in the Eighteenth Century: War and the Bourbon Reforms, 1713–1796* (Cambridge University Press, 2014), p. 216.

[18] R. García Cárcel, *Historia de España Siglo XVIII: La España de los Borbones* (Cátedra, 2002), p. 122.

what he does is right; and that His Conscience is at ease, when He reposes it on His Ministers and counsellors; and these assurances will always have more weight, the less He knows of the matter before Him, or cares to enter into the necessary Inquiries for their determination.[19]

Despite enjoying a very friendly relationship with the Spanish monarch, Keene was critical of, and clearly frustrated by, Ferdinand's reliance on the sycophantic behaviour of his ministers to guide him through matters upon which he was ill informed. If the 'certain persons' to whom Keene referred were uniformly pro-British and in favour of Spanish neutrality, there would have been no problem. However, given that accusations of Anglophilia sometimes caused Wall to remain silent, and given D'Abreu's lack of opinion, the men easing the king's conscience were not always vocal champions of Anglo-Spanish friendship.

As a whole, the impressions made on British ministers by the dynamics of the Spanish Court at the beginning of the war were twofold. There was a running theme of maintained friendship, and thus neutrality, but there was also a fragility to the relationship caused by a lack of strong pro-British leadership from the king. Much of the recent historiography contains the same impression, with Keuthe, Andrien, and Ricardo García Cárcel all coming to similar conclusions.[20] The dynamics of the Spanish Court would change dramatically with the death of Ferdinand and the succession of his half-brother, Charles III, in 1759. More belligerent than his brother, and no friend to Britain, the Court under Charles looked to actively diminish Britain's growing maritime power and to shift the balance of power in the Americas.

The Grievances: Logwood Cutting

From the official opening of hostilities with the French in 1756 to the death of Ferdinand in 1759, William Pitt and his allies negotiated with a Spanish Court of both allies and enemies led by a benign but friendly king. Long-standing grievances became inflamed and were unresolved, which left Charles with a desire and an excuse for war when he assumed the throne. The three primary grievances – logwood cutting in Honduras, prize affairs, and access to the Newfoundland fisheries – were mostly left over from previous wars and were brought back into the

[19] CL M-66, Shelburne Papers, vol. 22, Letter from Keene to Pitt, 21 April 1757, ff. 515–21.
[20] García, *Historia de España*, p. 123; and Kuethe and Andrien, *Spanish Atlantic World*, p. 216.

spotlight by Britain's war with France and by unsatisfactory treaties that had failed to bring resolution to Anglo-Spanish disagreements.

The right to cut logwood on the remote Honduran shore may appear, at first glance, an odd matter over which to have an almost century-long diplomatic dispute. Far from any permanent European settlement, the region in question spanned the coast of the south-eastern tip of modern-day Honduras and most of the eastern coast of modern-day Nicaragua. It was generally considered a hostile environment by Europeans, both in terms of climate and the indigenous inhabitants, referred to as the Moskitos by the Spanish. It was from the name given to the local indigenous population that the area received its other moniker, the Moskito Shore or Moskito Coast. British traders and smugglers from Jamaica began to establish semi-permanent littoral settlements there in the seventeenth century in order to trade with Spaniards on the South American coast.[21] Both the settlements and the trading were condemned by the Spanish Crown. The treaties of 1667 and 1670 had officially ended an Anglo-Spanish war begun under Cromwell and had given formal recognition to British territory already held in the Americas (including Jamaica). The treaty of 1667 allowed British traders established in Spain to trade with Spanish dominions. However, the treaty of 1670 prohibited inter-colonial trade between British and Spanish territories, as was the norm amongst the European empires at the time.[22] It was a prohibition that the Spanish extended to other European countries and would serve as part of the British argument for why the Rule of the War of 1756 should be applied to neutral Spanish ships.

Despite the emphatic wording of the 1670 treaty forbidding inter-colonial trade, enforcement was lacklustre and almost impossible.[23] The inaccessibility of areas like the Moskito Shore rendered any type of constant policing impractical and costly. More importantly, however, the contraband trade between British subjects and Spanish colonies was highly profitable for all involved and channelled much needed bullion into British trade networks. Adrian Pearce, in his book *British Trade with Spanish America 1763–1808*, determined that in the fourteen years from 1747 to 1761 (roughly the time between the War of the Austrian Succession and the Spanish entrance into the Seven Years' War), the

---

[21] A. Pearce, *British Trade with Spanish America 1763–1808* (Liverpool University Press, 2007), p. 28.

[22] CL M-1773, Charles Townshend Papers, Box 29 (entire); and Pearce, *British Trade in the West Indies*, p. 12.

[23] Treaty between Great Britain and Spain, signed at Westminster July 1670, Oxford Historical Treaties, http://opil.ouplaw.com/view/10.1093/law:oht/law-oht-11-CTS-383 .regGroup.1/law-oht-11-CTS-383?rskey=SEaUpo&result=3&prd=OHT.

British contraband trade was worth around £200,000 per year.[24] British and Spanish colonial governors and officials had little interest in ending the contraband trade between colonies. Ministers in London, who were well aware of the profits being made, did little more than vocally condemn the smuggling and make empty promises to the Spanish Court that the perpetrators would be stopped. In response to the ongoing smuggling, Spanish officials unleashed the '*Guarda Costas*' (coast guards) to capture British contraband ships and bring them to justice. If a smuggler were caught, the men in power in Jamaica or Britain could make little protest. However, the *Guarda Costas* preyed on licit and illicit British commerce, which caused the British Court to clamour against the injustice of Spanish law enforcement in the Americas.

Two years after the War of the Austrian Succession, in 1750, a new commercial treaty was concluded between Britain and Spain, which the Duke of Newcastle and Ricardo Wall hoped would solidify the mutual trading interests of both countries. Unfortunately, the new treaty did not resolve the matter of the zealous *Guarda Costas*, nor did it eradicate the controversy over British settlements on the Moskito Shore.[25] British ministers demanded that the *Guarda Costas* not stop, search, or capture legitimate British commercial ships, whilst the Spanish ministers, in turn, demanded that British settlements in Honduras be permanently removed before any measure could be taken to restrain the *Guarda Costas*.[26] Ultimately, neither the ministers in Madrid, nor those in London, had much control over the actions of the smugglers or the *Guarda Costas*, but the demands of British colonial officials for a resolution, as well as the refusal by either Court to grant concessions, led to a diplomatic stalemate on the issue in the early 1750s, which was broadly encompassed by the phrase 'Logwood cutting in Honduras'.[27]

The stalemate in negotiations and the simmering discontent that remained needed very little impetus to turn into a fully fledged diplomatic incident. Once Britain and France went to war in 1756, Spain feared the expansion of British power in the Americas, which made British settlements on the Moskito Shore seem more of an imminent threat. Smuggling profits therefrom increased during wartime, which led British merchants and traders to more flagrantly violate existing Anglo-Spanish treaties. Spanish ships, not only the *Guarda Costas*, took

---

[24] Pearce, *British Trade with Spanish America*, p. 31.   [25] Ibid. p. 528.
[26] Ibid. pp. 540–51.
[27] The treaty of 1667 did attempt to resolve the issue of *Guarda Costas* capturing British ships because it prohibited visitation and seizure except in limited circumstances, but enforcement of the newer treaty remained problematic.

advantage of the tumult caused by the Anglo-French conflict to capture British ships indiscriminately, and accuse them of smuggling. British merchants and privateers accused Spanish traders of carrying goods for the French and seized their ships as prizes. The altered circumstances in the Americas were enough to ignite the logwood controversy and turn it into one of the most important factors threatening Spanish neutrality and Anglo-Spanish relations during the Seven Years' War.

The Grievances: Prize-Taking

Like the logwood cutting in Honduras, prize-taking had been a bone of contention between the Spanish and British Courts for much of the eighteenth century and was, in part, tied to the logwood controversy. Disputes over prize affairs between Spain and Britain can be broken down into two categories. There were prizes taken whilst Spain and Britain were at war, and prizes taken in the Americas and Europe whilst the two countries enjoyed peaceful relations. The first category of prizes did not create political tensions over the seizures themselves, since commerce predation was an expected form of maritime warfare, but it did exacerbate difficulties because of the lengthy process of adjudication in the prize courts. By the end of the Seven Years' War, many ships seized by the British navy and privateers were still mired in the prize court system; indeed, the last cases were not completed until the early 1770s.[28] The possibility and reality of such long delays eroded Spanish merchant and ministerial confidence in the British prize court system and its ability to deliver timely decisions. If there was little confidence that the owner of an illegally seized ship would have their property returned quickly, then the act of seizure presented a much bigger threat to owners and merchants. Goods and ships detained for months or years became a costly loss to their owners, and led to clamours against governments who would not, or could not, curb illegal maritime predation.

When Britain and France renewed hostilities in May of 1756, Spanish shipping in American and European waters was once again at risk from illegal seizures and, with confidence in the prize system running low from experience in previous wars, Spanish ministers showed little patience when it came to indiscriminate British prize-taking. Even though the British ministers prosecuting the war against France were greatly invested in preserving Spanish neutrality, they had very little control over

---

[28] R. Pares, *Colonial Blockade and Neutral Rights 1739–1763* (Porcupine Press, 1975), p. 144.

the actions of privateers operating in American waters.[29] When a Spanish merchant or shipowner complained of illegal action by British colonial privateers, it was often impossible for British officials to find out in which colony the privateer was commissioned, let alone who the owner and captain actually were. If the Spanish owners lodged an appeal after condemnation by a colonial Vice Admiralty court, it could take months, or years, for the case to come before the Court of Prize Appeal where ministers had influence. Despite the desire of the government in London to instruct and control colonial privateers and prize courts, the means of addressing illegal seizure were slow, limited, and reactive. Colonial privateers received their commissions from governors or judges of the Vice Admiralty courts in the colonies, and it was not until 1760 that William Pitt requested a yearly list of privateers commissioned in the colonies for the purpose of having some oversight and ability to better respond to their potential illegal seizures.[30]

It was slightly easier for British authorities to manage illegal prize-taking in European waters. One of the most lucrative areas for British privateers to cruise was the Bay of Biscay, where Spanish ships carrying French colonial cargoes from the West and East Indies could be found. Privateers who frequented the Biscayan waters were likely to be smaller craft that had received their commission from authorities in Britain and were, thus, more easily identified. David Starkey has termed these types of ships 'Channel Privateers'.[31] Egregious episodes of violent or illegal activity towards neutral shipping were easier to stop when the perpetrators were known to British authorities and based in Britain. In terms of the prize court system, were a capture made by a Channel privateer off the coast of northern Spain, as was the case for both the *San Juan Baptista* and the *Jesus, Maria, y José*, the closest Admiralty court was the High Court of Admiralty in London. Going straight to the High Court of Admiralty avoided the time spent in Vice Admiralty courts, and Spanish ships brought into British ports could reasonably expect a somewhat shorter adjudication process than ships taken in the West Indies. However, there was still no guarantee that the process would not take months or even years. British ministers did not have the ability to interfere with the proceedings of the High Court of Admiralty and, until the Privateers Act of 1759, the Lords of the Admiralty had no

---

[29] R. Pares, *War and Trade in the West Indies 1739–1763* (Frank Cass and Co., 1963), p. 563.
[30] Pares, *Colonial Blockade*, p. 46. Governorships and Vice Admiralty judgeships were offices often held by the same man.
[31] David Starkey, *British Privateering Enterprise in the Eighteenth Century* (Exeter University Press, 1990), p. 39.

discretionary powers over granting letters of marque.[32] Therefore, except for extra-legal means, British ministers generally had to wait until a case came before the Court of Prize Appeal in order to influence the outcome in favour of a Spanish owner and the preservation of neutrality.

The long delays inherent in the British prize court system, coupled with ministerial impotence in curbing the behaviour of privateers towards Spanish shipping, left the officials of the Spanish Court increasingly frustrated and with little faith in their British counterparts. Much of the back and forth between the two ministries in the early stages of the war revolved around the Anglo-Spanish treaty of 1667 and whether it protected French goods shipped in Spanish bottoms; in other words, did the treaty truly grant the Grotian concept of 'free ships make free goods'? Spanish officials such as D'Abreu and Wall insisted that it did, whereas Keene resolutely argued that it did not.[33] The interpretation of the treaty of 1667 determined, in large part, whether the actions of some British privateers were legal or illegal in the eyes of the prize courts.

By 1757, Ricardo Wall considered the abuse of neutral Spanish shipping to be his chief grievance with the British Court.[34] The Duke of Newcastle, William Pitt, and Benjamin Keene, were all well aware that Spain's neutrality was important to British success in the war lest Spain should ally with France. Pitt attempted to use his status as the 'Champion of the Privateers' to rein in their captures of neutral shipping whilst Newcastle urged the Spanish ministers to use the Court of Prize Appeal to address their grievances with the privateers. Keene, who interacted directly with Wall, attempted to quell the Spanish minister's anger with assurances that action was being taken in London. Richard Pares went so far as to blame prize affairs for Keene's death: '[the seizure and molestation of Spanish vessels] continued to incense Wall to such a pitch of fury that even his old friend Keene could do nothing with him. Poor Keene can truly be said to have died of these disputes.'[35] With no agreement on either prize or logwood affairs, the two Courts continued to build upon pre-existing grievances as the war progressed. Trust between Spanish and British ministers continued to erode and a third grievance, the question of fishing rights off the Newfoundland coast, emerged not long after the prize disputes began.

[32] Ibid. p. 163.
[33] CL M-66, Shelburne Papers, vol. 22, Letter from Fox to Keene, 11 July 1756, ff. 256–63.
[34] Pares, *War and Trade in the West Indies*, p. 559.   [35] Ibid. p. 563.

The Grievances: Fishing Rights

Access to the Newfoundland fisheries was an important matter in British, Spanish, and French foreign policy of the mid-eighteenth century, not so much because of the fish – at that time there were plenty to go around – but because of the strategic importance of such access to empires with maritime ambitions. The fisheries, as many British ministers firmly believed, were one of the bedrocks of maritime power, because they provided training for sailors. A country with a large number of consistently employed sailors would be able to swell the ranks of its navy during wartime with well-trained crews. In the mid-eighteenth century, Spain perpetually suffered from a shortage of manpower in the navy.[36] If Britain controlled the Newfoundland fisheries to the exclusion of France and Spain, then the Royal Navy would always be able to outman its enemies. Given the hegemonic implications of a British monopoly in Newfoundland waters, neither Spain nor France would be happy to relinquish their claims to the fisheries.[37]

As with the other grievances between Britain and Spain, that of the fisheries was partially rooted in the interpretation of treaties. D'Abreu argued that Spain had a right to fish in Newfoundland as granted by the Treaty of Utrecht from 1713, and the Treaty of Madrid from 1721.[38] Pitt disagreed and wrote to his ambassador in Spain that the treaties of Utrecht and Madrid 'only [give] to the Spaniards such privileges as they are able to make claim to by right, *jure sibi vindicare poterunt* and the latter simply confirming the stipulation of the Treaty of Utrecht, without giving any new right whatever.'[39] The debate over Spain's 'right' to fish would never be settled to either Court's satisfaction, but would always be mentioned as one of the top grievances that Spain had with Britain, and as one of the reasons for ultimately joining France in the war. Interestingly, the debate around the Newfoundland fisheries only re-emerged in August 1758, due to the seizure of two Spanish ships by a British privateer. The Spaniards claimed that they were seized illegally

[36] Kuethe and Andrien, *Spanish Atlantic World*, p.198.
[37] J. S. Corbett, *England in the Seven Years' War: A Study in Combined Strategy*, 2 vols. (Longmans, Green, and Co., 1907), vol. I, p. 172.
[38] Kuethe and Andrien, *Spanish Atlantic World*, p. 72. The Treaty of Utrecht negotiated terms between Britain and Spain at the end of the War of the Spanish Succession. Amongst other concessions, it granted to Britain the Asiento de Negros and the right for one 500-ton ship per year to trade at annual fairs of Veracruz and Portobello. The Treaty of Madrid of 1721 reaffirmed Spanish and British commitment to the Treaty of Utrecht.
[39] BL Add MS 36807, Negotiations with Spain, Letter from Pitt to Bristol, 1 August 1758, ff. 18–27.

whilst fishing off of Newfoundland with a passport from the Court of Spain.[40] Since their defence depended on the legality of their fishing activities, the case brought Newfoundland fishery rights to the renewed attention of both British and Spanish ministers.

Spanish Merchants and the Importance of Trust

The grievances that eventually led to the Anglo-Spanish conflict of 1762 were not solely discussed at the ministerial level in Spain. In order for events to influence Spain's foreign policy and relations with Britain, they first had to affect the merchants upon whose trans-Atlantic trade the Spanish empire depended. Spanish merchants and traders, on both sides of the Atlantic, relied on networks of family and friends to safeguard goods and to ensure profits as trade moved between Spain and the Americas. Trust in the efficacy of these networks was of the utmost importance and, according to Xabier Lamikiz, was predicated on

three major factors: first, the efficiency of the legal system in enforcing contracts; second, the availability of information ...; and, lastly, the risks associated with the system and pattern of trade, including the distance and difficulty of navigation, the opportunities for the marketing of goods, the level of competition and the use of credit.[41]

Lamikiz makes no specific distinction in his factors regarding times of war and times of peace. However, if his factors are considered in a specifically wartime context, they can be expanded to take into account more international aspects. After 1756, when Spain became a neutral nation in Britain and France's war, Spanish merchants had to adapt to shifting international maritime conditions. The emergence of British privateers, an increase in British naval operations, and the opening of the French carrying trade, meant that Spanish merchants had to trust not only in Spanish legal systems, but in French and British systems as well. Access to information on British affairs and operations became important in order to trust that Spanish voyages could be conducted without British interference. The risks involved in wartime commerce for Spanish merchants were high because success depended, in part, on British interpretation and protection of Spain's neutral rights. The capture of Spanish ships by British privateers, the denial of fishing rights, and a continued British presence on the Moskito shore, all threatened the safe

---

[40] Ibid.

[41] X. Lamikiz, *Trade and Trust in the Eighteenth-Century Atlantic World* (Boydell Press, 2013), p. 13.

prosecution of Spanish merchants' wartime commerce. As their trust in the British government and Britain's legal system eroded during the war, Spanish merchants turned to the Spanish Court, and therefore a political avenue, for protection of their neutral rights. The grievances of the merchants became those of the ministers.

The Biscayan merchants who lived on Spain's northern shore did not have much interaction with French West and East Indian trade during times of peace. Bilbao, one of the biggest redistribution ports on the northern coast, traded mostly in north Atlantic goods from Britain, Holland, and France, as well as fish from the North American fisheries.[42] However, once the Seven Years' War began, the Biscayans became involved in shipping France's colonial trade. The French navy was unable to protect its coasts from the commercial predation of British privateers and warships. French ships travelling from the East and West Indies would consequently put into Galician and Basque ports, on the north-western coast of Spain, rather than risk running the gauntlet to France. At this point, Spanish ships, like the *Jesús, María, y José* could take the French colonial cargo on board and try to get through to France.[43] These strategies for avoiding British capture were perfect embodiments of 'free ships make free goods' and the question of whether transhipment turned a neutral ship into an enemy ship. Not long into the war it became clear that transhipment in neutral bottoms would not necessarily protect French colonial goods at sea, as British privateers seized neutral ships as well as French ships.[44] As shown by the tens of Spanish ships that came before the High Court of Admiralty, and those that came before the Court of Prize Appeal, the Biscayan merchants did not believe that British ships had the right to capture and condemn their wartime trade with France.

Spanish merchants in the Americas also benefited from a wartime trade with the French. Whilst usually forbidden to trade with French colonies by both French and Spanish law, Spanish ships were welcomed into the French colonies once the British navy began to blockade the French islands. The success of the British blockade was not always absolute, but it did have a sufficiently detrimental effect on the French colonies that neutral ships were welcomed to pick up French trade.[45] As was the case off the coast of northern Spain, British privateers in the West Indies preyed on Spanish ships that they accused of trading with France illegally. Condemnations in the colonial Vice Admiralty courts

---

[42] Ibid. p. 17.   [43] Pares, *War and Trade in the West Indies*, p. 360.   [44] Ibid. p. 373.
[45] Ibid. pp. 384–9.

abounded, and Spanish merchants became further incensed towards British authorities.[46]

From the early years of the Seven Years' War there is evidence of petitions sent from Spanish colonial officials in the Americas to the government in Madrid, complaining about British behaviour. In 1757, Ricardo Wall passed on to an unnamed Spanish minister a letter from the governor of Yucatán, Melchor de Navarrete, regarding the presence of British subjects in the Rio Hondo. In his letter, Navarrete described an attempt to remove the British subjects and the subsequent letter of protest he received from the governor of Jamaica regarding the harsh treatment that the British subjects had received at Spanish hands. Navarrete asked the king for support in the matter, and also asked that British ministers be made aware of their citizens' behaviour. Wall wrote to the unnamed minister that the king had asked him to pass on the letter and do what was required to ease the situation.[47] Given that the governor of Yucatán petitioned the Spanish king to bring the matter to the attention of the British ministers, it is likely that Spanish trust in British colonial officials, embodied, in this case, by the governor of Jamaica, had already been lost. By appealing directly to the Spanish king, the onus of resolving the grievance was placed with the government in Madrid and its ability to negotiate with the government in London. This type of petition was not uncommon when it came to Anglo-Spanish interactions and grievances during the period, in part because the right of all Spanish subjects to directly petition the king was a well-established cultural norm.[48] The use of petitions by merchants in the Americas and northern Spain in order to make their plight known would be a sensible and recognised course of action.

At a time when Ferdinand was looking towards internal reform, listening to the plight of Spanish colonial officials and maritime merchants would have been prudent. As Regina Grafe points out, every territory or individual in Spain was historically privileged with a veto, granted through constitutional tradition, which allowed a law, and therefore monarchical authority, to be recognised but not carried out (*la ley se obedece pero no se cumple* [the law is obeyed but not fulfilled]).[49] In a

---

[46] Ibid. p. 463.

[47] AGI MEXICO 3099, Letter from Wall to undisclosed minister, 7 February 1757.

[48] A. Irigoin and R. Grafe, 'Bargaining for Absolutism: A Spanish Path to Nation-State and Empire Building', *Hispanic American Historical Review*, 88 (2008), 173–209, pp. 182 and 175.

[49] R. Grafe, 'Polycentric States: The Spanish Reigns and the "Failures" of Mercantilism', in P. Stern and C. Wennerlind (eds.), *Mercantilism Reimagined: Political Economy in Early Modern Britain and Its Empire* (Oxford University Press, 2013), p. 252.

period of reform, such a veto could be a valuable bargaining chip in domestic politics. The protection of Spanish merchants' neutral rights was, therefore, not simply a matter of defending the Spanish empire from growing British maritime hegemony, it was also a matter of demonstrating to Spaniards that the Spanish Court could, and would, protect its maritime merchants in far-flung colonies. In exchange, colonial officials and merchants could be expected to both obey and to carry out the laws established by the Court in Madrid.

The Inevitable War?

It is unlikely that any one of the Anglo-Spanish grievances discussed in this chapter would have been enough, on its own, to drive Britain and Spain into a state of war. Nor is it likely that the disagreements around logwood cutting, prizes, and fishery rights would have come to a head without being considered threats to Spanish neutral rights during the Anglo-French conflict. Ferdinand's desire for peace, his friendly attitude towards Britain, and Wall's pro-British stance during the first years of the Seven Years' War led to a Spanish strategy based on neutrality. But, as Kuethe and Andrien point out, British and Spanish interests in the Americas were not compatible.[50] As Britain's war with France dragged on, Spanish colonial interests were threatened on two sides. Britain's growing maritime hegemony and creeping defeat of France threatened the balance of power in the Americas, which Spain held dear. Coupled with this shifting balance of power, was the apparent disregard and abuse of Spain's neutrality by British privateers and prize courts. Unsurprisingly, it is Julian Corbett's understanding of maritime strategy that offers the best analysis for Spain's progression from a neutral nation to a belligerent one: 'every step toward gaining command of the sea tends to turn neutral sea powers into enemies'.[51] If Corbett's idea is expanded to the political and legal realm and joined to Lamikiz's arguments on the necessity of trust in maritime commerce, then command of the sea can be exchanged with command of international maritime law. Corbett's maxim can then be altered and extended to 'every step a state takes toward gaining command of maritime law tends to turn neutral sea powers into enemies unless there is absolute trust in the maritime legal system of the state dictating the law'. Sophus Reinert argues that much of Europe feared

[50] Kuethe and Andrien, *Spanish Atlantic World*, p. 197.
[51] Corbett, *England in the Seven Years' War*, vol. I, p. 5.

it would be Great Britain to give the world its laws, either through the power of its navies or of its manufactures. Given the assumption that liberty was to live in a state of laws rather than license or arbitrariness, then precisely who set those laws – and under whose government – was of cardinal importance.[52]

As Britain gained command of the seas during the war and, by extension, as British laws became international maritime laws, the neutrality of other maritime countries became dependent on faith in the British government and legal system. Without proper legal and diplomatic redress for Spain's grievances, trust in the British government would disappear, and so would the desire to remain neutral. When the new Spanish king came unexpectedly to the throne in 1760, Spain's strategy of neutrality would be replaced with one of hostility towards Britain and an alliance with France.

---

[52] S. Reinert, 'Rivalry: Greatness in Early Modern Political Economy', in P. Stern and C. Wennerlind (eds.), *Mercantilism Reimagined: Political Economy in Early Modern Britain and Its Empire* (Oxford University Press, 2014), p. 352.

7   Forging Arguments
Spanish Ships in the High Court of Admiralty

As the cases of the *Jesús, Maria, y José* and the *San Juan Baptista* made their way through the High Court of Admiralty, the arguments that would eventually be laid before the Court of Prize Appeal took shape. Examining the cases closely offers a micro-level understanding of how Britain tried to maintain Spanish neutrality during the Seven Years' War through a mix of close diplomatic negotiation and decisions in the Court of Prize Appeal. Lord Hardwicke and his colleagues on the appellate court were conscious of the possible national and international political ramifications of their decisions, as well as any possible legal precedents that might be set and which could affect treaty interpretation in the future. The legal arguments made before the judges were addressed in ways that would be beneficial to Britain's maritime interests in both the short and the long term. However, they also had to be addressed in such a way that the Spanish Court would not perceive the decisions as unfair, or as proof that Britain was an untrustworthy or unjust international arbiter. Perceptions of British judicial decisions as unfounded or unfair would only serve to push Spain further away from a position of neutrality and into a closer friendship with France.

By the time appeals had been lodged in both the case of the *Jesús, Maria, y José* and that of the *San Juan Baptista*, Anglo-Spanish relations were already greatly deteriorating. In fact, negotiations over the legal parameters of Spain's neutrality were rocky from the outset of the war. Henry Fox, Secretary of State for the Southern Department at the beginning of the conflict, and Ricardo Wall, Secretary of State for Spain, did not see eye to eye on the interpretation of the Anglo-Spanish treaty of 1667 and what it meant for Spanish neutrality. Once William Pitt succeeded Fox in 1757, the disagreements over the treaty continued and were exacerbated by the diplomatic and public turmoil over Spain's treatment of a British privateer, the *Antigallican*, which had sought shelter from bad weather in Cádiz with two captured French prizes. There was little to no public reaction to Fox's earlier negotiations with Spain, but the *Antigallican* affair created a large anti-Spanish response in much of the British press. This elevated interest in Anglo-Spanish negotiations would last through the war, making it more difficult for ministers and judges to thread the needle of neutrality in the case of Spain.

Ministerial Politics, Treaties, and Anglo-Spanish Affairs

At least a year before hostilities officially broke out between Britain and France, the British government had issued orders to the commanders of warships concerning how they were to treat Spanish ships based on the treaty of 1667. The orders briefly stated that 'you are hereby most strictly required and directed ... to refrain from molesting or obstructing the trade and navigation of any Spanish vessels, but also from stopping or detaining them, unless loaded with such goods, as are declared contraband by treaty'.[1] In July 1756, two months after the British declaration of war against France, the Spanish called for the orders to be renewed and applied to privateers as well as warships.[2] In addition to sending out instructions to British privateers and warships in the summer of 1756, the British Secretary of State for the Southern Department, Henry Fox (soon to be replaced by William Pitt), made an attempt to show the Spanish Court that the government's words would be backed by action. Given the drawn-out process of the prize courts, any quick demonstration of action against illegal seizures of Spanish ships would have to be done through extrajudicial means. Whilst neither British ministers nor the British monarch could legally order a captured prize to be released, the commander of the capturing vessel could be persuaded, usually through monetary inducement, to settle the affair out of court.[3] In early July of 1756, Fox negotiated the release of a recently captured Spanish snow (a two-masted sailing vessel). In a letter to Keene, written on 11 July, largely dedicated to discussing the treaty of 1667, Fox described the release of the Spanish ship, and ordered Keene to make sure that the Spanish minister, Wall, was aware of the story:

Messr. D'Abreu [Spanish envoy to Britain] has seen ... an instance of the King's particular disapprobation of improper captures, by ordering the immediate release of a Spanish Snow ...: this was done without waiting for a representation from Messr. D'Abreu, and indeed without any certain account of the fact; which your Exc will truly represent to Ministro Wall as a mark of His

---

[1] CL M-1216, James Douglas Papers, vol. F., Letter to Capt. Douglas from Office of Lord High Admiral, 20 August 1756. Please note that though the date of these orders is 1756, they are a reissue of the orders from 1755. An original from 1755 was not found.

[2] CL M-66, Shelburne Papers, vol. 22, Letter from Fox to Keene, 11 July 1756, ff. 256–63.

[3] See the Introduction for an explanation of British prize law and the conditions for release of a captured prize.

Majesty's punctilious regard and attention to these points [of the treaty of 1667], the neglect of which, on either side, would be too likely to endanger the good correspondence between the Two Nations.[4]

By specifically mentioning that the snow was released without a request from D'Abreu and before the true circumstances of the capture were known, Fox represented the British ministry as ready to uphold and defend Spanish neutrality without reference to legal procedures, the treaty of 1667, the facts of the event, or Spanish demands for justice. It was an attempt, no doubt, to instil confidence in British commitment to Anglo-Spanish friendship. Such direct involvement from the British king might ensure that the Spanish monarch would also take an interest in maintaining good relations with Britain. In his enthusiasm, however, Fox made two errors. He made the mistake of making it seem as though the British king had the authority to order the release of captured Spanish ships, and he made the mistake of not rooting the release of the ship in a legitimate legal procedure that could clarify how Britain defined the limits of Spanish neutrality. Whether Keene repeated Fox's words verbatim to Wall is uncertain, but Spanish confusion over the British king's right to order extrajudicial releases became a recurring theme in Anglo-Spanish negotiations, and often led to Spanish anger when the British ministry declared that the King was powerless to order an extrajudicial release.

Unfortunately for Fox, Pitt, and Keene, Wall was less interested in one-off shows of British commitment to Spanish neutrality than in current British interpretations of the 1667 treaty. In the same letter of 11 July 1756, in which Fox gave an account of the release of the Spanish snow, he also recounted a misunderstanding over the wording of the 1667 treaty. D'Abreu had recently presented a memorandum to Fox, drawn up by Juan de Arriaga, the Spanish Minister for the Americas, concerning the treatment of Spanish ships. According to Fox's letter, the memorandum quoted Article 23 of the 1667 treaty, which dealt with the difference between contraband and free goods on board neutral ships. Fox accused D'Abreu and Arriaga of misquoting part of Article 23. According to Fox, the wording of the last line of this article, as written in the Spanish memorandum, was: 'toutes les autres marchandises [i.e. merchandise not deemed as contraband but found on neutral ships] seront libres et affranchies'.[5] The true wording of the article, as stated by Fox, was actually: 'les marchandises libres et

---

[4] CL M-66, Shelburne Papers, vol. 22, Letter from Fox to Keene, 11 July 1756, ff. 256–63.
[5] Translation: 'all the other merchandise shall be free and allowed'.

affranchies ne seront confisquées'.[6] The implication of Fox's wording was that goods deemed free and allowed by other articles of the treaty would not be liable to confiscation; a very restricted version of 'free ships make free goods'. The implication of Arriaga's wording was that any goods, including French owned ones, not deemed contraband, were free and allowed; a much broader and open-ended definition, which Fox considered akin to an unacceptably open definition of 'free ships make free goods'.[7] The Spanish wording could cause problems for Britain's strategy of commercial predation against France, because it would allow Spanish ships to carry French goods, as long as they were not on the treaty's list of contraband goods.

Whether Fox was aware of Hardwicke's thinking, which would even-tually become the Rule of the War of 1756, Arriaga's wording could have implications for more restrictive arguments based on the premise that commerce prohibited in peacetime should be prohibited in wartime. Unlike the Anglo-Dutch treaty of 1674, the Anglo-Spanish treaty did not contain an ambiguous phrase about goods carried in times of peace. If Spanish ships were allowed, by treaty, to freely carry any goods except those specifically mentioned, then it would be harder for British prize courts to argue that Spanish neutral rights should be limited to protecting only the types of goods that were allowed to be carried during times of peace.

Britain, as Fox made clear in his letter, did not acknowledge or allow the Spanish wording. When Fox raised the matter of the wording with D'Abreu, the Spanish representative, true to his unremarkable nature, agreed that it was a mistake, but that he was unable to change Arriaga's wording on his own authority. Confident of his victory, Fox informed Keene that: '[D'Abreu] is quite satisfied with my answer, and I hope his Catholick Majesty and His Ministers will, in like manner, acquiesce in it, ... not doubting but that his Catholick Majesty will, on His part, require, from his subjects, the due observance of His own laws, and an exact conformity to the Treaty of 1667.'[8] The difference between the British and Spanish interpretations of Article 23 was no small matter of mere semantics; it proved to be the fulcrum upon which the legality or illegality of many British seizures, including those of the *San Juan Baptista* and the *Jesús, Maria, y José*, would depend. Unlike D'Abreu, Wall, who had a better understanding of the political and strategic importance of clearly defined and mutually understood legal limits to

---

[6] Translation: 'the free and allowed merchandise shall not be seized'.
[7] CL M-66, Shelburne Papers, vol. 22, Letter from Fox to Keene, 11 July 1756, ff. 256–63.
[8] Ibid.

neutral rights, did not agree with Fox's interpretation, and he continued the debate.

Keene met with Wall on 25 July, after the latter had been absent from the Spanish Court due to illness. In Keene's presence, Wall had asked his secretary to read D'Abreu's dispatch from August 1755, which gave an account of his discussion with Fox over the instructions to be sent to British ships based on Arriaga's interpretation of Article 23. He then asked his secretary to read D'Abreu's more recent dispatch from July 1756, which discussed the orders again, but incorporated Fox's interpretation of Article 23.[9] Keene recounted, in a letter to Fox, that after having heard both dispatches, Wall was furious that the Spanish representative in London had agreed with Fox and stated that: 'He [Wall] would never authorize it with his own consent, or deviate from his opinion, by any assurances of the [British] King's firm intention to prevent illegal and vexatious visitings.'[10] Wall's uncompromising stance on the treaty caused Fox great anxiety and, in late August 1756, Fox penned a long letter to Keene arguing, once again, for his interpretation as the right one. He wrote that Article 23 of the treaty was made specifically to vary from a part of the law of nations which stipulated that the unlawful portion of a cargo infects the rest of the cargo and the ship itself. Therefore, it was only a clause inserted to safeguard clearly lawful goods.[11]

Fox himself appears to have misunderstood the implications of the law of nations, at least from a Grotian perspective. In terms of neutral and enemy goods, the law of nations was about the presumption of property. Goods found on board a neutral ship were presumed to be neutral unless proven otherwise. Goods found on board an enemy ship were presumed to belong to enemies unless proven otherwise.[12] The treaty deviated from this presumption by stating in Article 23 that

any merchandize hereunder mentioned, being of contraband and prohibited, they shall be taken out and confiscated, before the Admiralty or other competent Judges; but for this reason the ship, and the other free and allowed commodities which shall be found therein, shall no wise be either seized or confiscated.[13]

[9] CL M-66, Shelburne Papers, vol. 22, Letter from Keene to Fox, 27 July 1756, ff. 307–9.
[10] Ibid.
[11] CL M-66, Shelburne Papers, vol. 22, Letter from Fox to Keene, 18 August 1756, ff. 311–24.
[12] H. Grotius, On the Law of War and Peace (Anodos Books, 2019), p. 196.
[13] Article 23, Anglo-Spanish treaty of 1667, Oxford Historical Treaties, http://opil.ouplaw.com/view/10.1093/law:oht/law-oht-10-CTS-63.regGroup.1/law-oht-10-CTS-63?rskey=ALzNqM&result=4&prd=OHT.

When a British privateer or warship encountered a Spanish ship at sea and stopped it for search or questioning, certain assumptions were being made. The ship could be presumed to be French (an enemy) and the goods inside therefore presumed to be enemy goods. In this case the ship and its goods could be seized and brought before a prize court. The court would then determine whether the seizure had been legitimate and whether the ship and goods were indeed enemy property.[14] Alternatively, the ship could be presumed to be Spanish (neutral) but also presumed to be carrying contraband or enemy goods. From a Grotian and law-of-nations perspective, the initial legal presumption would be that all of the goods within the neutral ship were also neutral, so the captors would have to prove that the suspected contraband goods were indeed contraband. The captors could also challenge the presumption that the ship and the rest of the cargo were neutral and try to prove that they were (or should be considered) enemy property, as happened in some Dutch cases. The Anglo-Spanish treaty altered, or constrained, the presumption about neutral ships and goods inherent in the law of nations so that a neutral ship and goods not deemed contraband could not be 'seized or confiscated'. If the ship and part of the cargo could not be brought before a prize court because they were always deemed 'free' by the treaty, then its presumed neutrality could not be challenged, nor could it be condemned as lawful prize. The practical implications of this were huge, because if British warships and privateers had adhered to an agreed Anglo-Spanish interpretation of the article, it is possible that many fewer Spanish ships and their entire cargoes would have been taken as prize and gone through the prize court system. Fox argued that whilst the article allowed that free goods could be found on board the same ship as unlawful goods, the wording of the article ('aliaeque libera merces et permissae, quae, in istius modi navis reperiuntur'[15]) did not imply that all other cargo which was not deemed 'unlawful' or 'contraband' was free from possible condemnation in a prize court. Only expressly permitted goods were to go free from confiscation and seizure, thus limiting Spanish neutral rights to carry non-contraband French goods.[16] After dedicating most of his letter to making this argument, Fox admitted that it had been hoped within the ministry that a discussion of the treaty

---

[14] Ibid. Article 26.

[15] CL M-66, Shelburne Papers, vol. 22, Letter from Fox to Keene, 18 August 1756, ff. 311–24. Translation: 'and the other free and permitted merchandise likewise found in the ship, shall not be seized or confiscated for any reason'.

[16] Ibid.

would never arise between the two Courts and that, despite the British interpretation,

his Majesty has the friendship of Spain most warmly at heart, and is convinced of its utility and importance to the general fate of Europe, at this time, the King has given orders to His Ships of War to treat all Spanish Ships with a peculiar Regard. The former answer to M. D'Abreu's memorial being withdrawn ...[17]

Fox ended his letter with a request to Keene that his argument over the interpretation of the treaty not be conveyed to Wall and to avoid disputes with the Spanish minister. Orders were sent out, on 20 August 1756, to British ships to avoid detaining or annoying Spanish ships unless contraband goods were on board. These were the same orders that had been issued the previous year.[18] Despite months of anguished negotiations over the interpretation of the treaty, Fox backed down in the face of Wall's refusal to compromise and appeared to offer the Spanish special treatment. Though Fox was unwilling to allow the Spanish Court's interpretation of the treaty, he was willing simply to ignore the matter and give orders for Spanish ships to be treated favourably. Wall, however, continued to have little faith in Britain's promises of special treatment when it came down to the actual actions taken by British ships, and the Spanish minister did not let the matter rest.

Wall's scepticism was vindicated on 4 September, when news arrived in Madrid that a British privateer had taken some Spanish vessels off the coast of northern Spain in mid-August and carried them into Bristol as prizes.[19] The *Jesús, María, y José* was one of the captured ships. Keene wrote to Fox on 8 September, that before news of the captured Spanish ships had arrived, Wall had rejected Fox's offer of special treatment and answered that: 'Spain must not, can not, take for a Grace, or Permission, what is due to her, by treaty, and what she has observed all along, towards powers that had such treaties with her.'[20] From a Spanish strategic point of view, any favourable treatment which was granted by a maritime hegemon purely out of friendship, rather than grounded in a mutual understanding of a treaty, could be rescinded as soon as that friendship ceased to be beneficial. From a more practical point of view, and as proven by the capture of the *Jesús, María, y José*, the promise of favourable treatment was difficult to enforce amongst the privateers.

---

[17] Ibid.
[18] CL M-1216, James Douglas Papers, vol. F., Letter to Capt. Douglas from Office of Lord High Admiral, 20 August 1756.
[19] CL M-66, Shelburne Papers, vol. 22, Letter from Keene to Fox, 8 September 1756, ff. 357–61.
[20] Ibid.

Subsequent to the August captures, Keene declared that 'no methods, but open rules, could ever contain our people [the British] of falling upon all they met with'.[21] It was also clear to Keene that Wall would continue to demand a clarification of the treaty of 1667 until he received a satisfactory answer from the British government that addressed both the behaviour of the privateers and Spanish dependence on Britain's favour.

Faced with the reality that British privateers continued to plague Anglo-Spanish relations and that Wall would not compromise on the treaty of 1667, Fox had little choice but to further appease Spain or risk pushing her into a closer relationship with France. On 5 October, Fox wrote to Keene that '[Fox's] Palliatives ... with regard to the interpretation of the twenty-third article [had] proved insufficient ...'[22] Fox enclosed a memorandum for Wall within his letter to Keene, that acknowledged the Spanish interpretation of Article 23 (any goods not deemed contraband were free and allowed). Fox also penned a set of instructions, which were to be given to all captains who were granted a letter of Marque. These instructions were almost word for word those issued in 1755 and August 1756 but, instead of merely declaring that Spanish ships could only be stopped if they contained contraband goods, there was an added clause which stipulated that every part of the treaty of 1667 had to be observed.[23] The instructions, Fox noted, would be upheld by the Court of Prize Appeal should any Spanish ship come before it.[24] With the acknowledgement of Wall's interpretation and explicit instructions given to British privateers to adhere specifically to the entirety of the treaty, Fox hoped that

The Court of Spain will see how entirely the King has yielded to their earnest demands altho the consequence with regard to other powers ... may be very troublesome and extensive: the future conduct of the Court of Spain, by declining any connection with that of France, will best justify these – generous proceedings; and His Majesty relies upon their rigid discouragement of any abuses that may be made of it by their own subjects, who may now attempt, with impunity, to be the great and frequent carriers ... of the French Trade.[25]

Spain, and more specifically Wall, was the undoubted winner of this early round of wartime negotiations with Britain. Fox and Keene, in an

---

[21] Ibid.

[22] CL M-66, Shelburne Papers, vol. 22, Letter from Fox to Keene, 5 October 1756, ff. 381–91.

[23] BL Add MS 32611, Hardwicke Papers, Notes on the *Jesús, Maria, y José*.

[24] CL M-66, Shelburne Papers, vol. 22, Letter from Fox to Keene, 5 October 1756, ff. 381–91.

[25] Ibid.

attempt to keep Spain from furthering its friendship with France, had granted everything Spain had asked for regarding Article 23 of the treaty and the conduct of the privateers.

The Press and Anglo-Spanish Affairs

The decisions made in the Court of Prize Appeal were not made in isolation from the political events of the Seven Years' War, so it is important to place the two ships into the context of Anglo-Spanish affairs in the first few years of the war. Between the original capture of the *Jesús, Maria, y José* in August 1756, and the appeal lodged in April 1758, Anglo-Spanish relations at the ministerial level began to focus on the limits of Spanish neutrality, given the disputes around logwood cutting in Honduras, and prize-taking. However, ministers, kings, and ambassadors were not the only men concerned with Spanish affairs in the early years of the war. In the taverns and coffee houses of London, Anglo-Spanish relations were also being discussed by ordinary British citizens who had access to printed material either through their own reading or by having it read to them.

However, in complete contrast to the reaction towards the seized Dutch ships which were coming before the High Court of Admiralty around the same time as the *San Juan Baptista* and the *Jesús, Maria, y José*, there was seemingly little public response or engagement in the press to the seizure of Spanish ships by British privateers or to the logwood affair. This was in no way due to a lack of opportunity for arguments to find their way into printed material: by the 1750s there were at least six London daily newspapers, six newspapers which came out three times a week, six weekly papers, ten evening papers, and three newspapers published on Sundays. These numbers continued to rise for the rest of the century, providing the population with ample access to reading or listening material.[26] While it is difficult to determine exactly how often Anglo-Spanish relations were mentioned in print during the Seven Years' War, the Burney Collection, which contains 1,270 titles and 1 million pages of eighteenth- and seventeenth-century English newspapers, pamphlets, and books, and has been digitised by the British Library, offers a good indication. Searching the collection for material printed between 1 March 1756 and 1 May 1758 (roughly the opening of Anglo-French hostilities and Ezenarro's appeal to the Court of Prize Appeal) for the key words 'Spain' and 'Spanish' yielded 1,573

---

[26] J. White, *London in the 18th Century: A Great and Monstrous Thing* (Random House, 2012), p. 253.

articles of which 212 actually discussed Anglo-Spanish affairs.[27] This number is likely very far under the real number of articles discussing Anglo-Spanish affairs for two reasons. The Burney Collection is in no way a comprehensive collection of all British newspapers printed during the period, though it is a vast and useful one because of its digitisation. It is also a collection that represents primarily London publications.[28] Secondly, keyword searches that use Optical Character Recognition, such as the Burney Collection, can have an extremely low hit rate, meaning that there were likely many articles that did not come up in the search.[29] Nonetheless, a sample base of more than 1,500 articles is enough to show that discussions of Anglo-Spanish affairs during the early years of the war were not very prominent. Of the 212 articles, one discussed the *Jesús, Maria, y José* directly, and none discussed the *San Juan Baptista*. This dearth of reporting was not peculiar to the two ships in question. Very few of the Spanish ships which came before the Court of Prize Appeal during the War were mentioned between May 1756 and May 1758.

The first indirect mention of the *Jesús, Maria, y José* was in the *Middlewich Journal*, a weekly compilation of articles taken from six London-based newspapers published by the town of Middlewich, about 40 kilometres south-east of Liverpool.[30] Given its proximity to Liverpool, it is not surprising that the chosen articles often had a maritime theme. In the edition of 31 August 1756, there is a brief article titled 'Extract of a Letter from Bristol, dated August 21' in which it was stated that the *Britannia* privateer had brought in two Spanish ships on their way from San Sebastián to a French port carrying French East India goods.[31] Whilst the *Jesús, Maria, y José* is not named as one of them, given the dates, privateer, and location, it is highly unlikely to be any other ship. The article concluded 'But it's not certain whether she will be condemned.'[32] It is interesting to note the claim (put forward as fact) that the ship was bound from San Sebastián to a French port with French goods, as this was the contention of the English captain, Charles Davids, but not the Spanish master, José Ezenarro. Through publishing only Davids's claim, the author had biased the reader against expecting any outcome other than one favourable to Davids. In presenting Davids's

---

[27] British Library, 17th–18th Century Burney Collection Newspapers, Gale Cengage Learning, http://find.galegroup.com/bncn/start.do?prodId=BBCN&userGroupName= kings.

[28] S. G. Brandtzæg, P. Goring and C. Watson (eds.), *Travelling Chronicles: News and Newspapers from the Early Modern Period to the Eighteenth Century* (Leiden: Brill, 2018), p. 21.

[29] Ibid. p. 22.   [30] *Middlewich Journal*, 31 August 1756, no. 8.   [31] Ibid.   [32] Ibid.

claim as a true and legitimate cause for seizure and mentioning that the outcome of the case was not certain, the reader was left to speculate about the motives and justice doled out by the prize courts. If the case were as clear-cut as the article laid out – Davids had stopped French goods from reaching France via means of a deceptive, supposedly neutral, ship and should therefore to be rewarded by the prize courts – it would be easy for a reader to assume that any ruling that reflected otherwise would be unjust to British privateers in general and overly favourable to Spain, who seemed to prefer France's friendship over Britain's. Such possible speculation could have led, as in the case of captured Dutch ships, to a further discussion in the press about Spanish neutrality and how much British ministers and the prize courts were willing to curtail the rights of privateers in order to maintain it. However, this discussion barely took place regarding Spain at this time.

After the article concerning the capture of the *Jesús, Maria, y José* appeared in the *Middlewich Journal*, interest in the case seems to have disappeared. There is seemingly no article within the Burney collection that mentions the case further or reports on the ruling of the High Court of Admiralty. This appears to be true for almost all Spanish ships that came before prize courts. By the end of 1756, 131 prizes had been condemned by the High Court of Admiralty, 42 of which had been brought in by privateers.[33] Of those 131, at least 18 were Spanish ships.[34]

Despite the lack of reporting on Spanish prize cases, one article did appear on 31 December 1756, concerning Anglo-Spanish relations. The *Gazetteer* and *London Daily Advertiser* published what reads like a modern 'letter to the editor' detailing the author's concerns over a Spanish allegiance with France. The author was noticeably hostile towards Spain and declared in the opening sentences: 'I cannot help declaring that I greatly distrust them [Spain]. Though we have done every thing for that nation that they have desired for these thirty years past, what have they done equivalent to it?'[35] The article continued by mentioning the conflict over British rights to trade in logwood in Honduras and bemoaning the increasing trade between Spain and France to the detriment of British trade. The article ended by predicting an alliance between France and Spain predicated on the Catholic interest. 'Have we not had accounts from Marseilles, that the Spaniards have already

---

[33] David Starkey, *British Privateering Enterprise in the Eighteenth Century* (Exeter University Press, 1990), p. 178. Though Table 16 in that book gives the numbers for prizes condemned at Doctors' Commons, the Court of Prize Appeal did not meet in 1756, and thus the figures for this year can only apply to the High Court of Admiralty.
[34] BL Add MS 36208–11, Hardwicke Papers, Notes on Prize Cases.
[35] *Gazetteer and London Daily Advertiser*, 31 December 1756, no. 4772.

made large remittances to the court of Vienna? If this proves true, can we longer doubt of the junction of these three great Catholic powers?'[36] As far as the author of the *Gazetteer* article was concerned, Britain would have been much better off to regard Spain as an enemy in 1756, as she was a poor friend in trade and almost an assured enemy in Britain's war with France. With the backdrop of the loss of Minorca and the infamous trial of Admiral Byng (which was described in the very next article of that day's *Gazetteer*) the hostility towards Spain fuelled by the fear of a Franco-Spanish alliance is not surprising. However, as with the article in the *Middlewich Journal*, what is surprising is the lack of follow up. Except for one small notice on 13 January 1757, in the *London Intelligencer*, the press remained largely silent on Spanish affairs until March.[37] It is possible, though difficult to prove directly, that British ministers and judges wished for silence in the press on Anglo-Spanish affairs. An active discussion in the press could have added to the difficulty of maintaining Spain's neutrality, keeping Britain's merchant lobby friendly towards the ministry, and maintaining the faith of British financiers in the government's ability to successfully prosecute the war. Any excessive hostility towards Spain or discussions of the ministry's negotiations in the press could have had the potential to adversely affect the precarious balance that ministers strove so hard to maintain.

It is true that, if taken as a conglomerate force, the 'press' in Britain ultimately had little ability to bend politics to its various wills.[38] Nonetheless, many ministers still cared about what was printed and worried about its effect. Newcastle had wanted to prosecute the printer of the *London Evening Post* (a patriot leaning paper) in 1756 over an article about the militia.[39] In the first weeks of 1757, Charles Townshend, a member of the Board of Trade, received a letter from his informant, Mr Husk, that described the effect of a pamphlet published in support of Admiral Byng:

I enclose you a pamphlet in favour of Mr. Byng what has been given away to every Coffee House in town, and sells very well. It makes a great noise, and a great impression in his favour. It is astonishing what a horn it has given in his favour,

[36] Ibid.   [37] *London Intelligencer*, 13 January 1757, no. 1700.
[38] Jeremy Black, *The English Press 1621–1861* (Sutton Publishing, 2001), p. 44; Anna Brinkman-Schwartz, 'The *Antigallican* Affair: Public and Ministerial Responses to Anglo-Spanish Maritime Conflict in the Seven Years War, 1756–1758', *The English Historical Review*, 135: 576 (2020), 1132–64.
[39] Black, *The English Press 1621–1861*, p. 128.

and what prejudice it has done the ministry, 'tho I think it far from an able performance, and it passes over his behaviour on the day of action entirely.[40]

Though the controversy over Byng's execution was a particularly heated affair, open discussion and debate of Anglo-Spanish affairs also had the potential to inflame the public, as would become apparent in March 1757.

Ministers were not, however, powerless before the press, and it was possible for them to have a bearing on what was printed in some papers. The *Daily Gazetter*, amongst others, was financed and shaped by the ministry.[41] Other papers also had direct connections with the ministry; *The Monitor* was run by William Beckford, the rich West Indian planter who helped finance the war, MP for the City, future Mayor of London, and close ally of Pitt.[42] Ministers clearly had the ability to influence some of the papers published in Britain, and it seems unlikely that they would not have used this influence in order keep Anglo-Spanish affairs from being discussed too publicly whilst negotiations over neutrality and the interpretation of the Anglo-Spanish treaty of 1667 were ongoing.

The *Antigallican* Affair

In December 1756, William Pitt replaced Henry Fox as Secretary of State for the Southern Department, giving Britain's foreign policy a much more belligerent stance. In January 1757, questions about Spain's adherence to the treaty of 1667 and about her friendship with France, arose when a British privateer, the *Antigallican*, was seized in a Spanish port and its two French prizes were returned to the French. This event and the subsequent fall-out would become known as the *Antigallican* affair, and it galvanised the British press into action. Anglo-Spanish affairs became more widely discussed in the newspapers with a distinctly anti-Spanish rhetoric emerging in September 1757. News of the *Antigallican*'s activities appeared, like those of many successful privateers, in British newspapers as accounts of glorious battles against French privateers which were brought into port along with prizes to be tried in the Admiralty courts. Announcements of prize good auctions, mostly held in City coffee houses, sometimes included the name of the capturing ship and its captain. Any citizen who kept up with what was

---

[40] CL M-1773 B1/5/1, Charles Townshend Papers, Bowhill Papers, Letter from Mr Husk to Charles Townshend, no date.

[41] Ibid. f. 37.

[42] S. Kinkel, *Disciplining the Empire: Politics, Governance and the Rise of the British Navy* (Harvard University Press, 2018), p. 139.

printed about Britain's maritime war would likely have been at least vaguely familiar with the fortunes and misfortunes of Britain's privateers.

The *London Evening Post*, a patriot-leaning paper, printed a small article on 18 January 1757, which described the engagement of a British privateer, the *Antigallican*, against a French East Indiaman, *Le Duc de Penthievre*, off the coast of Spain the day before. In true sensational fashion, the article highlighted that the crew of the privateer held off their attack until they were close enough to the French ship to fire their small arms directly into the cabin windows.[43] The *Post*'s article was fairly typical for a description of British privateering success and concentrated more on the adventure of the encounter rather than any type of political or anti-French message. Unbeknownst to the writers and publishers of the London newspapers, however, bad weather had forced the *Antigallican* and its prize into Cádiz, where the Spanish governor claimed that the capture had taken place within cannon-shot of the Spanish coast – that is, in neutral waters – and was, therefore not legal. The governor ordered the British Captain Foster to give up his prize to the French consul, despite protestations from the French crew that it had been a legal capture. Foster refused, and two Spanish warships opened fire on the prize (now commanded by a British prize crew) until they surrendered to Spanish authority.[44]

Hints of a looming controversy emerged eighteen days later, in the edition of 5 February of the *London Chronicle*. In a section dedicated to the mail recently arrived from abroad, there were two articles of interest regarding Anglo-Spanish relations. The news from Madrid was that, due to the continued harassment of Spanish ships by the British, Spain's warships were being readied for sea in order to protect its commerce.[45] The news from Paris declared that the *Le Duc de Penthievre* was taken within range of a Spanish fort and that: 'The Court of Madrid reclaims her, and insists that she shall be restored.'[46] Whilst there is no direct discussion of neutrality in either article, nor any call to arms, the implication of both pieces was that Spanish neutrality was being undermined. In the first article, Britain was the abuser. In the second, Spain was guilty of abusing its own neutrality by showing preference to the French. The news from Madrid implied that, as far as Spanish authorities were concerned, the instructions issued by the British government to all privateers and ships of war were still not having the desired effect of

---

[43] *London Evening Post*, 18 January 1757, no. 4556.
[44] *London Evening Post*, 26–29 March 1757, 'Extract of a Letter from Cádiz, March 2', no. 4540.
[45] *London Chronicle*, 5 February 1757, no. 582.   [46] Ibid.

curbing egregious and illegal behaviour against Spanish shipping. The news from Paris implied that the Spanish Court had unilaterally decided the British capture of the French prize to be illegal and had decided the case in favour of the French. Whether any of the British ministers read, or were made aware of, what was printed in the newspapers is a matter of speculation, but William Pitt and Benjamin Keene were very much aware of, and concerned by, the actions taken against the British privateer, the *Antigallican*.

Pitt's concern, as expressed in a letter to Keene on 25 February 1757, was that the *Antigallican* affair showed an alarming partiality towards France on the part of the Spanish government. As the governor of Cádiz had alleged that his orders to take the *Antigallican*'s prize had come from superiors, Pitt concluded that Spain's violation of both neutrality and Anglo-Spanish treaties, was condoned by the Spanish Court.[47] From the British perspective, the actions of the Spanish governor of Cádiz were a violation of the 1667 treaty, and of Spanish neutrality, because, as a neutral port, Cádiz should have offered safety to the British privateer and her prize when they were fleeing bad weather.[48] As an official of a neutral port, the governor of Cádiz had no authority to declare the seizure illegal. From the Spanish point of view, the governor of Cádiz had every authority to declare the seizure a violation of Spain's neutrality because it had taken place within neutral waters where both British and French ships were safe from each other.

In an attempt to stave off a diplomatic crisis, Keene, on his own initiative, had remonstrated with Wall and hoped soon to acquire the orders for the release of *Le Duc de Penthievre* to the British captors.[49] Whilst Pitt had to wait for a reply from Keene to see how the small crisis would play out, the British newspapers indulged in rampant speculation. On 22 February, the *Middlewich Journal* published an article in which it was claimed that the influence of the French ambassador on the Spanish king, in combination with the preference shown to France in the case of the *Antigallican*, seemed to 'presage a Declaration of War against Great Britain ... orders either have, or will be given to our Ambassador [Keene], to re-demand the abovementioned prize [*Le Duc de Penthievre*], and, in

[47] CL M-66, Shelburne Papers, vol. 22, Letter from Pitt to Keene, 25 February 1757, ff. 467–9. NB: The date on this copy is wrongly penned as 25 March 1757. The correction was pencilled in by the compiler or by an archivist.

[48] Articles 10 and 13 of the Anglo-Spanish treaty of 1667, Oxford Historical Treaties, http://opil.ouplaw.com/view/10.1093/law:oht/law-oht-10-CTS-63.regGroup .1/law-oht-10-CTS-63?rskey=ALzNqM&result=4&prd=OHT.

[49] CL M-66, Shelburne Papers, vol. 22, Letter from Pitt to Keene, 25 February 1757, ff. 467–9.

case of a Refusal, he may perhaps immediately be recalled'.[50] As the British ministers were still trying to understand exactly what had been, and was, happening in the case of the *Antigallican*, the writers and publishers of the *Middlewich Journal* had falsely escalated the affair to one of impending warfare. Though the article had no discernible effect on the actions of British ministers, and had no direct anti-Spanish phrasing, it did convey to its readership a sense that war with Spain was inevitable and would be caused by French and Spanish connivance. This narrative would continue to play out in the British press with increasingly vehement anti-Spanish sentiment.[51]

The reality of the *Antigallican* affair, as related by Keene in a letter from early March, turned out to be much more pernicious than anything yet being printed in Britain. Wall had presented Keene's complaints about the treatment of the *Antigallican* to the Spanish king, who was seemingly unaware of the extent of the violence that had transpired. It came to light that the Spanish Minister for War, and captain general of the army, Sebastián de Eslava,[52] along with the French consul at La Coruña, had presented Ferdinand with a version of events in which *Le Duc de Penthievre* had been seized illegally by the *Antigallican*, and that painted the actions of the British captain as a violation of Spanish neutrality. The king, with these facts before him, gave Eslava leave to order that the prize be secured at Cádiz until more information could be gathered.[53] Ferdinand, however, had not authorised the use of force against Captain Foster or his prize. Nor had he authorised the return of the prize to French authorities; that order had been entirely orchestrated by Eslava, upon the urging of French representatives in the Spanish Court. Keene described Ferdinand's reaction upon learning of Eslava's cavalier actions: 'The King railed at Eslava, asked Wall why he was not turned out. He would discard the old Radoteur immediately; ... and then ordered the Letter to be wrote to stop further Proceedings.'[54] The damage, however, had been done. Ferdinand, unable, or unwilling, to bare to the world that he could not control his ministers, neither censured nor publicly contradicted Eslava. Wall, who feared further accusations of Anglophilia, remained silent. Keene bemoaned the dynamics of the Spanish Court and feared for Spanish neutrality: 'Messr. Wall hates his office, and suffers at these matters as much as myself; he sees, as well

[50] *Middlewich Journal*, 15–22 February 1757, no. 33.
[51] Brinkman-Schwartz, 'The *Antigallican* Affair'.
[52] Kuethe and Andrien, *Spanish Atlantic World*, p. 211.
[53] CL M-66, Shelburne Papers, vol. 22, Letter from Keene to Pitt, 6 March 1757, ff. 471–7.
[54] Ibid.

as I do, the Danger Two Great Crowns are in, from matters of so insignificant a nature compared with their peace, and a good correspondence.'[55] The 'danger' – namely, descent into a state of war – to which Keene alluded, was not, in the end, precipitated by the controversy over the *Antigallican*. In fact, there was limited immediate ministerial political fall-out other than the continued deterioration of Anglo-Spanish relations and an increasing unease, demonstrated by both Keene and Pitt, that British allies in the Spanish Court would prove unable to champion the cause of neutrality. In the last substantive letter concerning the *Antigallican* affair, Keene wrote to Pitt:

You will be tired, Sir, with this long dull tale ... I shall put an end to it ... on the consideration that the Sum and Substance of the whole would amount to no more than that those, who would assist us, are discouraged for want of Power, or the exercise of it, from Ideas of their own safety, in providing for their retreats; that there is no resolution in the chiefs to stop the measures that are contriving and machining by our enemies ...[56]

As the war continued, Pitt's negotiations with the Spanish Court over the logwood affair, the Newfoundland fishery, and prize court affairs, confirmed Keene's observation that the members of the Spanish Court were indeed discouraged from upholding and abetting British interests.

Correspondence between the two Courts over the *Antigallican* continued, intermittently, for the next several months. However, once Pitt and Keene's outcry put a stop to Eslava's plan to have the prize handed over to French authorities, the matter was given over to the Spanish court system and there was little the British ministers could do but wait for a decision on the legality of the *Duc de Penthievre*'s seizure. The British press, on the other hand, had only just begun to relish the *Antigallican*'s story.

One of the first detailed accounts of the *Antigallican*'s tribulations at Cádiz was published by the *Evening Advertiser* on 5 April 1757, in the form of extracts from Captain Foster's journal and letters.[57] The newspaper dedicated half a page to the story, beginning with the capture of *Le Duc de Penthievre*, going into meticulous detail about the Spanish warship that fired on the British prize, and culminating in the orders from Madrid to stop all hostile proceedings.[58] A week later, in the *London Evening*

[55] Ibid.
[56] CL M-66, Shelburne Papers, vol. 22, Letter from Keene to Pitt, 21 April 1757, ff. 515–21.
[57] Without access to Captain Foster's original journal and letters it is impossible to verify whether the *Evening Advertiser* was reprinting his actual account or a fabricated version.
[58] *Evening Advertiser*, 5 April 1757, no. 481.

Post's edition of 14 April, an article was reprinted from the *Utrecht Gazette* giving the news from Madrid concerning the 'affair of the *Antigallican's* Prize',[59] dated 11 March. This article gave another in-depth account of Spanish aggression and the honourable behaviour of Captain Foster but was of more political relevance because it addressed the question of Spanish neutrality from a Spanish point of view. As was often the case with articles printed as the 'news from abroad', the one appearing on the 14th was in the first-person plural, which had the effect of personifying Spain. The article mentioned Keene's objections about the treatment of Captain Foster issued on 6 March: 'Our [the Spanish] Ministry have made answer, "That they have canvassed, with all possible attention, the circumstances of this prize ... they had judged it proper that she should be restored ... [to the French] ... to the end that the Neutrality of the Spanish Ports should be no way violated on this account ...".'[60] The article was problematic, as much because of what is omitted as what is included. From 5 April's edition of the *Evening Advertiser*, it is clear that news of Ferdinand's orders to stop proceedings against Captain Foster had reached Britain in a public capacity and that the printers of the *London Evening Post* chose not to include the infor-mation. The personification of Spain also presented a problem, as it lent unity to the Spanish ministry and Spanish officials that, from the obser-vations in Keene and Pitt's letters, clearly did not exist. The overall impression given by the article was that the Spanish ministry and Spanish officials were in agreement on the fact that the neutrality of Spanish ports should be defended even at the price of violence towards British ships and citizens. It also gave the impression that the Spanish ministry had carefully considered the facts of the case and believed that it had acted justly to preserve Spanish interests and neutrality. Both impressions were based on partial truths and only half of the story, but it publicly put Anglo-Spanish relations on a hostile footing. Perhaps to the newspaper's credit, the article did not speculate over the influence of French officials in Spain, but rather attributed Spanish action only to the issue of neutrality. The article was perfectly in keeping with the paper's patriotic leanings, as the Patriot Whigs had been advocating a war with Spain that would allow Britain to acquire Spanish territory in the Americas since the 1730s.[61]

Public interest in the *Antigallican*'s plight seemed to grow as the printers of several newspapers in London continued to publish articles concerned with the affair. Between 18 January, when news of the

---

[59] *London Evening Post*, 14 April 1757, no number.   [60] Ibid.
[61] Kinkel, *Disciplining the Empire*, pp. 78–84.

Antigallican and *Le Duc de Penthievre* first appeared in the *London Evening Post*, and the middle of April when British ministerial correspondence about the issue tapered off, at least eleven articles appeared about the affair. This averages out to roughly one every two weeks, which is a marked increase in the public discussion of Anglo-Spanish affairs from the first year of the war. Towards the middle of April 1757, there was optimism in the press that the affair, despite Spanish depredations, would be resolved favourably. In the *London Evening Post*'s edition of the 19th, a copy of a letter from the managers and owners of the *Antigallican* to William Pitt was printed. The letter was, more than anything, a 'thank you' note to the minister for his treatment of the affair: 'as well knowing that your undertaking this affair was more than an omen of its success ... your whole behaviour in the affair has been so noble, so steady, and uniform, that we are at a loss where to admire you most, in the design, the prosecution, or the event'.[62] The letter ends with a more general exaltation of Pitt's negotiations with Spain: 'His Majesty may never want a Minister like you to hear with impartiality, to advise with candour and judgement, and with the most steady resolution to procure a proper redress for the Grievances of his Majesty's subjects.'[63] Given the tone of the correspondence between Pitt and Keene, the optimism in this letter, along with the promise of favourable resolution, seems misplaced. If, as the letter claimed, the owners of the privateer had met several times with Pitt, it is possible that he gave them more hope than he conveyed in his letters to Keene. As the 'Champion of the privateers' and a Patriot Whig, it may have been in his interest to keep the owners and managers of the *Antigallican* optimistic. Publishing the letter made it either a public vote of confidence, or an attempt by the privateering lobby to pressure Pitt into action. In either case, the letter would have impressed upon readers that Pitt looked after British interests when it came to negotiations with the Spanish Court.

Optimism in the *Antigallican* affair peaked on 26 April, when news was spread through Lloyd's Coffee House and other City establishments that *Le Duc de Penthievre* had been restored to Captain Foster by the Spanish Court, and that both the *Antigallican* and her prize had left Cádiz.[64] This news was completely false, as the Spanish Court did not decide the matter until August. However, between 26 April and mid-September 1757, there was almost nothing in the press about the *Antigallican* affair – presumably because it was believed that there had been a resolution. The illusion of a British triumph in Anglo-Spanish negotiations was dispelled

---

[62] *London Evening Post*, 19–21 April 1757, no. 4595.   [63] Ibid.
[64] *Middlewich Journal*, 26 April 1757, no number.

with the distribution of the *London Evening Post* on 17 September 1757.
An article was printed as the 'news from Madrid' dated 25 August, and
gave the impression that not only had the British ministry failed to defend
the British privateer, but that they had also capitulated and supported the
Spanish decision:

> [T]he sentence pronounced … against Capt. Foster … for having violated the
> Neutrality of the Coasts of Spain … the King [Ferdinand] … hoped that the
> Privateers of that Nation [Britain] would for the future abstain from all
> proceedings that might be contrary to the dispositions which the two Crowns
> have expressed towards each other … the British Ambassador has repeated
> assurances … that pursuant to these dispositions, if the Captain of the
> *Antigallican* had violated the Neutrality of this Crown, it was just that the Laws
> of the Monarchy should have their due effect against him; and that in this case his
> Britannick Majesty abandon'd him to the course of justice.[65]

This was an extremely damning portrayal of the entire affair. Pitt, who six
months before had been lauded as a hero by the owners of the
Antigallican, was now implicated in the 'abandonment' of the British
captain to Spanish justice because he and the rest of the ministry had
conceded that Spain's neutrality had been violated.

As far as the writer of the article was concerned, the king and the
ministry were more interested in appeasing the Spanish government than
in supporting British citizens against Spanish injustice. Whilst vitriolic
publications against Pitt and the rest of the government remained minimal, condemnation of the Spanish increased and remained fairly constant for the rest of the war. It is possible that it was the final outcome of
the *Antigallican* affair that acted as the catalyst for some of the most anti-
Spanish publications after September 1757. One long-running epistolary
series in particular, the '*Antigallican* letters' was clearly a direct result of
the unfavourable outcome in the case.

Beginning on 1 October 1757, the *London Evening Post* ran a series of
'Letters to the Editor', which were always signed as being from 'An
Antigallican'. There was an Antigallican society in London which often
published anti-French articles in the newspapers, but the author, or
authors, of the '*Antigallican* letters' was more likely drawing on the name
of the privateer, as they were dedicated, at first, to the *Antigallican* affair
and later to Anglo-Spanish affairs in general. The first letter told the story
of the *Antigallican* affair, with several patriotic embellishments and inac-
curacies up until the Spanish man of war fired upon the British prize.
Three aspects of the letter are of particular interest to the development of

---

[65] *London Evening Advertiser*, 17 September 1757, no number.

a public discussion around Anglo-Spanish relations. The article explicitly condemned French influence on the governor of Cádiz as a violation of neutrality:

Whatever external appearance of friendship the inhabitants of Cádiz might show to the British Captain, the Governor of that City soon carried another face, and from a neutral friend, acted like a public Enemy ... when we shall find him [governor of Cádiz] so much influenced by France, as to make no scruple of ... violating the Laws of Nations, and of insulting the Flag of that Kingdom [Britain], whose fleet has so often brought Spain to the brink of destruction.[66]

Unlike the authors of most of the articles that had appeared about the affair to date, the author of the first *Antigallican* letter made a direct link between French influence on Spanish officials and Spanish violation of neutrality as understood through the 'Laws of Nations'. Whilst Pitt and Keene had been discussing French influence in the Court of Spain for some time, this article was one of a very few instances of it until then in the public record. By making reference to British victories over Spain in past wars, the author threatened that Spanish behaviour in this affair was ill-advised.

In contrast to the 'news from Madrid' printed on 17 September, the *Antigallican* letter once again gave support to Pitt's government by insinuating strongly that the ministry would not suffer Spain's insults:

Our present ministers surely will never suffer the Spaniards to seize a legal prize ... though a former ministry suffered them to be destroyed on the Ocean ... but I hope they will be soon compelled to acknowledge their injustice, and to make proper retribution for the violence they have committed; or that they will once more feel the resentment of that Nation which they have so contemptuously treated, so greatly injured, and so perfidiously alarmed.[67]

Given that Pitt and Keene made but few protestations to the Spanish Court after *Le Duc de Penthievre* had been declared an illegal prize, it is unlikely that they were heavily influenced by such publications. However, for the interested public, it was a further call to arms against the Spanish, and one that evoked the strength and competence of Pitt's ministry by assuring the reader that, unlike previous ministries, Pitt's would not stand idly by as British maritime rights were trampled upon. The author was to be disappointed, however, as Pitt's ire did not turn belligerent until late 1760.

Whoever wrote the first *Antigallican* letter was aware of several bilateral treaties that existed between Britain and Spain and was keen to use them in the publication to further anti-Spanish sentiment. The reader was

[66] *London Evening Post*, 1 October 1757, no number.   [67] Ibid.

made aware, through implication, that the commercial Treaty of Seville of 1732 had been 'blundered' and had led to the many ship seizures that helped spark the Anglo-Spanish war in 1739.[68] The author next mentioned the Treaty of Aix la Chapelle of 1748, which had put an end to the war, and wrote: 'but what will follow that of Aix la Chapelle is uncertain; for the Spaniards seem no ways inclined to observe that which the numerous plenipotentiaries then so ostentatiously called, a *christian, universal, and perpetual peace*'.[69] A vague parallel had been drawn between the events that led to the war of 1739 and those of the *Antigallican* affair. Anyone who was aware of Britain's recent belligerent history with Spain would have understood that, as far as the author was concerned, Spain's contravention of existing treaties and cavalier actions with regard to British shipping had led to a victorious war in the past and could, or should, lead to a justified and victorious war again.

The first *Antigallican* letter was, without doubt, a scathing public indictment of Spain's role in the *Antigallican* affair. However, it was also a wider indictment of Spain's behaviour concerning neutrality and Britain's privateering rights in general. The recourse to international law and recent history for its arguments, along with a strong (if misguided) vote of confidence for the ministry's imminent action, made it one of the most compelling articles on Anglo-Spanish affairs published in Britain up to that date. It is perhaps all the more important because the letter was only the first of a series. At the conclusion of the article there was printed a notice which is worth quoting in full:

The whole unprecedented proceedings of the Court of Spain, regarding the Antigallican and her Prize, will, from time to time, be impartially set forth in the paper, in a regular series of letters, for the satisfaction of the public in general.[70]

No other diplomatic crisis during the war sparked such a dedicated reaction from the press, and public interest in the affair must have been high enough to justify the *Post*'s commitment to the project. The series, however, soon went well beyond the *Antigallican* affair, and within a few months had become the most constant and vitriolic commentary on Anglo-Spanish affairs in the war, with more than forty letters printed before the declaration of war in 1761. Many other authors followed suit and began to publish articles discussing Anglo-Spanish relations. After the publication of the first *Antigallican* letter, public discussion on the issue was constant, which marked a dramatic change from the first year-and-a-half of the war.

[68] Ibid.   [69] Ibid.   [70] Ibid.

The British public's increased interest in Anglo-Spanish affairs, prompted by the *Antigallican* affair, meant that foreign policy decisions taken by Pitt's ministry might be much more heavily scrutinised in newspapers or pamphlets. Such scrutiny could be extended to the affairs of the prize courts and the decisions handed down by the Court of Prize Appeal. The affair had demonstrated to Pitt and Keene that Spain was not as dedicated to its neutrality as Britain wished and, as such, the grievance of illegal prize-taking had to be treated with more care in order not to antagonise the Spanish Court. On the flip side, the new attention of the press, particularly that controlled by the Patriotic Whigs, meant that care also had to be taken by the ministry to not be seen as bending and cowering too much before Spanish demands.

The concept that the British press had the ability to influence the ministry's actions should be approached with caution. The relationship between the ministry and the press was complicated, and whilst some ministers clearly cared about what was printed, it is unlikely that something like the '*Antigallican* letters' would significantly change how the ministry approached Anglo-Spanish relations. Any oppositional figures in Parliament might use the press to highlight and disseminate their views, but it is unlikely that it would be a deciding factor in any power struggle.[71] The press could be a useful political tool to exert pressure on the public or the government, but it was not a coherent or independent force on its own. The *Jesús, Maria, y José* had come before the High Court of Admiralty before the *Antigallican* affair, but it was in the post-*Antigallican* political atmosphere that the *San Juan Baptista* would come before the High Court of Admiralty.

Two Spanish Ships in the High Court of Admiralty

When the crew of the *Britannia* successfully brought the *Jesús, Maria, y José* into Bristol in early October 1756, all of the proper protocols seem to have been followed. The Spanish ship's papers were handed over to Charles Davids, the commander of the *Britannia*. The Spanish master, José Pedro Ezenarro, as well as several crew members, were given the preparatory examinations (a standard set of questions about their personal details and the details of the voyage). On 4 October, the examinations and ship's papers were handed over either to Admiralty authorities in Bristol or to the High Court of Admiralty in London (the court records are vague on the location).[72] More than two weeks later, on 22 October,

---

[71] J. Black, *The English Press, 1621–1861* (The History Press, 2001), p. 44.
[72] BL Add MS 36211, Hardwicke Papers, Notes on the *Jesús, Maria, y José*.

Ezenarro put in a claim with Admiralty officials on behalf of the owners of the *Jesús, Maria, y José* and her cargo that the ship and goods were Spanish property, and that Davids should be made to pay all costs and damages resulting from the capture.

According to a certificate signed by the consul of San Sebastián, the owner of the Spanish vessel was Don Juan Ignacio Valez de Lavalla, a resident of San Sebastián and a subject of the Spanish king. A bill of lading, also found amongst the ship's papers, declared that the cargo was shipped by Don Francisco Gonzales of La Coruña and consigned to Don Pedro Larralde Dieusigny of San Sebastián. Ezenarro filed his claim in the names of Valez de Lavalla and Larralde. Davids's counterclaim, filed on or around 23 November, was that the ship's papers proved that, at the time of seizure, the ship was not a Spanish ship, and that the goods belonged to the French East India Company. David's claim also asserted that the *Jesús, Maria, y José* was bound for a port in France and that the goods had been placed onto the ship directly from a French East Indies ship without being first landed in Spain – a detail that would be very important when it came to the decision taken by the Court of Prize Appeal. The ship and goods, David's insisted, should be condemned as lawful prize. Many of the arguments presented in the High Court of Admiralty, and later in the Court of Prize Appeal, would focus on whether the men named by Ezenarro were, in fact, the true owners of the ship and property or, whether, as Davids claimed, they belonged to French subjects.

Prize court bureaucracy moved slowly, and the plaintiffs had to wait a month after Davids's claim before their case was heard in the High Court of Admiralty. The judge of the High Court was Sir Thomas Salusbury, who enjoyed the contempt of Lord Hardwicke when it came to his legal abilities. However, as Salusbury was appointed for life, he decided the outcome of all cases brought before the High Court during the Seven Years' War. In the case of the *Jesús, Maria, y José*, his decision left both parties wanting. The saltpetre, being named in the treaty of 1667 as contraband, was condemned as lawful prize, and the seizure, therefore, justified. The rest of the goods and the ship were returned to Ezenarro, but he was condemned to pay expenses, which, after three months in port and with court fees, would have been considerable.[73] Given the outcome of the case, it is not surprising that the participants chose to appeal the decision handed down by Salusbury. Ezenarro lodged his appeal with the Court of Prize Appeal on 14 April 1758. The court records do not

[73] Ibid.

stipulate why it took approximately one year and three months for the Spaniard to appeal his case. However, given that he owned neither the ship nor the cargo, it is likely that he had to return to Spain and consult with his employers before returning to try his luck in the appellate court. Assuming that Ezenarro was not footing the bill or, at least, not all of it, Valez de Lavalla and Larralde would have had to pay the considerable court and retainer fees without any guarantee that the decision would go their way. In a worst-case scenario, if the decision were to go completely against them (i.e. the ship and all goods were condemned), they would have been liable to pay all of Davids's legal expenses, lose the ship, and lose the value of the cargo. By the same token, Davids could have ended up in a similar scenario and have had to pay all of the Spaniards' expenses and 'losses' (which in this case would have been the net value of an original completed voyage). The decision to appeal was not one to be made lightly, and a lag time of several months was not uncommon.

Whilst those involved in the case of the *Jesús, María, y José* were readying their appeal, the British privateer *Tartar* sailed into Bristol with her recently acquired prize, the *San Juan Baptista*. On 22 June 1757, the master of the Spanish ship, José Arteaga, was given the preparatory examinations. The ship's papers, along with the examinations, were submitted to the High Court of Admiralty in London on 27 July, by the captain of the *Tartar*, John Shaw. On the same day, Arteaga submitted a claim to the High Court on his behalf and on behalf of Don Joachim de Irumbarbia as joint owners of the *San Juan Baptista*. The claim was also submitted on behalf of Don Vicente de Zavaleta as the owner of the cargo. An important part of the Spanish argument was to contest the manner in which the preparatory examinations had been administered, and to declare that Arteaga, his mate, and one sailor, had been intimidated by the long examination and forced to falsely depose that the cargo was owned by Frenchmen. Arteaga also stated that, in the same examination, the bills of lading, which named Don Vicente de Zavaleta of San Sebastián as the sole owner of the cargo, were true and accurate.[74] In addition to pointing out the glaring contradiction in the examinations, the Spanish claimed that the ship and goods belonged to Spaniards, had been purchased in Spain, carried all the correct passes as prescribed by the treaty of 1667, and should, therefore, be released with costs and damages to be paid by Captain Shaw.[75]

The arguments put forward on behalf of the *Tartar* were that the bills of lading were false as alleged in the examination of Arteaga, and that the

---

[74] BL Add MS 36208, Hardwicke Papers, Notes on the *San Juan Baptista*, ff. 246–67.
[75] Ibid.

passes on board the ship did not adhere to the form prescribed by the 1667 treaty. The privateers also claimed that the goods not only belonged to Frenchmen but, also, were put directly onto the *San Juan Baptista* from a French East Indies ship without first being landed in Spain. Shaw's contention was entirely at odds with the Spanish claim of ownership and cargo origin. The final argument put forward on behalf of the British privateer was that the voyage was unlawful because French East India goods, according to French law, could only be legally imported into France by a Frenchman and, as the ship was destined for a French port, the goods must belong to Frenchmen.[76] The parallels with the reasoning behind the Rule of the War of 1756 are fairly clear. Mercantilist-influenced laws did not allow French East India goods to be imported by foreigners, so if the voyage of the *San Juan Baptista* was legally sailing to a French port, the goods must belong to Frenchmen. If the French were using Spanish ships to tranship (taking goods directly from one ship and placing them into another without changing the destination or ownership of the goods) and to disguise their goods in order to avoid capture, then the Spanish ship could be accused of violating the spirit of Spanish neutrality. The hope of the *Tartar*'s crew was that both the ship and goods would be condemned by the High Court as lawful prize.

The case of the *San Juan Baptista* was heard by the High Court of Admiralty on 27 September 1757, four-and-a-half months after it had been captured. The judge, Sir Thomas Salusbury, condemned the cargo as lawful prize for being part of a French East India voyage and French property. The ship, however, was declared to be a Spanish ship and was restored to its owners. Because the capture had been deemed lawful, costs were to be paid by the Spaniards.[77] Without hesitation, Arteaga lodged an appeal. The court records are unclear as to when, exactly, the Spanish appeal was lodged, but it was very soon after the initial condemnation. It is possible that, as part owner of the ship, Arteaga, unlike Ezenarro, felt more comfortable lodging an appeal without first corresponding with the other owner of his ship, Irumbarbia, and with Zavaleta, owner of the cargo.

The *San Juan Baptista*'s appeal was lodged on three grounds. The first was that the goods were Spanish, as proved by the ship's papers, and that the coerced testimony of a witness through intimidation did not invalidate that fact. The second contention was that, even if the cargo of the ship had belonged to an enemy of Britain, it would have been protected

[76] Ibid.   [77] Ibid.

by being carried in a Spanish ship, an argument which invoked the concept of 'free ships make free goods', which could be justified using either the Anglo-Dutch treaty or the Anglo-Spanish treaty.[78] The third ground was that it did not matter who owned the cargo before it was brought to Spain, because once it was on Spanish soil and lawfully purchased, the property became Spanish.[79] This third argument, much like the one presented in the case of the *Jesús, Maria, y José*, presupposed that the goods in the *San Juan Baptista* were not taken directly out of a French East India ship whilst at anchor. It was a legal question of transhipment that was partly rooted in Hardwicke's Rule of the War of 1756. At the time the appeal was first lodged, the Rule of the War of 1756 had not yet come to fruition through the cases of the *Maria Theresa* and subsequent Dutch ships, but it had by the time the case was heard by the Court of Prize Appeal in 1759, and both Charles Pratt and George Hay (two of the advocates involved in the cases of the *Maria Theresa* and the *America*) worked as advocates on the case.[80] If the court accepted Captain Shaw's argument that the goods were taken from a French ship, then any ruling would have to address the issue of transhipping French goods in Spanish bottoms and would, consequently, be a reflection of Britain's position on the limits of Spanish neutrality and the wider applicability of the precedents set by the Dutch cases. Either a liberal or constrictive ruling on Spain's rights to tranship French goods under the banner of neutrality had the potential to enrage the Spanish Court or the British privateering lobby. If the court rejected Captain Shaw's argument, it would not have to make a ruling on transhipment but would still have to address the question of 'free ships, free goods' and therefore, again, make a ruling on the limitations of Spanish neutrality as it had done on Dutch neutrality with the cases of the *Maria Theresa* and the *America*.

Captain Shaw welcomed the Spanish appeal, as he believed that the ship, as well as the goods, should have been condemned but, unlike the captain of the *Britannia* in the case of the captured *Jesús, Maria, y José*, he did not lodge his own cross-appeal. Hoping to see costs and cargo restored, the Spaniards involved in the case of the *San Juan Baptista* had to wait about a year and ten months for their case to be heard in the Court of Prize Appeal.

---

[78] See the Introduction for an explanation of 'free ships, free goods'. As stated in the previous chapter, Article 38 of the Anglo-Spanish treaty of 1667 granted Spanish subjects the same privileges as those granted by Anglo-Dutch treaties.

[79] BL Add MS 36208, Hardwicke Papers, Notes on the *San Juan Baptista*, ff. 246–67.

[80] Ibid.

Death Comes for the Ambassador

Anglo-Spanish Diplomacy and the San Juan Baptista *in the Court of Prize Appeal*

A Death Hardly Noted

Whilst the British public had been concerned with the plight of Captain Foster and the *Antigallican* crew, the cases of the *San Juan Baptista* and the *Jesús, Maria, y José* were waiting to be heard in the Court of Prize Appeal. The months between the appearance of the first *Antigallican* letter on 1 October 1757 and the first appellate hearings for the *San Juan Baptista* on 12 and 15 July 1759 were eventful in the realm of Anglo-Spanish relations. The death of Sir Benjamin Keene in the first part of December 1757 was a severe blow to the relationship between the two Courts, as were the various failed attempts by William Pitt and the new British ambassador to Spain, Lord Bristol, to ease the tensions over maritime seizures.

Pitt and Keene were not the only officials to have complained about illegal seizures in the autumn of 1757. While they had expressed their dissatisfaction over the mistreatment of Captain Foster by Spanish authorities, D'Abreu, the Spanish representative in London, had penned a similar complaint to Pitt in September 1757. He claimed that the king of Spain despaired of the violence still being committed against Spanish ships by British privateers. He wrote that the prize courts in Britain worked too slowly, and that not enough was being done to ensure the illegal activities of the British privateers were dealt with swiftly and efficiently. The letter closed with a fairly passive-aggressive passage in which D'Abreu informed Pitt that he had enclosed a copy of a letter from the vice governor of New York 'in which you will see the agreeable effect of the King's orders [George II's orders to privateers from 1756], in rendering justice to Spanish subjects without them having to make a complaint to His Catholic Majesty [Ferdinand VI]'.[1] D'Abreu's jibe at the courts in Britain was hardly subtle, and was meant, perhaps, to pre-empt the argument often put forward by Pitt and Keene that the prize

---

[1] TNA PRO 30/8/92, Letter from D'Abreu to Pitt, 9 September 1757.

courts worked slowly because they were thorough, and because of the
nature of the prize system. If a Vice Admiralty court across the Atlantic
could produce justice to the satisfaction of Spanish merchants, why could
the courts in London not do the same? If Pitt responded directly to
D'Abreu, there is no record of it in his papers, and his opportunity to
address D'Abreu's accusations with Keene and Wall was cut short by the
news of Keene's death at Madrid on 15 December 1757.[2] The death of
this most experienced and trusted ambassador and colleague of Wall
heralded a further and steeper decline in Anglo-Spanish negotiations
over neutrality.

There was very little sentimentality about Keene's death in the correspondence of those who knew and worked with him. Pitt, Wall, and
Newcastle hardly seemed to mark the occasion; and only Hardwicke, in
an undated note to a collection of papers relating to Anglo-Spanish
negotiations, made a direct reference to his death and character as a
brilliant ambassador.[3] However, one of London's more popular newspapers within the maritime sector, *Lloyd's Evening Post*, used the occasion
of Keene's death to propagate both anti-Spanish and anti-French sentiment. In the edition of 17 February 1758, there is an article entitled 'Part
of a letter from a Jesuit at Madrid, to his correspondent at Frankfort,
Jan. 16.'[4] There is no mention of who the Jesuit is or why the newspaper
had his letter, and it is possible that it was merely a device to lend
credence to the article. The author claimed that Keene's death led to
new intrigues in the Spanish Court and that ministers from both France
and Austria were vying for the influence once held by Keene. In a
conspiratorial tone, the author wrote that he did not know in which
direction the Spanish Court would lean, but that 'the vast warlike preparations in all the ports of the kingdom, give room to think that it will not
long remain neuter, but declare in favour of Vienna and Versailles'.[5]

The allusion to 'vast warlike preparations' happening in Spanish ports
was an ill-informed exaggeration at best. Spanish production of ships of
the line had decreased steadily since 1754, in large part due to Keene's
influence on Wall, who managed the navy budget. According to Kuethe
and Andrien, Spain had produced fifteen ships of the line in 1754, and
only three in both 1757 and 1758.[6] Even had Spain produced a

---

[2] R. Lodge (ed.), *The Private Correspondence of Sir Benjamin Keene* (Cambridge University Press, 1933), p. xxiii.
[3] NYPL Hardwicke Papers 126, Note on the Character of Sr Ben. Keene, no date.
[4] *Lloyd's Evening Post and British Chronicle*, 15–17 February 1758, no. 91.   [5] Ibid.
[6] A. J. Kuethe and K. Andrien, *The Spanish Atlantic World in the Eighteenth Century: War and the Bourbon Reforms, 1713–1796* (Cambridge University Press, 2014), p. 214.

significant number of warships, there were not enough sailors to man them.[7] The article in *Lloyd's Evening Post* ended with a damning accusation of Ricardo Wall, claiming that it was 'looked upon as a thing certain, that Mr. Wall keeps his place only because he has entered into the views of France'.[8] The implications behind the accusation would have been very concerning for a reader interested in Anglo-Spanish relations. If Wall had to shift from supporting a position of neutrality to that of a French ally in order to keep his ministerial position, then it would be reasonable to assume that the Spanish king and his Court now looked upon France as an ally, and upon Britain as an enemy. Furthermore, if the shift in the king and Court's attitude was tied to the death of Keene, as the article implied, then it was only Keene's diplomatic efforts which had kept Spain friendly towards Britain. Whilst there was truth in the notion that Keene had been instrumental in preserving Britain's relationship with Spain, and truth in the speculation that Wall would now alter his support for Spanish neutrality, Keene's death did not precipitate an imminent rupture between the two states; war was still almost four years away. The article in *Lloyd's Evening Post* was likely capitalising on Keene's death as an opportunity to fear-monger and spread anti-Spanish feeling amongst London's maritime community. It is true, however, that Keene's death was a great loss to Britain's ability to negotiate with the Spanish Court. The man sent to replace Keene, Lord Bristol, was an inferior diplomat who, as will be shown, was less trusted by Pitt, Hardwicke, and Newcastle to defend Britain's interests in the Spanish Court and to keep Spain as a neutral actor in the Anglo-French conflict.

Part of Keene's success as an ambassador to Spain during the war was due, in addition to his comfort with the Spanish language and culture, to his training in the law, which he received first at Cambridge and then at Leiden.[9] Keene had understood the importance of engendering Spanish faith in Britain's prize court system as a safeguard for Spanish neutral rights. He had tried, through his good rapport with Wall, to convince the Spanish minister that grievances over maritime neutrality were best addressed by the Court of Prize Appeal, even though the process was often long and drawn out. Keene, Pitt, and Hardwicke worked towards creating a system where the limits of legal authority at sea (preventing abuses of neutrality by British privateers and Spanish merchants while at the same prosecuting the legal destruction of French commerce) were to

---

[7] Ibid. p. 198.
[8] *Lloyd's Evening Post and British Chronicle*, 15–17 February 1758, no. 91.
[9] Lodge (ed.), *The Private Correspondence of Sir Benjamin Keene*, p. xi.

be consistently addressed by the Court of Prize Appeal. What Keene failed to do before his death was to convince Wall that the discretionary judicial authority employed in the Court of Prize Appeal was the best method of addressing the limits of legal authority at sea and would eventually result in the resolution of Spanish displeasure over ship seizures. Lord Bristol, in contrast to Keene, did not have international diplomatic experience or the legal training enjoyed by the former ambassador. He had a brief career in the army before moving into diplomacy. He was unequipped to navigate the delicate political negotiations necessary to carry on Keene's work in the realm of international maritime law and neutral rights as ambassador to Spain.

The Untested Ambassador

Lord Bristol did not arrive in Madrid until late August 1758, more than eight months after Keene's death and did not meet with Ricardo Wall until 11 September. At their first meeting, the Spanish minister expressed his delight and renewed hope (presumably for Anglo-Spanish negotiations) now that Bristol had arrived in Spain.[10] One of the first written instructions that Bristol received from Pitt, dated 1 August, either just before he left Britain or soon after he arrived in Spain, concerned, in large part, a memorandum which Pitt had received from D'Abreu on 16 June 1758. D'Abreu's epistle contained, as usual, a complaint about the behaviour of British privateers. In this particular case, two Spanish fishing ships from San Sebastián, sailing to Newfoundland, were captured by two British privateers. D'Abreu professed that he could understand no reason for the capture, as the Spanish ships had all of the passes required which granted fishing rights by the Treaty of Utrecht, the treaty of 1667, and the treaty of 1721.[11] Having declared the innocence of the Spanish ships D'Abreu wrote:

I ask your excellency [Pitt] to arrange the most prompt and immediate restitution of these ships, and the reparation of all the incurred expenses ... The recourse through the courts in this kingdom is long ... one cannot count on it but very little for compensation ... I work constantly to bring to conclusion through appeal, all the cases that are judged by Doctors' Commons against the Spanish.[12]

It is interesting to note that, at the time that D'Abreu wrote his memorandum, no Spanish ships had yet come before the Court of Prize

---

[10] D. Alarcia Téllez, *El Ministerio Wall: La 'España discreta' del 'ministro olvidado'* (Ediciones de Historia, 2012), p. 98.
[11] TNA PRO 30/8/92, Letter from D'Abreu to Pitt, 16 June 1758.   [12] Ibid.

Appeal. If D'Abreu was constantly working to bring Spanish ships before the appellate court, then he was failing to convince owners or captains to do so; a possible indication of how little faith Spanish merchants had in the appellate process. The Spanish minister's request could have had two meanings. Either he was asking Pitt to have the two Spanish ships released extrajudicially with payment to the Spanish for incurred costs, or he was asking Pitt to intervene in the proceedings of the prize courts in order to speed up the process and to ensure a favourable outcome for the Spanish. In the case of the former, the move was not unheard of. Earlier in the war, Newcastle had interfered and paid privateers to release their Dutch prizes and not bring the cases to court. Whilst Pitt could have followed in Newcastle's footsteps, due to his good reputation amongst the privateers, he was also able to threaten them with a general reminder that, should they bring in illegal prizes, they would pay for it dearly in the courts. Such a threat could, theoretically, have served to induce privateers to drop certain prize cases.[13] There is seemingly no record of Pitt having directly asked or ordered a privateer to drop a court case until August 1759, and he clearly did not do so in the case of the two Spanish ships referred to in D'Abreu's letter, as it was their defence of the right to fish off Newfoundland that would later inflame the controversy over access to fisheries between the two Courts.[14]

If D'Abreu had instead meant to imply that Pitt should intervene in the prize court proceedings, the implication behind his request was that without direct interference from a British minister such as Pitt, the Spanish ships would not seek justice because of the long duration of cases in the prize courts and the great expense that could be accrued if the lowers courts or the appellate court did not find in their favour. The Court of Prize Appeal, therefore, could not be counted on by the Spanish to grant proper compensation or uphold Spanish neutral rights. By asserting that he worked closely with the Spanish cases that went through Doctors' Commons, D'Abreu gave himself an air of speaking from constant and direct experience which had left him with little faith in the British prize court system. Pitt made sure, in his letter to Lord Bristol about D'Abreu's memorandum, that the new minister was well equipped to face D'Abreu's master, Ricardo Wall (whose own faith in the British legal system was at a low ebb at this point in the war).

[13] R. Pares, *Colonial Blockade and Neutral Rights 1739–1763* (Porcupine Press, 1975), p. 70.
[14] R. Pares, *War and Trade in the West Indies 1739–1763* (Frank Cass and Co., 1963), p. 563.

Pitt's letter began with what was possibly a vote of no-confidence in Bristol's untested abilities as the ambassador to Spain. An opening overview of the logwood-cutting negotiations culminated in instructions not to discuss or make comments of any kind on that subject to anyone in the Spanish Court.[15] Negotiations between Pitt and Wall over the logwood affair had reached a stalemate by the end of 1757, when both ministers refused to grant concessions over their perceived rights to the Moskito Shore.[16] If Pitt remained unwilling to negotiate until Wall conceded, it is possible that he did not want to renew the antagonism over logwood cutting when Bristol was first sent to Spain. However, given how much free rein Keene had generally been granted in handling all Anglo-Spanish negotiations at the Spanish Court, it seems odd that Bristol would be given such a heavy restriction, unless Pitt did not fully trust in his abilities to firmly, but diplomatically, defend British interests. Whatever Pitt's motivation, Bristol adhered to his orders, and logwood affairs were not discussed again until 1760.[17]

The second part of Pitt's letter contained instructions relevant to D'Abreu's memorandum, prize courts, and fishing rights in Newfoundland. Having described the memorandum and the case of the two Spanish ships with passes to fish in Newfoundland, Pitt went on to explain that the Treaty of Utrecht granted the Spanish only 'such privileges, as they are able to make claim to by right'[18] and that the Treaty of Madrid from 1721 confirmed the Treaty of Utrecht but did not grant any additional rights. As far as Pitt was concerned, the Spanish had no claim to the Newfoundland fishery. He closed the section on fisheries with the observation that D'Abreu's memorandum was entirely founded on the complaints from the two Spanish ships which had been detained, and that D'Abreu had received no orders from the Spanish Court to raise the point with British ministers. Pitt believed, erroneously, that the ministers at the Spanish Court would not support D'Abreu in his complaint about fishing rights.[19]

The last, and longest, section of Pitt's letter was about privateering and the prize courts. Bristol was informed that all of Keene's papers that had to do with British privateering were being kept for him, and that he should familiarize himself with the negotiations conducted by the previous ambassador. Pitt wrote that

---

[15] BL Add MS 36807, Hardwicke Papers, Letter from Pitt to Bristol, 1 August 1758, ff. 18–27.
[16] Pares, *War and Trade in the West Indies*, p. 553.   [17] Ibid.
[18] BL Add MS 36807, Hardwicke Papers, Letter from Pitt to Bristol, 1 August 1758, ff. 18–27.
[19] Ibid.

His Majesty sees with real concern, the irregularities which many Privateers have, doubtless, committed and no opportunity, that the nature and constitution of this government allows, has been neglected, not only to give the Spanish sufferers all possible satisfaction, by the immediate release of their ships, in such cases where the same could be obtained ...[20]

Pitt's reference to the constitution is likely a response to D'Abreu's request for quick restitution. By overtly stating that everything had been done to satisfy Spanish complaints within the confines of the constitution, Pitt was making it clear to the new ambassador, and by extension, to the Spanish Court, that the release of any Spanish ship would occur only if the process were legal under the 1708 Prize Act, which had taken away the Crown's right to interfere in prize cases outside of the prize court system. However, Pitt also inserted a loophole. By including the vague phrase 'immediate release of their ships, in such cases where the same could be obtained' under the umbrella of instances which conformed to British law, he allowed that extrajudicial releases and political interference in the prize courts (the only two ways to obtain an immediate release given the long processing times of the courts) could occur. Privateers could be persuaded to drop their claims by ministers as long as the 1708 Act was not violated.

The 1708 Act had granted a statutory right to prizes taken by warships or privateers, and took away the Crown's right to control or influence the captors through administrative order.[21] In 1710, the judge of the High Court of Admiralty interpreted the Act as granting captors the right to have prizes prosecuted because it granted them the entirety of the prize after condemnation, and there could be no condemnation without a prosecution. In the same instance, the judge claimed that 'it is not advisable for the crown to interpose so as to discharge proceedings at the instance of a foreign minister, though his representations seem just and reasonable'.[22] This meant that no Crown official could instruct, or command, a privateer to relinquish their claim to a prize. However, if the prize were to be released voluntarily by the captor (with or without some unofficial persuasion from the Crown) then such a release was not in violation of the Act. Hardwicke was never satisfied with this concession to the rights of captors, and wanted to restore the Crown's ability to release captured neutrals without reference to the captors in the Prize Act of 1756 (which renewed the 1708 Act), and the Privateers Act of 1759. He was not successful in either case.[23]

---

[20] Ibid.   [21] Pares, *Colonial Blockade*, p. 66.   [22] Ibid. p. 67.   [23] Ibid. p. 68.

Conveniently for the government, the men assessing and justifying the legality of any extrajudicial releases would likely be either Pitt himself, the Duke of Newcastle (Secretary of the Treasury), Lord Hardwicke (ex-Lord Chancellor), Charles Yorke (Solicitor General), Charles Pratt (Attorney General), Charles Hay (King's Advocate), or Lord Mansfield (Lord Chief Justice of the King's Bench). Since it was, for the most part, also these men who managed the legal and political negotiations with Spain, the decisions on whether to release a Spanish ship through extra-judicial means could be made by balancing the displeasure amongst the British maritime community with the displeasure of the Spanish Court. Whichever decision was taken could be justified through Mansfield and Hardwicke's interpretation of prize law. With Pitt as his guide, Bristol would be able to address concerns put forward by Ricardo Wall about extrajudicial releases by pointing out that Spanish grievances were addressed favourably whenever it was legally possible to do so. Pitt would take great advantage of his own loophole later in the war.

Bristol was also given direct instructions with regard to Wall about D'Abreu's accusation that the proceedings of the Court of Prize Appeal suffered numerous delays. After proclaiming that delays in prize matters occurred in all countries, Pitt wrote that

it were much to be wished, that Mons. Wall would suffer himself to reflect how many British subjects have been referred to the ordinary courts of justice, on occasion of their complaints of illegal capture ... and have been obliged ... to repair to different parts of the Spanish Settlements, to prosecute their causes ... where they have met with such obstructions and delays, that some of these claims are not finally adjusted, at this time, though depending for many years.[24]

Pitt wanted to put Wall on the defensive in order to stem criticism of the highest prize court. By bringing up delays suffered by British subjects due to the removal of cases from the Spanish prize courts to ordinary courts, Bristol could argue that long delays in a court system were natural when dealing with prize affairs. If Wall could be convinced that delays were not purely a British manifestation but, rather, inevitable, due to the inter-national nature of the cases and equity-based judicial process, then delays might cease to be a point of contention between the two countries, and Spanish faith in Britain's ability to protect neutral rights might be increased. As ammunition, Pitt furnished Bristol with the details of two English sailors who had been imprisoned in Spain for offences against Spanish ships, and with the particulars of the *Antigallican* affair.[25]

[24] BL Add MS 36807, Hardwicke Papers, Letter from Pitt to Bristol, 1 August 1758, ff. 18–27.
[25] Ibid.

A Spectre of Death in the Spanish Court

The new British ambassador found no immediate use for Pitt's information and remained unable to answer Pitt's letter until well into September of 1758. This was due to a sudden and extended paralysis in the functioning of the Spanish Court. A few days before Bristol's arrival in Madrid, King Ferdinand's wife, Maria Bárbara de Bragança, died. Though she had been seriously ill since late 1757 from uterine cancer, and her death was not wholly unexpected, the event pushed Ferdinand into ill health and a melancholy retreat at his castle in Villaviciosa in the north of Spain.[26] According to Alarcia, his retreat 'would tie the hands and feet of the Irishman [Wall] in the most critical moment of the war'.[27] Alarcia considers late 1758 a 'critical moment' for the Spanish during the war because Spain's position had become unstable and untenable vis-à-vis its policy of neutrality. He argues that Wall's grievances against Britain had produced little effect on Britain's behaviour towards Spain and that Wall intended to develop a much more bellicose position to prepare Spain for a possible war, as he no longer saw a peaceful way of resolving Anglo-Spanish disagreements. However, the king's retreat and illness put a stop to Wall's foreign policy plans and forced him to focus on domestic affairs, which included the possible return of one of his rivals to court. With his focus shifted to domestic problems, Wall softened his stance with Britain and became more conciliatory. He ceased to prepare for war and sought to buy time for the Court to become functional once again before entertaining war with Britain.[28] Ferdinand's withdrawal after his wife's death plunged the Spanish Court into uncertainty, and there was a direct correlation between the timing of the queen's death and a slightly more conciliatory Wall when it came to Anglo-Spanish grievances.

According to a letter Bristol wrote to Pitt on 25 September 1758, the Spanish king had not left his bed for seven days, and refused to see even his closest ministers, including Arriaga, Eslava, and Wall. He wrote that

The extraordinary situation in which this country now is from the Catholick King's indisposition is the cause that all business is at a stand ... There is a melancholy in the King, which nothing can divert; and such a settled taciturnity prevails, that no directions can be given nor any orders issued.[29]

---

[26] Alarcia, *Ministerio Wall*, p. 97.
[27] Ibid. Original Text: 'atará de pies y manos al irlandés precisamente en el momento más crítico del conflicto'.
[28] Alarcia, *Ministerio Wall*, pp. 94–8.
[29] BL Add MS 3432, Leeds Papers, Letter from Bristol to Pitt, 25 September 1758.

A collateral effect of the king's indisposition was that Wall did not meet with any foreign ministers that week, a change to the custom he had maintained previously throughout the war.

After commenting on the situation at the Spanish Court, Bristol's letter changed tack, and he entered into a diatribe against D'Abreu. Unlike many benign descriptions of the Spanish representative from the beginning of the war, Bristol's description is decidedly hostile. He accused D'Abreu of putting British intentions and actions in the worst light through his correspondence with Wall, and of misconstruing situations to paint Britain as an aggressor against Spain:

I believe that the less is transacted during Mon. D'Abreu's residing in England, the better prospect there will be of coming to a right understanding, and of laying down some plan for the removal of future altercations, and settling the difference now subsisting between the two Crowns.[30]

In support of his contention that negotiations were best done without D'Abreu, he went on to write that Wall and the Spanish Court were not deceived by the Spanish representative's letters, and that his reception when he returned to Madrid would be a cold one. This was one of the first, if not the first, reference to the imminent departure of D'Abreu from his post in London. His replacement, the Conde de Fuentes, had already been chosen, and was accorded the higher-ranking title of ambassador, which gave him more authority to negotiate on behalf of the Spanish Court. Fuentes had been chosen by Wall, as he was his close political ally. In reality, Fuentes was appointed at this time in order to stall negotiations with Britain and buy time for Spain to prepare for war once the Court had recovered from the havoc caused by the queen's death.[31] However, due to the turmoil that would be caused by Ferdinand's own illness and eventual death, Fuentes would not actually be sent to London until late May 1760. Bristol naively painted Fuentes as an ally of Wall and a friend to Britain:

I am impatient for the departure of the Conde de Fuentes; he has often told me that he was convinced, in such negotiations as ours a great deal depended on the representations the different ministers made to their respective courts; harsh conversations might, and ought to be softened, and the private views of Particulars were not to be put in competition with the general good. Allow me, Sir, to say, it would be difficult to decide which of us two is most inclined to promote the union of Our Courts ...[32]

How sincerely Bristol believed his own words is a matter of speculation but, given Fuentes's uncompromising attitude when he did finally arrive

---

[30] Ibid.   [31] Alarcia, *Ministerio Wall*, p. 97.   [32] Ibid.

in London, and his unrestrained desire to go to war with Britain as soon as possible after peace had been declared in 1763,[33] it is difficult to read Bristol's letter without accusing him of naivety. Alarcia goes so far as to claim that Bristol was purposefully duped by Wall and Fuentes to believe in their plan of reconciliation, and to unwittingly aid them in deceiving Pitt, thus buying time for the Spanish Court to put an end to its internal instability before joining France in a war against Britain.[34]

Pleased with the seemingly bright outlook for future Anglo-Spanish negotiations, Bristol ended his long letter to Pitt by laying out his tactics. He hoped first to gain Wall's confidence and trust. How he planned to do this was not revealed. His next step was to avoid, at first, matters which might anger Wall (such as the prize courts and the Newfoundland fishery) but to begin to discuss them as their friendship grew and 'lay before him [Wall] the series of established facts, as well as the uncontrovertable [*sic*] evidence, you have so completely furnished me with, to maintain all his majesty's just rights'.[35] However, his plan, he admitted was predicated on D'Abreu no longer being in London: 'at the same time I must own I have but little hopes of success, 'til Mons. D'Abreu's dispatches do not come to thwart all my attempts'.[36] His plans did not play out as he hoped and, unfortunately for Bristol, it would be more than a year until D'Abreu left London, by which time a new, more aggressive, and anti-British monarch would be sitting on the Spanish throne. If Alarcia's analysis of Wall and Fuentes's intentions is correct, then Bristol's plan was doomed from the start with or without D'Abreu's continued presence in London. The implications for negotiations over neutrality were bleak, because Bristol did not have Wall's trust, and with no Spanish appeals yet adjudicated in the Court of Prize Appeal there was no way to assure Wall that neutrality was still the best course for protecting Spanish interests in the maritime sphere.

Bristol's bright tone and cheer continued through the middle of November 1758. He wrote to Pitt of Wall's friendship and even 'affectionate behaviour'.[37] However, he also hinted at the internal anxieties Wall was facing which lend credence to Alarcia's contention that Wall was only being friendly to the new ambassador in order to buy time. Bristol described Wall as lamenting the Spanish king's indisposition but also dreading a change in the monarchy. He explained that, should

[33] AHN ESTADO 4119, Dispatch from Prince Maserano to Conde de Fuentes, 1764.
[34] Alarcia, *Ministerio Wall*, p. 98.
[35] BL Add MS 3432, Leeds Papers, Letter from Bristol to Pitt, 25 September 1758.
[36] Ibid.
[37] NYPL Hardwicke Papers 129, Letter from Bristol to Pitt, 13 November 1758.

Ferdinand die, the queen dowager, Elizabeth Farnese, would return to the Spanish Court, and with her would come the exiled minister, the Marquis de la Ensenada. Farnese's influence and place in the Spanish Court had ended when Ferdinand took the throne because, though she was Phillip V's widow, she was not Ferdinand's mother. She was, however, the mother of Charles III, Ferdinand's half-brother and heir. Ensenada's exile and fall from grace in 1754 had been orchestrated primarily by Keene and Wall. Ensenada believed that Britain was Spain's greatest rival, and that the two countries could not have compatible interests in the Americas.[38] As such, his return, along with that of the like-minded and overbearing queen dowager, was not desirable for either Britain or Wall. Until Wall's domestic concerns were allayed (some time after the ascension of Charles III), he continued to be portrayed by Bristol as Britain's greatest friend. Bristol quoted Wall in a letter to Pitt in order to demonstrate Wall's attitude:

believe me that before we had done, you and I will accommodate all things, by putting them upon all good footing, to the mutual advantage of our cause and the contentment of both our Royal masters ...[39]

Such professions of goodwill did not last, and there is a note scribbled by Lord Hardwicke on Bristol's surviving copy of the letter quoted above where he wrote 'Mr. Wall appears to me by no means to have made good these propositions in the next Reign [Charles III's reign].'[40] If Wall was indeed buying time to resolve internal affairs by claiming to favour neutrality, then he performed his deceit admirably. It was within the atmosphere of uncertainty in the Spanish Court, and an atmosphere of hope created by Bristol in the British Court, that the *San Juan Baptista* came before the Court of Prize Appeal in the summer of 1759.

Wall's Ire

In terms of prize affairs, the British ministry spent the early months of 1759 discussing, drafting, and passing what would come to be known as the Privateers Act of 1759. The Act had been drafted mainly as a way to appease Dutch anger over the conduct of British privateers, but the new restraints it imposed on privateers would benefit any neutral ships. However, it is important to note that there is no indication that British ministers intended for the Privateers Act to appease Spain. In fact, Wall

---

[38] Kuethe and Andrien, *Spanish Atlantic World*, p. 197.
[39] NYPL Hardwicke Papers 129, Letter from Bristol to Pitt, 13 November 1758.
[40] Ibid.

had made it abundantly clear in his communications with the British Court that he was not interested in promises of future better conduct. Wall was interested in actions that would right the wrongs already committed by British privateers in the current war, and the only way that could be addressed was through the release of captured Spanish ships, not simply the creation of a new Act that restrained future behaviour.

The wider Spanish Court had nothing to say about the passing of the Privateers Act. Consumed by the illness and decline of Ferdinand VI, the Spanish ministers never mentioned or discussed the Privateers Act or the British contention that it was created in the service of protecting the ships of neutral nations. Part of the reason the Act had little impact on negotiations over neutral rights with Spain was that it was a corrective measure that limited the freedoms of privateers rather than address the perceived failings of the prize court system. Its most significant curb on privateers was to nullify all commissions that had been granted to vessels under 100 tons burthen with fewer than forty men. Future commissions for such vessels were at the discretion of the Lords of the Admiralty.[41] Unfortunately for Anglo-Spanish relations, negotiations over neutral rights had never really focused on how privateers could be prevented from illegally capturing neutral ships. The focus had always been on the British prize court system, and the Court of Prize Appeal, in particular, as the protector of Dutch and Spanish neutral rights. By 1759, there were very few ships being captured, because French seaborne commerce had been largely destroyed, but the Court of Prize Appeal had yet to demonstrate to the Spanish government that it was capable of protecting Spain's rights as a neutral nation.

About a month after the Privateers Act was passed, and three days before the *San Juan Baptista* came before the Court of Prize Appeal, Wall wrote a letter to D'Abreu that clearly showed his annoyance at D'Abreu's handling of Spanish affairs, his continued preoccupation with the Spanish Court's internal upheaval, and his ever-present concern over the failure of the British prize courts to restore Spanish ships. The letter was a response to one sent by D'Abreu in June 1759 about the British conquest of Guadeloupe and his subsequent conversation with the Duke of Newcastle in which, according to D'Abreu, Newcastle had touted the advantages that Britain's allies might derive from such conquests. Newcastle had also expressed a desire to 'cultivate' Spain's friendship.[42] The subtext of Newcastle's comments was not subtle; as Britain made

[41] David Starkey, *British Privateering Enterprise in the Eighteenth Century* (Exeter University Press, 1990), p. 163.
[42] TNA PRO 30/8/92, Letter from Wall to D'Abreu, 9 July 1759.

territorial gains against the French in the West Indies, it would behove Spain to consider carefully whether Britain or France would make the better ally. Newcastle's posturing was not without some merit; Britain had yet to enjoy the successes against France that would be achieved later in 1759, but British forces had captured Louisbourg (in Nova Scotia) in July 1758, Gorée (in West Africa) in December 1758, and Guadeloupe (in the West Indies) in January 1759. French West Indian commerce had also fallen to less than a quarter of its pre-war value by the end of 1758 and would fall even further by 1760.[43] Wall's window for an advantageous war against Britain was shrinking.

D'Abreu's letter had been sent by an express messenger rather than through the normal channels of correspondence, and it was this aberration, or the speculation that might arise in both Courts over what news would necessitate an express, which incensed Wall the most. The minister wrote with thinly veiled displeasure:

I am extremely surprised at your not waiting for the regular post, and at your dispatching a messenger upon so frivolous an occasion. In our melancholy situation, it can only serve to engage the curiosity of the foreign ministers, who are informed of this arrival.[44]

Wall's reproach was yet another vote of no confidence in D'Abreu's ability to manage Spanish interests at the British Court. The 'melancholy situation' was a clear reference to Ferdinand's worsening illness; he would be dead within a month of Wall's writing this letter and his death would cause a dramatic upheaval and change of dynamics in the Spanish Court. Given the precarious, if seemingly friendly, state of relations between the two Courts in 1758–9, Wall's desire to keep rumour and speculation about the stability of Anglo-Spanish relations in check was understandable. Speculation about possible Franco-Spanish or Anglo-Spanish alliances arising in all the Courts of Europe, at a time when the Spanish government was unstable, could complicate Wall's relationship with other European ministers wanting to know whose side Spain was going to take.

Wall continued his short letter with a second admonishment that demonstrated both his lack of faith in D'Abreu and his belief that it was Pitt, and Pitt alone, who ruled in the British government. In reference to D'Abreu's conversation with the Duke of Newcastle, Wall '[w]ish[ed] … that you had discovered with certainty, whether or not Mr. Pitt who is in reality the ministry thinks in the same manner with

[43] D. Baugh, *The Global Seven Years' War, 1754–1763* (Pearson, 2011), p. 321.
[44] TNA PRO 30/8/92, Letter from Wall to D'Abreu, 9 July 1759.

the Duke'.[45] By expressing that he 'wished' D'Abreu had sought out Pitt's opinion on the important matter of Anglo-Spanish friendship, he was making it clear that D'Abreu should have known Pitt's mind before rushing an express to Wall because, in Wall's opinion, it was Pitt who would guide the British ministry's actions.

Despite Newcastle's protestations of mutual and beneficial friendship, Wall remained sceptical of how Britain's calls for friendship would translate into action. None of the grievances that existed between the two Courts had been resolved. The few concessions that Britain had granted at the start of the war in the realm of prize affairs had had little effect on the actions of privateers or the prize courts. Wall expressed his scepticism to D'Abreu at the end of his scathing letter: 'If they really wish to live in amity with us, there are sufficient opportunities of showing it instead of the fair words they are so prodigal of, by restoring the great number of vessels so shamefully taken by their privateers ...'[46] Though it is unlikely Wall was making a reference to the recent Privateers Act, his letters serve as an example of the unsubstantiated promises which Wall believed the British ministry gave out so freely, but never translated into a discernible benefit for Spain. At this point in the war, with the logwood affair still off the negotiation table, only the restoration of Spanish ships would satisfy Wall and convince him that heeding Britain's calls for friendship was in Spain's interest. Ships would have to be restored by the Court of Prize Appeal if Wall was to be won over to trust the British prize system and Britain's commitment to Spanish neutrality.

The Spanish Appellate Case

A few days after Wall penned his letter to D'Abreu, the Lords Commissioners for Prize Appeal had the chance to restore a Spanish ship and demonstrate that the abuses of British privateers could be corrected by the highest authority in the British prize court system. On 12 July 1759, at eleven in the morning, the case of the *San Juan Baptista* was heard before the Court of Prize Appeal. There is no record of which commissioners were in attendance other than Lord Hardwicke. The absence of such a record is partly due to the fact that there was very little discussion of the case before the sentence was handed down. Lord Hardwicke's notes are minimal, and do not contain the opinions of other members of the court. A record of which commissioners attended is also missing because, unlike the cases of many of the Dutch ships that came

---

[45] Ibid.   [46] Ibid.

before the Court of Prize Appeal, there was seemingly no mention of the case in British newspapers either on the day it went to court, or in the preceding or subsequent days.

The two advocates who represented the Spanish Appellants (José Arteaga, Don Joachim de Irumbarbia, and Don Vincente de Zavaleta) were Dr Charles Pratt, Attorney General, and Dr Richard Smalbroke. The arguments they presented before the Court of Prize Appeal were derived from Articles 13, 14, 23, and 24 of the Anglo-Spanish treaty of 1667, and from Article 17 of the 1713 Treaty of Utrecht. However, the issue at the heart of the appellate case was whether the goods found on board the *San Juan Baptista* were purchased in Spain, as claimed by the Appellants, or whether they had been put on board the Spanish ship directly from a French East India ship, as claimed by the British captain, John Shaw, the Respondent in the case. It was, in other words, a question of transhipment.

After stating the facts of the case from the Spanish point of view (i.e. that the goods had been purchased and loaded in Spain) Pratt and Smalbroke unleashed a list of articles from the treaty of 1667 which they claimed had been violated by the British privateers. They first called on Article 13, which stated that if the lawfulness of a ship's voyage of either nation were questioned when met at sea only 'Letters of safe Conduct, or other papers of their intended voyage, and certificate of their cargo'[47] needed to be produced in order for the ship to remain unmolested and allowed to pass. Article 14, which went hand in hand with Article 13, clearly stipulated that ships of war and privateers were to remain outside of cannon-shot of the merchant vessel being questioned, and that only a boat with, at most, three men could be sent to ask for a ship's papers. Should the veracity of a ship's papers be doubted, a certificate signed by the king (Spanish in this case) would further authenticate the voyage.[48] The Spaniards' advocates claimed that they had adhered strictly to both articles by having on board one single bill of lading, one expired pass from the Spanish king for a previous voyage, a current pass signed by the Spanish king for the voyage in question, and one muster book. Since these documents had been presented to the privateer and were in accordance with the treaty, the *San Juan Baptista* should have been allowed to continue her voyage to Nantes unmolested.

The point of Articles 13 and 14, within the larger context of the treaty, was to avoid any controversy or violence over the visiting and searching of ships by limiting the contact of the ships' crews, and through a

[47] BL Add MS 36208, Hardwicke Papers, Notes on the *San Juan Baptista*, ff. 246–67.
[48] Ibid.

verification system that did not require a ship to be actively searched for contraband or hidden documentation. Unfortunately, the system put in place by the treaty of 1667 ultimately relied on mutual trust, especially during times when one of the countries was at war. The trust implied that Spanish and British merchants would not carry multiple sets of documentation which masked the carriage of contraband goods, and that the documentation reflected what was actually in the hold and who owned it. Trust also meant that privateers and ships of war would not board a merchant ship without cause and search until they found a 'reason' for taking the ship as prize. Without this trust between Spanish and British sailors, it was impossible for the treaty to preserve Spanish neutrality at sea.

The second argument put forward by Pratt and Smalbroke revolved around Articles 23 and 24 of the 1667 treaty. Article 23 was the same article which had proved so contentious in Anglo-Spanish affairs in the summer of 1756, when Charles Fox, one of the Secretaries of State at the time, conceded that Wall's interpretation (which deemed all goods that were not designated as contraband to be free) was the correct one. In the case before the appellate court, the advocates conceded that any contraband goods were liable to confiscation.[49] However, they claimed that any contraband goods were to be taken out of the offending vessel and then proceeded against separately in court, leaving the ship itself, and any other goods found within, free and able to sail away: 'but so as the ship itself, and the other free and allowed goods found in such ship, shall in no wise be seized or confiscated on that account'.[50] This wording was very close to the French-language version of the same portion of the article put forward by Wall and accepted by Fox: 'toutes les autres marchandises seront libres et affranchies'.[51] In relation to the events in the case of the *San Juan Baptista*, both versions of Article 23 would have put Captain Shaw's seizure of the Spanish ship in contravention of the 1667 treaty. No contraband goods were found on board and any other goods found on board could not be confiscated and seized as prize. None of the East Indian goods that made up the *San Juan Baptista*'s cargo were on the list of contraband goods from the treaty. Thus, the *San Juan Baptista* and her cargo should have been left unmolested by Captain Shaw and the crew of the *Tartar*. The interpretation and wording of Article 23 used by the Spaniards' advocates was the acknowledged correct interpretation according to both the British and Spanish Courts, due to Fox's

---

[49] Which were explicitly named in Article 24 and are broadly covered by the term *war supplies*.
[50] Ibid.   [51] Translation: 'all the other merchandise shall be free and allowed'.

concession in the 1756 dispute. It is likely that Hardwicke would have been aware of the dispute and its implication upon the legality of the *San Juan Baptista*'s capture.

The final treaty-based argument that was presented on behalf of the Spaniards was grounded in the Anglo-French Treaty of Utrecht of 1713 and the Anglo-Spanish treaty of 1713. The latter was a crucial piece of legislation which, as quoted by Pratt and Smalbroke, granted to both signatories 'the same privileges, liberties, immunities, as to all ... goods, and merchandizes, ships, freight, seamen, navigation and commerce; and shall have the like favour in all things as the subjects of France'.[52] In other words, Spaniards could claim the same benefits as the French were given by the Anglo-French Treaty of Utrecht. In the specific case of the *San Juan Baptista*, the advocates interpreted the 1713 Anglo-Spanish treaty as applying to the privileges granted to the French by Article 17 of the Anglo-French Treaty of Utrecht, which stipulated that ships of either country would enjoy 'liberty and security' when trading from any port to a port deemed to belong to an enemy of either sovereign or from one enemy port to another. The article also stipulated that neither the ownership nor the nationality of the cargo made any difference to the 'liberty and security' of the ships in which it was laden:

> it is now stipulated concerning Ships and Goods, that free ships shall also give a freedom to goods, and that every thing shall be deemed to be free and exempt which shall be found on board the ships belonging to the subjects of either of the Confederates, although the whole lading, or any part thereof, should appertain to the enemies of either of their Majesties, contraband goods being always excepted ...[53]

By using the Treaty of Utrecht, Pratt and Smalbroke challenged the Court of Prize Appeal to make a statement on the Grotian maxim of 'free ships make free goods' and whether it would apply to Spanish ships. As stated before, Grotius's maxim was really about the *presumption* of ownership. The goods found on board a ship were presumed to have the same privileges as the ship itself unless proven otherwise. Article 17 of the Anglo-French treaty could be interpreted as taking Grotius's maxim to an extreme, where the privilege of the ship actually *granted* its privileges to the goods on board, rather than just create the presumption of privilege. The implications of the article would affect transhipment, because if privilege was granted, and not just presumed, then transhipment ceased to be a viable argument for confiscation. It would not matter if the goods

---

[52] BL Add MS 36208, Hardwicke Papers, Notes on the *San Juan Baptista*, ff. 246–67.
[53] Ibid.

were French or Spanish; the ship itself, by virtue of being Spanish, would protect the French goods. If the commissioners of the appellate court believed, as Captain Shaw claimed, that the goods found on board the *San Juan Baptista* belonged to the French East India Company and were being sent on account of Frenchmen, then any sentence handed down would be either an endorsement or a condemnation of the notion of 'free ships make free goods' as espoused by the Treaty of Utrecht. If, on the other hand, the commissioners wanted to avoid any decision based at least in part around Article 17 (this was likely, given Hardwicke's role in their recent decisions on the Dutch ships *Maria Theresa* and *America* which had gone some way to formalising the Rule of the War of 1756, which would have prevented the Spanish ship from carrying French East India goods because it was a trade that was prohibited to the Spanish during peacetime) then they would have to acknowledge the Spaniards' contention that the goods belonged to a Spaniard and originated in Spain. Since the *San Juan Baptista* was still on a voyage to a French port, any sentence would have an effect on the part of Article 17 which claimed that French (or in this case Spanish) ships could freely trade to the ports of British enemies.

Pratt and Smalbroke also reminded the court that all British privateers had been issued specific instructions not to molest Spanish shipping unless contraband were on board. They then rehashed the argument that the men of the *San Juan Baptista*, who testified that the goods were French and had been loaded from a French East Indies ship, had been intimidated by the privateers into making such claims. At the end of stating their case, the advocates asked that the sentence handed down by the High Court of Admiralty be reversed, and the cargo restored to the Appellants.

The British Respondent's Case

On the same day, 12 July 1759, the arguments on behalf of the Respondent in the *San Juan Baptista* case were presented before the commissioners of the appellate court. Captain John Shaw was represented by Dr George Hay and Dr A. Forrester. Like Pratt and Smalbroke, Hay had argued before the Court of Prize Appeal in several instances during the Seven Years' War, including the cases of the *Maria Theresa* and the *America*. Unlike the arguments presented on behalf of the Appellants, Hay and Forrester did not rely on any treaties to make their case. Instead, they relied solely on convincing the commissioners that the goods on board the Spanish ship had been placed therein directly from a French East India ship in the river near the Basque town of Pasajes and then carried towards Nantes. Their arguments were essentially rooted in transhipment and in the intentional collusion of the French and Spanish to deceive the British and protect French East India goods. As a consequence of Hay and Forrester's strategy, the arguments and evidence they presented differed little from those which had been employed in the High Court of Admiralty, and were contrastingly vague as compared to those put forward by the Appellants' advocates.

The most concrete evidence that the Respondent possessed was the Preparatory Examination of the *San Juan Baptista*'s master, José de Arteaga, taken on 22 June 1757, in which the Spaniard had claimed

> that when she [*San Juan Baptista*] arrived at Passage [*sic*], a French East-India Ship was lying at anchor in the Road or River, about half a mile from the Town of Passage; from on board which French East-India Ship this examinant [Arteaga] took in a loading of tea, coffee and logwood on freight, to go therewith to Nantz in France ... immediately from on board the said India ship ...[54]

The examination continued in a similar vein and Arteaga claimed that a merchant of San Sebastián, Don Pedro Delaraldy, had recommended to him that he take on the cargo from the French East India ship and deliver it, in Nantes, to Don Pedro Mitchel. Arteaga did not know on whose account the cargo had been shipped, but he did know it was shipped on account of French subjects. The advocates, without the support of Arteaga's testimony, declared that after the cargo had been loaded, Arteaga signed a counterfeit bill of lading that named Don Vincente de Zavaleta, one of the Appellants, as owner of the cargo. In order to support this claim, Hay and Forrester argued that the ship had to be carrying a pass written under oath as required by the treaty of 1667 and that the actual pass found on board the *San Juan Baptista* was not written as prescribed by the treaty nor written under oath.[55]

Once the Respondent's advocates had laid these arguments before the commissioners, they asked that the appellate court uphold the decision made in the High Court of Admiralty in regard to the cargo, because it belonged to Frenchmen, and, therefore, Don Vincente de Zavaleta had no claim to it. They also asked that the ship itself be condemned as lawful prize because the pass carried by the ship was incorrect and therefore the ship was not protected under the 1667 treaty. However, even had the pass been correct, the advocates claimed at the very end of their case, the ship should still have been condemned because 'she could not be protected in carrying on a French East-India Trade'.[56] It was a very vague statement to end a vague and lacklustre case. It is possible that Hay and

---

[54] Ibid.   [55] Ibid.   [56] Ibid.

Forrester were trying to imply that, since the Spanish ship had been allowed to carry French East India Goods (a trade prohibited to Spanish ships) that it should be treated as a French ship; an implication that could be used to call upon the Rule of the War of 1756 and the precedents set by previous Dutch ships like the *Maria Theresa* and the *America*. Such an action could then set a further precedent, but this time based on a Spanish case. However, if this was the intention, the question remains as to why they were not more explicit. The contrast between the Appellants' and the Respondent's case is interesting to note, and the possible reasons behind the discrepancy are worthy of further comment.

It is possible to glean insight into the reasoning of the four advocates involved in the case of the *San Juan Baptista* by linking it to the cases of two Dutch ships, the *Maria Theresa* and the *America*, and to the Rule of the War of 1756. The rule decreed that any trade that was prohibited to a country in times of peace would be prohibited during times of war. French law prohibited other countries from trading with its colonies in the West or East Indies, which effectively put all French colonial trade under Hardwicke's Rule of the War of 1756, and allowed the Court of Prize Appeal to condemn neutral ships that carried French colonial goods without treading on any existing Anglo-Spanish treaties. In the case of the *Maria Theresa*, the Rule of the War of 1756 had been used in order to restore both the ship and cargo, through a determination that the cargo had not belonged to an enemy, nor had the ship been engaging in French colonial trade. Smalbroke, Pratt, and Hay had served as advocates in that case. In the case of the *America*, the Rule of the War of 1756 was used to condemn both the ship and the cargo because the West Indian goods had been found to belong to Frenchmen and had been placed directly into the Dutch ship without ever touching land, a clear case of transhipment. The ship had been condemned on the argument that in cases of transhipment, effectively, free ships did not make free goods, and further, unfree goods made unfree ships.[57] This was, fundamentally, because if French colonial goods were transhipped into a non-French ship, then the ship could be considered French as only French ships were allowed to carry French colonial goods. Pratt and Hay had also served as advocates in the cases of the *Maria Theresa* and the *America*. Hardwicke had presided over the two Dutch cases as an appellate judge, so lines of argument based on those first Dutch cases would have been easy to employ and to lend consistency to decisions handed down by the Court of Prize Appeal.

---

[57] See Chapter 3 for a full discussion of the case of the *America* and the arguments made during the sentencing.

The *San Juan Baptista* case was heard exactly three months after the case of the *America*, and it is reasonable to assume, given the participants, that the proceedings in the latter affected those of the former. But Ricardo Wall's faith in British friendship and the prize court system was at its nadir, not to mention the ever-increasing probability that the friendly Spanish king would soon be replaced by his less benign brother, so the case of the *San Juan Baptista* offered an opportunity to boost Spanish confidence in Britain's intentions to safeguard Spanish neutrality. Given that there is a copy of Wall's letter to D'Abreu from 9 July, in Pitt's papers, it is more than likely that he was keenly aware of just how disenchanted Wall was with the state of Anglo-Spanish affairs at exactly the time the *San Juan Baptista* was to be tried. It was the first Spanish case to come before the Court of Prize Appeal during the war, and there was a chance to make real headway in gaining Spanish trust in Britain's repeated promises to protect Spanish neutral rights. It was not an opportunity to be wasted.

The 'Ifs' and 'Buts' of the Case

As mentioned, Hardwicke left almost no notes on the case of the *San Juan Baptista*. However, scribbled on the cover page of the group of documents termed the 'Appellant's Case' under the phrase 'at eleven in the forenoon', the time at which the case was heard, there is a single word in bold letters, 'Reversed'. The cargo was restored to the Spaniards and the ship was deemed to be a Spanish ship.[58] There are two possible reasons why Hardwicke's papers contain no notes about his reasoning on this case: either they are no longer extant, or the case was decided quickly and without much discussion, requiring no notes for contemplation. The former, though possible, is not the most likely, as other cases amongst his prize court papers also lack thorough documentation of a discussion between the commissioners. This points, rather, to its being a case that required little debate and was quickly decided.

Hardwicke's choice to reverse the decision handed down by the High Court of Admiralty in the case of the *San Juan Baptista* was entirely in keeping with Pitt's policy of upholding Spanish neutrality without committing to any firm definitions of what privileges neutrality actually granted to Spanish shipping. One of the first factors that would have had to be decided was the issue of whether the goods originated in Spain and were owned by Spaniards, or whether they were French East India

---

[58] BL Add MS 36208, Hardwicke Papers, Notes on the *San Juan Baptista*, ff. 246–67.

goods owned by Frenchmen. The most straightforward and only option that would lead to a reversal of the original sentence was to accept the Appellants' argument that the goods were Spanish. From the arguments made in the Appellants' and Respondent's cases, Hardwicke's sentence would have been easy to justify. The only concrete evidence to support Spanish ownership was the bill of lading signed by Zavaleta and the only support for French ownership was the testimony in which Arteaga had declared the goods to be French. That testimony was, however, marred by the claim that Arteaga had been intimidated into giving his answers. Given the behaviour of privateers during the war and the many claims that had been made against them over excessive violence, it was not a stretch to believe that the Spanish master had been coerced.[59] In terms of the bill of lading, it was the Spaniards' word against the privateer and, other than Arteaga's evidence, possibly tainted by intimidation, there was no reason to believe that the bill was false.

In the case of the *San Juan Baptista*, Hardwicke's previous precedent setting experience in prize cases, as well as in Chancery, likely helped him pursue British strategic aims through the Court of Prize Appeal. Precedents had become increasingly important in Chancery during the early-modern period, and the authority of the judges who set precedents was highly regarded.[60] Hardwicke appreciated the importance of precedents to the functioning of the Court of Prize Appeal and to achieving British aims regarding neutrality in the long term. The cases decided during the current war could, and would, be used in future conflicts in order to defend British strategic interests in the maritime world. Given the available and conflicting 'facts' of the case, Hardwicke could choose which 'facts' his reasoning would be built upon. Strategically, the case of the *San Juan Baptista* needed to assuage Spanish distrust. This meant finding in favour of the Spanish litigants, but it also meant showing that there was no discrepancy between the outcome of this case and the precedents that had been set by the early Dutch cases with regard to transporting French colonial goods. Hardwicke was free to accept that the goods were French or Spanish because the facts or evidence supporting either contention were not concrete and turned largely on hearsay. The desired outcome was clear, and Hardwicke's reasoning that would lead to a precedent-affirming, non-treaty-based, outcome is fairly simple. It is important to note here that usually, in order for a precedent to be set, a reasoned judgment needs to be left behind. Hardwicke did not write

[59] Starkey, *British Privateering*, p. 163.
[60] E. Koops and W. K. Zwalve (eds.), *Law and Equity: Approaches in Roman Law and Common Law* (Brill, 2013), pp. 7–8.

such a judgment in the case of the *San Juan Baptista*, so it cannot strictly be classified as a precedent-setting case. However, because the judgment from the High Court of Admiralty does exist, and Hardwicke reversed the outcome of the High Court case, the *San Juan Baptista* could still be used as a case that began to create a *communis opinio* for what types of Spanish cases, and lower court judgments, could, or should, be reversed through the appellate process. The small, and often related, pool of advocates and judges that were involved in prize appellate cases make it more likely that collective legal opinions and understanding would emerge from cases like that of the *San Juan Baptista*. In the same vein, the case could be used to affirm the precedents set in the previously examined Dutch cases, because the ship and goods were declared to be Spanish property and thus not in violation of the Rule of the War of 1756. This left open the possibility in subsequent cases that, should goods in Spanish ships be found to be French property, the goods and/ or the ship could be condemned under the Rule.

Having a large number of cases upon which precedents and *communis opinio* were based proved to be useful for prize court judges in future conflicts. Sir William Scott, who became judge of the High Court of Admiralty court in 1798 and is recognised for the quantity and quality of judgments he produced in prize affairs, relied heavily on precedents set by the Court of Prize Appeal.[61] Scott, who understood that British prize court decisions were not divorced from British maritime strategic interests, pulled from a great variety of cases and precedents that best allowed him to adjudicate new cases within the framework of a British law of nations that had grown over the century and now included the Rule of the War of 1756.[62] Scott, and his fellow civilians operating in the Admiralty and prize courts, also relied heavily on the philosophy produced by law-of-nations thinkers such as Grotius, Vattel, and Bynkershoek. However, when adjudicating difficult and politically sensitive cases, they put more stock in precedent and previous opinion than in the reasoning of philosophers.[63]

What then, might have been Hardwicke's reasoning in the case of the *San Juan Baptista*? If the goods were accepted to be Spanish, then the Court of Prize Appeal's reversal would have no significant bearing on any of the treaties invoked during the case or decisions passed in previous cases. Articles 13 and 14 of the treaty of 1667, which called for the respect of Spanish ships when stopped by a British privateer, would

---

[61] H. Bourguignon, *Sir William Scott, Lord Stowell: Judge of the High Court of Admiralty 1798–1828* (Cambridge University Press, 1987), pp. 165–6.
[62] Ibid. pp. 195 and 197.   [63] Ibid. p. 141.

remain unaltered by the decision – although the privateers might be censured for stopping and searching a Spanish ship without reason. Wall's interpretation of Article 23 would have been confirmed by the reversal, and therefore have served as an endorsement of his interpretation – but this had already been accepted by British politicians near the start of the war. No contraband goods had been found on board, which meant, according to Wall's interpretation, that the ship and the rest of her goods should have been free to proceed on their voyage. Returning the goods in the appellate case rectified the abuse of Article 23 by the privateers.

A decision based on the goods being Spanish and originating in Spain nullified all discussion of the Treaty of Utrecht, because there were no enemy goods involved and no question of transporting goods to France from the French East Indies. This would equate with the case of the *Maria Theresa*, but avoid any similarities with the *America*, and avoid any need to bring in the Rule of the War of 1756. Since the Respondent's case was not based on any treaties, the reversal was only a commentary on the over-zealous actions of privateers who erroneously took ships as prizes and intimidated witnesses to make their case. Such a judgment might have annoyed privateers, but it did not change their legal rights to take prizes.

If, on the other hand, Hardwicke and the commissioners had taken the option to believe Captain Shaw and accept Arteaga's testimony at face value, the decision to reverse the High Court of Admiralty's sentence would have been impossible to justify. It could still have avoided having a significant bearing on the treaties involved, but the reasoning would have had to address the Rule of the War of 1756 as it had begun to emerge with the precedents set in previous Dutch cases. With the goods acknowledged to be French and originating in the French East Indies, Hardwicke would have had to get round the stipulation in Article 17 of the Treaty of Utrecht (a ship could trade to and from the ports of Britain's enemies without being hindered), which was one of the cornerstones of the Appellants' case. The only way to avoid making a judgment on the treaty would have been by using the Rule of the War of 1756. As had been established in the case of the *America*, the Rule of the War of 1756 had been Hardwicke's way of nullifying the argument that 'free ships absolutely make free goods' by arguing that commerce which was prohibited during peacetime could not be allowed during wartime. Or, put another way, neutral countries should neither be penalised for their neutrality nor should they gain by it. France's laws did not allow other countries to carry their East India goods during times of peace, so Britain would not allow it during times of war. Restoring the goods to the

Appellants if the goods were considered to be French, would have been incompatible with the Rule of the War of 1756 and the previous decisions handed down by the Court of Prize Appeal.

If the Court had taken Arteaga's testimony as true and acknowledged that the goods had been placed directly into the Spanish ship from the French ship, the question of transhipment would have arisen. The commissioners would have had to decide whether the French goods, which had never touched Spanish soil, infected the ship and made it, for all intents and purposes, a French ship. As the case was extremely similar to that of the *America*, where the ship and the goods had been condemned because of transhipment, the court would have been hard pressed to find a way around condemnation without bringing into question the Rule of the War of 1756 and previous decisions made by the Court of Prize Appeal. However, the arguments presented by the advocates on either side of the *San Juan Baptista* case were seemingly set up perfectly for an easy reversal of the original sentence handed down by the High Court of Admiralty. The Appellants' case was rigorously assembled using Anglo-Spanish treaties that had been topics of contention between the British and Spanish ministries during the war. Such rigour, when dedicated to Spanish Appellants by British advocates, could only serve to boost Spain's confidence in the British prize court system and its 'fairness' in terms of legal representation. The Respondent's case had been set up without the same level of rigour afforded to the Appellants and was wholly dependent on a questionable testimony. Such an argument was easy to strike down, as it was entirely at the discretion of the judges whether to believe Arteaga's testimony. Given that three of the four advocates had been involved in the cases of the *Maria Theresa* and the *America*, it makes sense that they could take a case like that of the *San Juan Baptista*, which was in many ways very similar, and formulate their arguments in such a way that decisions made in the Dutch cases would both serve, and not serve, as precedents to help Hardwicke restore the ship and cargo.

The decision in the *San Juan Baptista* case was handed down on the same day it came before the Court of Prize Appeal, and Hardwicke's lack of notes points to an easy decision requiring little to no discussion. It is, of course, impossible to prove that the case of the *San Juan Baptista* had been planned to play out as described in this chapter, because there is no tell-tale document laying out such planning. However, the circumstantial evidence is fairly suggestive, and Hardwicke's approach to prize appeals clearly served the purpose of Pitt's foreign policy with neutral nations. In one day, the Court of Prize Appeal had delivered a decision in a Spanish prize case showing that Spaniards could seek justice for the wrongs committed by British privateers, if only they would take their cases to the Court of Prize Appeal. It also showed that Wall's scepticism of the British prize court system was, perhaps, misplaced. It was an encouraging development for Anglo-Spanish relations but did not set any precedents based on treaties that might curtail Pitt's policy of commerce predation. The case did, however, contribute to the nascent corpus of cases that supported the newly emerging Rule of the War of 1756. As was the norm during the Seven Years' War in Anglo-Spanish affairs, the decision in the appellate case caused very few ripples in the British press.

The day after the case of the *San Juan Baptista* had been decided, a single notice related to the event was printed in three of the London newspapers. The *London Evening Post*, the *London Chronicle*, and the *Whitehall Evening Post* all printed the following:

> Thursday came on before the Lords of Appeal the cause of a Spanish ship, called the St. Juan Baptista, Joseph Arteaga Master, taken in her passage from [*sic*] to Nantz; when after a long hearing; and many learned Arguments, their Lordships were pleased to decree the restitution of both Ship and Cargo; but from an Irregularity in the Pass, no Costs were given the Claimants.[64]

The short description is entirely unremarkable and offers no opinion on Anglo-Spanish affairs. It is merely a statement of facts and events, which puts it in stark contrast with the printed reactions to the Dutch cases of the *Maria Theresa* and the *America*. The article omitted the story about the French East India ship, which made the reversal seem like a routine case in which Spanish neutrality had been violated by a British privateer. The name of the capturing privateer is also omitted which, along with the absence of the transhipment story, made the article uncontroversial and therefore unworthy of comment. Whether these omissions were intentional, the effect was that, after the appearance of this notice, the subject did not arise again in the press. Given the anti-Spanish rhetoric that had greatly increased in the press since the *Antigallican* affair, it is odd that a case so favourable to the Spanish did not cause more of a commotion in the London press.

It is also interesting to note the comment about the 'irregularity' of the pass in the newspaper article. As Captain Shaw declared that the Spanish pass had not been in the correct form as prescribed by the treaty of 1667, it seems that Hardwicke and the commissioners agreed, and used it as a way to justify not awarding the Appellants any costs. This may have been a prudent move, as Captain Shaw would have had to give up the value of

[64] *London Evening Post*, 12–14 July 1759, no. 4944.

the cargo as well as all of the court fees incurred by the appellate process, usually a not inconsiderable sum for a privateer. By not awarding costs, the court was able to appease the Appellants and keep Captain Shaw's losses to a minimum. With the facts presented as they were in the article, the outcome of restoration without costs would likely have seemed a fair response and one that required no further discussion. The case of the *San Juan Baptista* had played out perfectly for Pitt's strategic needs regarding neutrals. Spain had been granted a victory in the prize courts to appease their anger, and neither the privateering lobby nor the public was stirred into action. From a legal perspective, the reasoning behind the Rule of the War of 1756 had survived its first contact with a Spanish appellate case, because the reversal of the High Court judgment did not contradict or undermine the principles of the Rule. The case had also successfully avoided setting a precedent rooted in the Anglo-Spanish treaty. Unfortunately for Pitt and Hardwicke, just a week after the *San Juan Baptista* case was heard, the *Jesús, Maria, y José* came before the commissioners of prize appeal. Hardwicke's new case proved the opposite of the previous one, as it was anything but quick and simple. It dragged on until February of 1761, and offered no easy way for the sentence to support Pitt's strategy. The case was also beset by outside complications, such as the death of Ferdinand VI, the arrival of the Conde de Fuentes as the Spanish ambassador in London, and the unexpected death of the British monarch, George II.

9   Reactive Foreign Policy and the
End of Spanish Neutrality
The *Jesús, Maria, y José* in the Court of Prize Appeal

Another Chance for Neutrality

Britain's maritime strategy throughout the Seven Years' War was often plagued by acrimonious relations with neutral maritime nations who could threaten to renounce their neutrality at any given time and join France as allies against Britain. Having secured Dutch neutrality by the end of 1759, Britain's ministers still faced the more daunting task of maintaining Spanish neutrality. The latter years of Spain's neutrality during the war (1759–62) saw an even greater deterioration in Anglo-Spanish relations. Ministers from both Courts attempted to preserve and salvage Spanish neutrality, but unresolved diplomatic grievances, as well as the deaths of both the Spanish king, Ferdinand VI, and the British monarch, George II, foiled their efforts.

The increasing decay and eventual breakdown of Anglo-Spanish relations during the war demonstrates that the tactics used to ensure Dutch neutrality could not so easily be transferred to maintain Spanish neutrality, particularly in the face of so many unexpected deaths of key figures. This chapter begins with the appellate case of the *Jesús, Maria, y José* and a very close look at the legal arguments presented for both the Spanish shipowners and the British privateers who took the ship as prize. The proceedings of the court are analysed alongside the political developments between the Spanish and British ministries and illustrate how they influenced one another. In the end, decisions made in the Court of Prize Appeal failed to engender Spanish confidence in Britain's prize court system. British ministers were unable to convince Spain that it was Britain's aim to preserve and respect Spanish neutrality, rather than to violate it and shift the balance of power in the Americas heavily in Britain's favour.

The appellate court's efforts were not all in vain, however. Despite the Anglo-Spanish war that broke out in 1762, the early Spanish appellate cases served to establish *communis opinio* around how the Rule of the War of 1756 could be applied outside of a Dutch context in future cases.

They also served to affirm the precedents for the rule that had already been set during the war. The case of the *Jesús, Maria, y José* provided a huge amount of written material that laid out Hardwicke's thinking and reasoning based on Grotian philosophy, and his own ideas about the Rule of the War of 1756. The case helped turn the Rule of the War of 1756 from a Dutch-specific rule to one that could be applied to all neutral nations by future jurists.

The Legal Mire

The legal journey of the Spanish ship *Jesús, Maria, y José* from its capture by the British privateer *Britannia* in September 1756, through two trials in the British prize court system was protracted, and convoluted. After condemnation of part of the cargo, and condemnation to pay court costs by the High Court of Admiralty in December 1756, the Spanish captain lodged an appeal in April 1758, and the case came before the Court of Prize Appeal in July of 1759. The appellate case may have seemed straightforward, at first glance, but as it progressed and new facets emerged, the case morphed into a complicated legal conundrum with the potential to upset already precariously positioned Anglo-Spanish relations.

A cursory look at the case of the *Jesús, Maria, y José* reveals many similarities to that of the *San Juan Baptista*. Both ships had been accused of transporting French East India goods into France in supposed contravention of international treaties, and both had seen part – or all – of the Spanish cargo condemned as prize by the High Court of Admiralty. The two appellant cases were largely based on the Anglo-Spanish treaty of 1667, but the *Jesús, Maria, y José* case also called on the Anglo-Dutch treaty of 1674. Three of the advocates involved in the *Jesús, Maria, y José* had also worked on the *San Juan Baptista* case: George Hay, R. Smalbroke, and A. Forrester. Lord Hardwicke produced tens of pages of notes on the problematic arguments and situations provoked by the *Jesús, Maria, y José*. As the case evolved, it became increasingly clear that the Spanish ship had carried French goods owned by Frenchmen and was destined for a port in France. These revelations made it more difficult for Hardwicke to hand down a sentence that would not condemn both the ship and the goods as legal prize, thus risking Spanish ministerial anger and possibly pushing Spain closer to renouncing her neutrality in the war.

The first complication that faced the Court of Prize Appeal was that appeals had been lodged by both the Spanish master, José Ezenarro, and by the British captor, Charles Davids, the captain of the *Britannia* privateer. The owners of the *Jesús, Maria, y José* had been condemned to pay all the expenses incurred by the trial in the High Court of Admiralty, and wished for this to be reversed. They also wished for the owners and captain of the *Britannia* to be condemned to pay damage costs for lost revenue. The owners of the privateer had only been awarded the saltpetre portion of the Spanish cargo as prize by the court but wanted the entire cargo and the ship awarded as lawful prize by the appellate court.[1] The entire case, therefore, was open to scrutiny, not just the sentence handed down by the High Court of Admiralty concerning the saltpetre. On 19 July 1759, the *Jesús, Maria, y José* came before Lord Hardwicke and the commissioners of prize appeal. There is, unfortunately, no record of who was present at this first hearing besides Hardwicke. For the sake of clarity, the Spaniards were considered the Appellants because they had lodged their appeal first, and Captain Davids was considered the Respondent.

The Spanish appellate case was put together by the advocates John Bettesworth and A. Forrester. The argument put forward by the Appellants' advocates was that the *Britannia* should have allowed the *Jesús, Maria, y José* to continue on its voyage unmolested after first boarding it and being presented with the ship's papers, which indicated Spanish ownership and a voyage from La Coruña to San Sebastián. According to Articles 13 and 14 of the 1667 treaty, and to the specific instructions issued to privateers about Spanish ships in 1756, a Spanish ship carrying an official patent or passport from the king of Spain was not to be molested or questioned by a British ship in any way.[2] This was the same argument and the same articles used in the case of the *San Juan Baptista* to claim that stopping a Spanish ship and seizing it was illegal. The Appellants' advocates also claimed that Article 21 granted that Spanish ships 'may with all Security navigate and traffic throughout all the Kingdoms, States and Countries, cultivating Peace, Amity or Neutrality, with either of the said Kings [British or Spanish]'.[3] Since the voyage of the *Jésus, Maria, y José* was supposedly between two Spanish ports carrying Spanish owned goods, there was nothing that contravened the cultivation of 'peace, amity or neutrality'.

The next article to be invoked by the advocates was the twenty-second, which specified that the liberty of British or Spanish ships could not be

---

[1] BL Add MS 32611, Hardwicke Papers, Notes on the *Jesús, Maria, y José*.

[2] Anglo-Spanish treaty of 1667, Oxford Historical Treaties, http://opil.ouplaw.com/view/10 .1093/law:oht/law-oht-10-CTS-63.regGroup.1/law-oht-10-CTS-63?rskey=pcFr3u& result=3&prd=OHT.

[3] BL Add MS 32611, Hardwicke Papers, Notes on the *Jesús, Maria, y José*.

interrupted 'by reason of any Hostility which now is, or may be hereafter between either of the said Kings, and any other Kingdoms, Dominions and States, being in Friendship or Neutrality with the other party'.[4] It is interesting to note that Article 22 could have been employed to argue against the Rule of the War of 1756, as it declared that the freedom of commerce between two countries was not affected by one of them becoming either an enemy of Britain or a neutral in a British conflict. The Rule of the War of 1756 declared, imperiously, that commerce prohibited to a country in peacetime could not be allowed during war-time. In the specific case of Spain, it meant that Spaniards and their ships could not transport or import French colonial goods during the present war because they were not allowed to do so when France was at peace. If Spanish ships attempted to bring French goods into French or Spanish ports, it could be taken by British prize courts to be a violation of their neutrality. The advocates representing the Spanish could have argued that Article 22 refuted the Rule of the War of 1756 and safeguarded Spanish neutrality even if France specifically opened up its commerce to Spanish shipping during the war, because the article protected the freedom of France and Spain to conduct commerce regardless of France's belligerent status. This would be a very broad interpretation of the article, but the wording is vague, and 'freedom of commerce' is a term open to broad interpretation. Were such an interpretation to be supported by the Court of Prize Appeal, it would have broadened Spain's neutral rights and expanded their ability to carry French commerce. This, in turn, would have made it more difficult for Britain to pursue its strategy of commerce predation. It is difficult to say why Article 22 was not used in the case of the *San Juan Baptista*, but was used in that of the *Jesús, Maria, y José*. It is possible that Hardwicke and his allies were seeking to do something similar to what had been done with the first two Dutch cases that came before the appellate court. In the Dutch cases, the first to come before the court was decided in a manner that was favourable to Dutch interests and the second was decided in a manner such that it was made clear that the Rule of the War of 1756 would be used in adjudicating cases involving French colonial commerce. The case of the *San Juan Baptista* had been decided in favour of the Spanish, with the ship and goods restored. That of the *Jesús, Maria, y José*, with the argument around Article 22, was possibly being set up to make a ruling that would send a clear signal about the Rule of the War of 1756 and how it would be applied to Spanish ships. If this was indeed

[4] Ibid.

Hardwicke's design, it certainly did not play out the way the first Dutch cases did.

Article 23, which dealt with contraband and 'free ships make free goods', was used as it had been for the *San Juan Baptista*. The argument was that any contraband goods found in a Spanish ship should be taken out of the ship and taken to the prize courts separately. The offending ship was then supposed to be left to continue its voyage unmolested. The definition of contraband goods had been set by Britain's Secretary of State for the Southern Department, Charles Fox, in 1756. He had conceded that the Spanish government's interpretation of Article 23 was the correct one. Spain's interpretation was that all goods not designated as contraband by the treaty were free. Saltpetre, a designated contraband good, had been found in the *Jesús, Maria, y José* and, according to the Appellants' advocates, the privateer should only have confiscated the saltpetre and let the ship and the rest of the cargo continue the voyage unmolested. The advocates stretched the meaning of Article 23 quite far by arguing that contraband goods could only be designated as such if the ship in question were voyaging to an enemy port; this had not been agreed to in the negotiations of 1756.

Discussions over the breadth and application of such treaty articles were not confined to court documents and court proceedings. Treatises and pamphlets that discussed the meaning of neutrality treaties circulated in the public domain. One in particular, *A Discourse on the Conduct of the Government of Great Britain in Respect to Neutral Nations*, was written by Charles Jenkinson and published in 1758. Jenkinson would go on to become Baron Hawkesbury and Earl of Liverpool, as well as an MP and President of the Board of Trade. His political career began in 1761 under the new monarch, George III. In 1758, however, he was paid (possibly by Newcastle or Holderness) to write the pamphlet, though he did not have any formal legal training.[5] Jenkinson directly addressed the interpretations of Articles 21 and 22 of the Anglo-Spanish treaty. He argued that the law of nations granted people of every country the right to trade to the ports of any other state, even if that state was engaged in a war, so long as the goods were their own or being traded on their account. The goods could also not be contraband. However, Jenkinson went on to claim that the law of nations was not always adhered to in previous conflicts and that warring states had abused the rights of neutrals granted by the law of nations. As a response to these abuses in the mid-seventeenth century, commercial treaties began to be made wherein the rights granted by the

---

[5] BL Add MS 32889, Newcastle Papers, Memorandum for the King, 5 April 1759, f. 363.

law of nations were laid out in specific articles, such as Articles 21 and 22 in the Anglo-Spanish treaty. But, he continued, the general language of the articles was not meant to imply that enemy trade could be freely carried because this was not the intention behind the law of nations. A treaty article had to expressly state that enemy trade could be freely carried because it was a deviation from the general rights granted by the law of nations. Jenkinson cited the Anglo-Dutch treaty of 1674 and the Anglo-French treaty of 1677 as examples where an explicit right to carry enemy goods had been granted.[6] According to Jenkinson's reasoning, Article 22 could not have been used to refute the Rule of the War of 1756 because it did not grant Spain the right to trade enemy goods as it was only included to make sure the law of nations was safeguarded. Jenkinson's reasoning would also not allow for Article 23 to be interpreted as had been agreed between Wall and Fox in 1756 because that interpretation granted that all goods, except those specifically designated as contraband, could be freely carried. It is not clear whether the advocates arguing the case, or Lord Hardwicke, ever read Jenkinson's treatise, but the purpose of it was to argue against a neutral's right to indiscriminately carry French trade.[7] Much like Hardwicke and his political allies, Jenkinson was trying to define the limits of neutral rights and root those limits within the legitimacy of international legal philosophy.

The final argument in the Appellants' case, based on the treaty of 1667, called upon Article 38 and, in the court documents, Hardwicke underlined the following wording of that article:

the people and subjects of both the said Kings, shall have and enjoy in the Lands, Seas, Ports, Havens, Roads, and Territories of the other, and in all other Places whatever, all the same Priviliges [sic], Securities, Liberties and Immunities, whether they concern their persons or Trade, which have been already granted ... to the Most Christian King [the king of France], or to the States General of the United Provinces ...

It is Article 38 that inspired the Appellants' advocates to also use the Anglo-Dutch treaty of 1674 as part of their argument, and it was clearly an article that Hardwicke considered important to the case. The Anglo-Dutch treaty had been used in many appellate cases lodged by disgruntled Dutch merchants and had been the subject of tense Anglo-Dutch

---

[6] Charles Jenkinson, *A Discourse on the Conduct of the Government of Great-Britain, in Respect to Neutral Nations, During the Present War* (R. Griffiths, Pater-Noster Row, 1758), pp. 32–4.
[7] There are instances of Jenkinson's treatise appearing in the collections of some civilians such as Sir William Burrel, who took annotated notes of Admiralty cases including prize cases during the Seven Years' War. Burrel's copy of Jenkinson's treatise can be found in TNA HCA 45/3/1.

negotiations over its interpretation since the start of the war. The use of the 1674 treaty in the Appellant's case was, however, contentious. The phrase 'already granted' from Article 38 of the Anglo-Spanish treaty of 1667 could be taken to mean that only pre-1667 treaties were covered by the article. This interpretation would have nullified the portion of the Appellants' case based on the 1674 Anglo-Dutch treaty.

From the Anglo-Dutch treaty of 1674, the Appellants' case drew on Articles 5 and 6. The former stipulated that Dutch ships could not be molested, detained, or searched by British privateers or ships of war as long as they carried the passport prescribed by the treaty.[8] The liberties granted by Article 5 were the same as those in Article 14 of the Anglo-Spanish treaty of 1667, but the advocates invoked the Dutch treaty in order to argue that the capture of the *Jesús, Maria, y José* was a violation of two treaties that applied to Spanish ships. Article 6 of the 1674 treaty drew a distinction between when a Dutch ship was obliged to show a passport and when it was necessary to show a passport and a bill of lading. If a Dutch ship were sailing to the port of an enemy of Great Britain, then it would be required to show a bill of lading in order to ensure that no contraband goods were being carried. However, if the Dutch ship were sailing to a port that was not under the control of an enemy, then the only documentation that needed to be shown was the passport. The advocates claimed that since the *Jesús, Maria, y José* was sailing from a Spanish port to a Spanish port, the privateer did not have the right to demand a bill of lading, and that, therefore, regardless of what the *Jesús, Maria, y José* carried as cargo, or what the bill of lading said, it was illegal for Captain Davids to have asked for it, and any argument made by the privateer using the bill of lading was irrelevant. Based on the two treaties, and the fact that the *Jesús, Maria, y José* carried the correct passport, the advocates representing the owners of the Spanish ship argued that the entire seizure and subsequent proceedings had been illegal. They claimed the saltpetre should be returned to them and all the costs and damages incurred during the trials should be awarded to them; that is, paid by the captain or owners of the *Britannia*.[9]

The Respondent's case was heard on the same day as the Appellants', and the argument made on behalf of Captain Davids was also founded on the treaty of 1667. However, Captain Davids's version of the journey of the *Jesús, Maria, y José* was dramatically different. Whilst the Appellants' case avoided any specific mention of the origin of the *Jesús, Maria, y José*'s cargo, the advocates representing Davids made it the crux of theirs.

[8] BL Add MS 32611, Hardwicke Papers, Notes on the *Jesús, Maria, y José*.   [9] Ibid.

Hay and Forrester claimed, first, that the ship was not bound to San Sebastián but, rather, to a port in France. They further claimed that the entire cargo was made up of French East India goods which had been placed on board the Spanish ship from a French ship, without first being landed in Spain. Additionally, and in contravention of the treaty of 1667, the passport of the ship had not been obtained by oath and was, therefore, false. As proof, Davids claimed that Ezenarro and other witnesses had sworn in the interlocutories (interrogations of the crew brought in on the prize ship) that the shipper was not a Spaniard, but the son of the French consul at San Sebastián known as Bosinack. They had also sworn that the cargo was the property of French subjects.[10] There was, however, a problem with Ezenarro's testimony, because a month after it was given, he contradicted it with new testimony.

More Evidence Needed

When the *Jesús, Maria, y José* was first brought into Bristol, Ezenarro and his crew were questioned, on 4 October 1756, per the interrogatories required by prize law.[11] In one of his responses, Ezenarro claimed that from San Sebastián, the ship would continue to either Bayonne or Bordeaux and there end her voyage. He also testified that Bosinack, the French consul's son, had travelled from San Sebastián to La Coruña in order to act as the shipper of the East India goods, and that Pedro de Larralde, the man to whom the goods were consigned, was a Frenchman by birth, not a Spaniard. Ezenarro then declared that he was made to sign four bills of lading and send two of them, by land, to France: a highly irregular procedure. Lastly, he offered the observation that the Spanish vessels were used only to protect the French goods from capture by British ships. His testimony was corroborated by five other members of the crew.[12] Whilst Ezenarro's interrogatories were damning to the Spanish case, their credibility was challenged when, on 22 October 1756, he submitted a claim on behalf of Larralde and Valez de Lavalla challenging the seizure of the *Jesús, Maria, y José*. Part of the claim was an affidavit, sworn to by Ezenarro, that declared the ships and goods to be owned by Spanish subjects, and that he supported Larralde and Valez de Lavalla's claim against Captain Davids.[13]

If Ezenarro's original testimony was true, and the Spanish ship had indeed been bound for a French port, then Article 13 of the treaty of 1667 (dealing with contraband) would have indisputably come into effect

[10] Ibid. [11] See the Introduction for an explanation of interrogatories and monitions.
[12] BL Add MS 32611, Hardwicke Papers, Notes on the *Jesús, Maria, y José*. [13] Ibid.

and the seizure of the ship could have been justified due to the presence of contraband goods. It was also noted by the advocates that importing French East India goods into Spain was prohibited by the laws of both France and Spain. This would have meant that the destination of San Sebastián was illegal, and therefore unlikely to be the actual intended terminating port. As a response to the Appellants' claim that the Anglo-Dutch treaty of 1674 applied to Spanish ships, the Respondent's advocates countered:

> yet it is known, that the great Freedom of Trade granted to the subjects of the States General, by the Treaty of 1674, is, by the 2nd Article of that Treaty, extended only to those commodities which might be carried in Time of Peace; and therefore, that the Dutch themselves are not permitted to carry the Goods of an Enemy, or even their own, to or from any of the Ports of an enemy, to which they could not trade in Times of Peace ...[14]

Such an interpretation of Article 2 meant that no Dutch ship, and therefore no Spanish ship, could carry French East or West Indian goods into any port, because such commerce was prohibited by French law, and a state of war between Britain and France did not make the commerce legal. Therefore, if the *Jesús, Maria, y José* was transporting French East India goods, she was in violation of the Anglo-Dutch treaty. It was an argument that essentially backed the Rule of the War of 1756 with which Hay, as one of the advocates involved in several Dutch cases, would have been intimately familiar. The Respondent's case ended by asking that the entire cargo of the *Jesús, Maria, y José* be condemned as enemy property, and that the ship itself be condemned as an adopted French ship. For a Spanish ship to be considered an adopted French ship, the court would have to be satisfied that it was being used to complete a French voyage in order to avoid capture by the British. If the Court of Prize Appeal were to decide to uphold the arguments put forward in the Respondent's case, it would further strengthen the Rule of the War of 1756 and limit the neutral rights of Spanish ships in terms of carrying French colonial goods. Such a decision would likely not be looked upon favourably by the Spanish Court and could further inflame Anglo-Spanish tensions.

The question of adoption often went hand in hand with that of transhipment, the action of transferring French goods from a French ship into a Spanish ship in order to complete a French voyage but evade capture by the British. Both of these concepts were tied up with Hardwicke's original thinking on the need for the Rule of the War of

---

[14] Ibid.

1756. By requesting that the ship be treated as a French ship, the advocates forced the commissioners of prize appeal to open a discussion about transhipment and the Rule of the War of 1756. It is important to note that there is an important distinction between declaring a ship to be an adopted French ship and declaring a ship to be Spanish, engaged in the act of transhipping and fraud. The distinction came in the sentencing. Ships condemned as adopted French ships would usually be declared fair prize and awarded to the British captors. Spanish ships engaged in transhipping French goods could be restored to their Spanish owners with only the goods awarded as prize to the British captors. These distinctions could matter greatly when handing down politic sentences that could either appease or anger the Spanish merchant community and the British privateering lobby. During the war, about twenty-six cases came before the Court of Prize Appeal in which discussions over adoption formed part of the sentencing decision as to whether a ship should be condemned as lawful prize.[15]

By the end of the Appellants' and Respondent's arguments, the case looked very much like that of the *San Juan Baptista*, in that the commissioners of prize appeal would need only believe Ezenarro's second allegation that the goods were Spanish, heading to a Spanish port, in order to easily decide the case in the Spaniards' favour. However, before the commissioners could convene for the decision, the Appellants petitioned to be allowed time to make further proof of the ownership of the cargo and vessel. The court granted the request and decreed a commission be sent to San Sebastián to examine witnesses and return by 1 April 1760. The commission did not return until May 1760.[16] There is no record of who was sent as part of the commission or why the request was allowed. However, it was likely that the request was granted both because the facts of the case were contentious, and because it was a sign of good faith towards the Spanish. Hardwicke was demonstrating that the court was interested in deciding cases based upon having all the possible facts at its disposal and that it was willing to postpone sentencing until all relevant evidence had been presented.

The British press gave its own reason for the commission granted by the Court of Prize Appeal. Both the *Whitehall Evening Post* and the *London Evening Post* mentioned the trial of the *Jesús, Maria, y José* in its

---

[15] Cases in the Court of Prize Appeal where this distinction and line of argument can be seen include: *America* (1759) BL Add MS 36208; *Resolutie* (1760) BL Add MS 36211; *Vrow Anna* (1760) TNA HCA 45/2/8; *Good Christian* (1760) TNA HCA 45/1/55; *Johannes* (1760) TNA HCA 45/2/42; *Maria Johanna* (1760) TNA HCA 45/2/29; and *San Vicente* (1760) TNA HCA 45/2/28.

[16] BL Add MS 32611, Hardwicke Papers, Notes on *Jesús, Maria, y José*.

first hearing before the appellate court, and they both ran the same notice in their 19–21 July edition. The notice gave the destination of the Spanish ship as San Sebastián, and claimed that the commission had been granted due to it being 'not improbable, that some mistakes had been made by the interpreter who assisted in taking down the answers of the Spanish Master and crew'.[17] There is no mention in the court documents of any mistakes committed by interpreters, and the reason for the commission is clearly stated as the Appellants' desire to provide more proof of Spanish ownership. The notice is a fabrication, which painted the case in a very straightforward light and painted the court as being sensitive to mistakes made within the prize system. Whether the notice was published out of ignorance, or by intention in order to avoid speculation, is impossible to say. It may also be that the intention behind the notice was to indirectly address accusations about Ezenaro's testimony being coerced, ignorance of language usually being a lesser sin than coercion. Either way, anyone who read this account of the first hearing would have been left with the impression that the commission was only in search of correcting an interpretation error. This did not prepare the reader to expect a possible lengthy trial based on new evidence found in Spain.

The Death of a King

During the ten months that the commission was being fulfilled, Anglo-Spanish relations changed more dramatically than they had over the course of the entire war. The first dramatic event came on 10 August 1759, with the death of Ferdinand VI and the ascension of his anti-British half-brother, Charles III, to the throne of Spain. It took three months for Charles to arrive in Spain from Naples, where he ruled as king of Naples and Sicily, but with a new healthy and politically engaged monarch on his way to Madrid, the Spanish Court was immediately invigorated, and Ricardo Wall, first minister of Spain, was able to cast off the guise of desiring to fix Spain's broken friendship with Britain.

Wall took up the policy left behind when Ferdinand got sick, that Alarcia describes as an 'armed neutrality … which was continued at a forced march'.[18] Even before Charles arrived in Madrid, the effect of the new monarch on the attitudes of Spanish ministers towards Britain and the abuse of Spanish shipping by British privateers was obvious.

---

[17] *Whitehall Evening Post*, 19–21 July 1759, no. 2081.
[18] D. Alarcia Téllez, *El Ministerio Wall: La 'España discreta' del 'ministro olvidado'* (Ediciones de Historia, 2012), p. 106.

On 17 August 1759, only a week after Ferdinand's death and a month after the *Jesús, María, y José* arguments were presented at the Court of Prize Appeal, D'Abreu, Spain's representative in London, wrote a letter to Pitt concerning three Spanish ships which had been taken by the British privateer *Drake* on 15 July. The three ships, just like the *San Juan Baptista*, had been carrying loadings of sugar, coffee, and indigo from La Coruña to Bordeaux. One of the ships was carried into Bristol and the master, Julian Lopez, wrote to D'Abreu about the captures and to complain about being taken as a prize. According to D'Abreu, what he found 'remarkable in this affair, is that the privateer justified the right of his capture on the goods being French disregarding the spirit of conventions, and even decisions previously made by the Court of Prize Appeal in consequence of treaties'.[19] Given the date of the letter, the cargoes, and the destinations of the ships, it is highly likely that one of the previous decisions to which D'Abreu referred was the case of the *San Juan Baptista*. D'Abreu ended his letter by wishing that Pitt, upon the principles espoused by recent court decisions, treaties, and conventions between the two countries, would give orders for the prompt restitution of the three ships, the cargoes, and payment for any damages.[20] It is fairly clear from D'Abreu's letter, as well as his request, that, as far as the Spanish representative was concerned, the decision in the case of the *San Juan Baptista* set a precedent, and that all such Spanish ships captured by British ships would be restored, either by the courts or the ministry. Sensible perhaps of how long disputes took to settle in the prize courts, it made sense for D'Abreu to try to take advantage of Britain's professed desire for friendship and to push for an extrajudicial resolution. His attempt paid off, and a week after D'Abreu wrote the letter, Pitt wrote his own letter to William Read and Edward Charlton, the owners of the *Drake* privateer.

Pitt's letter to the owners of the privateer left no doubt as to his expectation that they would release their captured Spanish ships. He openly explained that D'Abreu had complained of their behaviour and asked them to provide the reasons for their capture. He then continued by stating that if the ships had been taken contrary to the treaty of 1667 or the additional instructions of October 1756, he

---

[19] TNA PRO 30/8/92, Letter from D'Abreu to Pitt, 17 August 1759. Original in French: 'remarquable dans cette affaire, c'est que l'armateur fondoit le droit de sa capture sur ce que les Marchandives etaient Francoises meprisant ainsi la Foy des conventions, et même des decisions dernierement donnés par le conseil d'appel de S.M.B. en consequence des traités'.

[20] Ibid.

[did] not doubt but you will immediately order the same to be released, and thereby avoid giving just cause of complaint to the subjects of His Catholick Majesty, and to prevent the inconveniencies that may arise to yourselves in case the capture shall, upon trial, prove to have been illegal.[21]

The threat in Pitt's letter is thinly veiled. If the ships were not released, the privateers' actions would likely be found illegal in a subsequent trial. Though this was not the first time Pitt had directly intervened in a prize court case, it is one of the few documented examples of Pitt, Secretary of State, de facto prime minister, and acclaimed leader of Britain's wartime victories, writing directly to the owners of a privateer. It must have been an intimidating letter to receive, and one that was not easily ignored.

The owners of the *Drake* did as Pitt asked and released all three of the Spanish ships within six days of Pitt's writing. On 31 August, Pitt wrote a short letter to D'Abreu informing him that the ships had been released, and enclosing a copy of the privateer's letter as proof.[22] Wall did not seem to be involved in the affair of the *Drake* privateer, and it is possible that Pitt acted with such celerity in order to stave off Wall's involvement and avoid further delay and annoyances to the Spanish Court and its new king. The fact that Pitt considered D'Abreu's complaint important enough to take care of the affair himself, and to D'Abreu's satisfaction, is indicative of the importance that Pitt attached to Spanish neutrality and its role in his wartime strategy. It is also possibly a testament to Pitt's own incipient loss of faith in the Court of Prize Appeal as the best vehicle to preserve Spanish neutrality because of the delays. Though the case of the *San Juan Baptista* had been decided favourably for the Spanish, the case of the *Jesús, Maria, y José* was now delayed, and no other Spanish ships would come before the Court of Prize Appeal until the Spring of 1760.

Charles III's Requests

One of Charles III's first steps vis-à-vis negotiations with Britain was to send a memorandum to the British Court which contained expressions of friendship and, at the same time, concern, when it came to British conquests in the Americas. The memorandum was sent before Charles reached Madrid and, therefore, before he was able to consult with most of his ministers. In a letter to Lord Bristol, ambassador to Spain, from

---

[21] TNA PRO 30/8/92, Letter from Pitt to Wm Read, Edw. Charlton, Owner of the Drake Privateer, 25 August 1759.
[22] TNA PRO 30/8/92, Letter from Pitt to D'Abreu, 31 August 1759.

14 December 1759, Pitt expressed both his surprise and annoyance at the contents of Charles's memorandum:

> I will, therefore, only observe, that it could not but administer a matter of no small surprise here [British Court], that, before His Catholic Majesty had reached His Capitol, or so much as seen the ministers of Spain, as well as before an ambassador had been appointed for the Court of England, Mr. D'Abreu should receive orders of so delicate and important a nature; but, above all, I am to let your excellency understand, that that part of the memorial, which declares His Catholic Majesty cannot see with indifference our successes in America, seems here very little consistent with the expressions in other parts of that piece, where Spain desires to be considered as in a pure neutrality, and as a disinterested equal friend ...[23]

Charles's concern about British successes in America stemmed from his desire, and that of most members of the Spanish Court, to maintain a balance of power in America. By the end of 1759, the British had seized Quebec and were driving the French out of Canada. In the West Indies, Guadeloupe had been taken, with more islands falling to the British in the following months. Pitt wanted all of North America and as much of the West Indies as could be conquered in order to have a strong hand at the negotiating table with France. 'By conquering one French colony after another, he [Pitt] must necessarily make England the strongest power in that part of the world, and bring her face to face with Spain.'[24] If the French were truly swept from the Americas, there would be no balance of power, and any colonial grievances between the British and Spanish Courts, should it come to war, would have to be fought without French assistance. Given the disparities between British and Spanish sea power, such a contest would not end well for the fledgling Spanish king. In an attempt to avoid the balance of power tipping any further in the direction of Britain, Charles concluded his memorandum by offering to mediate a peace between Britain and France.[25]

Whilst Pitt was happy to appease the Spanish when it came to the actions of British privateers, he did not accept that Charles's claims of neutrality and concern about the balance of power were compatible. He also, clearly, did not believe in the sincerity of Charles's friendship towards Britain, and asked Bristol to find out who, and what, was driving the king's actions:

---

[23] BL Add MS 36807, Negotiations with Spain, Extract of a letter from a letter from Pitt to Bristol, 14 December 1759, ff. 43–4.

[24] R. Pares, *War and Trade in the West Indies 1739–1763* (Frank Cass and Co., 1963), p. 556.

[25] BL Add MS 36807, Negotiations with Spain, Abstract of Spanish Dispatches previous to the late negotiations with France, no date, ff. 254–7.

[Y]our excellency should be extremely attentive to discover what may have given rise to a measure of such high moment ... and whether this step may not be the result of the French Ambassador's infusions, since their Catholic Majesties left Naples; ... and whether ... Mr. Wall, may not in consequence of French intrigues, be struck at in this measure, taken whilst the Court was at so great a distance and perhaps even without the previous participation of that able minister, of whose wise and upright intentions for the well being of Two Countries so naturally connected by mutual interests ...[26]

Pitt's suspicions would largely prove justified. The new French ambassador to the Spanish Court, the Marquis D'Ossun, was highly competent, close to the new king, and had an acrimonious relationship with Wall. In the coming months, Wall would become more and more isolated within the Spanish Court after the new king replaced his allies with mostly pro-French ministers. As negotiations between Spain and Britain continued over the possibility of mediating a peace, Wall became convinced that the time for Spain to enter the war was past, because Britain had grown too strong and France too weak to make a formidable ally.[27] Kuethe and Andrien sum up the trajectory that the new Spanish king took in this way:

Charles had few diplomatic alternatives. Acting through the increasingly discredited Ricardo Wall, the king sought to restore equilibrium thorough Spanish mediation, but London held the upper hand and was in no mood to be conciliatory. Fearing that he would be left to face the British alone, Charles found himself drawn closer to Versailles.[28]

Pitt's response to Charles's memorandum was sent on 13 December, a day before his letter to Bristol. Pitt referred to the Treaty of Utrecht of 1713, which had been used in Charles's memorandum to justify his call for a balance of power in America. Pitt pointed out that there was nothing in the treaty that was meant to establish or maintain a balance of power between the three empires in the Americas.[29] He also declined Charles's offer of mediation, as Britain had committed itself to treat for peace jointly with Prussia. Pitt, perhaps sensible that shutting down any legal precedent for a balance of power in the Americas was important in order to carry out his strategy of sweeping the board clean of French

---

[26] BL Add MS 36807, Negotiations with Spain, Extract of a letter from Pitt to Bristol, 14 December 1759, ff. 43–4.

[27] Alarcia, *Ministerio Wall*, p. 108.

[28] Allan J. Kuethe and Kenneth Andrien, *The Spanish Atlantic World in the Eighteenth Century: War and the Bourbon Reforms, 1713–1796* (Cambridge University Press, 2014), p. 219.

[29] BL Add MS 36807, Negotiations with Spain, Extract of a letter from Pitt to Bristol, 14 December 1759, ff. 43–4.

possessions in the West Indies and in North America, asked Lord Hardwicke for his advice in the matter. It was only after Hardwicke had approved his answer that he dared send it to the Spanish Court. He wrote to Hardwicke, 'I am not a little easier, as well as flattered, by the honour of your Lordship's approbation of the latter [answer to the memorandum], on a matter where I should justly fear to stand upon my own judgments ...'[30] The letter undoubtedly reflects the hyperbole which is found in so many eighteenth-century epistolary styles, but there is also likely much truth to Pitt's thanks. Hardwicke was a man of unprecedented legal knowledge and ability. In matters of international treaties and negotiations of peace, it would have been foolish not to consult either him or Lord Mansfield.

A New Ambassador in London

After the rejection of Charles's memorandum, Anglo-Spanish negotiations dealing with neutrality and prize court affairs were relatively quiet between late December 1759 and the arrival in London of Spain's ambassador, the Conde de Fuentes, on 24 May 1760. He had, at long last, been sent to his post in an attempt to resolve the grievances between Britain and Spain. A month before Fuentes's arrival, three Spanish ships came before the Court of Prize Appeal starting with the *San Vicente* (misidentified in court documents as *San Vincente*) on 26 March 1760. The ship and goods had been condemned as lawful prize by the High Court of Admiralty and the Court of Prize Appeal upheld the sentence because the ship was considered to have been an adopted French ship.[31] As in the case of the *Jesús, María, y José*, the advocates for the Spanish Appellants invoked the privilege granted by the Anglo-Spanish treaty which granted the privileges of the Anglo-Dutch treaty of 1674. This in turn allowed the advocates for the Respondents to invoke the ambiguously worded Article 2 that allowed the transport of goods carried in times of peace. This offered continuity with previous Dutch cases such as that of the *America*. The advocates acting for the British privateer claimed that since carrying French colonial goods was prohibited to Spanish ships during peacetime, it remained prohibited during wartime. It was, in other words, an argument that perfectly conformed with the Rule of the War of 1756 and previous decisions in Dutch cases. It was presented, in this case, as an established rule that could be used to substantiate the call

---

[30] BL Add MS 35423, Hardwicke Papers, Letter from Pitt to Hardwicke, 12 December 1759, f. 199.
[31] TNA HCA 45/1/21, Case of the *San Vincente*.

for the ship to be condemned as an adopted French ship. The Respondent's reasoning was as follows. Many of the ship's papers that declared the goods and the ship to be Spanish-owned were provable forgeries. The real owner of the goods and the ship, as claimed by several of the deposed witnesses, was a Frenchman by the name of Monsieur Reje. Several witnesses also claimed that the ship had been engaged in a voyage from and to the French port of Bayonne rather than San Sebastián. The Appellants claimed that the voyage was lawful and the ship was Spanish. If this was accepted by the court, then the ship must be considered a French ship by adoption. Alternatively, the court could accept that the ship and goods belonged to a Frenchman and therefore should be declared French and lawful prize. Interestingly, the advocates in this case were the same four who acted as advocates in the case of the *Jesús, Maria, y José*. Hardwicke's one page of notes mostly focuses on which set of witnesses is to be believed and therefore whether the ship and goods were owned by Spaniards or Frenchmen. Without deep explanation, he concluded that the goods should be considered to be Spanish. He gives no indication as to whether the ship should be considered an adopted French ship but goes on to state that the ship and goods will be condemned as lawful prize. Though questions of adoption were raised by the Respondents, they do not appear to have been addressed in written form by Hardwicke and therefore it is difficult to draw out any hard-and-fast rules about adoption in this instance. However, as the ship and goods were condemned, as requested by the Respondents, the case could be referred to in future as an example of Spanish ships being condemned for engaging in French colonial trade based on the Rule of the War of 1756 and as a case where a Spanish ship was treated as an adopted French ship.[32]

On the next day, two Spanish ships came before the Court of Prize Appeal, the *San José* (also named as the *San Joseph* in court documents) and the *San Joachim*. Both ships had been taken by the same British privateer and were owned by the same Spanish merchant. Both ships and their cargoes had been condemned as lawful prize by the High Court of Admiralty and both ships and cargoes were restored by the Court of Prize Appeal. The advocates in both cases were Charles Pratt, J. Bettesworth, George Hay, and Charles Yorke. The same quartet of advocates who had presided over almost every Dutch case, and most Spanish cases, to come before the appellate court. In the case of the *San José*, it was captured leaving San Sebastián and potentially heading to French colonies in

---

[32] BL Add MS 36209, Hardwicke Papers, Notes on the *San Vicente*.

North America. However, as there were no French colonial goods found on board and it was not certain that the voyage was to a French colony, the court was able to reverse the original sentence and not invoke the Rule of the War of 1756.[33] The circumstance of the *San Joachim* were almost identical to those of the *San José*.[34] If Hardwicke and the British ministers presumed that the outcomes in the appeal cases of these three ships would produce similar results in Spain's attitude towards its neutral rights as the *Maria Theresa* and the *America* had produced in the Dutch Republic's outlook, they were to be sorely disappointed. The restoration of the *San José* and the *San Joachim* did nothing to appease Spanish anger, nor did the Spanish see the cases as having established any sort of useful precedents or limits to neutral rights based on the Rule of the War of 1756.

Within a month of his arrival, on 20 June, Fuentes presented a memorandum to the British Court detailing the complaints that his Court harboured against British privateers and warships. Three particular grievances were highlighted by the memorandum and subsequently in Pitt's notes. The first was the disregard shown by the prize courts to the pass granted by the Spanish king to Spanish merchants. The second concerned Spanish ships that took in French East India Goods directly out of French ships (i.e. transhipment). The last was the protection of saltpetre bound to France.[35] The memorandum also demanded reparations for the Spaniards who had suffered at the hands of British privateers and warships.[36] Pitt, Mansfield, and Hardwicke spent a portion of July coming up with an adequate response to the memorandum, and the British Court gave its official answer to Fuentes on 1 September 1760. Whilst the three men were working on their answer, another Spanish ship named the *San José* came before the Court of Prize Appeal. The advocates were once again Pratt, Yorke, Hay, and Bettesworth. Once again, the ship and goods were restored to the Spanish owner along with costs and damages to be paid by the British privateer.[37] This case, like those that came before it, seemingly had no effect in appeasing Spanish anger, and the correspondence about the response to Fuentes's memorandum makes it clear, through omission, that British ministers were beginning to

---

[33] BL Add MS 36209, Hardwicke Papers, Notes on the *San Joseph*.

[34] BL Add MS 36209, Hardwicke Papers, Notes on the *San Joachim*.

[35] TNA PRO 30/8/80, Three of the Principal Points Appealed to the Rt Hon. the Lords Comm. of Appeals for Prizes, 1759.

[36] BL Add MS 36807, Negotiations with Spain, Extract of a letter from Pitt to Bristol, 14 December 1759, ff. 43–4.

[37] TNA HCA 45/1/37, Case of the *San Joseph* [English translation as it appears in the HCA documents].

realise that what had worked to appease Dutch anger in 1758 was not working with the Spanish in 1760.

It is clear from Pitt and Hardwicke's correspondence that an answer to the memorandum required a considerable amount of research into how previous, and still active, Anglo-Spanish treaties had been negotiated. However, a good portion of that September was also taken up by a large load of Dutch cases coming before the Court of Prize Appeal. Hardwicke and Mansfield's correspondence in this month was dominated by discussions of Dutch appellate affairs. Given that the final form of the British Court's response to Fuentes's memorandum was largely written by Mansfield, it seems likely that the discussions about the memorandums were done more in person than via letter. Since they were often in court together, they would likely have had several opportunities to meet and discuss the memorandum.[38]

By August of 1760, the correspondence about Fuentes's memorandum shifted and was dominated by letters between Pitt and the Lords of the Admiralty. This presumably occurred because Pitt, Mansfield, and Hardwicke had come to an agreement over how to respond to the memorandum, and the next task was to make the Admiralty aware of the ministers' decisions. On 1 August, Pitt wrote a letter addressed to the Lords of the Admiralty in which he reiterated Fuentes's complaints about the preferential conduct of British prize courts, particularly in Gibraltar and America, which favoured British privateers over Spanish merchants. Pitt wrote:

I am commanded to signify to your Lordships the King's pleasure, that you do forthwith cause the strictest Enquiry to be made, whether there is any, and what foundation for the representation abovementioned, and that you do give the strongest directions, as far as shall be consistent with Law, to the judges of all the Courts of Admiralty, that they do, without the least unnecessary delay, give immediate justice to any Spanish ships brought before them; and that, in all their judgments they have the strictest regard to the stipulations, and true meaning of the treaty of 1667 subsisting between the Crowns of Great Britain and Spain, and to His Majesty's orders and instructions founded thereon, to all ships of war and privateers[39]

Such writing was, by this stage in the war, beginning to smack of tooth-less repetition but, at the same time, if the Court of Prize Appeal was having no effect in terms of assuring that Spain remained a neutral

[38] BL Add MS 35596, Hardwicke Papers, Entire. Unfortunately, no copy of Mansfield's answer was found in the archives used for this book. It is possible that a copy exists in Mansfield Papers at Scone Palace, Scotland or in the Collection on Legal Change at Olin Library, Wesleyan University, which contains a large Mansfield collection.

[39] TNA ADM 1/4124, Letter from Pitt to Lords of the Admiralty, 1 August 1760, f. 10.

nation, it is possible that Pitt saw little alternative but to try to demand change in the behaviour of the lower prize courts. Prize law, however, had not changed, and Pitt still had no actual jurisdiction or authority over the lower courts. He always stopped just short of commanding the prize court judges to make judgments that would not anger the Spanish Court, because legally he could not. All he could do was direct the judges to resolve Spanish cases quickly and to adhere to the 'true meaning of the treaty of 1667', a laughable request, as the Spanish and British Courts could not agree on a 'true meaning' of any treaty, particularly in the realm of the right to carry French colonial goods. Nonetheless, by writing the letter, Pitt was able to convey to the Spanish ministers, once again, that he was actively engaged in making sure that Spanish ships received justice when they entered the British prize system.

Once Fuentes arrived at the British Court and the response to his memorandum had been agreed by Pitt, Hardwicke, and Mansfield, Pitt began to interfere personally in several prize cases involving Spanish ships. On 11 August, he requested that the Lords of the Admiralty send him information regarding eleven Spanish ships that had been taken by British warships between January 1757, and June 1760. In the case of all eleven, the Spaniards had complained of the captures. Pitt wanted to know which ships had been restored and when. The letter made it clear that the information was of the utmost importance and was to be delivered to his office by the next morning.[40] The next day, Pitt addressed another letter to the Lords of the Admiralty on the subject of Captain Dalrymple, commander of HMS *Postilion*, who had lodged an appeal with the Lords Commissioners of Prize Appeal after capturing a Spanish ship trading between San Sebastián and Dublin. The case had first been tried at the Vice Admiralty court in Dublin, where the Spanish ship was restored. Pitt wrote that the ship 'was to have been released according to the sentence of the Vice Admiralty court at Dublin, where the cause was heard, had not this affair been protracted by an appeal, which, in the opinion of the Conde de Fuentes, can only be productive of unnecessary expense and delay'.[41] Pitt continued by instructing the Lords of the Admiralty to acquaint Captain Dalrymple with the 'disadvantageous consequences to himself'[42] if the appellate court confirmed the sentence passed by the Vice Admiralty court. The wording of the letter is worth quoting in full, as the language left no doubt that the

---

[40] TNA ADM 1/4124, Letter from James Rivers to Lords of the Admiralty, 11 August 1760, f. 19. Note that James Rivers was secretary to Mr Pitt.
[41] TNA ADM 1/4124, Letter from Pitt to Lords of the Admiralty, 12 August 1760, f. 21.
[42] Ibid.

captain was being ordered by Pitt to drop the appeal, without ever actually giving an order to either the Lords of the Admiralty or Dalrymple:

> should it appear that the circumstances of this capture are such, as cannot justify the additional delay and trouble which he gives to the subjects of His Catholic Majesty by an appeal, which it would be more to his credit and advantage to drop, unless he is thoroughly founded in the clearness of his legal pretensions.[43]

By inserting the Conde de Fuentes's opinion in the letter, Pitt turned it into a situation where it was Fuentes's position against that of Captain Dalrymple. There was little doubt that it was the Spaniard's position that would be heeded. The appellate case was couched in terms of delay rather than legality, which demonstrated both Pitt's and Fuentes's priorities. The affair was about Spanish displeasure, not the legality of the capture. By explicitly writing that it would be to the captain's advantage to drop the case, Pitt came as close to an order as possible, and the implied threat to the captain's career, should he proceed, was hard to miss. Dalrymple's case does not show up in the records of the Court of Prize Appeal, which suggests that he was not 'thoroughly founded' in his legal pretensions and withdrew the appeal as Pitt wished. At least four similar letters with similar outcomes crop up in Pitt's correspondence until the break with Spain in 1762. All of them make reference to specific complaints from the Conde de Fuentes to Pitt. Whilst it was impossible for the Secretary of State to control the actions of the Royal Navy at sea, it was possible for him to make sure that the Conde de Fuentes's complaints were addressed quickly and without the long process of the prize courts. Though this may not have engendered trust in the British legal system, it showed the Spanish ambassador that British ministers were willing to act quickly during prize disputes in order to appease the Spanish Court and maintain Spanish neutrality.

Nine days after the answer to the prize affairs memorandum had been returned to Spain, the Conde de Fuentes presented two further memorandums to the British Court. One memorandum was about Spanish claims to the Newfoundland fisheries, and the other was about British logwood-cutting settlements in Honduras. Neither memorandum was particularly welcomed by British ministers, and Pitt considered the Newfoundland fishery memorandum insulting, because a copy of it had been given by the Spanish Court to the Court of France.[44] As in

---

[43] Ibid.

[44] BL Add MS 36807, Negotiations with Spain, Abstract of Spanish Dispatches previous to the late negotiations with France, no date, ff. 254–7.

most of his diplomatic dealings with the Spanish Court, Pitt consulted Lord Hardwicke on both memorandums, and it was Hardwicke's opinion that a copy of the Newfoundland memorandum had been sent to France in order to gain French support for Spanish claims. Hardwicke wrote that 'One idea meant to be conveyed by that extraordinary step [sending the memorandum to France], so unusual between friendly Courts, I conjure, was that France was to be hurried in as a bishop to support the Spanish Claim.'[45] Interestingly, Fuentes added that his Court did not require an immediate answer to the Newfoundland memorandum but did require an immediate answer to the logwood memorandum. It is likely that by calling on French support but not forcing a British answer, the Spanish Court was merely demonstrating that it was willing to involve the French in its disputes with Britain but was also still open to resolving disputes without French aid, should Britain choose to co-operate.

The dispute over logwood cutting demanded more immediate attention than that over the fishery because it was ultimately a territorial dispute on Spanish soil in Central America and was, therefore, a threat to the balance of power, which was increasingly tilting in Britain's favour as the war progressed. Pitt's response to both memorandums was sent to Lord Bristol on 26 September 1760, along with a set of secret instructions. Bristol was to read Pitt's response in full to Ricardo Wall as often as was requested but he was not ever to hand a copy of the response to the Spanish minister. Bristol was also instructed to 'observe to Him [Wall] that you do it [the readings], as a more open and confidential manner of acting with Him, from yourself, and not by any order from your court'.[46] Pitt likely wanted to foster a relationship between Wall and Bristol that was similar to that between Keene and Wall. However, such effort was, according to Hardwicke, misplaced. In his letter advising Pitt about the memorandums he wrote, 'I much fear that Mr. Wall's influence in the Court of Madrid is not the same as it has been, and that his having been insinuated as partial to England, will make him too cautious and afraid to open himself upon such points ...'[47] Since Hardwicke wrote his letter three days after Pitt sent the response for the memorandum, it is possible that he simply did not receive Hardwicke's warning about Wall in time, though it is unlikely that he was unaware of Wall's fading influence. With

---

[45] BL Add MS 35423, Hardwicke Papers, Letter from Hardwicke to Pitt, 29 September 1760, ff. 207–8.

[46] Clements Library M-66, Shelburne Papers, vol. 22, Letter from Pitt to Earl of Bristol, 26 September 1760, ff. 528–38.

[47] BL Add MS 35423, Hardwicke Papers, Letter from Hardwicke to Pitt, 29 September 1760, ff. 207–8.

the new Spanish king and a Spanish Court that was ever more hostile to Britain, Wall was likely one of the only Spanish ministers left whom Pitt considered could be an ally to Britain.

The response which Bristol was to read aloud to Wall is nineteen pages long. In terms of the fishery, the response is well summarised by the following:

> to make the court of Madrid sensible of the imprudence as well as indecency of so strange a step; and that the Spanish Ministers will receive, before it is too late, an useful hint, given (with no unfriendly intentions) namely, that, hoping to intimidate, they will only indispose a Court which in general, most sincerely means every thing that is just and friendly towards Spain ...[48]

It was a clear signal to the Court of Spain that calling on the aid of the French would not make Britain back down on her claims of monopoly over the Newfoundland fishery which was, according to the British ministers, granted by the Treaty of Utrecht.

The response to the logwood-cutting memorandum was more complicated. In this dispute, Pitt was willing to back down and concede to some of Spain's demands. Pitt agreed to order the abandonment of all British fortifications and establishments in Honduras as requested by the memorandum, as long as the Court of Spain was willing to negotiate on the actual cutting and harvesting of the logwood. Pitt considered that Fuentes's memorandum 'far from proposing to open a negotiation, absolutely shuts the door to any; and denying to the subjects of Great Britain, all colour of privilege, or liberty, to cut logwood on the American coasts'.[49] Pitt was unwilling to completely give in to Fuentes's demands because the previous Court of Spain under Ferdinand had promised that 'all such differences and accidents [over logwood] as might otherwise interrupt good harmony, and friendship, were to be amicably adjusted, This, beyond all contradiction supposes negotiation, and something to be agreed between the Two Powers.'[50] With such a justification, Pitt proceeded to go on the offensive and threatened that, if the Spanish Court continued to insist on the terms as presented in Fuentes's memorandum,

> the answer of His Majesty can ... be such only, as the dignity of His Crown, and the just cause of the essential interests of His subjects, suggest. Interposing this delay, therefore, in such a circumstance, is not only wise in His Majesty but surely it is also friendly, in order to give time thereby for sounder policy, and more

[48] CL M-66, Shelburne Papers, vol. 22, Letter from Pitt to Earl of Bristol, 26 September 1760, ff. 528–38.
[49] Ibid.   [50] Ibid.

temperate councils to prevail at Madrid: If the desired effect follows, the conclusion may be happy for both countries: if not, England will have nothing to reproach herself.[51]

Pitt made it very clear that if Fuentes cut off negotiations in terms of logwood cutting, then there was no guarantee that British actions would be favourable to the Spanish Court, and that Britain would not be bullied into giving up all access to logwood cutting without an attempt at negotiation. By directing his answer to Wall, Pitt was communicating with a minister who had been instrumental in previous Anglo-Spanish negotiations over logwood cutting, and who had always favoured negotiations over ultimatums in this subject. As a parting threat, Pitt played on Spanish fears over the balance of power in the Americas. Unless the disputes over logwood cutting were resolved to the satisfaction of both courts they 'may otherwise continue to give to Spain serious and lasting uneasiness; and fatally prove an obstruction to the cordial friendship of a power, best able and most willing to contribute to the great views of His Catholic Majesty'.[52] Pitt not only threatened continued vexation when it came to Spanish sovereignty in America, he also threatened that Spain's intransigence could lead to war. With British victory in Canada in early September 1760 and the crippling of French sea power in the battle of Quiberon Bay in 1759, British threats were not idle. The balance of power in the Americas had already shifted greatly in favour of the British, and France's ability to aid Spain in a conflict against Britain were greatly diminished.

On receiving Pitt's answers to the various memorandums, Wall considered the language so insulting and combative that he did not even show them or discuss them with the Spanish king.[53] Wall worried that Spanish neutrality was becoming impossible to maintain, and he turned his efforts towards encouraging an Anglo-French peace lest Spain become involved in the war. The Spanish Court, in the meantime, was becoming more anti-British, and not long after Pitt responded to the Spanish memorandums, the Spanish ambassador to the French Court, Wall's friend and ally in supporting Spain's neutrality, was replaced with the anti-British Duke of Grimaldi. Grimaldi returned to Spain in 1763 to become one of the Court's prime ministers, and a proponent of rebuilding Spanish power in order to seek out another war with Britain when the opportunity arose.[54]

---

[51] Ibid.   [52] Ibid.   [53] Alarcia, *Ministerio Wall*, p. 112.
[54] AHN ESTADO 4119, Letter from Grimaldi to Wall, 15 April 1763.

Further Anglo-Spanish negotiations over grievances or memorandums were delayed when the British Court was rocked by the unexpected death of King George II on 25 October 1760. The positions and favour of Britain's ministers suddenly depended on the young King George III and his favourite, Lord Bute. In terms of the four men who were most closely involved with Anglo-Spanish relations – Pitt, Newcastle, Hardwicke, and Mansfield – only Pitt, a close friend of both Bute and George III, would remain in favour during the transition to a new monarch. The other three men, who had served the new king's grandfather for so long and retained his confidence, were no longer favoured.[55] However, nothing was firmly settled, and Pitt, Newcastle, and George III faced political uncertainty through the end of the war. George III and Lord Bute wanted the war to come to an end swiftly. Pitt became ever more belligerent and would not be satisfied until France's ability to wield a navy was destroyed, and more of her lands conquered.[56] Newcastle became consumed with his treatment at the hands of Bute and George III, alternately threatening to resign and going to great lengths to garner support from Parliament and the rest of the government. Lord Mansfield soon found his way into the favour of the new king but, in doing so, lost the trust and friendship of his one-time patron, Newcastle.[57] In the new, uncertain environment of George III's ascendency, the affairs of the Court of Prize Appeal were, understandably, put aside for a time, and the court did not meet again until late November of 1760, when the case of the *Jesús, Maria, y José* was finally resumed.

The Trial Resumes

By the time the Court of Prize Appeal met on 20 November, the commission that had been sent to Spain on the Appellants' request had been back for exactly six months. It had returned in May with the depositions of eight Spanish witnesses who claimed that the *Jesús, Maria, y José* was a Spanish ship. Six of those witnesses also claimed that the goods had been shipped by, and belonged to, Don Pedro de Larralde.[58] The arguments presented at the second hearing of the case were short and revolved entirely around the new depositions. The Appellants presented the new evidence to the court in support of the original arguments made in 1759.

---

[55] J. S. Corbett, *England in the Seven Years' War: A Study in Combined Strategy*, 2 vols. (Longmans, Green, and Co., 1907), vol. 2, p. 101.

[56] Ibid. p. 142.

[57] N. S. Poser, *Lord Mansfield: Justice in the Age of Reason* (McGill-Queen's University Press, 2013), p. 137.

[58] BL Add MS 36211, Hardwicke Papers, Notes on the *Jesús, Maria, y José*.

The depositions had been taken in San Sebastián, but there was no written explanation given for the choice of witnesses, and at no point did Hardwicke reference any account in his notes. Two of the deponents were public notaries of San Sebastián: one was a master shipbuilder, another was the Captain of Port and of the Quay of San Sebastián, and the other four were given only by name. What is most interesting about the depositions is that none of the men offer any concrete or written proof for their statements about the ownership of either the vessel or the goods. Each deposition is full of language such as 'that he knew well', or 'that he well and certainly knew'. The master shipbuilder deposed 'That he had really heard, that when the said ship should be laden at La Coruña, she should return with the lading to this City of St. Sebastiáns [sic].'[59] All of the 'evidence' produced by the depositions was hearsay or based on what the witnesses said they believed to be true. Nonetheless, at the end of the eight depositions the advocates, Bettesworth and Forrester, told the court that it was clear that the ship and the goods belonged to Spaniards and should be restored, with costs and damages, to the Appellants. There was never any mention of, or attempt to refute, the prior accusation that the goods were put on board the *Jesús, Maria, y José* from a French East India ship; this was an interesting omission given that the Respondent's case was built upon an argument of transhipment. Without depositions that specifically gave proof that the goods were bought by Spaniards after they had been landed on Spanish soil, then the argument of transhipment could still be made against the Spanish Appellants.

In reply to the depositions taken at San Sebastián, the advocates for the Respondent, Hay and Smalbroke, questioned the lack of material evidence presented in support of the claims made by the Spanish witnesses. Why was it, the advocates posed to the court, that a commission sent to San Sebastián, the supposed home of Larralde and the owners of the *Jesús, Maria, y José*, did not return with proof, on paper, which showed the ship to be Spanish, or which showed that the cargo had been legally purchased by Larralde? They also questioned why Larralde and the owners of the ship had not given depositions. As far as Hay and Smalbroke were concerned,

the cause ... remains exactly in the same state as before, on the part of the Appellants, the preparatory Examinations directly contradicting the ship's papers, and the additional evidence; and there not being any clear

---

[59] Ibid.

uncontradicted proof, that the said ship was not trading for the account of the enemy, and bound to an enemy's port ...[60]

In order to clearly show the contradiction between the preparatory examinations and the evidence presented by the Appellants, some extracts from the preparatory examinations were presented to the Lords Commissioners. They contained parts of the depositions of Ezenarro and four other crew members. Whilst Ezenarro had contradicted his deposition when the appeal was first filed, the other crew members had not, and their depositions supported the Respondent's contention that the goods on the ship came from a French East India ship. Hardwicke's annotations on the extracts were all in the sections having to do with whether the goods were French and had come from a French East India ship. Hardwicke was clearly annotating all the sections that supported the Respondent's argument. In the deposition from Alexander de Rosa, a foremast-man, Hardwicke underlined two different sections: 'all the said lading was put on board her [*Jesús, Maria, y José*] at one time at the Port of Corunna [*sic*] ... directly from on board a French East India ship, then lying in the said Port, without having been landed or put on shore there',[61] and 'That at the time the said goods were putting on board the said Snow [*Jesús, Maria, y José*] from the French East India ship, as aforesaid, this examinant heard the said Consul's [Bozinack] said son say or declare, that the said goods were to be delivered at Bayonne or Bordeaux in France.'[62] From the deposition of Baptist de Arenter, a mariner, Hardwicke highlighted a section about an overheard conversation between one of the owners of the Spanish ship, Valez de Lavalla, and Ezenarro

[t]hat before they sailed from St. Sebastián's, he heard the said Ignatius de Lavalla tell both the said Pedro de Ezenarro ... that they must sign Four Bills of Lading for their Cargoes, and send Two or Three of them over Land to France; and saith, That afterwards, whilst at Corunna [*sic*], he heard the said Pedro de Ezenarro ... that Two of the Bills of Lading ... were sent over Land to France.[63]

The depositions of the witnesses presented by the Respondent's advocates provided multiple and damning counters to the depositions put forward by the Appellants' case. With the lack of concrete evidence put forward by the Appellants, despite the voyage to San Sebastián to gather such evidence, much of the appellate court's sentence would depend on which depositions were weighted more heavily by Hardwicke and his fellow commissioners. The larger implications of which depositions were

[60] Ibid.   [61] Ibid.   [62] Ibid.   [63] Ibid.

to be believed was how the Spanish ambassador and the Spanish Court would receive any sentence given in this case. Given Fuentes's response to previous prize court issues, it is likely that any sentence condemning the voyage as fraudulent would provoke outrage and would further damage Anglo-Spanish relations. This placed Hardwicke and British ministers in a complicated position because, although Fuentes could respond poorly to a sentence favouring the British privateer, he had shown no sign of being appeased by previous outcomes favourable to Spanish appellants.

When all the advocates had finished presenting their arguments, the commissioners retired to discuss the case and the sentencing. Hardwicke's notes of the sentencing process indicate that the commissioners began by going through the arguments presented by the advocates. After a brief summary of the Respondent's and Appellants' arguments, Hardwicke concluded that there were four vital questions to answer: whether the ship should be considered a Spanish or French ship; whether the goods were French property or Spanish property; if the property was French, was it protected by the ship being Spanish; and whether the case was one of transhipment and fraud in order to assist the French against a lawful capture by British ships?[64] Hardwicke understood that the evidence could be evaluated in a variety of ways, and he sought to reason through the various possibilities of the conflicting statements and evidence. To answer the first two questions, he picked aspects from both the Respondent's and Appellants' submitted depositions. From the Appellants' he began with the assumption that the ship was clearly Spanish. In his notes, Hardwicke called on the case of the Dutch ship *Novum Arartum* which had been tried by the appellate court in May 1760. The *Novum Arartum* had been sailing from St Eustatius to Amsterdam and was presumed to be carrying French colonial goods. The question arose as to whether the ship should be considered an adopted French ship. Charles Yorke, one of the advocates, sought the advice of John Berens (a well-connected Hamburg merchant who specialised in Anglo-Dutch trade and went on to establish the successful Muilman and Berens Co. in 1772) on the question of adoption and transhipment. In a letter written to Yorke the day before the case came before the appellate court, Berens explained that transhipment was a process used by many nations in times of peace for a variety of legal and practical reasons. In St Eustatius specifically, the geography of the port was such that landing and shipping goods was considered dangerous

---

[64] Ibid.

because the road between the anchorage and the shore had very high surf. As such, transhipping was practiced whenever possible (via permit or the permission of the governor) in order to avoid the dangerous passage from ship to shore. In times of peace, Berens wrote, the French traded sugar and coffee at St Eustatius, making use of transhipment, and this continued during the current war. As far as Berens was aware, the property being transhipped did not always change ownership but 'I believe in general it must be presumed there is, and that the transhipping is done by order and for account of the person resident in the port where it is performed.'[65] The exception to this, was French ships carrying West and East India goods that came to Spanish ports in order to transfer their cargo into Spanish ships with the intention of carrying them safely to French ports in Europe. Berens indicated that he and Yorke had discussed this exception previously. This last point was of particular interest to the case of the *Jesús, Maria, y José*, because it indicated that the Spanish ship was most likely engaged in transhipment in order to avoid capture. Though Yorke was not an advocate in the case of the *Jesús, Maria, y José*, his partner in the case of the *Novum Arartum*, George Hay, was. It is also worth noting that a copy of Berens's letter was in Hardwicke's notes for the *Novum Arartum*. Yorke and Hay argued that the *Novum Arartum* could not be considered a French ship by adoption because it engaged in transhipment that was allowed during peacetime and because it was travelling between two Dutch ports and never traded at an enemy port. Hardwicke accepted this reasoning, and it was in line with the decision made in the *Maria Theresa*.[66] If, as claimed by the Spanish Appellants, the *Jesús, Maria, y José*, had been travelling between two Spanish ports, then the circumstances of the *Novum Arartum* could apply. If, however, the ship was travelling to a French port, then it could be considered a continuation of the original French journey and could be considered a French ship. Hardwicke also noted that East India goods could only be imported into France on French ships which would make the ship French if it were travelling to a French port. Hardwicke did not resolve this question at this stage in his notes but shifted to considering the question of who owned the goods on board.

Hardwicke began with the assumption from the Respondent's case that the cargo of French East India goods was French property and that the ship was bound, ultimately, to a French port. Hardwicke acknowledged that the various witness statements and written evidence created confusion as to whether the goods belonged to Spaniards through the process of being landed on Spanish soil and/or being purchased by Spaniards. There was also contrary evidence as to whether the ship was bound to a French port or to a Spanish port. Hardwicke even wrote at the end of the summaries 'I admit there is great contrarity of evidence.'[67] However, in this section of his notes on the ownership of the goods, he did not refer to any previous cases. He did make the point that the Spanish had had the opportunity to prove that the goods had been purchased by Spaniards and had not done so. The property, he concluded, would be assumed to be French property.

With the above reasoning, Hardwicke had granted some credence to both the Spanish and the British Privateer's cases and set it up so that arguments could address transhipment and the Rule of the War of 1756. From here, Hardwicke had to answer whether the French property was protected by the Spanish ship, and whether the voyage was intentionally fraudulent. In other words, was it a case of transhipment or a case of adoption, and how did the Rule of the War of 1756 apply, as Spaniards were prohibited from carrying French colonial trade during peacetime?

Hardwicke proceeded by asking whether the case was one of transhipment by the Spaniards in order to help the French deceive the British and avoid lawful capture and whether such actions would make the ship and cargo lawful prize. If the circumstances of the case determined that it was indeed a case of transhipment, then Hardwicke claimed that there was no precedent in print set by previous prize cases that fit the circumstances of the *Jesús, Maria, y José*. Given that many Dutch and Spanish ships were brought before the prize courts under accusations of fraudulently carrying on French trade, Hardwicke's claim at first glance seems to lack credulity. However, he was making a distinction between neutral ships condemned as 'adopted French ships' of which there had been many instances, and neutral ships condemned as lawful prize for transhipping enemy goods without being considered 'adopted French ships', which had not occurred.[68] Hardwicke called on the case of the Dutch ship *America*, where the ship had been declared French by adoption because it was trading French colonial goods to French ports, a trade only open to French ships. But the *America* had been in a French port (St Domingue) before it was taken as prize.[69] In the present case, the ship was bound for a French port but had not actually visited one before capture. Hardwicke

[67] BL Add MS 36211, Hardwicke Papers, Notes on the *Jesús, Maria, y José*.   [68] Ibid.
[69] TNA HCA 45/2/12, Case of the *America*.

questioned whether a ship could be cast as an adopted French ship if it had not been in a French port during its voyage.[70]

Before the case of the *Jesús, Maria, y José* came before the Court of Prize Appeal, approximately thirty cases (most involving Dutch ships) came before the Court of Prize Appeal in which questions of adoption arose. In twenty-seven of those cases, the ships and the goods were condemned as lawful prize. Of those twenty-seven, eighteen appear in Hardwicke's notes.[71] The common thread between the cases where the ship was designated an adopted French ship was whether it had been in a French port prior to capture. There were three exceptions, the case of the *Vrow Anna*, the case of the *Nassau*, and the case of the *Anna and Elizabeth*. In these three cases, the ships were condemned as adopted French ships due to the evidence of being engaged in a voyage to transport or pick up French goods at a French port. In two cases, the evidence was a French passport and evidence of French duties being paid.[72] In one case, that of the *Anna and Elizabeth*, the ship was taken near a French colonial port and the evidence from the crew and letters relating to the voyage were deemed enough to prove that the ship was engaged in a voyage to a French port to engage in French colonial trade.[73] All of these cases supported the precedent begun with the *America* that came to be known as the Rule of the War of 1756, and made it clear that the Court of Prize Appeal would condemn 'neutral' ships as lawful prize via adoption if they had been in a French port.

If the *Jesús, Maria, y José* were not considered an adopted French ship, but the goods were considered French, then the court had to address whether the transhipment was fraudulent through the attempt to pass French goods off as legitimate Spanish trade (not just French trade protected by treaties covering neutral rights). For this, there was indeed no precedent. Hardwicke thus called upon the Anglo-Spanish treaty of 1667 and the Anglo-Dutch treaty of 1674 (invoked by the Appellants' case) as his guide. If Hardwicke concluded that the ship should indeed be considered Spanish property and lawful prize, then any sentence handed down in the case of the *Jesús, Maria, y José* could set a precedent that

[70] BL Add MS 36211, Hardwicke Papers, Notes on the *Jesús, Maria, y José*.
Ibid.
[71] BL Add MS 36208–11, Hardwicke Papers, Cases of the *America* (1760); *De Resolutie* (1760); *Vrow Anna* (1760); *Nassau* (1760); *Juffrow Alida* (1760); *Isaac Galley* (1760); *Speedwell* (1760); *Stad Rotterdam* (1760); *Rotterdam* (1760); *De Snip* (1760); *Den Amstel* (1760); *San Vicente* (1760); *Maria Agnes* (1760); *Geregtigheit* (1760); *Peter John* (1760); *Anne and Elizabeth* (1760); *De Hoop* (1760); *Maria Johanna* (1760).
[72] BL Add MS 36210, Hardwicke Papers, Case of the *Vrow Anna* (1760), and Case of the *Nassau* (1760).
[73] BL Add MS 36210, Hardwicke Papers, Case of the *Anna and Elizabeth* (1760).

would address Spanish attempts to fraudulently claim French colonial goods as Spanish goods in Spanish ships. If the sentence were linked to the Rule of the War of 1756 (which might be done by arguing that Spaniards could not tranship French goods into Spanish ships in order to complete a French East India voyage ending in a French port because this type of trade was not allowed during times of peace) then the remit of the rule could be expanded.

Hardwicke allowed that the Spanish could invoke the privileges of the Anglo-Dutch treaty of 1674 and that, therefore, the privileges of the ship protected cargo that was not designated as contraband. However, he added the proviso that 'Whoever will claim the privilege of such a treaty must bring himself within the terms and conditions of it.'[74] In other words, according to Hardwicke, the privileges of the ship were curtailed by Article 2 of the Anglo-Dutch treaty of 1674 which declared that 'the cargo must be such goods as the Friend's [Dutch] ships might have carried and had right to carry in times of peace'[75] (the basis of the Rule of the War of 1756). If the Spanish wanted to claim the privileges of the Dutch treaty, they would also have to adhere to its limitations and, for the Court of Prize Appeal, that meant being bound by the Rule of the War of 1756. Referring again to the case of the Dutch ship *America*, Hardwicke stated that, 'the object and instruction of such a treaty is ... you shall not be ... put in a worse condition by our war but you shall not be put in a better condition by it'.[76] Therefore, since the French East India trade was not open to Spaniards or Spanish ships in times of peace and the goods on board the *Jesús, Maria, y José* were French property, the privileges of the Spanish ship did not protect her cargo from condemnation. Hardwicke's reasoning was also to be found in the philosophy and thinking of the law-of-nations scholar, Cornelis van Bynkershoek, who argued for a distinction between trading with the enemy, which meant engaging in trade that was not designed to deceive a belligerent nation (trade allowed during times of peace), and trading for the enemy, which meant engaging in fraudulent trade that would benefit one belligerent at the expense of another (trade that was prohibited during times of peace).[77]

Hardwicke took time in his notes, at this point, to make clear that the Appellants had been given ample opportunity to prove that the goods had

---

[74] BL Add MS 36211, Hardwicke Papers, Notes on the *Jesús, Maria, y José*.   [75] Ibid.
[76] Ibid.
[77] K. Stapelbroek. 'The Foundations of Vattel's "System" of Politics and the Context of the Seven Years' War: Moral Philosophy, Luxury and the Constitutional Commercial State', in K. Stapelbroek and A. Trampus (eds.), *The Legacy of Vattel's Droit des Gens* (Palgrave Macmillan, 2019), pp. 115–16.

been purchased by Spaniards and had become Spanish property at some point during the transition from the French ship to the Spanish ship. However, since no concrete proof of Spanish ownership was provided to the court, and the goods had never touched Spanish soil, they were still considered French. Furthermore, Hardwicke considered the nature of the trade and whether it was 'bona fide' or 'fraudulent to avoid the just Rule of England against her enemy, arising from her war'.[78] He called upon the depositions of the Spanish sailors about Bozinack (the French consul at San Sebastián) and how his sons had managed the transhipment of the goods from the French East India ship into the *Jesús, Maria, y José*. He also called upon the five bills of lading, four of which had been sent overland to France, presumably in an attempt to hide the true ownership and destination of the property. These facts alone, Hardwicke noted, had been enough to condemn ships and goods as lawful prize.[79] It is interesting to note here that Hardwicke chose not to call on specific cases where this had been the case, particularly when three Dutch ships had been condemned in 1760 as adopted French ships by the Court of Prize Appeal based on documentation and the intent to travel to a French port (rather than having been in a French port before capture) in order to engage in fraudulent trade. These three ships were the aforementioned *Vrow Anna*, the *Nassau*, and the *Anne and Elizabeth*. Was Hardwicke trying to avoid calling upon precedent that could logically lead to declaring the *Jesús, Maria, y José* an adopted French ship? This seems like a possibility given that he had repeatedly called on the case of the *America* and made the point that declaring a ship an adopted French ship was based on that ship having been in a French port.

Hardwicke then turned to whether the transhipment itself was fraudulent. Hardwicke considered that there was a clear case for fraudulent transhipment as the French goods had been placed directly from a French ship into a Spanish ship, with an intended destination in France. It is interesting that here he did not once again bring up the case of the *Novum Aratrum* and Dr Hay's letter about the fraudulent nature of transhipment practices on the North coast of Spain in regard to French goods. As the goods remained French property, there was, arguably, no difference between this voyage and that of a French East India voyage, except for the change of ship, indicating that it was done only to escape capture by British ships. The Spanish ship was used in lieu of a French ship and 'must ... be subject to the like impediments and hazards [as a French ship]'.[80] For Hardwicke it became increasingly clear that the

[78] BL Add MS 36211, Hardwicke Papers, Notes on the *Jesús, Maria, y José*.   [79] Ibid.
[80] Ibid.

intended fraud was, essentially, to complete the French East India voyage using a Spanish ship in order to avoid capture. The ship could, therefore, be treated as an adopted French ship rather than a Spanish ship and there was certainly precedent to make such a decision. However, Hardwicke ended his notes by stating that declaring the *Jesús, Maria, y José* an adopted French ship would be 'carrying it too far' because the ship had never been in a French port. He did not describe in his notes how this case differed from those where documents describing the intent to go to a French port had been enough to condemn the ship. It is possible that one of the differences Hardwicke took into account was that the *Vrow Anna*, the *Nassau*, and the *Anne and Elizabeth* were captured in the West Indies rather than European waters. What is clear from his notes, is that Hardwicke's reasoning had led him to a circumstance where there was precedent from previous cases to condemn the ship as an adopted French ship, but that Hardwicke chose not to call upon these cases. Between the writing of his notes and the writing of the declared sentence on the cover sheet of the case documents, however, Hardwicke appears to have altered his thinking on the point of adoption.

The end of Hardwicke's sentence, which comes at the end of his notes on the case, reads as follows: 'That therefore the Lords are of opinion that this was a grossly fraudulent transhipping and a continuation of the original French voyage from the East Indies to France. Therefore presumed Fr.'[81] Such a sentence would have led to the condemnation of the ship and all of the goods as lawful prize and to the Appellants being condemned to pay all of the expenses incurred over the course of a five-year trial. In terms of Anglo-Spanish affairs and the tension that existed between the two Courts over the recent memorandums, the sentence of the Lords Commissioners was less than desirable. Fuentes, who took a very close interest in prize affairs, would likely have condemned the decision as a display of favouritism and bias, of which he had so often accused the British prize courts. From a speculative legal perspective, condemning the *Jesús, Maria, y José* as an adopted French ship would have strengthened the precedent that neutral ships could be condemned as lawful prize in the British prize system even if they had not been in a French port. It would also have become only the second Spanish ship to be condemned as an adopted French ship (the other was the *San Vicente*[82]) therefore creating more precedent for Spanish ships to be condemned as adopted French ships if they were carrying French colonial goods with the intent to visit a French port. In terms of the Rule of

[81] Ibid.   [82] BL Add MS 36209, Hardwicke Papers, Notes on the *San Vicente.*

the War of 1756, the case would have added to the now long list of cases that upheld the British prize court precedent that trade prohibited to a neutral country during peacetime would be prohibited during wartime. It would also have established that Spanish ships would not be treated differently from Dutch ships and that transhipment of French colonial goods into a Spanish ship was not enough to avoid condemnation in the prize court system, even if captured in European waters rather than colonial waters. All of this would also have been in keeping with the ideas put forward by Charles Jenkinson in his treatise *A Discourse on the Conduct of the Government of Great Britain in Respect to Neutral Nations*. However, the sentence was never pronounced, either officially in the court, the court documents or, seemingly, in the British press.

A Convenient Petition and the Collapse of Anglo-Spanish Negotiations

There is no note or correspondence left by Hardwicke to indicate why the sentence in the case of the *Jesús, Maria, y José* was not pronounced. Three handwritten notes offer some explanation: an undated petition from Charles Davids, captain of the British privateer *Britannia* that had taken the Spanish ship as prize, was attached to the end of the court documents, an annotation in Hardwicke's hand on the cover sheet of the first set of court documents relating to the case, and a handwritten note on another copy of the case's documents filed with the Court of Prize Appeal's documents. Captain Davids's petition briefly recounted the progression of the trial from the High Court of Admiralty through the Court of Prize Appeal. He described how the appeals had raised doubt as to the particular circumstances of the case and 'That your Lordships had therefore taken time to deliberate and have not yet given Judgment therein or intimated when you shall please to give judgment ...'[83] Sentences were normally handed down the same day as the final hearings. Assuming that the *Jesús, Maria, y José* followed the same pattern, Hardwicke's notes and the sentence he recorded should have been given on 20 November 1760. However, either the deliberation was conducted on the 20th and not made public, or the deliberations were delayed. Either way, it was an abnormal occurrence. Even more abnormal was the fact that the court met two more times in fairly quick succession (quick for the prize court system). On 17 December 1760 the court met again, and for this meeting there is a list of the attendees. Thirteen members

---

[83] BL Add MS 36211, Hardwicke Papers, Notes on the *Jesús, Maria, y José*.

were present – amongst them Hardwicke, Mansfield, Lord Royston (Hardwicke's son), Lord Sandys (friend of Hardwicke and future head of the Board of Trade), and Robert Nugent (friend of Newcastle and recent appointee to a lucrative sinecure). The only note left behind after the 17 December meeting was that the commissioners were taking more time to deliberate and would meet after the holidays.[84]

Even though the court chose to continue deliberations on the *Jésus, Maria, y José* into the new year, they still met on the 19 and 20 December to decide the fate of three other Spanish ships. On 19 December, the court met to deliberate on the case of the ship *La Virgen del Rosario y el Santo Cristo de Buen Viaje* and restored the ship and goods to the Spanish owner along with costs to be paid by the British privateer.[85] This case was ultimately about inter-colonial disputes between inhabitants of Havana and Port Royal. It was on appeal from the vice-Admiralty court in New York.[86] The next day, two Spanish ships, owned by the same woman and taken on the same day by two different British privateers, came before the Court of Prize Appeal. The ships *Los Buenos Amigos* and the *San Antonio*, along with their cargo, had been condemned as lawful prize by the Admiralty court in Gibraltar. The Court of Prize Appeal reversed both sentences and awarded costs to be paid to the Spanish owner by the privateers.[87] *Los Buenos Amigos* had been voyaging from Spain to London with no colonial goods on board.[88] The circumstances of the *San Antonio* were almost identical to those of the *Los Buenos Amigos*, in that it carried no colonial goods and was bound from a Spanish port to London.[89] In all three of these cases it was, once again, Yorke, Pratt, Hay, and Bettesworth who acted as advocates, continuing the practice of having the three legal officers most concerned with international law and diplomacy consistently participate in prize appeal cases. These three ships added to the tally of seven Spanish ships that had come before the Court of Prize Appeal since the *Jésus, Maria, y José* first appeared before the appellate court in July 1759. Only the first of those cases had been found in favour of the British plaintiffs, and the decisions were consistent with British strategic aims. Only the Spanish ship that had carried French colonial goods was condemned; the other six were restored and had very

---

[84] TNA HCA 45/3, Case of the *Jesús, Maria, y José*, Appendix to the Appellant's Case.
[85] TNA HCA 45/1/51, Case of *La Virgen del Rosario y el Santo Cristo de Buen Viaje*.
[86] BL Add MS 36210, Hardwicke Papers, Notes on *La Virgen del Rosario y el Santo Cristo de Buen Viaje*.
[87] TNA HCA 45/1/49, Case of *Los Buenos Amigos* and TNA HCA 45/1/48, Case of the *San Antonio*.
[88] BL Add MS 36210, Hardwicke Papers, Notes on the *Buenos Amigo*.
[89] BL Add MS 36210, Hardwicke Papers, Notes on the *San Antonio*.

little impact on the disagreements between Britain and Spain concerning neutral rights. Nonetheless, neither the Conde de Fuentes nor his masters in Spain seemed to take any comfort from the fact that what the British had been promising for most of the war (resolving prize disputes and defending neutral rights through the appellate process) was finally playing out. This is likely because, though Spanish ships were being restored, the decisions mostly did not contribute to clarifying Anglo-Spanish disputes. It is also likely that it was simply too little too late, and that the window of opportunity for gaining Spanish trust in Britain's commitment to upholding neutral rights had closed nearer the time when the *San Juan Baptista* had come before the appellate court. However, without quicker success in the case of the *Jesús, Maria, y José*, and without a quick succession of Spanish cases to build on the Spanish victory in the *San Juan Baptista* case, Spanish trust was not won. It was, of course, also made more complicated by other diplomatic incidents such as the *Antigallican* affair, disputes over logwood cutting, and the succession of Charles III. Hardwicke, likely aware of Fuentes's attitude and the ill feeling in the Spanish Court, made the strategic decision to postpone announcing the sentence of the *Jesús, Maria, y José* and instead hear, and decide, cases that might still serve to appease Spanish ire.

The delay in the case of the *Jesús, Maria, y José* between 20 November and the vague timing of 'after the holidays' was long enough to prompt Captain Davids to write his petition. Davids was worried about the case and his financial situation, and at the end of his petition he wrote 'to avoid any further delay and expense he [Davids] is willing and ready to withdraw and waive his Appeal ... and therefore most humbly pray your Lordships Speedy judgment upon the original decree of the Judge of the High Court of Admiralty'.[90] The petition was presented to the Court of Prize Appeal on 5 February 1761 when the commissioners next met. It is unclear if they met because the petition had been submitted or on prior arrangement. Only nine commissioners were present in the February meeting, but of those nine, Hardwicke, Mansfield, Sandys, and Nugent were once again present. The note next to the list of attendees says only two things: the petition was submitted and accepted by the court, and that the commissioners then made a final decree which affirmed the sentence handed down by the High Court of Admiralty.[91]

By withdrawing his appeal, Davids changed the entire case and, therefore, the sentencing possibilities. Davids had originally appealed to the appellate court because he believed that the Spanish ship and all of the

---

[90] BL Add MS 36211, Hardwicke Papers, Notes on the *Jesús, Maria, y José*.
[91] TNA HCA 45/3, Case of the *Jesús, Maria, y José*, Appendix to the Appellant's Case.

goods within should have been condemned as lawful prize. It was upon his appeal that the questions of French ownership and transhipment had been opened up for debate. Ezenarro and the Spanish owners had only appealed the decision of the High Court of Admiralty, which had condemned the saltpetre as contraband and condemned the Spaniards to pay costs. The Spanish appeal, on its own, compelled the Court of Prize Appeal only to uphold or reverse the decision on the saltpetre and costs, with no need to investigate questions of French ownership. It is not possible to say with certainty that the Court of Prize Appeal deliberately delayed their sentence knowing that it might cause Captain Davids to grow apprehensive about costs and the outcome of the case. However, it would have been a tactic completely in keeping with previous behaviour exhibited by the court and Pitt's government. Unlike in the situation of naval captains, where Pitt could threaten their careers if they pursued a prize case, privateers and merchants were more independent of government interference. One of the few ways to force the hand of a privateer was through delays in the prize court system that would cost money. The Court of Prize Appeal, after deliberating and crafting a sentence based on transhipment and then adoption, took the chance offered by an impoverished Captain Davids to deliver a sentence which would not cause yet another incident between the British ministry and the Spanish ambassador. The decision was taken with no indication of further deliberation once Davids's petition had been withdrawn. It is well to note, once again, that only commissioners who had attended all hearings relating to a case were able to contribute to the final judgment. Attendee lists are only available for the last two sessions, but the overlap in the two lists puts the decision-making power completely in the hands of Hardwicke and three of his allies. It seems likely that of the possible four members able to contribute to the judgment, all were eager to pronounce a judgment that would not plunge Anglo-Spanish relations further into disarray.

Once again, it is important to point out that Hardwicke's leadership and his approach to prize appeal cases was critical to this final outcome in the case. Though Captain Davids had withdrawn his appeal, there is no indication in Hardwicke's notes or in court documents that the sentence arrived at by the Commissioners had to be reconsidered. Hardwicke and the court could have chosen to hand down their original sentence, which favoured Captain Davids and was based on the available gathered evidence. However, on 5 February 1761, two-and-a-half months after the last arguments had been presented in the case, Hardwicke penned a quick note 'The cross appeal was withdrawn on the petition of the Captor ... and on the original appeal the sentences were affirmed with costs.'[92] The ship, along with all of the cargo, save the saltpetre, was returned to the Spanish, though they had to pay all of their own court costs, which were likely not insignificant. Davids received the saltpetre as lawful prize.

By upholding the sentence of the High Court of Admiralty, the Court of Prize Appeal upheld the spirit of Pitt's strategy. Saltpetre was named as contraband by both the Anglo-Spanish treaty of 1667 and the Anglo-Dutch treaty of 1674. No other aspect of the treaties needed to be invoked, because the detention of the ship could be justified through the presence of contraband. Since the Spanish ship had been captured in July 1756, it predated the special instructions to leave Spanish shipping alone issued by the Admiralty in October of 1756. If Fuentes complained to Pitt about the sentence handed down by the Court of Prize Appeal, there seems to be no record of it and that is consistent with his silence on previous cases that were decided in Spain's favour. There was also, seemingly, no mention of the final sentence or any fall-out from the sentence in the press. It is, of course, impossible to say that Hardwicke and Pitt planned for Davids's financial situation to prompt the withdrawal of his appeal. Nonetheless, from the delay in the sentencing it is possible to speculate that Hardwicke and his fellow commissioners were uncomfortable with the original sentence and sensitive to the fact that it would worsen an already rocky relationship with the Spanish Court. Hardwicke's reasoning had upheld British interpretations of Anglo-Spanish and Anglo-Dutch treaties as well as demonstrated consistency in the application of the Rule of the War of 1756. However, with the evidence indicating French ownership of the goods, the evidence of transhipment for the sake of avoiding capture, and the reasoning for considering the ship an adopted French ship, the court had been left in a difficult position. Not condemning goods as French and the voyage as fraudulent would have set a precedent that opened the door for all French East India trade to be carried into European French ports, and protected by, Spanish ships, an outcome that was anathema to British maritime strategy. Davids's petition and subsequent withdrawal allowed the court to avoid a contribution to worsening Anglo-Spanish relations whilst not conceding additional rights to neutral carriers of seaborne goods. Given the attitude in the Spanish Court towards Britain in late 1760 and early 1761, it was the best possible outcome for the British ministry to the case of the *Jesús, Maria, y José.*

---

[92] BL Add MS 36211, Hardwicke Papers, Notes on the *Jesús, Maria, y José.*

War with Spain, however, could not be staved off any longer by the Court of Prize Appeal and Hardwicke's meticulous sentencing. Pitt and Hardwicke had successfully managed the intertwining threads of Spanish neutrality and the British prize court system such that they had been able to keep a Franco-Spanish alliance from being formed in the early years of the war. One of the issues with Hardwicke's approach to appellate cases is that they could take months or years to decide. Nonetheless, unable to control the actions of British or Spanish citizens at sea or in the lower courts, they could only ever alleviate crises of neutrality after the fact and late in the war, which was too little and too late to win the trust and faith of the Spanish Court. From a legal perspective, however, the case of the *Jesús, Maria, y José* was not a wasted intellectual effort. It could not strictly create precedent for the Rule of the War of 1756 because the sentence that incorporated the relevant reasoning was not the one pronounced. Nonetheless, Hardwicke's detailed notes, the oral arguments made during the case, and discussions held amongst the small community of prize court judges and advocates, were enough to create a *communis opinio* around how the rule could be used in a Spanish or non-Dutch context. This *communis opinio* supported and strengthened the reasoning used in Dutch cases to create precedent around the rule. The early cases decided by the Court of Prize Appeal served to create enduring constructs like the Rule of the War of 1756 which would continue to play a large role in British prize courts through the Napoleonic Wars. The precedents and *communis opinio* created in the prize cases involving neutral ships would be called upon again and again by future judges and legal thinkers looking to further Britain's maritime strategic interests.[93]

The disputes over logwood cutting and prizes had existed between the two empires for over a century, and as Britain's sea power grew more hegemonic, those disputes became ever-greater threats to the safety of the Spanish empire and her American colonies. Six months after the sentence in the case of the *Jesús, Maria, y José* was pronounced, the British Cabinet was fractured by conflicting views on ending the war with France, and Spain had signed the Family Compact with France on 15 August 1761. Perceiving the Family Compact as a renunciation of Spanish neutrality, Pitt pushed Britain to declare war on Spain on 4 January 1762. The new Anglo-Spanish war, like the three that had

---

[93] See in particular H. Bourguignon, *Sir William Scott, Lord Stowell: Judge of the High Court of Admiralty 1798–1828* (Cambridge University Press, 1987); S. Neff, 'James Stephen's *War in Disguise*: The Story of a Book', *Irish Jurist*, 38 (2003); and G. Frei, *Great Britain, International Law, and the Evolution of Maritime Strategic Thought, 1856–1914* (Oxford University Press, 2020). See the discussion in Chapter 10.

come before it, did not resolve any of the existing grievances, and by 1778, a new war would break out over the same old disputes. Hardwicke and the Court of Prize Appeal had, ultimately, delivered what was needed in order to support Britain's strategy with neutral nations. Hardwicke's reasoning around international law philosophy, particularly the ideas of Hugo Grotius, resolved disputes with the Dutch Republic and helped keep Spain neutral until an alliance with France no longer presented an insurmountable threat. However, the legal flexibility required to support Britain's strategy meant that disputes over neutral rights were not resolved in a concrete fashion that altered or clarified treaties. Prize law had not been officially changed, though new legal norms backed by precedent did emerge. International maritime law remained a murky realm of interpretation that could be used, left aside, and bent, to fit strategic aims.

Conclusion

Legal Traditions

The Court of Prize Appeal during the Seven Years' War was a singular institution combining the civil law traditions of an Admiralty court, the ideas and philosophies of high-ranking judges who had legal careers outside of the prize system, and the political and maritime strategic concerns of the government. The combination was not necessarily a given, because there were no specified rules on how the appellate court judges should conceive of, or operate, the court, and because the combination flourished under Lord Hardwicke's guidance and network of allies. The purpose of the court was to make a final determination whether ships, and the goods they transported, had been legally captured. There was little to guide the judges outside of this mandate other than what previous iterations of the court had done and what previous judges thought should be done. Hardwicke understood that the court had a political role to play and that it was part of a strategy to further British maritime interests. Part of furthering Britain's strategic interests was to generate a British view of international law and neutral rights that could be accepted by other European nations. To this end, he helped drive the conception and development of the Rule of the War of 1756, and to shape a practice that demarcated under what circumstances the rule should, or could, be applied.

To keep Spain and the Dutch Republic as neutral nations without limiting Britain's ability to destroy French colonial commerce, the court had to be trusted by neutrals as an institution that protected neutral rights and dealt with prize cases in a consistent, equitable, manner. There were two key elements to achieving Britain's strategic aims through the appellate court. First, negotiations over the interpretation of treaties that governed Anglo-Dutch and Anglo-Spanish relations regarding neutrality had to prevent either neutral country from gaining specific and wide-ranging rights to carry enemy commerce. Whilst this could cause issues and diplomatic flashpoints in British negotiations with neutrals, it also meant that Britain could tailor its interpretations of the treaties to the strategic needs of a conflict. Secondly, the decisions handed down by the appellate court had to foster trust in the British prize court system as an arbiter of neutral rights. One way to do this was to set precedents and establish new legal norms that would lead to clear expectations on the part of neutral governments and predictability from the court. Hardwicke's long experience as a judge and Lord Chancellor, his close familial relationships within the legal and diplomatic world, and his close relationships with those in government, set him up perfectly to guide the appellate court and to help realise Britain's wartime strategy.

To avoid the issue of firmly interpreting Anglo-Dutch and Anglo-Spanish treaties on neutrality, Hardwicke developed his Rule of the War of 1756, which was rooted in Article 2 of the Anglo-Dutch treaty of 1674. The rule laid out that commerce which was prohibited to a neutral during peacetime would remain prohibited during wartime. The aim of the rule was to prevent neutral nations from carrying French colonial commerce and to allow the appellate court to forge a practice that would be understood and accepted by neutral nations. Whilst the rule is rooted in the Anglo-Dutch treaty, it never became codified, nor was it integrated into the Anglo-Dutch or Anglo-Spanish treaties after the war. This meant that subsequent prize court judges could choose to apply it in future conflicts or not, without altering or calling into question the existing treaties. If new interpretations or 'rules' needed to be developed to fit changing strategic circumstances, the court had the flexibility to do so. If the court wanted to preserve the use of the rule in future conflicts (as indeed turned out to be the case) then the precedents and Hardwicke's (or other judges like Lord Mansfield's) cases and case notes were there to be invoked. Prize cases and case notes or opinions in this period were not formally published (though this would change with Sir William Scott) and many civilians relied on the notes they took whilst sitting in on cases. These notes could be shared, or not, amongst friends and colleagues; the sharing of legal opinions was largely an informal process. Attending cases and listening to arguments was a large part of passing on traditions, ideas, and precedents.[1]

Hardwicke initially demonstrated the utility of the rule through the first two Dutch cases to come before the court, the *Maria Theresa* and the *America*. He knew that he could use these two cases to both appease Dutch anger and foster Dutch trust, while laying out a precedent that would make it clear that Dutch ships trading with French colonies under

---

[1] H. Bourguignon, *Sir William Scott, Lord Stowell: Judge of the High Court of Admiralty 1798–1828* (Cambridge University Press, 1987), pp. 41–2 and 48.

certain circumstances would be condemned by the prize system as per the Rule of the War of 1756. The circumstances of the two cases, and the evidence presented, were such that judicial interpretation could have resulted in different sentencing decisions. However, with Britain's strategic aims in mind, Hardwicke was able to use legal reasoning and call on Hugo Grotius's philosophy (as illustrated in his case notes and his engagement with existing treaties) on the law of nations and neutral rights in order to deliver sentences that made legal sense, were comprehensible to merchants and diplomats, and which would help preserve Dutch neutrality.

Hardwicke tried to employ the same approach when the first Spanish cases came before the appellate court. However, a combination of factors rendered his efforts less efficacious. Prize affairs were one of three main grievances that existed between Britain and Spain, and very little progress was made during the war in negotiating over the other two: fishing rights and logwood cutting in Honduras. It is very clear from the effort put into negotiating neutral rights and prize-taking by British officials that, at the time, they considered such efforts a viable and critical avenue for the preservation of Spain's neutrality. It is possible that Hardwicke's efforts through the Court of Prize Appeal might have succeeded, but the unexpected deaths of Ambassador Keene and King Ferdinand VI produced immediate detrimental effects to Anglo-Spanish relations. Hardwicke's labours were further plagued by a series of Spanish appellate cases (*La Virgen del Rosario y el Santo Cristo de Buen Viaje*, *Los Buenos Amigos*, and the *San Antonio*) that were not conducive to the further setting of precedents based on the Rule of the War of 1756, and to limiting Spain's rights to carry French colonial commerce. Despite his best efforts, Hardwicke was unable to do more than delay Spain's entry into the war.

The achievement of delay should not be dismissed as unimportant to British strategy, because it had great strategic implications. By the time Spain entered the war in 1762 as France's ally, it was unable to salvage a French victory, and the months of war brought to Spain the fall of Manila and Havana at the hands of British naval forces. From this perspective, Hardwicke's efforts to maintain Spanish neutrality through the appellate court helped create a strategic environment in which Spain becoming a belligerent did not have a detrimental effect on Britain winning the war.

From a legal perspective, the Spanish cases that came before the court involving debates or decisions based on the Rule of the War of 1756 (like the *San Juan Baptista* and the *Jesús, Maria, y José*), helped to create a *communis opinio* that could be used to address the parameters of the new rule outside of the Anglo-Dutch context. This helped create a collective understanding that could take the new rule from something that was only applied to Dutch ships to something that applied to neutral ships in general. The specific case of the *San Juan Baptista* made it clear that a Spanish or neutral ship that proved it carried Spanish-owned goods (even those that were originally French East India goods) from a Spanish port into a French port, would not be condemned by the appellate court. This showed that the Rule of the War of 1756 would not be applied just because French colonial merchandise was involved and was borne out in subsequent rulings on Spanish ships during the war. In terms of the *Jesús, María, y José*, had the British privateer captain not withdrawn his appeal, it seems that the ship and her cargo would likely have been condemned as an adopted French ship and legally seized prize goods. Such an outcome would have strengthened the precedent set by the Dutch ships for the Rule of the War of 1756 to be applied in cases where the ship had not yet been in an enemy port at the time of capture but was provably on a covert voyage to an enemy port, carrying enemy goods. Nonetheless, because Hardwicke's notes on the second Spanish case were so extensive, and the reasoning itself was not undone by the withdrawal of the appeal, the case could still be of use to future jurists looking to deal with similar cases.

Anglo-Spanish Negotiations Re-Set

In terms of diplomacy, it was the Treaty of Paris of 1763 that formally brought the Seven Years' War to an end. It consisted of twenty-seven articles, five of which addressed Anglo-Spanish grievances that had contributed to the outbreak of war in 1761. The state of war between Britain and Spain had nullified previous Anglo-Spanish treaties, which included the treaty of 1667, the interpretation of which had caused friction during negotiations over Spain's neutral rights. The Treaty of Paris, in Article 2, renewed many of the treaties that had existed between Spain and Britain before Spain's entry into the Seven Years' War. Among the renewed treaties were the treaty of 1667, and the 1713 Treaty of Utrecht. The article ended with the following: 'all the said parties declare, that they will not suffer any privilege, favour, or indulgence to subsist, contrary to the treaties above confirmed, except what shall have been agreed and stipulated by the present treaty'.[2] The problem was that the rest of the 1763 treaty did not in any way address the issues over neutral rights that had led to the Anglo-Spanish war. This left Anglo-Spanish relations over

---

[2] Treaty of Paris 1763, https://avalon.law.yale.edu/18th_century/paris763.asp.

neutral rights in the same place they had been at the start of the Seven Years' War. Even the decisions made in the British Court of Prize Appeal had not improved long-term Anglo-Spanish understanding or agreement on the two treaties.

Given the nature of the Spanish cases that came before the court, from the *San Juan Baptista* to the conclusion of the *Jesús, Maria, y José*, Hardwicke and his fellow judges had been unable, or unwilling, to set firm precedents around the treaty of 1667 or the Rule of the War of 1756. In the case of the *San Juan Baptista*, where French East India goods had allegedly been transferred from a French ship onto a Spanish ship, the treaties were explicitly avoided by the advocates of both sides and the restoration of the cargo and ship were based on Hardwicke's decision that a single Spanish witness who claimed the cargo to belong to Frenchmen rather than Spaniards was not enough for a condemnation. The question of the transhipment of French East India goods and the rights of Spain, as a neutral country, to carry such goods, did not arise in the final decision. Aside from the *San Juan Baptista* and the *Jesús, Maria, y José*, only the case of the *San Vicente* involved French colonial goods, and it was deemed an adopted French ship, as it had been travelling to and from a French port. The case conformed to previous Dutch-based decisions involving the Rule of the War of 1756, but Hardwicke's notes did not delve into the specifics of why the ship should be considered an adopted French ship. The case did, however, set up the potential for Spanish ministers to accept that cases where adoption could be reasonably argued would not be decided in favour of Spanish plaintiffs. A discussion between British and Spanish ministers about adoption after the *San Vicente* case, however, did not take place, likely because British ministers were more concerned with responding to the Spanish ambassador's memorandum regarding other issues, or because the Spanish ambassador, the Conde de Fuentes, did not wish to have a discussion to negotiate limits on Spain's neutral rights.

The arguments presented by the advocates in the case of the *Jesús, Maria, y José*, had relied heavily on the treaty of 1667; but the sentence eventually handed down by the Court of Prize Appeal (as well as the sentence written by Hardwicke, but not handed down that would have declared the ship an adopted French ship) still did not set any precedents based on the treaty of 1667. As in the case of the *San Juan Baptista*, the crux of the arguments was whether the goods on board the Spanish ships were French property, and whether such transhipment rendered the Spanish ship a French ship for legal purposes. The advocates on the Appellant's side had made the argument that the Anglo-Spanish treaty of 1667 allowed the Spaniards to call on the privileges of the Anglo-Dutch treaty of 1674. Bringing in the Dutch treaty then allowed Hardwicke to formulate a decision which would have condemned the Spanish ship and cargo based on the Rule of the War of 1756, and the precedents of previous Dutch ships condemned by the court.

Hardwicke's approach to prize appeal cases granted him flexibility in terms of interpreting cases and handing down sentences, but there were limits to this flexibility. Hardwicke could not choose which cases the Spanish wished to appeal and, as most of the cases between the sentencing of the *San Juan Baptista* and the *Jesús, Maria, y José* demonstrated, they could not always be used to address the pressing issue of neutral ships carrying French colonial trade. Even in the case of the *Jesús, Maria, y José*, it became apparent that, though the Rule of the War of 1756 could be applied, the evidence was so clearly stacked against the Spanish that, at the time the sentence was devised, it was deemed politically prudent not to pronounce it. Through a stroke of luck, or excellent machinations on the part of ministers and Hardwicke, the British Respondent in the case withdrew his appeal, leaving the court with only the decision of whether to uphold the High Court of Admiralty's sentence, which had condemned the saltpetre on board the *Jesús, Maria, y José* as contraband. The decision was duly upheld by the court and, therefore, no firm interpretation on neutral rights based on the treaty of 1667, or the Rule of the War of 1756, was made.

Nonetheless, the decisions handed down by the Court of Prize Appeal in regard to Spanish ships captured at sea, illustrated by the cases of the *San Juan Baptista* and the *Jesús, Maria, y José*, fulfilled the strategic aims of the British ministers prosecuting the war against France, because they attempted to bolster Spanish confidence in the British prize court system's ability to uphold neutral rights, while at the same time allowing privateers and warships to freely pursue commerce predation against French ships and neutral ships that might be carrying French goods. As shown in Part III, boosting Spanish confidence in the prize court system's ability to uphold neutral rights was, ultimately, not enough to keep Spain out of the war, because of grievances outside the purview of the Court of Prize Appeal and because of the nature of most of the Spanish cases that came before the appellate court. By never concretely interpreting the treaty of 1667 or establishing precedents based on the Rule of the War of 1756, the British prize courts and the ministers from both countries never concretely agreed the limits of Spanish neutral rights. British negotiations and prize court cases did not resolve any of Spain's enduring concerns over their neutral rights though the *communis opinio* created by Hardwicke's decisions, and notes laid the groundwork for a framework to be set up around the Rule of the War of 1756 for the next time neutral rights would become a point of contention between Britain and Spain. The Treaty of Paris of 1763 re-established the treaty of 1667 and did not incorporate the Rule of the War of 1756. There was a lacklustre attempt to have the Treaty of Paris address prize cases specifically, but it brought no new clarity as to how neutral rights might be addressed in future conflicts. Article 16 of the Peace of Paris stipulated:

The decision of the prizes made in times of peace by the subjects of Great Britain, on the Spaniards, shall be referred to the Courts of Justice of the Admiralty of Great Britain, conformably to the rules established among all nations ... according to the law of nations, and according to treaties ...[3]

The implication of the article was that rules about the legality of prize-taking were uniformly understood by the signatories of the treaty, and that previous treaties were also uniformly understood when it came to prize affairs. There was no acknowledgement that Hardwicke and the Court of Prize Appeal had evolved in their understanding of neutral rights around the Rule of the War of 1756 and the rights of Spanish ships to carry French colonial goods. This meant that Anglo-Spanish relations were effectively re-set by the new 1763 treaty to their pre-war condition. This does not mean, however, that the work of the Court of Prize Appeal had no meaning. Whether the Spanish government chose to acknowledge it or not, Britain's politicians, judges, and advocates who were involved in prize affairs now had new collective knowledge, understanding, and thinking to draw upon when next confronted with issues surrounding the limits of Spanish neutrality.

Logwood Cutting and Fishing Rights

In terms of the other two grievances which led to Spain entering the Seven Years' War – logwood cutting in Honduras and fishing rights off Newfoundland – the Treaty of Paris addressed them in two separate articles. Article 17 dealt with the rights of British citizens to cut logwood along the shore of Honduras. British citizens were allowed to cut logwood in Honduras and in any part of Spanish America as long as they dismantled any fortifications which had previously been built by British settlers, and as long as no more fortifications were erected. Houses and settlements could be established.[4] The stipulations in the article (whilst seemingly sensible from the point of view of Spanish officials who were already planning for the next war and from the point of view of British officials who wanted access to the trade in logwood) were completely

[3] Ibid.   [4] Ibid.

unenforceable due to the remoteness of the Honduran coast. They also relied entirely on the good faith of the Spanish *Guarda Costas* and British settlers. As tensions between the two countries arose in the 1760s and 1770s, complaints on both sides over breaking Article 17 arose with them. War was declared in 1779, and Spain soon attacked British settlements in Honduras, after which the British governor of Jamaica launched an ill-fated expedition of revenge.[5]

Article 18 of the Treaty of Paris addressed fishing rights off Newfoundland as follows:

> His Catholic Majesty [King of Spain] desists, as well for himself as his successors, from all pretention which he may have formed in favour of the Guipuscoans [Guipuscoa was part of the Basque Country in northern Spain], and other his subjects, to the right of fishing in the neighbourhood of the island of Newfoundland.[6]

Once again, enforcement of this article would be almost impossible unless both Spanish and British officials agreed about the definition of 'neighbourhood'. Spanish ships would continue to be taken as prize for illegal fishing in Newfoundland, and tensions over such seizures would increase throughout the 1760s and 1770s.

One last article of the Treaty of Paris of 1763 is worth noting, because of its effects on Anglo-Spanish tensions and grievances. Article 7 of the treaty granted both Britain and France complete freedom to navigate the Mississippi river. However, Louisiana and New Orleans had been ceded by the French to the Spanish, so when Anglo-Spanish tensions increased in the interwar period, British ships navigating along the Mississippi were often stopped and seized by Spanish officials. This produced a decidedly negative contribution to negotiations over neutrality once Britain's North American colonies rebelled, and France joined the war in 1778.[7]

Overall, despite the Anglo-Spanish experiences in the Seven Years' War with negotiations over neutrality, and despite the difficulties in regulating the behaviour of citizens at sea or in the colonies, the treaty which ended the war did little to directly address the causes of the war or address Spanish concerns about the British prize court system. These same issues would soon lead the two countries into another round of

---

[5] A. J. O'Shaughnessy, *An Empire Divided: The American Revolution and the British Caribbean* (University of Pennsylvania Press, 2000), p. 189.

[6] Treaty of Paris 1763, https://avalon.law.yale.edu/18th_century/paris763.asp.

[7] CL M-66, Shelburne Papers, Case of the Seizure of the British vessels by the Spaniards in the river Mississippi, 1778. Also see A. Brinkman, 'Merchants of Fortune', in D. Morgan-Owen (ed.), *Economic Warfare and the Sea* (Liverpool University Press, 2020).

tense negotiations over neutral rights and into another war. The cases adjudicated in the Court of Prize Appeal during the war, and the negotiations over neutral rights, furthered British strategic aims by contributing to Spain's late entry into the war. However, Spanish trust in the British prize court system was not increased and no attempt seems to have been made to capitalise on Britain's stronger position at the negotiating table after the war to formalise a more concrete and mutual understanding of neutral rights, either in the treaty or during the leisure of peacetime.[8] Each empire, instead, focused on domestic policies within their empires and, in the case of Spain, on preparing for the next war with Britain.

Anglo-Dutch Negotiations

In contrast to Anglo-Spanish relations, post-war Anglo-Dutch negotiations were not marked by a new treaty or by the redistribution of territory. Whereas the decisions made in the Court of Prize Appeal regarding Spanish ships had been unable to prevent Spain's entry into the war, the decisions handed down concerning Dutch ships in the midst of the Anglo-Dutch crisis had greatly contributed to maintaining Dutch neutrality. Because the Dutch did not enter the Seven Years' War as belligerents, negotiations over the treaty of 1674, and negotiations over neutrality, were left as they had been at the end of the Anglo-Dutch crisis in 1759.

Though the decisions made in the Court of Prize Appeal in the cases of the *Maria Theresa* and the *America* had alleviated the Anglo-Dutch crisis at the time, true to the intentions of Newcastle and Holdernesse's policy, the decisions did not make any concrete contributions to further defining Dutch neutral rights, or establishing mutually understood interpretations, based on the treaty of 1674. The cases did, however, create precedent based on the Rule of the War of 1756, which was accepted by Dutch officials during the Seven Years' War. The Rule of the War of 1756, though, was never made binding by a treaty between Britain and the Dutch Republic. By accepting the rulings of the Court of Prize Appeal after the Anglo-Dutch crisis period, the Dutch were signalling that they accepted the limits imposed by the Rule of the War of 1756, but its use in defining the limits of Dutch neutral rights was, ultimately, at the mercy of those in power during the next maritime war in which Britain was a belligerent and the Dutch Republic was a neutral actor. Future

---

[8] The correspondence of ministers in the immediate aftermath of the war is filled mostly with domestic affairs, and little to no discussion about neutrality or alterations to the prize court system.

Dutch ministers were not bound by the Rule of the War of 1756 in the same way that the British prize court judges and advocates would claim to be bound by the precedents created in Dutch prize cases like those of the *Maria Theresa* and the *America*.

The advocates in both the cases of the *Maria Theresa* and the *America* had based their arguments on the treaty of 1674, but the decisions in both cases turned on whether the cargoes in the Dutch ships were made up of French West Indian goods and whether, if they were, that transformed the ship into a French ship. For the *Maria Theresa*, Hardwicke evaded basing the decision on the treaty of 1674 by declaring that the treaty was an inversion of the law of nations which, he claimed stipulated that the goods of an enemy found on board the ship of a neutral were free, but goods of a neutral found on board the ship of an enemy were not free. Though Hardwicke here invoked the law of nations (the legitimate behaviour between States in the absence of specific agreements), he was, ultimately, referring to Grotius's maxim that free ships were presumed to make free goods unless proven otherwise. Any change to that presumption would require an agreement, such as a treaty, between two nations. The specific form of the maxim that Hardwicke was calling on came from Article 2 of the 1674 treaty. Hardwicke's interpretation was that only trade allowed in peacetime was allowed in wartime and protected by 'free ships make free goods'. As the only 'proof' that the cargo of the *Maria Theresa* was of French provenance was the hearsay of one of the sailors, Hardwicke claimed that both the ship and cargo were Dutch, and therefore did not come under Grotius's maxim or the 1674 treaty. Hardwicke's sentence had helped to relieve Anglo-Dutch tensions by making it clear that ships trading between the Dutch Republic and Dutch colonies would not be condemned out of hand. However, by design, to help maintain the flexibility of the Court of Prize Appeal, no lasting clarification had been made on the 1674 treaty. A clarification had been made, however, allowing Dutch merchants to have confidence that, if they were trading between Dutch colonies in Dutch ships, their rights would be protected by the Court of Prize Appeal during the war.

The case of the *America*, similarly to that of the *Maria Theresa*, focused on whether it was a Dutch ship carrying French West Indian goods and therefore should be classed as a French ship. One of the main differences in the cases was that the *Maria Theresa* had made its voyage from the Dutch Republic to St Eustatius and back, whereas the *America* had voyaged from the Dutch Republic to the French colony of St Domingue in order to pick up French West Indian goods. Hardwicke's inversion argument was called upon in order to stipulate that the ship and the goods should not be condemned because French West Indian goods (goods of the enemy) found on board a Dutch ship were within the bounds of the law of nations and therefore within the treaty of 1674, which inverted the law of nations and protected the goods of an enemy found on board a neutral ship. When it came time to deliberate, Hardwicke's case notes made it clear that he focused on the argument that would prove that the Dutch ship could, and should, be considered a French ship. If this were the case, then the goods and the ship could be condemned by the Court of Prize Appeal without recourse to the treaty of 1674, because French goods inside a French ship had nothing to do with neutrality. To establish that the ship should be considered a French ship, Hardwicke called on the Rule of the War of 1756, which did not allow neutral countries to trade in wartime in a fashion prohibited to them during peacetime. Since French colonies were not open to Dutch ships for trading during times of peace, the *America* was considered a French ship, for being allowed to trade to St Domingue during the war. Both the ship and the goods were condemned by the Court of Prize Appeal, and the Rule of the War of 1756 was thereafter applied in the Court of Prize Appeal, with the Dutch acquiescing to the limits it had placed on Dutch neutral rights.

Hardwicke's decision, once again, served British policy, because it alleviated Anglo-Dutch tensions (by clarifying that the Rule of the War of 1756 would be applied by the British appellate court) but made no concrete interpretations of the treaty of 1674 that might bind Britain to a certain definition of Dutch neutral rights in future conflicts. The Anglo-Dutch crisis of 1758–9 had been defused in large part by the success of Newcastle and Holdernesse's policy of upholding Dutch neutral rights through decisions made in the Court of Prize Appeal. However, the flexibility needed by the court to make decisions that adhered to British strategy meant that any trust in Britain's prize court system was not necessarily going to last into future conflicts, because it was not founded on mutually agreed interpretations of existing bilateral treaties. Trust, rather, was dependent on precedents set in British prize courts that had been accepted, and understood, by Dutch officials. Mutual agreement between the Dutch and British officials who had negotiated during the war would not necessarily be carried into future conflicts. This created new 'law' for the British prize court system in terms of the precedents establishing the Rule of the War of 1756, but it also created a political understanding between British and Dutch officials that was not codified. Both were necessary for maintaining Dutch neutrality in future maritime wars.

Out with the Old War, In with the New

Britain's victory over France and Spain in the colonial sphere of the Seven Years' War was exemplified by the long list of French and Spanish colonies that succumbed to British conquest. When peace negotiations began between France, Spain, and Britain, British forces had already successfully conquered all of French Canada, the French West Indian colonies of Martinique and St Lucia, as well as Spain's most important possessions in the West Indies and the Pacific: Havana and Manila. Once Martinique had been conquered in February of 1762, the rest of the French islands in the West Indies submitted to British control.[9] Both Baugh and Corbett described France as a broken and completely defeated maritime power at the end of the Seven Years' War. Baugh wrote 'France had nothing left but Saint-Domingue, no active navy, no money to activate one ...'[10] Similarly, Corbett wrote 'For France to recover her broken navy from the blows which Hawke and Boscawen had dealt was beyond the national power so long as the war lasted ... the study of revenge was all that was left, and for that peace must be had.'[11] Spain and France both went into the negotiations with the notion that peace would only last until the next opportune moment to wage another war against Britain.

The negotiations would eventually culminate in the 1763 Treaty of Paris. At the negotiating table, the colonial map of America was largely redrawn in Britain's favour in terms of territorial acquisitions. In return for the island of Martinique, the French minister, Choiseul, agreed to cede to Britain all territory in North America east of the Mississippi, excluding New Orleans. The West Indian islands of Grenada, St Vincent, Dominica, and Tobago, along with all French conquests made since 1749 in the East Indies, were also ceded to Britain.[12] Spain came away from the conflict better than did France. Havana and Manila were returned to Spain, but most of Florida was ceded to Britain. France gave Spain Louisiana and New Orleans, but Britain retained free navigation of the Mississippi River.[13] As Spain had feared ever since the start of the war, the balance of power in America had shifted dramatically in Britain's favour. Britain emerged with more territory and the only

---

[9] D. Baugh, *The Global Seven Years' War, 1754–1763* (Pearson, 2011), p. 580.
[10] Ibid. p. 609.
[11] J. S. Corbett, *England in the Seven Years' War: A Study in Combined Strategy*, 2 vols. (Longmans, Green, and Co., 1907), vol. I, p. 325.
[12] R. Pares, *War and Trade in the West Indies 1739–1763* (Frank Cass and Co., 1963), p. 597.
[13] Treaty of Paris 1763, https://avalon.law.yale.edu/18th_century/paris763.asp.

credible navy out of the three belligerents. None of the ministers in Spain, France, or Britain expected the new peace to last. Pares put it eloquently at the end of his book *War and Trade in the West Indies*: 'He [Choiseul] spoke of a peace as a rest, or a truce, necessary for the reform and repair of the French and Spanish fighting machines. Pitt called the peace a ten years' armed truce; Choiseul only expected it to endure for five.'[14] In fact, the peace lasted for fifteen years. The breakout of a revolt in Britain's mainland American colonies would give Spain and France the opportunity to restart the war that had ended so unsatisfactorily for them in 1763.

The Interwar Years

With the new colonies that Britain had acquired through the Peace of Paris, the British government (and Britain's new young king) had to contend with the question of how to integrate the new territories into the existing empire. British colonists largely believed that their autonomy was defended by the English constitution, and that it protected them against the intrusion of governors, ministers and Parliament in administering the colonies.[15] P. J. Marshall argued that the Seven Years' War made colonial reform necessary, in part, because the conflict had exposed the 'limitations of an imperial authority based on negotiation'.[16] Marshall's argument is easily applied to negotiations over neutral rights and commerce predation in the Seven Years' War. The abuses by British privateers and the treatment of prize cases in the colonies and lower prize courts had, in large part, led to the Anglo-Dutch crisis and contributed to the deterioration of Anglo-Spanish relations. The ministers in London tried to uphold neutral rights (as defined by British ministers) at the start of the war and issued instructions to privateers and warships in the hope that they would not abuse Dutch and Spanish neutral commerce. Unfortunately, the orders had little effect in quelling what the Dutch and Spanish considered abusive and over-zealous behaviour. It was not until prize cases started coming before the Court of Prize Appeal that British ministers could concretely address the abuses committed at sea, in the colonial prize courts, and in the High Court of Admiralty. Even then, it was a reactive solution for maintaining neutrality, not a preventive one. If neutral rights were to be better protected in the next war, then the construction of British imperial authority would require, at least,

---

[14] Pares, *War and Trade in the West Indies*, p. 611.   [15] Ibid. p. 50.
[16] P. J. Marshall, *The Making and Unmaking of Empires: Britain, India, and America c.1750–1783* (Oxford University Press, 2007), p. 85.

more stringent colonial obedience. Whilst British ministers and policy makers acknowledged the necessity of broader imperial obedience at the end of the Seven Years' War, they did not connect it with upholding neutral rights during wartime in a way that would be preventive as well as reactive.[17] Nor did they connect it with the possibility of reform in the prize system, particularly in the lower courts.

In the fifteen years between the Seven Years' War and the American War of Independence, Marshall describes British ministers and officials who concerned themselves with the colonies and with empire as driven by an urgent need to defend the colonies from Bourbon revenge, and to curb public expenditure. As part of the strategy to reduce public expenditure, there was a shift from working with the colonies on commercial and legal matters, to a focus on enforcing colonial obedience to British law.[18] However, the drive for colonial obedience in legal matters did not translate into legal reform in prize law. Such reform might have helped prevent subversion by colonial actors and lower court judges. Instead, when the next war broke out, prize law and prize courts remained in the same state they had been at the end of the Seven Years' War.

British ministers were not the only agents of empire concerned with how colonial affairs developed between the Seven Years' War and the next expected conflict. Dutch and Spanish colonial policy also developed in the interwar years.

During the 1760s, Dutch colonial policy did not change very much from what it had been before and during the Seven Years' War. The island swaps between Spain, France, and Britain, along with Spanish and British experiments with free ports, had very little effect on how Dutch colonies were managed. In the Republic itself, the largest issue of the 1760s was a battle between the Orangeists and the anti-stadtholderians over whether the Dutch army should be built up or whether more ships of war should be made ready for convoy duty in the event that another colonial war made the protection of Dutch shipping paramount.[19] Because the Dutch and the British had not become enemies during the Seven Years' War, the treaties of 1674 and 1678 were still in place and

---

[17] Ibid. p. 85.

[18] Ibid. p. 285. Ministerial focus on colonial defence and colonial obedience is perhaps best illustrated by the archival collections of William Petty, 2nd Earl of Shelburne, who served as Secretary of State for the Southern Department from 1766 to 1768. His collection of papers (held at the Clements Library in the University of Michigan) from his time as Secretary of State is full of documents relating to the defence and commerce of the colonies with an emphasis on past and present treaties and laws. Clements Library. Shelburne Papers, vol. 13-168.

[19] A. C. Carter, *Neutrality or Commitment: The Evolution of Dutch Foreign Policy 1667–1795* (The Pitman Press, 1975), p. 93.

would, theoretically, remain in effect in the event of another war. Carter attributed Dutch desire to continue a policy of neutrality similar to that of the Seven Years' War to an expectation that there were profits to be made out of such neutrality. When France and Britain next went to war, the Dutch expectation was that it would be, once again, Dutch ships that carried the colonial commerce of the belligerents, within the agreed legal parameters that Anglo-Dutch negotiations and Court of Prize Appeal cases had set.[20] However, Dutch thinking changed in the mid-1770s in the face of Britain's increasing tensions – and eventual break – with its American colonies. Before Britain's North American colonies openly declared a rebellion in 1775, the Dutch West Indian islands were already providing the rebels with war materials such as guns and ammunition. St Eustatius stockpiled guns and ammunition, but none of this trade was illegal, or covered by existing treaties, until Britain officially declared war. The trade was lucrative for the Dutch, but created heightened tensions with British officials who viewed it very much as a case of unwanted Dutch interference in British colonial affairs.[21] As a result, in 1774, Anglo-Dutch negotiations began to look very much like the ones that had taken place in 1756 over Dutch rights to carry enemy commerce. Anglo-Dutch negotiations deteriorated quickly when Britain entered into hostilities with its North American colonies. Britain launched a campaign of maritime commerce predation against the Americans that, once again, affected Dutch ships and was, in theory, regulated by the treaties of 1674 and 1768.[22]

In contrast to the Dutch Republic, the Spanish empire, with its new king, dedicated much of the 1760s to enacting colonial reforms which would, in large part, allow the young monarch to wage a more effective war against Britain.[23] In 1763, Charles III created the Junta de Ministros, also sometimes known as the Committee of Imperial Defence or the Interministerial Junta. The Junta de Ministros was a group of the king's closest advisors; they met weekly to guide colonial policy and to improve its integration with Iberian policy.[24] A crucial aspect of better integration between colonial and Iberian policy was the creation of more frequent, and more reliable, communications across the Spanish empire. In the summer of 1764, a mail system, run and administered by the Crown, was launched. Monthly mail ships would depart from La Coruña for Havana;

---

[20] Ibid. p. 95.   [21] Ibid. p. 96.   [22] Ibid. p. 97.
[23] Allan J. Kuethe and Kenneth Andrien, *The Spanish Atlantic World in the Eighteenth Century: War and the Bourbon Reforms, 1713–1796* (Cambridge University Press, 2014), p. 272.
[24] Ibid. p. 235.

from Havana, small mail ships proceeded to other areas of the empire.[25] A year after the mail system had been launched, a limited free port system was introduced in the Americas. Havana, Santo Domingo, Puerto Rico, Margarita, and Trinidad were opened up to direct commerce with nine ports in Spain. Inter-island trade was also opened, but only to colonial products.[26] Both reforms were pursued to boost commerce within the empire and provide revenue for the Spanish Crown. The mail system also allowed Charles III and his ministers to, theoretically, better enforce the Crown's command and hold Spanish colonial officials accountable for their actions. In the long term, the reforms helped prepare the Spanish empire for its next colonial war, through increased integration. By 1769, military reforms which boosted ship building, in both Havana and in Spain, had brought Spain's operational navy to approximately sixty ships of the line.[27] Spanish reforms throughout the 1760s meant that, when a new conflict broke out in 1779, Spain's colonial empire was in a much stronger position to wage war against Britain than it had been in 1761.

Spain's reforms did not go unnoticed by the British, and the Free Port Bill of 1766, which opened up two ports in Jamaica and two in Dominica was, in part, a response to the opening of Spanish free ports. One of the aims of the bill was to encourage Spanish traders to bring bullion to the British free ports in exchange for slaves and British manufactured goods.[28] The reaction of many Spanish merchants to both the Spanish and the British free port experiments was that they produced new and more opportunities for the Anglo-Spanish smuggling trade in the Americas.[29] Whether the free port experiments did allow for more illegal trading between Spanish and British colonies is still up for debate, and Adrian Pearce, in his book *British Trade with Spanish America 1763–1808*, cautions against making too strong a link between the two. However, Pearce does claim that, in response to the British Free Port Act, the Spanish colonial governments increased their coastal presence and often replaced local officers with officers sent out directly from Spain. Tensions between the two countries mounted as Spanish coastal vessels began to repeatedly seize British merchant vessels accused of smuggling. Spanish officials also clashed continuously with British logwood cutters on the Honduran shores. The British and Spanish governments had agreed, through the Treaty of Paris, that British citizens could cut logwood on the Honduran coast, but could not erect any permanent

---

[25] Ibid. p. 244.   [26] Ibid. p. 245.   [27] Ibid. p. 282.   [28] Ibid. p. 246.
[29] A. Pearce, *British Trade with Spanish America 1763–1808* (Liverpool University Press, 2007), p. 53.

structures or encampments.[30] Both the practice of capturing British merchant ships and the clashes over logwood-cutting rights would continue until the outbreak of war in 1779.[31] Spanish actions were in keeping with the reforms being enacted by Charles III to increase Crown control in the colonies, improve Spanish colonial commerce, and prepare Spain for a new war.

Dutch and Spanish colonial policies in the 1760s and early 1770s developed in the face of, and sometimes in response to, Britain's emergence as the post-Seven Years' War maritime hegemon of Europe and the Americas. As these policies developed, and as tensions increased between Britain and her North American colonies, it became increasingly clear that neither the Anglo-Dutch nor the Anglo-Spanish grievances which had sparked crises over neutral rights during the Seven Years' War had been resolved by wartime negotiations or the Treaty of Paris of 1763. The lack of resolution over past grievances and the failure to re-negotiate treaties meant to protect and define neutral rights, along with Spain's determination to go to war again, largely contributed to the next Anglo-Dutch and Anglo-Spanish crises, which emerge during the American War of Independence.

One Size Did Not Fit All

The court cases analysed in this book demonstrate that the Court of Prize Appeal could be an effective means of maintaining the neutrality of maritime nations when Britain was at war. However, they also demonstrate that it was a difficult strategy to implement effectively. In the case of Anglo-Dutch relations, there were relatively few grievances between the two countries other than the treatment of Dutch ships at sea. Dutch domestic policy was based on staying out of the war either at sea or on land in Europe. Both circumstances were favourable to the success of British policy, because the threshold of trust in the British prize system needed to maintain Dutch neutrality was not very high. Decisions in the Court of Prize Appeal, which calmed Dutch anger and clarified the boundaries of Dutch neutral rights, were enough to keep the Republic out of the war. In contrast, Anglo-Spanish relations were plagued by more than disputes over Spanish ships taken at sea by British privateers and warships. The grievances over logwood cutting in Honduras and fishery rights off Newfoundland accelerated the deterioration of Anglo-Spanish relations during the war. Added to the multitude of grievances

---

[30] Treaty of Paris 1763, https://avalon.law.yale.edu/18th_century/paris763.asp.
[31] Pearce, *British Trade with Spanish America*, p. 54.

was the change of monarch from the Anglo-friendly Ferdinand VI to the Anglo-phobic Charles III, and the change of ambassador from Ricardo Wall's trusted friend Benjamin Keene to the untested and untrusted Lord Bristol. Taken together, the factors which contributed to the outbreak of war between Britain and Spain were too numerous to be countered by decisions made in the Court of Prize Appeal and, as such, the policy of upholding neutral rights through the appellate court ultimately failed when applied to Spain. The threshold of trust in Britain's prize court system, and rule of law in general, was much higher for Spain, and trust could not be achieved through the Court of Prize Appeal. This became more evident when Britain went to war with Spain in 1779, and the Dutch Republic in 1780, after a similar strategy failed to secure the neutrality of either country while Britain was at war with its own colonies and France.

By the time of the American War of Independence, almost all of the men who had guided Britain through the Seven Years' War were either dead or out of political life. As such, there was no ministerial continuity, and very little legal continuity, between the two wars. Though a study of the British Court of Prize Appeal during the American War of Independence has not been undertaken, it is an important missing piece of mid-eighteenth-century British imperial historiography, and one that would be well supported by the work of historians such as Andrew Jackson O'Shaughnessy, Sam Willis, P. J. Marshall, David Hancock, and David Starkey, among others.[32] The two wars had very different political contexts both within, and outside, the British empire. However, they were intimately connected. The Seven Years' War and its political aftermath contributed directly to the deteriorating relations between Britain and the North American Colonies. The war also left Spain worried about the balance of power in the Americas and strengthened Franco-Spanish determination to engage Britain in a future war when the opportunity arose. Britain's relationships with, and policies towards neutral nations during the Seven Years' War and the American War of

---

[32] D. Hancock, *Citizens of the World: London Merchants and the Integration of the British Atlantic Community, 1735–1785* (Cambridge University Press, 1995); Marshall, *The Making and Unmaking of Empires*; P. J. Marshall, *Remaking the British Atlantic: The United States and the British Empire after American Independence* (Oxford University Press, 2012); O'Shaughnessy, *An Empire Divided*; A. J. O'Shaughnessy, *The Men Who Lost America: British Leadership, the American Revolution, and the Fate of the Empire* (Yale University Press, 2013); David Starkey, *British Privateering Enterprise in the Eighteenth Century* (Exeter University Press, 1990); E. S. van Eyck van Heslinga and J. A. de Moor (eds.), *Pirates and Privateers: New Perspectives on the War on Trade in the Eighteenth and Nineteenth Centuries* (University of Exeter Press, 1997); S. Willis, *The Struggle for Sea Power: A Naval History of American Independence* (Atlantic Books, 2015).

Independence are rarely studied and works which engage with eighteenth-century thinking on the concept of neutrality are exceedingly rare.

British policies for maintaining neutrality in the mid-eighteenth century were not one-size-fits-all, nor could they be stagnant. What worked in one war with a given neutral would not necessarily work in the next or with a different neutral country. Neutrality was not a passive state, but was, rather, something that had to be upheld and maintained through evolving policies that reacted to the changing domestic situations in the neutral countries. In the case of Britain as a hegemonic maritime empire in the mid-eighteenth century, policies meant to uphold neutral rights needed to foster a relatively high level of trust in Britain's legal system, and that system had to be accepted as the international arbiter for neutral rights. This book has described and analysed British policies on neutral rights through the detailed case studies of four ships from two neutral countries and their fates under the Court of Prize Appeal. It has shown that the success of the Lords Commissioners for Prize Appeal in engendering that trust depended on close management of diplomatic relations and people, as well as implementation or circumvention of treaties. While Lord Hardwicke and his ministerial allies had notable successes in this endeavour, they failed when the strengths of interpersonal relationships were interrupted. Entrenched fears for the colonial future of Spain overwhelmed Spanish ministers, who were ultimately inclined to reject the Court of Prize Appeal as a partial and unjust system which did not protect the rights of their ships at sea. The result was the loss of Spanish neutrality and the entry of Spain into the war. The end of the war would bring fifteen years of peace, but no solution to the difficulty of maintaining neutrality: a critical element of Britain's maritime success during times of war.

Legal Legacies

Hardwicke's thinking, and particularly the Rule of the War of 1756, had a lasting, but not continuous, impact on British maritime strategic thinking, British prize courts, and maritime international law. During the American War of Independence, the Rule of the War of 1756 was not used, and this was only partly because France, Spain, and the Dutch Republic all became belligerent nations. The judge of the High Court of Admiralty during this war was Sir James Marriott who served in the post from 1778 to 1798. Marriott had served as an advocate during the Seven Years' War and had written a pamphlet titled *The Case of the Dutch Ships Considered* (1758) which was very well received in British legal and commercial circles.[33] It was republished the year that Marriott became judge of the High Court of Admiralty. Marriott argued for the same position as Hardwicke and the ministry: that it was forbidden for Dutch ships to engage in French trade during the war because they were not allowed to do so during times of peace. Despite the positive reception of his pamphlet and his tenure as judge, Marriott does not enjoy the best reputation. E. S. Roscoe described him in 1932 as having 'neither a judicial temperament nor a logical intellect'.[34] Whilst Marriott's pamphlet was in agreement with Hardwicke's legal thinking and British maritime strategic aims, he does not seem to have attached importance to the precedents set by Hardwicke and the Court of Prize Appeal. Bourguignon stated that Marriott described prize law as rooted in equity, reason, and good sense, where cases were not determined by precedents.[35] In addition to Marriott's dislike of precedent, the French had declared at the start of the 1778 war that their colonies would be open to neutral trade and the British courts decided to treat this as a permanent change in France's mercantilist policies.[36] Though these circumstances might have spelled the end of Hardwicke's work and the newly laid precedents, the appointment of Sir William Scott as judge of the High Court of Admiralty after Marriott would bring the precedents of the Seven Years' War back into use.

Like Marriott, Scott had practiced as an advocate and argued cases before the Court of Prize Appeal and before the High Court of Admiralty. Unlike Marriott, Scott put great stock in precedent and was sensitive to the important relationship between prize law and British maritime strategic aims. In his analysis of Scott's development as a judge, Bourguignon describes the informal processes through which advocates and judges of the prize courts created and collected a body of precedents based on personal notebooks, papers, and judgments. Scott himself kept notebooks in which he not only took notes of cases he attended, but also of old prize appeal cases.[37] In the early 1790s, Scott was appointed as King's Advocate, and his brother served as Solicitor General, Attorney General, and eventually as Lord Chancellor in 1801. Scott's appointment meant that he and his brother drafted opinions for the foreign office and advised in matters such as neutral rights and trade disputes. Scott was keen to develop his intellect and, according to Bourguignon, saw

---

[33] T. Helfman, 'Neutrality, the Law of Nations, and the Natural Law Tradition: A Study of the Seven Years' War', *Yale Journal of International Law*, 30 (2005), 549–86, p. 564.

[34] E. S. Roscoe, *Studies in the History of the Admiralty and Prize Courts* (Stevens and Sons, 1932), p. 28.

[35] Bourguignon, *Sir William Scott*, p. 145.   [36] Ibid. pp. 227–8.   [37] Ibid. p. 48.

himself as the 'Mansfield of prize law'[38] (though a more apt moniker might have been the Hardwicke of prize law). Given Scott's career trajectory and his behaviour as a High Court judge, it is more than likely that he came into contact with Hardwicke's judgments from the Court of Prize Appeal and that they helped him to formulate his own judgments during the French wars.

In his role as King's Advocate arguing before the Court of Prize Appeal in the 1796 case of the American ship *Sally*, Scott argued that the ship was engaged in French trade that was prohibited to it during peacetime and that the Rule of the War of 1756 should be applied. He called on earlier precedents and on the fact that the Privy Council had issued instructions to naval commanders in 1793 that effectively applied the Rule of the War of 1756 by declaring that any ship carrying French colonial goods should be brought in for adjudication.

Evidence of Hardwicke's lasting influence can also be seen in the decisions taken on the doctrine of continuous voyage. In 1796 the Court of Prize Appeal determined that French goods which became American property and were carried to America in American vessels would be restored and not considered lawful prize. This caused a certain civilian observer whose notes survive to remark that the Rule of the War of 1756 had been relaxed, and that neutrals were now able to trade legally with the French islands. However, this was not quite the case. As was argued by Hardwicke in several of the cases analysed in this book, the final destination of the voyage, and the intention of the voyage, mattered. The High Court of Admiralty and the Court of Prize Appeal determined that if the original destination of the goods was a French port, and if the goods remained French property, then it would be treated as lawful prize and the Rule of the War of 1756 would continue to apply.[39] Scott understood, and supported, the government's need to be able to define and bend the limits of something like the Rule of the War of 1756 in order to serve a strategy of maritime predation and destruction of French colonial trade. A relaxation of the rule when it came to American vessels, to avoid war with the Americans, did not necessarily mean that any neutral nation could trade freely with the French islands. Nonetheless, as is argued by Gabriela Frei in her article on prize law in the War of 1812, the Americans challenged the Rule of the War of 1756 and, in part, went to war over what they considered an abuse of their neutral rights by British ships and prize courts.[40] Much like Hardwicke and his

---

[38] Ibid. p. 50.   [39] Ibid. pp. 228–30.

[40] G. Frei, 'Prize Laws in the War of 1812', in T. Voelker (ed.), *Broke of the Shannon and the War of 1812* (Barnsley, 2013). There is a wide body of literature on the war of 1812 and

governmental allies, Scott was not always able to convince neutral nations that British prize law protected, and upheld, neutral rights.

The Rule of the War of 1756 was not given up by Britain until the end of the Crimean War in 1856 and the Declaration of Paris. The purpose of the declaration was to create a multilateral agreement on how relations between neutrals and belligerents were to be governed. This represented a shift from the bilateral agreements that played a dominant role in negotiations over neutral rights in the long eighteenth century. The Declaration of Paris achieved the abolition of privateering; the protection of enemy goods under a neutral flag, except for contraband; and the agreement that neutral goods, except for contraband, could not be seized under an enemy flag.[41] Though the Declaration of Paris did not end Britain's attempts to reconcile international law and maritime strategic aims, it did mark the end of the practical legal application of the precedents created by the Court of Prize Appeal during the Seven Years' War.

Law and Strategy

Although Britain's strategy succeeded in the case of the Dutch but only delayed Spain's entry into the war, it is important to remember that Hardwicke and his allies pursued their strategy because they believed it could, and would, succeed. They believed that the best way to guarantee Dutch and Spanish neutrality was to foster trust in the British prize system and set precedents based on rules that could bind the British prize courts but did not formally alter the treaties and thus did not bind the Dutch and the Spanish. It was a case, ultimately, of political needs working together with legal innovation and interpretation to deliver a British maritime strategy that addressed the dangers posed by neutral nations. Deliberately incorporating legal thinking and innovation into strategic thinking proved fruitful not only in the Seven Years' War, but throughout the conflicts of the first half of the nineteenth century. It proved particularly fruitful when jurists, such as Hardwicke, understood Britain's maritime strategy and the critical role that prize law played.

English legal traditions and Grotian philosophy, in the case of neutral rights during the war, were employed as a critical component of British strategy, forged by Hardwicke's skill set as a legal scholar and

the role of neutral rights but Frei's work and the work of John B. Hattendorf are excellent places to start.

[41] G. Frei, *Great Britain, International Law, and the Evolution of Maritime Strategic Thought, 1856–1914* (Oxford University Press, 2020), pp. 17–18.

government ally. The successes and failures of Hardwicke's work with the Court of Prize Appeal also demonstrate two potentially uncomfortable realities of international law. One is that international law only exists, and functions, so long as states agree that it does. The second is that, with the right combination of ministers and judges, international law can be successfully employed to further national strategic aims. International law does not exist in a strategic vacuum and, certainly in the eighteenth century, it needs to be considered as an important component of strategic thinking and an enabler of strategic aims.[42] This book is not the first, nor will it be the last, to make the link between international law and strategic thinking. Historians such as Gabriela Frei, Lauren Benton, and Lisa Ford have made this point about other periods and empires.[43] However, approaching international law as a historian, particularly a historian focused on law and strategic thinking, is by no means the only lens through which to approach international law and the Seven Years' War.[44] In a 2017 article, Valentina Vadi analysed the state of the history of international law as a discipline and the different approaches taken by historians and practitioners: 'While historians are interested in the past for its own sake and want to put it in context, lawyers tend to be "interested in the past for the light it throws on the

---

[42] M. Koskenniemi, 'Expanding Histories of International Law', *American Journal of Legal History*, 56 (2016), 104–12; V. Vadi, 'International Law and Its Histories: Methodological Risks and Opportunities', *Harvard International Law Journal*, 58 (2017), 311–52; A. Alimento and K. Stapelbroek (eds.), *The Politics of Commercial Treaties in the Eighteenth Century: Balance of Power, Balance of Trade* (Palgrave Macmillan, 2017); E. Cavanagh (ed.), *Empire and Legal Thought: Ideas and Institutions from Antiquity to Modernity* (Brill, 2020); A. Lambert, *The British Way of War: Julian Corbett and the Battle for a National Strategy* (Yale University Press, 2021); L. Benton and L. Ford, *Rage for Order: The British Empire and the Origins of International Law 1800–1850* (Harvard University Press, 2016); Frei, *Great Britain, International Law*.

[43] Benton and Ford, *Rage for Order*; and Frei, *Great Britain, International Law*.

[44] For instance, I have relied heavily on the work of Tara Helfman who has analysed neutrality and prize law in the context of the Seven Years' War. Her article 'Neutrality, the Law of Nations, and the Natural Law Tradition' has been invaluable to my understanding. Helfman focuses on the doctrinal development of the Rule of the War of 1756 and the doctrine of continuous voyage. However, her approach to the subject is based on the pamphlets written by James Marriott and Charles Jenkinson and a shift from Grotian thinking and philosophy to current positivism. She argues that this shift in legal thinking was achieved through the British prize courts and their use of Bynkershoek's ideas. Whilst Helfman and I engage with some of the same sources and come to some of the same conclusions, my research did not engage with the ideas of Bynkershoek because I did not see his thinking reflected in the writing of men like Hardwicke, or in the cases that helped develop the Rule of the War of 1756. Helfman, nonetheless, convincingly argues that a shift from Grotian thinking to a more Bynkershoek-like philosophy is demonstrated in the publications she examines. Helfman's purpose and mine were very different, and rather than being in opposition, our research enriches different aspects of legal history.

present".'[45] Ultimately, Vadi argues that different practitioners need to be in conversation with each other and aware of complementary expertise. The purpose of this book has been to examine the relationship between international law and strategic thinking during the Seven Years' War and to engage in a deep study of the court cases that were shaped by strategic thinking and, in turn, shaped legal doctrines and precedents. The aspiration for this book is that it will prove useful to historians and practitioners alike, by shedding light on how, why, and by whom, international law and national strategy are forged together to pursue victory in a maritime war.

---

[45] Vadi, 'International Law and Its Histories', 312.

Bibliography

Primary Sources

(In chronological order)

Archivo General de Indias (AGI) MEXICO 3099, Orders from His Majesty in America in the Province of Yucatan for the Deportation of the English Intruders in the Baliz River, no date

AGI MEXICO 3099, Proposals for Prohibiting the Extraction of Logwood by the English, 1733–67

AGI MEXICO 3099, An Historic Extract of All the Principal Occurrences in the Present Era that Give Light to Ulterior Determinations, 1737–58

AGI FILIPINAS 256, Letter from José de Carvajal y Lancaster to Official in Manila, 18 August 1750

AGI ESCRIBANIA 71B, Case of Spanish *Guarda Costa* Taking Two British Ships, 1755

AGI MEXICO 3099, Copy of a Letter from Don Jorge Bryan to Don Juan de Isla, 1755

AGI MEXICO 3099, Letter from Governor of Havana to Arriaga, 24 March 1755

AGI MEXIOC 3099, Letter to Governor Melchor de Navarrete, 10 June 1755

AGI MEXICO 3099, Letter to the Governor of Campeche Whose Obligation It Is to Expel the English, 10 February 1756

AGI MEXICO 3099, Letter from Ricardo Wall, 25 October 1756

AGI MEXICO 3099, Wall to Undisclosed Minister, 7 February 1757

AGI MEXICO 2998, Letter from Esteban José de Albanid to Arriaga, 21 August 1758

AGI MEXICO 2998, Letter to Marques de Squilace, 6 November 1761

Archivo Histórico Nacional (AHN) ESTADO 2891, Jaime Massones to Wall, 12 March 1756

AHN ESTADO 2891, Letter from Don Jaime Massones to Wall, 12 March 1756

AHN ESTADO 2891, Letter from D'Abreu to Wall, January 1760

AHN ESTADO 2891, Letter from D'Abreu to Wall, 29 February 1760

AHN ESTADO 4119, Packet of Documents Sent from Grimaldi to Wall on the State of the French Navy, 1763

AHN ESTADO 4119, Letter from Wall to Grimaldi, 2 January 1763

AHN ESTADO 4119, Letter from Grimaldi to Wall, 15 April 1763

AHN ESTADO 4119, Letter from Paris to Wall, 25 April 1763

AHN ESTADO 4119, Dispatch from Prince Maserano to Conde de Fuentes, 1764

Anonymous, *Arguments against a Spanish War* (London: E. Cabe, Ave-Mary-Lane, no date)

Anonymous, *Considerations of the Expediency of a Spanish War: Containing Reflections on the Late Demands of Spain; and on the Negociations of Mons. Bussy* (London: R. Griffiths, Strand, 1761)

Anonymous, *The Case of Going to War, for the Sake of Procuring, Enlarging, or Securing of Trade, Considered in a New Light* (London: J. Dodsley Pall-Mall, 1763)

British Library (BL) Add MS 36208–11, Hardwicke Papers Notes on Prize Cases

BL Add MS 36208, Hardwicke Papers, Notes on the *America*, ff. 180–98

BL Add MS 36208, Hardwicke Papers, Notes on the *Maria Theresa*, ff. 128–50

BL Add MS 36208, Hardwicke Papers, Notes on the *San Juan Baptista*, ff. 246–67

BL Add MS 36211, Hardwicke Papers, Notes on the *Jesús, Maria, y José*

BL Add MS 36807, Negotiations with Spain. Abstract of Spanish Dispatches Previous to the Late Negotiations with France, no date, ff. 254–7

BL Add MS 3431, Leeds Papers, Letter from Hardwicke to Holdernesse, 6 June 1756

BL Add MS 32997, Newcastle Papers, Note Written at the Cockpit by Newcastle, 1 July 1756, f. 22

BL Add MS 32997, Newcastle Papers, Note Written at Claremont by Newcastle, 29 August 1756

BL Add MS 32997, Newcastle Papers, Hardwicke's Notes Relating to the Dutch Trade with France, September 1756, ff. 48–51

BL Add MS 35423, Hardwicke Papers, Letter from Pitt to Hardwicke, 20 June 1757

BL Add MS 32997, Newcastle Papers, Memorandum Written by Newcastle, 29 August 1757

BL Add MS 36807, Negotiations with Spain, Letter from Pitt to Bristol, 1 August 1758, ff. 18–27

BL Add MS 3431, Leeds Papers, Letter from Hardwicke to Holdernesse, 7 September 1758

BL Add MS 3432, Egerton Papers, Letter from Bristol to Pitt, 25 September 1758

BL Add MS 32886, Newcastle Papers, Letter from Holdernesse to Yorke, 28 November 1758, ff. 54–65

BL Add MS 32886, Newcastle Papers, Letter from Yorke to Holdernesse Separate and Secret, 28 November 1758, f. 67

BL Add MS 32886, Newcastle Papers, Letter from Newcastle to Yorke, 1 December 1758, ff. 98–9

BL Add MS 32886, Newcastle Papers, Letter from Newcastle to Yorke, 8 December 1758

BL Add MS 32886, Newcastle Papers, Letter from Yorke to Newcastle, 8 December 1758

BL Add MS 32886, Newcastle Papers, Memorandum Written by Newcastle, 10 December 1758

BL Add MS 32886, Newcastle Papers, Letter from Newcastle to Yorke, 12 December 1758

BL Add MS 32886, Newcastle Papers, Letter from Yorke to Newcastle, 12 December 1758

BL Add MS 32886, Newcastle Papers, Letter from Newcastle to Bentinck, 15 December 1758

BL Add MS 32886, Newcastle Papers, Letter from Newcastle to Yorke, 15 December 1758, ff. 319–20

BL Add MS 32886, Newcastle Papers, Letter from Newcastle to Yorke, 22 December 1758, f. 429

BL Add MS 32886, Newcastle Papers, Memorandums for the King, 22 December 1758, f. 431

BL Add MS 32886, Newcastle Papers, Letter from Yorke to Newcastle, 22 December 1758

BL Add MS 32886, Newcastle Papers, Letter from Mr Calvert to Newcastle, 24 December 1758

BL Add MS 3432, Leeds Papers, Letter from Pitt to Holdernesse, 10 January 1759

BL Add MS 3432, Leeds Papers, Letter from Pitt to Holdernesse, 8 February 1759

BL Add MS 35595, Hardwicke Papers, Letter from Holdernesse to Hardwicke, 8 February 1759

BL Add MS 32889, Newcastle Papers, Newcastle Memorandum, 28 March 1759, ff. 272–3

BL Add MS 32889, Newcastle Papers, Memorandum for the King, 29 March 1759, f. 291

BL MS 3431, Leeds Papers, Letter from Hardwicke to Holdernesse, 30 March 1759

BL Add MS 32889, Newcastle Papers, Letter from Newcastle to Yorke, 30 March 1759, ff. 299–300

BL Add MS 32889, Newcastle Papers, Memorandum for the King, 30 March 1759

BL Add MS 32889, Newcastle Papers, Memorandum for the King, 5 April 1759, f. 363

BL Add MS 32889, Newcastle Papers, Letter from Yorke to Newcastle, 6 April 1759, ff. 372–3

BL Add MS 32890, Newcastle Papers, Newcastle Memorandum, 12 April 1759, ff. 41–3

BL Add MS 32890, Newcastle Papers, Letter from Yorke to Newcastle, 13 April 1759

BL Add MS 32891, Newcastle Papers, Letter from Newcastle to Hardwicke, May 1759

BL Add MS 35439, Hardwicke Papers, Letter from Pitt to Yorke, 2 May 1759

BL Add MS 32891, Newcastle Papers, Letter from Newcastle to Hardwicke, 6 May 1759

BL Add MS 32891, Newcastle Papers, Letter from Bentick to Newcastle, 8 May 1759

BL Add MS 32891, Newcastle Papers, Memorandums for the King, 9 May 1759

BL Add MS 32891, Newcastle Papers, Letter from Yorke to Newcastle, 15 May 1759

BL Add MS 32891, Newcastle Papers, Letter from Hardwicke to Newcastle, 18 May 1759

BL Add MS 32891, Newcastle Papers, Letter from Newcastle to Yorke, 18 May 1759

BL Add MS 32891, Newcastle Papers, Letter from Yorke to Newcastle, 18 May 1759, f. 165

BL Add MS 32891, Newcastle Papers, Letter from Newcastle to Yorke, 22 May 1759, f. 222

BL Add MS 32891, Newcastle Papers, Memorandum of What Passed with the Dutch Deputies, 22 May 1759

BL Add MS 32891, Newcastle Papers, Memorandum for the King, 22 May 1759

BL Add MS 32891, Newcastle Papers, Petition to House of Commons from Bristol Owners and Agents of Privateers, 22 May 1759

BL Add MS 32891, Newcastle Papers, Memorandum for the King, 24 May 1759

BL Add MS 32891, Newcastle Papers, Letter from Yorke to Newcastle, 1 June 1759

BL Add MS 32891, Newcastle Papers, Memorandum to the King, 5 June 1759

BL Add MS 32891, Newcastle Papers, Letter from Newcastle to Mansfield, 8 June 1759

BL Add MS 32891, Newcastle Papers, Letter from Newcastle to Yorke, 8 June 1759

BL Add MS 35596, Hardwicke Papers, Letter from Lyttleton to Hardwicke, 6 October 1759

BL Add MS 35423, Hardwicke Papers, Letter from Hardwicke to Pitt, 20 November 1759

BL Add MS 35423, Hardwicke Papers, Letter from Pitt to Hardwicke, 12 December 1759, f. 199

BL Add MS 36807, Negotiations with Spain, Extract of a Letter from a Letter from Pitt to Bristol, 14 December 1759, ff. 43–4

BL Add 35423, Hardwicke Papers, Letter from Hardwicke to Pitt, 15 January 1760

BL Add MS 35596, Hardwicke Papers, Letter from Mansfield to Hardwicke, 9 July 1760

BL Add MS 35423, Hardwicke Papers, Letter from Pitt to Hardwicke, 14 July 1760, f. 205

BL Add MS 35423, Hardwicke Papers, Letter from Hardwicke to Pitt, 29 September 1760, ff. 207–8

BL Add MS 35423, Hardwicke Papers, Letter from Pitt to Hardwicke, 12 October 1760

BL Add MS 35596, Hardwicke Papers, Anonymous Letter to Hardwicke, late 1760

BL Add MS 32917, Newcastle Papers, Letter from Devonshire to Newcastle, 9 January 1761

Blackstone, William, *Commentaries on the Laws of England. Book the First* (Oxford: Clarendon Press, 1765)

Caird Library ADM/L/S/407, Navy Board Lieutenants' Log, HMS *Squirrel*, 1756–63

Clements Library (CL) M-1773 B1/5/1, Charles Townshend Papers, Bowhill Papers, Letter from Mr. Husk to Charles Townshend, no date

CL M-1773, Charles Townshend Papers, Box 22, Letter from Andrew Symmer to Townshend on Exports from America, no date

CL M-1773, Charles Townshend Papers, Box 34, Remarks upon the Spanish Trade to Jamaica, no date

CL M-1216, James Douglas Papers, vol. P, An Account of Prizes Sent to Mr. Southwell by the *Acteaon* and *Falkland*, no date

CL M-66 Shelburne Papers, vol. 74, State of Turks Islands, no date

CL M-1773, Charles Townshend Papers, Box 29, Extracts from the Treaties between England and Spain, no date

CL M-66, Shelburne Papers, vol. 74, Letter from the Duke of Bedford to Capt. Hodgson Superintendent of the Mosquito Shore Settlement, 5 October 1749

CL M-66, Shelburne Papers, vol. 74, Letter from Duke of Bedford to Gov. Trelawney, 5 October 1749

CL M-1773, Charles Townshend Papers, Box 52, To the King's Most Excellent Majesty the Humble Address and Representation of the Council and Assembly of Jamaica, 20 November 1752

CL M-66, Shelburne Papers, vol. 22, Letter from Fox to Keene, 11 July 1756, ff. 256–63

CL M-66, Shelburne Papers, vol. 22, Letter from Keene to Fox, 27 July 1756, ff. 307–9

CL M-66, Shelburne Papers, vol. 22, Letter from Fox to Keene, 18 August 1756, ff. 311–24

CL M-1216, James Douglas Papers, vol. F, Letter to Capt. Douglas from Office of Lord High Admiral, 20 August 1756

CL M-66, Shelburne Papers, vol. 22, Letter from Keene to Fox, 8 September 1756, ff. 357–61

CL M-1216, James Douglas Papers, vol. F, Letter to Capt. Douglas from Boscawen, 26 September 1756

CL M-66, Shelburne Papers, vol. 22, Letter from Fox to Keene, 5 October 1756, ff. 381–91

CL M-66, Shelburne Papers, vol. 22, Letter from Pitt to Keene, 4 January 1757

CL M-66, Shelburne Papers, vol. 22, Letter from Pitt to Keene, 25 February 1757, ff. 467–9

CL M-66, Shelburne Papers, vol. 22, Letter from Keene to Pitt, 6 March 1757, ff. 471–7

CL M-1216, James Douglas Papers, vol. F, Letter to Capt. Douglas aboard the Alcide from Office of the Lord High Admiral, 5 April 1757

CL M-66, Shelburne Papers, vol. 22, Letter from Keene to Pitt, 5 April 1757, ff. 479–87

CL M-66, Shelburne Papers, vol. 22, Letter from Keene to Pitt, 21 April 1757, ff. 515–21

CL M-66, Shelburne Papers, vol. 22, Letter from Pitt to Earl of Bristol, 26 September 1760, ff. 528–38

CL M-1773, Charles Townshend Papers, Box 4, A Plan Proposed for Excluding the French from the Newfoundland Fishery, 12 May 1761

CL M-1773, Charles Townshend Papers, Box 29, Extracts from the Treaties between England and Spain, 1762

CL M-66, Shelburne Papers, vol. 74, Extract from Letters Relating to the Mosquito Shore, 1762

CL M-1216, James Douglas Papers, vol. N, Log Book, 10 March 1760–9 September 1762

CL M-1773, Charles Townshend Papers, Box 20, Letter Containing Some Strictures on Considerations on Trade and Finances, 1766

CL M-1773, Charles Townshend Papers, Box 20, Memoranda of Enquiries to be Made about Some Assertions in Mr G's Pamphlet, 1766

CL M-1773, Charles Townshend Papers, Box 34, Committees upon American Papers, 7 April 1766

CL M-66, Shelburne Papers, Case of the Seizure of the British Vessels by the Spaniards in the River Mississippi, 1778

Jenkinson, Charles, *A Discourse on the Conduct of the Government of Great-Britain, in Respect to Neutral Nations, During the Present War* (London: R. Griffiths, Pater-Noster Row, 1758)

Jenkinson, Charles, *A Collection of Treaties of Peace, Commerce, and Alliance Between Great-Britain and Other Powers, From the Year 1619 to 1784* (J. Almon and J. Debrett, Piccadilly, 1781)

Marriott, James, *The Case of the Dutch Ships, Considered* (R. and J. Dodsley in Pall-Mall, 1759)

Newspapers from the British Library, 17th–18th Century Burney Collection Newspapers, Gale Cengage Learning, http://find.galegroup .com/bncn/start.do?prodId=BBCN&userGroupName=kings

Middlewich Journal, 31 August 1756, no. 8

Gazeteer and London Daily Advertiser, 31 December 1756, no. 4772

London Intelligencer, 13 January 1757, no. 1700

London Evening Post, 18 January 1757, no. 4556

London Chronicle, 20–22 January 1757, no. 10

London Chronicle, 5 February 1757, no. 582

Middlewich Journal, 15–22 February 1757, no. 33

London Evening Post, 26 February–1 March 1757, no. 4573

London Evening Post, 8–10 March 1757, no. 4557

British Gazetteer, 12 March 1757, no. 3916

Middlewich Journal, 15–22 March 1757, no. 37

London Evening Post, 17 March 1757, no. 4580

London Chronicle, 17–19 March 1757, no. 34

London Evening Post, 26–29 March 1757, 'Extract of a Letter from Cádiz, March 2', no. 4540

Evening Advertiser, 5 April 1757, no. 481

London Evening Post, 12–14 April 1757, no. 4592

London Evening Post, 14 April 1757, no number

London Evening Post, 19–21 April 1757, no. 4595

Middlewich Journal, 26 April 1757, no number

London Evening Advertiser, 17 September 1757, no number

London Evening Post, 1 October 1757, no number

London Evening Post, 6–8 October 1757, no. 4668

The Public Advertiser, 31 October 1757, no. 7181

London Evening Post, 22–24 November 1757, no. 4688

Public Advertiser, 10 January 1758, no. 7245

London Evening Post, 26–28 January 1758, no. 4716

Lloyd's Evening Post, 15–17 February 1758, no. 91

London Evening Post, 18–21 February 1758, no. 4726

London Intelligencer, 10–12 August 1758, no. 1934

London Evening Post, 26–29 August 1758, no. 4809

Whitehall Evening Post Or, London Intelligencer, 2–5 September 1758, no. 1942

London Evening Post, 12–14 October 1758, no. 4827

Universal Journal, 23–30 December 1758, no. 39

Lloyd's Evening Post and British Chronicle, 21–23 March 1759, no. 262

London Evening Post, 29 March 1759, no. 4899

Gazetteer and London Daily Advertiser, Friday, 30 March 1759, no. 5456

Universal Chronicle or Weekly Gazette, 30 March 1759, no. 52

Lloyd's Evening Post and British Chronicle, 30 March–2 April 1759, no. 266

London Evening Post, 31 March–3 April 1759, no. 4900

Universal Chronicle or Weekly Gazette, 7–14 April 1759, no. 54

Lloyd's Evening Post and British Chronicle, 11–13 April 1759, no. 271

Gazetteer and London Daily Advertiser, Thursday 12 April 1759, no. 5460

London Chronicle, 19–22 May 1759, no. 37

Lloyd's Evening Post, 23–25 May 1759, no. 289

London Daily Advertiser, 28 May 1759, no. 5497

Lloyd's Evening Post, 28–30 May 1759, no. 291

London Chronicle, 2–5 June 1759, no. 380

London Evening Post, 12–14 July 1759, no. 4944

London Chronicle, 12–14 July 1759, no. 397

Whitehall Evening Post, 12–14 July 1759, no. 2078

Universal Chronicle, 14–21 July 1759, no. 68

London Evening Post, 19–21 July 1759, no. 4947

Whitehall Evening Post, 19–21 July 1759, no. 2081

Public Ledger, 27 March 1760, no. 65

London Chronicle, 28 June–1 July 1760, no. 548

Whitehall Evening Post Or, London Intelligencer, 4–7 October 1760, no. 2271

Public Ledger, 8 November 1760, no. 259

The Monitor or British Freeholder, 28 November 1761, no. CCCXXXII

London Evening Post, 16–18 December 1760, no. 5169

Whitehall Evening Post, 16–18 December 1760, no. 2302

London Gazette, 16–20 December 1760, no. 1006

Public Ledger, 17 December 1760, no. 292

Public Advertiser, 24 December 1761, no. 6456

London Chronicle, 29–31 December 1761, no. 783

Public Advertiser, 2 January 1762, no. 8475

London Chronicle, 2–5 January 1762, no. 785

St James's Chronicle Or, British Evening Post, 9–12 January 1762, no. 130

No Author, *The English Registry, for the Year of Our Lord, 1759; or A Collection of English Lists* (Printed for John Exshaw, 1759)

No Author, *The Annual Register, or a View of the History, Politics, and Literature, for the Year 1759* (J. Dodsley, Pall-Mall, 1783)

New York Public Library (NYPL) Hardwicke Papers 80, Project of a Memorandum in Answer to M. D'Affry, February 1758

NYPL Hardwicke Papers 126, Note on the Character of Sr Ben. Keene, no date

NYPL Hardwicke Papers 129, Note on the Character of Foreign Ministers, no date

NYPL Hardwicke Papers 129, Letter from Bristol to Pitt, Most Secret, 25 September 1758

NYPL Hardwicke Papers 129, Letter from Bristol to Pitt, 13 November 1758

NYPL Hardwicke Papers 129, Letter from Bristol to Pitt, 31 August 1761

NYPL Hardwicke Papers 129, Letter from Bristol to Egremont, 7 December 1761

Oxford Historical Treaties, Anglo-Spanish treaty of 1667, http://opil
.ouplaw.com/view/10.1093/law:oht/law-oht-10-CTS-63.regGroup.1/
law-oht-10-CTS-63?rskey=pcFr3u&result=3&prd=OHT

Postlethwayt, Malachy, *Britain's Commercial Interest Explained and Improved; In a Series of Dissertations on Several Important Branches of her Trade and Policy: Containing a Candid Enquiry into the Secret Causes of the Present Misfortunes of the Nation* (A. Millar in the Strand, 1757)

The National Archives (TNA) HCA 30/1041, Lord Stowell's Notebook 1 Case Notes, no date

TNA HCA 42/53, The Case of the *America*

TNA HCA 45/1, The Case of the *Maria Theresa*

TNA PRO 30/8/92, Memorandum of Spanish Partialities to France, no date

TNA PRO 30/8/92, Deduction of the State of the Treaties Between Great Britain and Spain, the Depredation in the West Indies and the Causes of Them, With Some Hints for Satisfaction and Prevention of the Grievances for the Future, January 1737/8

TNA PRO 30/47/12, Letter from Pitt to Keene, 23 August 1757

TNA PRO 30/8/92, Letter from D'Abreu to Pitt, 9 September 1757

TNA PRO 30/8/78, Letter from Anson to Pitt, 23 September 1757

TNA PRO 30/47/12, Letter from Keene to Pitt, 26 September 1757

TNA PRO 30/8/78, Bristol Memorandum, 1758

TNA PRO 30/8/92, Letter from D'Abreu to Wall, 17 March 1758

TNA PRO 30/8/92, Letter from D'Abreu to Pitt, 16 June 1758

TNA PRO 30/8/78, Letter from Commander of the HMS *Trydent* to Messrs. Bliss Harding and Clark Owners of the Privateer *Hibernia*, 19 July 1758

TNA PRO 30/8/78, Letter from H. Holding to Earl of Grenville, 28 July 1758

TNA PRO 30/8/80, The Humble Representation and Petitions of Several Merchants, Traders, and Others of the City of London and of the Owners and Agents of Private Ships of War, on Behalf of Themselves and Many Thousands of Seamen, 1759

TNA PRO 30/8/80, State of Ships Mentioned in the Conde de Fuentes's Recapitulation According to the Different Classes They Are There Divided Into, 1759

TNA PRO 30/8/80, Three of the Principal Points Appealed to the Rt Hon. the Lords Comm. of Appeals for Prizes, 1759

TNA PRO 30/8/92, Wall to D'Abreu, 9 July 1759

TNA PRO 30/8/92, D'Abreu to Pitt, London, 17 August 1759

TNA PRO 30/8/92, Letter from Pitt to Wm Read, Edw. Charlton, Owner of the Drake Privateer, Whitehall, 25 August 1759

TNA PRO 30/8/92, Letter from Pitt to D'Abreu, 31 August 1759

TNA ADM 1/4124, Letter from Pitt to Lords of the Admiralty, 1 August 1760, f. 10

TNA ADM 1/4124, Letter from Mr Wood to Mr Cleveland, 4 August 1760, f. 11

TNA ADM 1/4124, Letter from James Rivers to Lords of the Admiralty, 11 August 1760, f. 19

TNA ADM 1/4124, Letter from Pitt to Lords of the Admiralty, 12 August 1760, f. 21

TNA ADM 1/4124, Letter from Mr. Wood to Mr. Cleveland, 2 October 1760, f. 36

TNA ADM 1/4124, Letter from Mr. Wood to Mr. Cleveland, 7 July 1761, f. 96

TNA ADM 1/4124, Letter from Pitt to Lords of the Admiralty, 25 September 1761, f. 121

Treaty of Paris 1763, *The Avalon Project: Documents in Law, History and Diplomacy*, http://avalon.law.yale.edu/18th_century/paris763.asp

Secondary Sources

Abbenhuis, Maartje, *An Age of Neutrals: Great Power Politics, 1815–1914* (Cambridge University Press, 2014)

Alarcia, Diego Téllez, *El Ministerio Wall: La 'España discreta' del 'ministro olvidado'* (Ediciones de Historia, 2012)

Alimento, Antonella, and Koen Stapelbroek (eds.), *The Politics of Commercial Treaties in the Eighteenth Century: Balance of Power, Balance of Trade* (Palgrave MacMillan, 2017)

Anderson, Fred, *Crucible of War: The Seven Years' War and the Fate of the Empire in British North America, 1754–1766* (Faber and Faber, 2000)

Armitage, David, and Michael J. Braddick, *The British Atlantic World, 1500–1800* (Palgrave, 2002)

Baker, John, *An Introduction to English Legal History* (Oxford University Press, 2019)

  The Law's Two Bodies: Some Evidential Problems in English Legal History (Oxford University Press, 2001)

Barker, Hannah, *Newspapers, Politics, and Public Opinion in Late Eighteenth Century England* (Oxford University Press, 1998)

Baskes, Jeremy, 'Risky Ventures: Reconsidering Mexico's Colonial Trade System', *Colonial Latin American Review*, 14 (2005), 27–54

Baugh, Daniel, *The Global Seven Years' War, 1754–1763* (Pearson, 2011)

  'Great-Britain's 'Blue-Water' Policy, 1689–1815', *The International History Review*, 10 (1988), 33–58

  'Withdrawing from Europe: Anglo-French Maritime Geopolitics, 1750–1800', *The International History Review*, 20 (1998), 1–32

Bayly, C. A, *The Birth of the Modern World 1780–1914* (Blackwell, 2009)

Beaumont, Andrew D. M., *Colonial America and the Earl of Halifax 1748–1761* (Oxford University Press, 2015)

Benton, Lauren, *A Search for Sovereignty: Law and Geography in European Empires, 1400–1900* (Cambridge University Press, 2014)

Benton, Lauren, and Lisa Ford, *Rage for Order: The British Empire and the Origins of International Law 1800–1850* (Harvard University Press, 2016)

Benton, Lauren, and Richard J. Ross, *Legal Pluralism and Empires, 1500–1850* (New York University Press, 2014)

Black, Jeremy, *The English Press 1621–1861* (Sutton Publishing, 2001)

Parliament and Foreign Policy in the Eighteenth Century (Cambridge University Press, 2004)

Pitt the Elder (Cambridge University Press, 1992)

Bourguignon, Henry, *Sir William Scott, Lord Stowell: Judge of the High Court of Admiralty, 1798–1828* (Cambridge University Press, 1987)

Brand, Paul and Joshua Getzler (eds.), *Judges and Judging in the History of the Common Law and Civil War* (Cambridge University Press, 2015)

Brandtzaeg, Siv Gøril, Paul Goring, and Christine Eatson (eds.), *Traveling Chronicles: News and Newspapers from the Early Modern Period to the Eighteenth Century* (Brill, 2018)

Brett, Annabel, 'Natural Right and Civil Community: The Civil Philosophy of Hugo Grotius', *The Historical Journal*, 45 (2002), 31–51

Brinkman, Anna, 'Merchants of Fortune', in David Morgan-Owen and Louis Halewood (eds.), *Economic Warfare and the Sea: Grand Strategies for Maritime Powers, c.1600–1945* (Liverpool University Press, 2020)

Brinkman-Schwartz, Anna, 'The Antigallican Affair: Public and Ministerial Responses to Anglo-Spanish Maritime Conflict in the Seven Years War, 1756–1758', *English Historical Review*, Nov. (2020), 1132–64

'The Heart of the Maritime World: London's Wartime Coffee Houses 1756–1783', *Historical Research*, 94 (2021), 508–31

Brown, Brendan F., 'Lord Hardwicke and the Science of Trust Law', *Notre Dame Law Review*, 319 (1936)

Browning, Reed, *The Duke of Newcastle* (Yale University Press, 1975)

Campling, Liam and Alejandro Colás, *Capitalism and the Sea* (Verso, 2021)

Cannadine, David (ed.), *Empire, the Sea and Global History: Britain's Maritime World, c.1763–c.1840* (Palgrave, 2007)

Canny, Nicholas, and Philip Morgan (eds.), *The Oxford Handbook of The Atlantic World 1450–1850* (Oxford University Press, 2011)

Carter, Alice Clare, 'The Dutch as Neutrals in the Seven Years' War', *International and Comparative Law Quarterly*, 12 (1968), 818–34

The Dutch Republic in Europe in the Seven Years' War (MacMillan and Co., 1971)

Neutrality or Commitment: The Evolution of Dutch Foreign Policy 1667–1795 (The Pitman Press, 1975)

Cavanagh, Edward (ed.), *Empire and Legal Thought: Ideas and Institutions from Antiquity to Modernity* (Brill, 2020)

Clark, J. C. D., *English Society 1688–1832* (Cambridge University Press, 1985)

Corbett, Julian Stafford, *England in the Seven Years' War: A Study in Combined Strategy*, 2 vols. (Longmans, Green, and Co., 1907)

Some Principles of Maritime Strategy (Longmans, 1911)

Crow, Matthew, 'Littoral Leviathan: Histories of Oceans, Laws, and Empires', in Edward Cavanagh (ed.), *Empire and Legal Thought* (Brill, 2020)

Darwin, John, *The Empire Project: The Rise and Fall of the British World-System 1830–1970* (Oxford University Press, 2009)

Dunthorne, Hugh, *The Maritime Powers, 1721–1740: A Study of Anglo-Dutch Relations in the Age of Walpole* (Garland, 1986)

Du Plessis, Robert, *Transitions to Capitalism in Early Modern Europe: Economies in the Era of Early Globalization, c.1450–c.1820* (Cambridge University Press, 2019)

Encyclopaedia Britannica, 'States General', www.britannica.com/topic/States-General-Dutch-history

Findlay, Ronald, and Kevin O'Rourke, *Power and Plenty: Trade, War, and the World Economy in the Second Millennium* (Princeton University Press, 2007)

Frei, Gabriela, *Great Britain, International Law, and the Evolution of Maritime Strategic Thought, 1856–1914* (Oxford University Press, 2020)

'Prize Laws in the War of 1812', in Tim Voelker (ed.), *Broke of the Shannon and the War of 1812* (Barnsley, 2013)

García, Ricardo (ed.), *Historia de España Siglo XVIII: La España de los Borbones* (Cátedra, 2002)

Garvaglia, Juan Carlos, and Juan Marchena, *América Latina de los Orígenes a la Independencia, II: La Sociedad Colonial Ibérica en el siglo XVIII* (Crítica, 2005)

Gauci, Perry, *William Beckford: First Prime Minister of the London Empire* (Yale University Press, 2013)

Godfrey, Mark (ed.), *Law and Authority in British Legal History, 1200–1900* (Cambridge University Press, 2016)

Grafe, Regina, 'Polycentric States: The Spanish Reigns and the 'Failures' of Mercantilism', in Philip Stern and Carl Wennerlind (eds.), *Mercantilism Reimagined: Political Economy in Early Modern Britain and Its Empire* (Oxford University Press, 2014)

Graham, Aaron, 'Corruption and Contractors in the Atlantic World, 1754–1763', *English Historical Review*, 1333 (2018), 1093–119

Greene, Jack P, *Evaluating Empire and Confronting Colonialism in Eighteenth-Century Britain* (Cambridge University Press, 2013)

Grotius, Hugo, *The Free Sea*, ed. David Armitage (Liberty Fund, 2004)

On the Law of War and Peace (Anodos Books, 2019)

Haggerty, Sheryllynne, *Merely for Money? Business Culture in the British Atlantic, 1750–1815* (Liverpool University Press, 2012)

Hancock, David, *Citizens of the World: London Merchants and the Integration of the British Atlantic Community, 1735–1785* (Cambridge University Press, 1995)

Harris, Bob, 'The London Evening Post and Mid-Eighteenth British Politics', *English Historical Review*, 110 (1995), 1135–99

Hattendorf, John, 'Alfred Thayer Mahan and his Strategic Thought', in John Hattendorf and Robert Jordan (eds.), *Maritime Strategy and the Balance of Power: Britain and America in the Twentieth Century* (Palgrave Macmillan, 1989)

Helfman, Tara, 'Commerce on Trial, Neutral Rights and Private Warfare in the Seven Years War', in Koen Stapelbroek (ed.), *Trade and War: The Neutrality of Commerce in the Inter-State System* (Helsinki Collegium for Advanced Studies, 2011)

'Neutrality, the Law of Nations and the Natural Law Tradition: A Study of the Seven Years' War', *The Yale Journal of International Law*, 30 (2005), 549–86

'Trade and War: The Neutrality of Commerce in the Inter-State System', in Koen Stapelbroek (ed.), *Trade and War: The Neutrality of Commerce in the Inter-State System* (Helsinki Collegium for Advanced Studies, 2011)

Heuser, Beatrice, *Strategy Before Clausewitz: Linking Warfare and Statecraft 1400–1830* (Routledge, 2017)

Horn, D. B., *Great Britain and Europe in the Eighteenth Century* (Oxford University Press, 1967)

Horowitz, Henry and Patrick Polden (eds.), 'Continuity and Change in the Court of Chancery in the Seventeenth and Eighteenth Centuries?', *Journal of British Studies*, 35 (1996), 24–57

Howard, Michael, *The British Way in Warfare: A Reappraisal* (Cape, 1975)

Hull, Isabel, *A Scrap of Paper: Breaking and Making International Law during the Great War* (Cornell University Press, 2014)

Hunt, Barry, *Sailor-Scholar: Admiral Sir Herbert Richmond, 1871–1946* (Wilfrid Laurier University Press, 1982)

'The Strategic Thought of Sir Julian S. Corbett', in John Hattendorf and Roberty Jordan (eds.), *Maritime Strategy and the Balance of Power: Britain and America in the Twentieth Century* (Palgrave Macmillan, 1989)

Ibbetson, David, 'Authority and Precedent', in Mark Godfrey (ed.), *Law and Authority in British Legal History, 1200–1900* (Cambridge University Press, 2016)

Irigoin, Alejandra, and Regina Grafe, 'Bargaining for Absolutism: A Spanish Path to Nation-State and Empire Building', *Hispanic American Historical Review*, 88 (2008), 173–209

'A Stakeholder Empire: The Political Economy of Spanish Imperial Rule in America', *Economic History Review*, 65 (2012), 609–51

Israel, Jonathan, *Democratic Enlightenment: Philosophy, Revolution, and Human Rights 1750–1790* (Oxford University Press, 2012)

The Dutch Republic: Its Rise, Greatness, and Fall 1477–1806 (Oxford University Press, 1998)

Keene, Edward, *Beyond the Anarchical Society: Grotius, Colonialism and Order in World Politics* (Cambridge University Press, 2002)

Kinkel, Sarah, *Disciplining the Empire: Politics, Governance, and the Rise of the British Navy* (Harvard University Press, 2018)

Klinck, Dennis R, *Conscience, Equity, and the Court of Chancery in Early Modern England* (Routledge, 2016)

Klooster, Wim and Gert Oostindie, *Realm Between Empires: The Second Dutch Atlantic 1680–1815* (Cornell University Press, 2018)

Koops, E. and W. J. Zwalve (eds.), *Law and Equity Approaches in Roman Law and Common Law* (Brill, 2014)

Koskenniemi, Martti. 'Expanding Histories of International Law', *American Journal of Legal History*, 56 (2016), 104–12

Kuethe, Allan J., and Kenneth Andrien, *The Spanish Atlantic World in the Eighteenth Century: War and the Bourbon Reforms, 1713–1796* (Cambridge University Press, 2014)

Kulsrud, Carl, *Maritime Neutrality to 1780* (Little Brown and Co., 1936)

Lambert, Andrew, *The British Way of War: Julian Corbett and the Battle for a National Strategy* (Yale University Press, 2021)

'The Development of Education in the Royal Navy: 1815–1914', in Geoffrey Till (ed.), *The Development of British Naval Thinking: Essays in Memory of Bryan McLaren Ranft* (Routledge, 2006)

Lamikiz, Xavier, *Trade and Trust in the Eighteenth-Century Atlantic World* (Boydell Press, 2013)

Langbein, John H. 'Bifurcation and the Bench: The Influence of the Jury on English Conceptions of the Judiciary', in Paul Brand and Joshua Getzler (eds.), *Judges and Judging in the History of the Common Law and Civil War* (Cambridge University Press, 2015)

Langford, Paul, *Short Oxford History of the British Isles: The Eighteenth Century* (Oxford University Press, 2002)

Liddell Hart, Basil, *The British Way in Warfare* (Faber and Faber Limited, 1932)

Lincoln, Margarette, *London's Maritime World in the Age of Cook and Nelson* (Yale University Press, 2018)

Lodge, Richard (ed.), *The Private Correspondence of Sir Benjamin Keene* (Cambridge University Press, 1933)

McNair, Arnold D. et al. (eds.), 'The Debt of International Law in Britain to the Civil Law and the Civilians', *Transactions of the Grotius Society*, 39 (1953), 183–210

Mahan, Alfred T., *The Complete Works of Alfred Thayer Mahan* (Shrine of Knowledge, 2020)

The Influence of Sea Power upon History (Little Brown and Co., 1890)

Marichal, Carlos, 'Las Guerras Imperiales y los Préstamos Novohispanos, 1781–1804', *Historia Mexicana*, 39 (1990), 881–907

Marichal, Carlos, and Johanna von Grafenstein, *El Secreto del Imperio Español: Los Situados Coloniales en el Siglo XVIII* (El Colegio de México, 2012)

Marshall, P. J., *The Making and Unmaking of Empires: Britain, India, and America c.1750–1783* (Oxford University Press, 2005)

Remaking the British Atlantic: The United States and the British Empire after American Independence (Oxford University Press, 2012)

Modirzadeh, Naz K., 'Cut these Words: Passion and International Law of War Scholarship', *Harvard International Law Journal*, 61 (2020), 1–64

Murphy, Ann, 'Financial Markets: The Limits of Economic Regulation in Early Modern England', in Philip Stern and Carl Wennerlind (eds.), *Mercantilism Reimagined: Political Economy in Early Modern Britain and Its Empire* (Oxford University Press, 2014)

Namier, Lewis, *England in the Age of the American Revolution* (Macmillan, 1966)

Neff, Stephen, 'James Stephen's War in Disguise: The Story of a Book', *Irish Jurist*, 38 (2003), 331–51

Justice Among Nations: A History of International Law (Harvard University Press, 2014)

War and the Law of Nations (Cambridge University Press, 2009)

Oldham, James, *English Common Law in the Age of Mansfield* (University of North Carolina Press, 2004)

'Informal Lawmaking in England by the Twelve Judges in the Late Eighteenth and Early Nineteenth Centuries', *Law and History Review*, 29 (2011), 181–220

Orford, Anne, *International Law and the Politics of History* (Cambridge University Press, 2021)

Ormrod, David, *The Rise of Commercial Empires: England and the Netherlands in the Age of Mercantilism, 1650–1770* (Cambridge University Press, 2003)

O'Shaughnessy, Andrew Jackson, *An Empire Divided: The American Revolution and the British Caribbean* (University of Pennsylvania Press, 2000)

   The Men Who Lost America: British Leadership, the American Revolution, and the Fate of the Empire (Yale University Press, 2013)

Pares, Richard, *Colonial Blockade and Neutral Rights 1739–1763* (Porcupine Press, 1975)

   War and Trade in the West Indies 1739–1763 (Frank Cass and Co., 1936)

Pares, Richard, and Alan J. P. Taylor (eds.), *Essays Presented to Sir Lewis Namier* (Books for Libraries Press, 1956)

Pearce, Adrian, *British Trade with Spanish America 1763–1808* (Liverpool University Press, 2007)

Poser, Norman S., *Lord Mansfield: Justice in the Age of Reason* (McGill-Queen's University Press, 2013)

Prescott, Andrew, 'Searching for Dr. Johnson: The Digitisation of the Burney Newspaper Collection', in S. G. Brandtzaeg, Paul Goring, and Christine Watson (eds.), *Travelling Chronicles: News and Newspapers from the Early Modern Period to the Eighteenth Century* (Brill, 2018)

Prest, Wilfred, *William Blackstone: Law and Letters in the Eighteenth Century* (Oxford University Press, 2012)

Raven, G. J. A. and N. A. M. Rodger, *Navies and Armies: The Anglo-Dutch Relationship in War and Peace, 1688–1988* (John Donald Publishers, 1990)

Reinert, Sophus, 'Rivalry: Greatness in Early Modern Political Economy', in Philip Stern and Carl Wennerlind (eds.), *Mercantilism Reimagined: Political Economy in Early Modern Britain and Its Empire* (Oxford University Press, 2014)

Richmond, Herbert, *Sea Power in the Modern World* (G. Bell and Sons, 1934)

   Statesmen and Sea Power (Little Clarendon Press, 1946)

Rodger, N. A. M., *The Command of the Ocean* (Norton, 2004)

   'The Idea of Naval Strategy in Britain in the Eighteenth and Nineteenth Centuries', in Geoffrey Till (ed.), *The Development of British Naval Thinking: Essays in Memory of Bryan McLaren Ranft* (Routledge, 2006)

   The Wooden World: An Anatomy of the Georgian Navy (Norton, 1996)

Roscoe, E. S., *A History of the English Prize Court* (Lloyd's, 1924)

   Studies in the History of the Admiralty and Prize Courts (Stevens and Sons, 1932)

Rupert, Linda M., *Creolization and Contraband: Curaçao in the Early Modern Atlantic World* (University of Georgia Press, 2012)

Satsuma, Shinsuke, 'Politicians, Merchants, and Colonial Maritime War: The Political and Economic Background of the American Act of 1708', *Parliamentary History*, 32 (2013), 317–36

Index